Vinyar Tengwar

π 11

May, 1990

"Now I am a burglar indeed!" thought he

In This Issue

Editor's Musings

Welcome to *VT* #11. While last issue saw some dramatic changes (for the better, hopefully) in *VT*'s format, this issue sees a dramatic change for *VT*'s editor. My wife and I have finally beaten our way out of the rent trap, and are now the proud owners of a new townhouse (and the dubious parents of a bouncing baby mortgage). Please be sure to note my new address, which is given on the back cover.

The lack of suitable cover art has reached a crisis level. Surely there are some artists out there who would like to reach the teeming masses with their vision of Middle-earth. If something isn't done soon, I'll be forced to run a blank cover, or worse, a picture of myself!

— Carl F. Hostetter

"…. Archaeologists can as it were smell with the noses and feel through the skins of human beings long turned to dust. But one thing they cannot do: they cannot loosen the tongues of the dead.

"This is a severe handicap. A people is essentially a linguistic community. The man who first wished his wife good day in Celtic must count as the first Celt. But since an excavated piece of ankle-bone does not tell us what dialect its owner spoke, the results of archaeological enquiry often seem very abstract. The diggers themselves seldom speak of peoples but only of 'cultures': globular-urn people, Funnel-Beaker people, Battle-Axe people, Urnfield people. They leave open the question whether those who produced these objects had in common only their attachment to certain types of utensil, weapon, burial-rite, or whether they spoke a common dialect. There are good reasons for this. An archaeologist of the distant future would be grossly in error if he took the world-wide occurrence of huge quantities of Coca-Cola bottles as an indication of a unified world language."

— Gerhard Herm, in *The Celts* (New York: St. Martin's Press, 1977), pp. 70-71.

E.L.F. News

In Memoriam

VT is saddened to learn of the death on Dec. 17, 1989 of E.L.F. member Heiner Zech of Nürnberg, West Germany. The E.L.F. extends its condolences to Heiner's family and friends.

VT *Editor Moves*

I've bought my first house! Send all submissions and subscription checks to me at my new address:

• Carl F. Hostetter   2509 Ambling Circle, Crofton, MD 21114.

ELFCON III

ELFCON III will be held in conjunction with Mythcon XXI at the California State University at Long Beach, August 3 - 6, 1990. In addition to the usual nightly gatherings, events planned by the E.L.F. include classes on Elvish, a High-elvish vocal with harp recital of Chapter 8 of *The Silmarillion*, a panel on "The Future of Elvish", and several papers pertinent to Elvish studies. Membership for Mythcon XXI is $35.00. Room and board is $100.00 (double occupancy, including all meals from Friday dinner to Monday breakfast, except for the Banquet, the price of which will be determined later). Guests of honor are Patrick Wynne and Diana L. Paxson. To register or for more information write 2554 Lincoln Blvd., Suite 190, Marina del Rey, CA 90291.

Les Langues de la Terre du Milieu

The first volume of *Les Langues de la Terre du Milieu* will contain a "Telerin Glossary". For further information write Edouard Kloczko, 22 rue Victor Hugo, 78800 Houilles, France.

Other Changes of Address

The following E.L.F. members have changed their addresses:

• Chris Gilson   300 North Civic Drive, #304, Walnut Creek, CA 94596.
      [Chris is the editor of the oft-mentioned Parma Eldalamberon *—CFH]*
• Jean-Marc Rulier   223 rue de la Parx, 50120 Equeurdreville, France.
• Bill Welden   19419 Valerio Street, Reseda, CA 91335.

Letters to VT

• Patrick Wynne   Fosston, Minnesota

My thanks to Eli Bar-Yahalom and Craig Marnock for their comments on my article on "Lúthien's Song" *[which appeared in* VT *#9 — CFH].* They have raised several points which require clarifying.

Both Eli and Craig assert that *Hîr Annûn gilthoniel* in line 4 of "Lúthien's Song" refers to Varda rather than the Moon. This is unlikely for a variety of reasons, not the least of which is that it is clear that Tolkien conceived of *hîr* 'lord' as a masculine form (masculine sexually, not grammatically), with a feminine equivalent *híril* 'lady'. These Sindarin forms are given in the Appendix of *The Silmarillion [S]*, p. 359[*], entry *heru*. A glance at the entry **KHER-** in the *Etymologies (The Lost Road [LR]*, p. 364) will show that this yang-yin, masculine-feminine lord-lady distinction was the norm in other Elven tongues as well: Quenya *heru* 'master', *heri* 'lady'; Old Noldorin *khéro* 'master', *khíril* 'lady'; Noldorin *hîr, hiril*. Short of Tolkien also supplying us with accompanying anatomical sketches, I do not see how the sexual distinction in these pairs could be made any clearer. If line 4 of "Lúthien's Song" referred to Varda, we would see *Híril*, not *Hîr*.

I am not nearly ingenious enough to understand why Craig finds my gloss of *gilthoniel* as 'star-kindling' to be "a bit too ingenious", nor do I understand how his alternate gloss 'star-making' would require that this participle refer to Varda and not the Moon. Assuming, purely for the sake of argument, that *gilthoniel does* mean 'star-making' in line 4, Chris Gilson's explanation of its applicability to the Moon still holds valid: to Lúthien perhaps it seemed that the Moon "re-made" the stars after obscuring them as it passed.

Tolkien does gloss *Gilthoniel* (with variant *Gilthonieth*) as 'Star-maker' in the *Etymologies*, written *c*. 1937-38 (*cf. LR*, p. 390, entry **TAN-**). But this was not his last word on the subject. In *The Road Goes Ever On [RGEO]* (1967) he glosses *Gilthoniel* as 'Star-*kindler*' (p. 64) and this must represent his final conception of the name. The verb stem *thon-*, probably mutated from *ton-* due to the preceding *l* in *gil*, must be cognate with Q. *tunda-* 'kindle' given in *The Book of Lost Tales, Part One* (p. 270, entry *Turuhalmë*) as a derivative of the root **TURU** (**TUSO**) 'kindle', along with *turu* 'firewood, wood in general' and *turúva* 'wooden'. One or the other of these latter two words must provide the initial element in *Turuphanto* 'The Wooden Whale', a name from the Classical Corpus (it occurs in "Aldarion and Erendis", written *c*. 1965) which shows that **TURU** (**TUSO**) and its derivatives were retained in the late conception of the languages.

Just in case anyone does not yet consider this moribund equine to be thoroughly flagellated, I will note that it must be significant that *gilthoniel* in line 4 is not capitalized. Surely if it referred to Varda we would see *Gilthoniel*, since that was one of her names.

Both Eli and Craig object to the title "Lord of the West" being applied to Tilion, a Maia. Granted, the plural form "Lords of the West" is a synonym for the Valar. But the Maiar were essentially the same sort of beings as the Valar, only running on lower wattage: "… of the same order as the Valar but of lesser degree" (*S*, p. 3). We are told of the Maia Uinen that the Númenóreans "held her in reverence equal to the Valar" (*ibid.*), and it is entirely possible that the Elves of the First Age held Tilion in similarly high regard. It should be remembered

---

[*] As usual, all page references are to the Houghton Mifflin hardcover editions.

that the Moon was a very important symbol in Elvish thought, "for the Sun was set as a sign for the awakening of Men and the waning of the Elves, but the Moon cherishes their memory." (*S*, p. 99). Craig denigrates Tilion as "a not very important Maia", and it *is* a rather shocking oversight that the Horned One does not crop up in "The Valaquenta", where every Maia who's any Maia ought to be listed. Still, the fact that we know Tilion's name indicates he was a Maia of some importance, since the vast majority of the Maiar never were assigned names. The Valar must have held a high opinion of him — I can't imagine they would have handed over the task of forever tending the last flower of Telperion to just any old Joe who happened to have been loitering around Lórien looking unoccupied. And Tilion must have been a being of some potency, since he was able to emerge victorious from an assault by Morgoth, who sent spirits of shadow against him.

It should also be noted that the belief that "Lord of the West" was blasphemous when applied to anyone other than "one of the great Valar" is portrayed by Tolkien as being a concept particular to a specific culture (the party of the Faithful of Númenor) at a specific period in history (the late Third Millennium of the Second Age). There is no evidence to suggest that this belief was universal among all the cultures of Middle-earth during other historical periods, and to assert as Eli does that "Melian's daughter obviously knew" about this belief is to assume that Lúthien possessed a remarkable degree of prescience which she used to indulge an interest in Númenórean theology. I think not.

An important factor in determining the referent of **Hîr Annûn gilthoniel** which Eli and Craig ignore is *context*. Lúthien's song does not occur in isolation, it is set within the framework of a narrative. If you read lines 85-143 of "The Lay of Leithian Recommenced", you will find that the poem occurs in a scene awash with moonlight; there are at least four references to the Moon (lines 87, 111, 127, and 141), five if you count **Ithil** in the first line of the song itself. Stars or starlight are not mentioned even once in this scene. It is clear from the context that "Lúthien's Song" is a hymn to the Moon, not to Varda.

Craig attempts to explain the puzzling use of a Third Age Sindarin dialect by Lúthien with the proposal that this is due to Tolkien discarding the concept of a Noldorin *vs.* Doriathrin dialectical distinction in favor of Sindarin as described in Appendix F of *The Lord of the Rings*. It is indisputable that the language of Doriath is referred to as Sindarin in Tolkien's later writings. Had Craig taken the time to do a modicum of research, however, he would have found that Tolkien retained the concept of Doriath having its own peculiar dialect. In the *Narn i Chîn[*] Húrin* (which I presume to be a late work, perhaps contemporaneous with "Of Tuor" *c.* 1951, though I cannot find a date of composition listed and would be delighted to have one pointed out to me) Tolkien gives us some idea of the nature of the Doriathrin dialect of Sindarin: "From Nellas Túrin learned much concerning the ways and the wild things of Doriath, and she taught him to speak the Sindarin tongue after the manner of the ancient realm, older, and more courteous, and richer in beautiful words." (*Unfinished Tales [UT]*, p. 76) Further information is provided in the footnote (no. 6) to this quote — "… the speech of Doriath, whether of the King or others, was even in the days of Túrin more antique than that used elsewhere;… Mîm observed … that one thing of which Túrin never rid himself, despite his grievance against Doriath, was the speech he had acquired during his fostering." (*UT*, p. 147)

For an example of the "older" and "more antique" flavor of the Doriathrin dialect of Sindarin, we may turn to the inscription on the gravestone of Túrin: **Túrin Turambar Dagnir**

---

[*] For **Chîn** cf. *The Lost Road*, p. 322, §25.

Glaurunga. Here we see the genitive singular of *Glaurung* formed by the *démodé* addition of final *-a*, whereas all the truly trendy Sindar expressed the simple genitive by word order alone (as Tolkien tells us in *RGEO*, p. 67).

This archaic genitive in *-a* is also seen in Doriathrin as described in the *Etymologies*: "The name *Nauglamîr* is strictly Doriathric, in which genitive in *-a(n)* preceded." (*LR*, p. 375, entry **NAUK-**) Also note Doriathrin *(n)gold* 'one of the wise folk, Gnome' and its occurrence in genitive form in the compound *Goldamir* 'Gnome-jewel, Silmaril'. (*LR*, p. 377, entry **ÑGOLOD-**)

What the evidence seems to indicate is that Tolkien never changed his conception of Doriath having its own unique dialect of Low-elven. What did change was Tolkien's method of referring to this dialect, the term "Doriathrin" giving way to "Sindarin". This fits in with the assertion of Tom Loback and Chris Gilson in *Parma Eldalamberon* #8 that the term "Sindarin" was used by Tolkien to refer to "a *group* of mutually intelligible dialects, so called because most of the speakers who talked to each other using it were Sindar 'Grey-elves' in an ethnic sense." (p. 15, footnote 3).

Craig cites Tolkien's biographer, Humphrey Carpenter, as a valid source of information regarding changes taking place in the languages. I think it is unwise to rely on Mr. Carpenter as an authority in any matter pertaining to Elvish. Let us not forget that he is the man responsible for the Travesty Transcript of four lines of the poem "*Narqelion*" which appeared on p. 76 of *Tolkien: A Biography*. Of the 13 words in those four lines, Mr. Carpenter managed to get six, count 'em, *six* wrong. How many hours, I wonder, did Carpenter's carelessness cause Elvish linguists to waste studying and explaining Elvish words that *never existed*? When it comes to matters of Elvish linguistics, Humphrey Carpenter has proved that he is highly unreliable as a source of information.

Finally, I will return the baleful gaze of my Lidless Eye to Eli, and his suggestion that *lasto dîn* means 'listen to him'. This gloss did occur to me but was rejected as nonsensical — why would Lúthien urge the flowers and trees to listen to the Moon, a celestial luminary hardly noted (save in Hobbit nonsense-verse) for its tendency to hold forth with any sort of vocalizations?

• Tom Loback   New York, New York

My compliments on another fine issue. In anticipation of the huge sacks of mail you will undoubtedly receive saying *[with regard to Tom's cover art for* VT *#10,* "The Death of Caranthir" *— CFH]* "But it says in *The Book of Lost Tales, Part Two* (*BoLT2*), pp. 241-2, that '*Celegorm* was pierced by a hundred arrows, and Cranthor beside him'" (emphasis mine), I defend my resolution of the image as follows:

First and foremost I was struck by the power of the image of the "hundred arrows" because (my apologies to all Christian metaphorists — it does not relate to St. Sebastian's martyrdom) it reminded me of a very famous Japanese print by Utagawa Kuniyoshi at the Victoria and Albert Museum entitled 'The Last Stand of the Kusunoki'. Wanting to retain that image I had difficulty in rationalizing the retention with what is said in *The Silmarillion* (*S*): "There fell Celegorm by *Dior's hand*," (emphasis mine) since I regard *S* as the definitive source when confronted with directly contradictory statements — usually. I concluded that Tolkien's final word on this was that Dior slew Celegorm in personal combat and probably also Curufin, as those brothers were inseparable. But neither *S* nor *BoLT2* precludes Caranthir from falling in the Battle of Region that follows the sack of Menegroth. In fact, *BoLT2* suggests Cranthor (Doriathrin *epessë* for Noldorin *Caranthir*) fell in the same storm of arrows.

What can I say about Edouard Kloczko's remarks? I asked for criticism — he gave it. I do suggest he read *Unfinished Tales* p.263, where *lô* is stated to be a Sindarin word.

With regard to Edouard's Iron Crown Enterprises (ICE) comparison, I can only say that, having actually done work for ICE, I am acutely aware of the difference between my method of Middle-earth study and theirs. Mr. Kloczko's complete lack of footnoting, sourcing, or supporting evidence for his pontifications (however interesting) is more like ICE's methodology than anything I have seen in the fan community. I suggest Ed get off his soapbox and try proving, or at least demonstrating, the feasibility of some of his more bizarre conclusions about Elvish, if he thinks they can stand the test of debate from this bunch of linguistically misguided Americans.

Thimbault is taken from the earliest *Silmarillion* map. The word appears there *only*. I can't begin to imagine how Ed concludes that it is Númenórean from Sindarin **thara** (come on, Ed, show us how you did it: **thara > thimbault**; **th > mb**? **ara > ault**?) — talk about creating one's own world. I put it on the map because Tolkien had it on his map and I could find no reason to remove it, and several reasons to retain it. I wouldn't call that excessive creativity.

Ed has some interesting theories on the Elven languages, and I certainly have some sympathy for his views expressed in earlier issues, but if this current prestidigitation is an example of his methodology I can only hope that the editors of *VT* will keep him on a short linguistic leash in the future by insisting he provide the details of his generalizations *[I think Jorge did a sufficient job of that when Edouard's letter ran −CFH].*

• Edouard Kloczko   Houilles, France

Thank you for *VT* #10. The presentation of VT is improving fast. Bravo!

The main point in my last letter regarding **Thimbault** was not about its etymology but the rightness of its inclusion in the "Map of Beleriand" made by Tom Loback *[which appeared in* VT *#8 −CFH].* From an 'internal' point of view the name **Thimbault** *never existed* in Middle-earth; and from an 'external' point of view **Thimbault** was just a passing name *invented* by J.R.R. Tolkien and which was later *disregarded*. In his column "*Essitalmar*" in *VT* #10 Tom has again and deliberately distorted Tolkien's vision of Middle-earth to conform it to his own vision. Tom states that all of the Eldar used two given names, but in *Unfinished Tales*, p. 266, we read: "... the Eldar in Valinor ... had two 'given names' ...." In Valinor, Tom! Your discussion about a given name for Thingol (or even Beren?!) is quite irrelevant. As for the invented given name of Finduilas: I am in a state of shock; are we studying Tolkien's books or are we playing the "Middle-earth Role Playing Game"?

[I must point out that the fact that Tolkien "disregards" a word or name does not *mean that it has necessarily been* discarded. *Even the most casual reader of the volumes in* The History of Middle-earth *pertaining to the material which would become* The Silmarillion *can hardly escape the sad conclusion that much of beauty and import was lost over time through* compression, *not disposal. Second, the fact that Tolkien explicitly states only that the Elves in Valinor had two given names does not in any way indicate that the Elves in Middle-earth did not. From "A implies B" it does not follow that "not A implies not B". Finally, Tom presents his name for Finduilas as a speculative exercise, a suggestion, not as fact. He is perfectly within his rights to do so, as are you to offer specific and reasoned arguments as to why you disagree −CFH]*

Now for the question about the **-va** case in Quenya. I have called it the 'metaphorical case' because of **Taurë Huinéva** [The Lost Road, *p. 382, entry* **PHUY-** *−CFH],* which is a metaphor. In **Nurtalë Valinóreva** (*The Silmarillion*, p. 102) and **Mindon Eldaliéva** the morpheme **-va** expresses a 'comparison' between two nouns. But I am at a loss to explain the long *é* in **Huinéva** and **Eldaliéva**.

• Eli Bar-Yahalom   Haifa, Israel

VT is starting to behave like a real scientific journal/magazine. It makes me hope that Elvish studies will eventually be recognized as a scientific discipline in its own right. I may note, without offending *Quettar*, that *VT*'s higher frequency and regularity of publication, together with its specialized columns, variety of articles (in the Latin sense of the word — including letters, poetry, artwork and paraphernalia), together with the habit of careful treatment of the material, makes *VT* a formidable "opponent" to *Quettar* — but, as the Hebrew saying goes, "*kin'at sophrîm tarbeh ḥokhmâ*": rivalry between scholars multiplies wisdom. *[Thanks for the very kind words, and thanks especially for the apt quote and the softening quotation marks around "opponent" — I like to think that* VT *and* Quettar *complement, rather than compete with, one another —CFH]*

The new format of *VT* is absolutely stunning in its combination of elegance, legibility and effectiveness. My last sentence was a stunning combination of Latin words, so it'll be better to say the new *VT* is just *beautiful. [I blush —CFH]* The epigram on the contents page should become a fixed tradition. By the way, the vocative of *ego* is a must for all schizophrenics!

• Craig Marnock   Kirkcudbrightshire, Scotland

I thought the epigram from Bloomfield *[in* VT *#10]* was particularly apt considering the outline for "The Book" which appeared a couple of pages later, which seemed very Bloomfieldian in format. I hope these piquant epigrams become a permanent feature of *VT*.

I think I can reassure Eli that he is unlikely to receive rotten tomatoes through the mail from Chris and Tom, judging by my own experience. Or perhaps they just got lost in the post.

VT rapidly approaches its second birthday and has grown up quite a lot in that period. Keep it up!

Foreword to "The Fifth Battle"
by Tom Loback

This issue of *VT* marks the beginning of a four-part presentation of "The Fifth Battle", or the *Nirnaeth Arnoediad*. It is a black-and-white print which represents the climactic hours of the battle, during which the Elves, Men and Dwarves of the Union of Maedhros were tragically and utterly defeated by the Hosts of Morgoth, led by Gothmog, Lord of Balrogs, and Glaurung, the Father of Dragons.

While the *tengwar* border calligraphy uses a Quenya mode, the descriptions of the battle formations are Sindarin, written in the Mode of Beleriand. This could indicate the origin of the piece was in Eregion during the middle of the Second Age. However, the calligraphic and illustrative style point to a possibly later period.

Anyone interested in acquiring a print of this work should write me at 152 West 26th Street, #36, N.Y. City, N.Y. 10001, USA. The print is limited to 100 copies. Prices vary on the quality of the material: $100.00 for Maplewood veneer, $50.00 for Arches Cover bond (acid-free paper), and $20.00 for heavy white bond. Size: 27" wide by 18" high. Make checks and money orders payable to Tom Loback. Inquiries welcome.

This month's installment reproduces the northwest quadrant of the map. The northeast quadrant will be given next month.

[The first quadrant of "The Fifth Battle" appears as the center spread, pp. 10-11 —CFH]

Two Problematic Quenya Noun Cases
compiled by Jorge Quiñónez

The purpose of this article is to begin a discussion towards solving the linguistic puzzle of the two remaining noun declension cases about which the Quenyandili are still uncertain. In J.R.R. Tolkien's letter to Dick Plotz concerning "...the forms of "Classical" or Book Quenya..." (see *VT* #6, p. 14) we see these two problematic cases (here marked [*Vcase*] and [*Scase*] for ease of identification) along with the other eight well-known cases:[1]

[Case]	S[ingular]	Pl[ural] 1	Pl[ural] 2	Dual
(a) N[ominative]	*cirya*	*ciryar*	*ciryalī*	*ciryat*
A[ccusative]	*ciryā*	*ciryai*	"	"
G[enitive]	*ciryō*	*-aron*	*-alion*	*ciryato*
I[nstrumental]	*ciryanen*	*-ainen*	*-alīnen*	*ciryanten*
(b) All[ative]	*ciryanna*	*-annar*	*-alinna(r)*	*ciryanta*
[Dative]	*(ciryan)*	*(-ain)*	*(alin)*	*(ciryant)*
Loc[ative]	*ciryasse*	*-assen*	*-alisse(n)*	*ciryatse*
[*Scase*]	*(ciryas)*	*(-ais)*	*(-alis)*	
Abl[ative]	*ciryallo*	*-allon*	*-alillo(n)*	*ciryalto*
(c) [*Vcase*]	*ciryava*	—	*-alíva*	
(a) [Nominative]	*lasse*	*lassī*	*lasselī*	*lasset*
[Accusative]	*-ē*	"	[rest] as for	[rest] as for
[Genitive]	*lasseo*	*lassion*	*kiryalī* [above]	*kiryat* [above]
[Instrumental]	*-enen*	*-ínen*		
(b) [Allative]	*-enna*	*-ennar*		
[Dative]	*(-en)*	*(-in)*		
[Locative]	*-esse*	*-essen*		
[*Scase*]	*(-es)*	*(-is)*		
[Ablative]	*-ello*	*-ellon*		
(c) [*Vcase*]	*-eva*	—		

The following is an attempt to compile everything which has been said on the *Vcase*: Jim Allan was the first to recognize the *Vcase,* in *An Introduction to Elvish* (p. 16):

> The only published example [as of 1976] of the *–va* case marker is on the form *miruvóreva* in the phrase *yuldar...lisse-miruvóreva* 'draughts...of sweet-mead'. Here *–va* indicates that the noun to which it is attached comprises the substance from which something is COMPOSED. Accordingly, the case marked by *–va* may be labelled the COMPOSITIVE case pending further data demonstrating other uses.

Many years later *Quettar* #13 (Feb., 1982, p. 11) added the following:

> The "compositive" case has long been a very annoying form. The name was given in ItE, when the only published example was <u>miruvóreva</u>, in the Lament of

— *continued on page 18.*

---

[1] The declension table is presented here with cosmetic changes.

"The Love-song of Maglor"
by Eli Bar-Yahalom

Eli's poetic hero is Maglor. His "editions" of the first two Songs of Maglor "The Lament for Maedhros" and "Man ëa or menel" appeared in Quettar #30, *and the third,* "Ú-Hlapa hrestannar hairë" *appeared in* Quettar #38.

This song was sung by the Elves throughout Middle-earth, and became well-known, perhaps due to its bitter flavour, which distinguished it among the love-songs of the Eldar, usually carefree and merry. However, not everyone knew that its composer was actually Maglor — the last of the seven sons of Fëanor. It doesn't appear in the Lothlórien Manuscript of his *Noldolantë* (recently discovered by archaeologists), but may be counted as part of it, since Maglor himself declared that the term *Noldolantë* applied to everything he had ever written.

Who was the subject of Maglor's apparently unhappy love? This remains a mystery. Some speculate that it was none other than Altáriel of Laurelindórinan, known as Galadriel in the Grey-elven tongue; however, this speculation is supported only by line 16 of the Song. Its metre is a variant of *tolontë*, or eight-part rhythm, known as *thennath Maglor*.

Mellírë Métima Híno Fëanáro

Pella hísië, penna mar
2 Órenyan iltúvima lár.
Erya tenn' ambarónë sundar
4 Nályë
    fírië,
        nwalmë,
            nár.
Tular Valar mi silyë fanar,
6   Meldanya curuntanen tánar:
Minya — Vard' elerrillë anta,
8 Miruvórë Yavanna quanta
Ulmo — rossë ëaro, yallo
10 Aulë cára vanima canta.
   Nesso — lintessë, Váno — helma.
12   Tula Melkor ar anta melmo.
Erwa ná Fëanáro Hín —
14 Úner mára voronda nín.
Hlara, melda carmëo aina,
16 Laurefinda ve Laurelin.
   Ú-kenuvanyel tenn' Ardo metta.
18   Hlara enyo metima quetta.
Pella hísië, pella nen,
20 Tira iluvekéna hen.
Indis, engwa indëo olos,
22 Náva
    manina
       elyo
          men.

Notes:

Line 1:   **penna** 'without'; a reconstruction by analogy with Sindarin **Iarwain Ben-Adar**.

Line 2:   **lár** 'rest, pause', from *Unfinished Tales [UT]* and *cf. The Lost Road [LR]*, p. 353, entry **DAR-**.

Line 3:   **Erya** 'its' (also 'hers, his'). An earlier version of this poem had **Ehyo**, but Bill Welden's article in *Parma Eldalamberon* #8 persuaded me that Quenya had no gender, thus **–s** 'it' is from **–rye**

         ambarónë, plural of **ambaróna**, used by Treebeard. I feel it must mean 'doomed'.

Line 12:   **melmo** 'lover' is the object of the sentence (of course, Maglor means himself!).

Line 21:   **indëo**, genitive of **indë** 'mind' from root **IN(ID)-** (*UT*, p. 400), and *cf.* **indo** in "Fíriel's Song" (*LR, p. 72*).

Line 22:   **Náva**. I believe this, not ****nuva**, is the future of **ná**. The reason is that, when "Fíriel's Song" was written, the **–uva** suffix was already present; yet the future of **antar** is **antáva**. Patrick Wynne, in his fabled "Analysis" (*Parma* #8) brilliantly explains the difference between stems which end in consonants and those which end in vowels. **Na–** is given as a stem in the "late" *The Road Goes Ever On*, as well as the "early" *Etymologies* in *LR*, thus **na + uva > náva** (*cf.* **yéva** in "Fíriel's Song", *LR*, p. 72).

Translation: Love-song of the Last Son of Fëanor

         Beyond mist, without home

2   there is no rest which can be found for my mind.

         Down to its [the mind's] doomed roots

4   You are — death, torment, fire.

            The Valar come in shining *fanar*,

6   [and] shape my beloved one with their skills:

         First — Varda gives star-radiance,

8   Yavanna pours *miruvórë*-nectar,

         Ulmo — sea-foam, from which

10   Aulë fashions the beautiful form.

            From Nessa [comes] swiftness, from Vána — the skin;

12   Comes Melkor and gives [her] a lover.

         Alone is the Son of Fëanor;

14   None remains faithful to me.

         Listen, love, [a product] of holy art,

16   Golden-haired as the Golden Tree.

            I will not see you till the End of the World —

18   Listen to my last word.

         Beyond mist, beyond waters,

20   Watches an all-seeing eye.

         Woman, the dream of a feverish mind,

22   Be your road blessed.

Note on the translation: being literal, it acquires extra pathos which is undesired but inevitable. Surely I can't claim the Quenya original to be perfect, but I think it's more lyrical than the translation can express.

Northwest quadrant of Tom Loback's "The Fifth Battle".

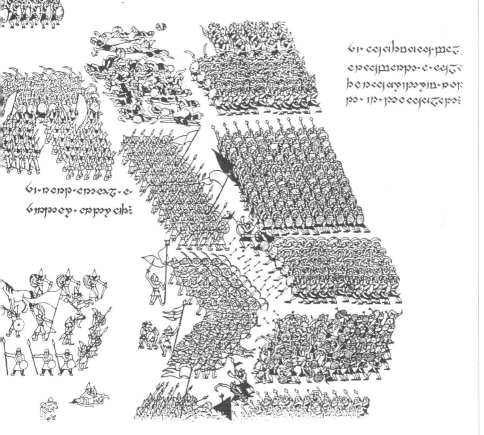

See page 6 for further information on this work.

Essitalmar
The Roots of Middle-earth Names and Places
A column edited by Tom Loback

This is a forum for the readers of VT *to submit their ideas and thoughts about names, both of people and places; their meanings and the story that the tell. All are encouraged to submit inquiries, short interpretations and discussions thereof, particularly those names still undefined. Send all correspondence for this column to the editor at 152 West 26th St., #36, N.Y. City, NY 10001, USA.*

The Longswordsman

Editor, writer, essayist.

These words, and words like them, are part of the English language. We all know what they mean: *editor* — one who edits; *writer* — one who writes; *essayist* — one who composes an essay. What most of us don't know is why each of these words takes the form it does instead of the form of the others. Why not *editor, writor, essayor*; or *editer, writer, essayer*; or *editist, writist, essayist*? Wouldn't one of these be simpler, more logical and easier to learn and use? One rule to explain all cases. And how to explain the rules to someone learning our language? Do we even know the rules governing these usages ourselves? We seem to. No one says *singor, singist* instead of *singer*; or *dictater, dictatist* instead of *dictator*. How did 'English' get into this situation when one ending would be so much more practical and convenient?

Generally speaking, the answer is that 'English' got into this situation because much of 'English' is not English at all. It is Latin, Anglo-Saxon, French and other languages. The rules governing the cases are often the rules of the other languages. Most nouns ending in *-or*, like *editor* and *dictator*, are derived from Latin; those like *singer* and *writer* are from Anglo-Saxon; *essayist* and *artist* are from French.

The Elven language 'Sindarin' may be in a similar situation. If the evidence of the *Etymologies* is accepted, as well as statements in *The Road Goes Ever On*, then Sindarin is made up of several languages, each having its own rules, combined in a very complex way that is unlikely to be finally codified. In comparison, Quenya is a piece of cake, regular and logical to a high degree that can only be found in 'dead' languages. Sindarin is as confusing and mysterious as English, probably as its inventor intended. Without trying to be anachronistic, it would appear that it has a noun situation similar to that in English.

'Sindarin' is further complicated in that it has two histories. One is the *Primary*, or *Real World*, history of its invention by Tolkien. The other is its *Secondary*, or *Sub-created World* history.

The Primary history may be seen, for convenience only, in basically four stages:

1. *The Book of Lost Tales, Parts One & Two (BoLT1* and *BoLT2)* (with the *Gnomish Lexicon [GL]*); early *Hobbit*.
2. *The Lost Road (LR)* (with the *Etymologies [Ety.]*) and closely contemporary works.
3. *The Lord of the Rings [LotR]*.
4. Post-*LotR* works.

The Secondary history is mainly that set out in the Appendices of *LotR*, *The Silmarillion*, and the *Lhammas* of *LR*, as well as many significant statements elsewhere. No single one is here considered wholly definitive or rejected.

As pointed out by Bill Welden in *Parma Eldalamberon* #8, the word 'Sindarin' first appears in the Appendices of *LotR*, not in the text, making the *name* a post-*LotR* element, but not the *concept* of a language formed from a mixture of tongues. The mixed-tongue concept goes back to the first stage of the Primary history, where Ilkorin loan-words are mentioned in *GL* (*BoLT1*, pp. 249, 252). It is in *GL* that this particular analysis will begin.

In *GL* are found a class of nouns similar to those mentioned above in English. The Gnomish words end either in **-on** or **-or**, but there is little to indicate why the word has one suffix or the other.

-on		**-or**	
Hothr-on	'captain'	*Theg-or*	'chief'
Dair-on	'fluter'	*Gald-or*	(? 'tall one')
Mel-on	'beloved'	*Nand-or*	'farmer'
Celebr-on	'moon' ('silvery one')	*Hend-or*	(? 'grey' or 'old one')
Tarn-on	'porter'	*Ind-or*	'master of house', 'lord'
Pelecth-on	'hewer'	*Drond-or*	'racer', 'messenger'
Ilath-on	Ilúvatar	*Ilad-or*	Ilúvatar
		Fion-or	'Goblet-smith'[1]

In the *Etymologies* the same situation exists. There names that are not compounds like *Celebrimbor* (*Celebrin* + *bor*) are found.

-on		**-or**	
Call-on	'hero' ('shining one')	*Bë-or*	'follower', 'vassal'
Mell-on	'friend'	*Maeth-or*	'warrior' ('fighter')
Lathr-on	'listener'	*Bach-or*	'pedlar'
Nessar-on	'young one'	*Goll-or*	'magician'
Nathr-on	'weaver'	*Magl-or*	
Dang-on	'slain' (plural *dangen*)		
Tor-on	'brother'		
Odhr-on	'parent'		
Gar-on	'lord'		

In addition are words using either suffix: **Hadr-on**, **Had-or** 'hurler'.

And there is a pair in which the two forms are derived from the same base but take the different suffixes in separate languages: Noldorin **Pethr-on**, Doriathrin **Cwind-or** 'narrator', 'speaker'.

It would be specious to conclude at this point on the basis of one pair of words that Tolkien was delineating a change or division in the usage of these two suffixes into two languages, with **-on** being the Noldorin form and **-or** the Doriathrin/Ilkorin. There is no direct statement or evidence to support this and even some that contradicts it: Noldorin **Thavr-on**, Ilkorin **Thav-on** (not **Thav-or**) 'carpenter'.

However, there is some indirect evidence to support this notion. First, and strongest, is that **-on** as a suffix is in frequent use in Doriathrin/Ilkorin for place names that are not compound words, *e.g.* **Cel-on**, **Brith-on**, **Niv-on**, **Lind-on**, **Radh-on**, **Tov-on**, **Uduv-on**. This strongly

---

[1] **Fionor** is quite possibly an *epessë* for Fëanor (see *Essitalmar* in *VT* #10 on the rules of names: "Gnomes delighted to give two similar-sounding names of dissimilar meaning…" [*BoLT1*, p. 267]).

suggests that the additional use of *-on* as a personal or occupational name suffix in Doriathrin/ Ilkorin is unlikely. Additionally, there is a bit of evidence that *-or* would be used for place- names that are not proper names, *e.g.* Noldorin *gadr*, *gador* 'prison'[2] (*LR*, p. 358) and *naðor* 'pasture' (*LR*, p. 374), *nandor* 'farmer' (*BoLT1*, p. 261). Second, the name *Elbor-on* (initially Ilkorin) is removed from Ilkorin and Ilkorin *Bor-on* is struck out (*LR*, pp. 351, 353). *Di-or* is positively identified as Doriathrin (*LR*, p. 375, entry **NDEW-**).

Third, Doriathrin/Ilkorin place names with an *-or* are invariably compounds containing *-dor*. While in Noldorin, most place names end not with *-on* but *-ion* or other suffixes (*-ian*, *-en*, *-an(d)*), including *-or*. Fourth, those forms that do contradict this division can be seen as loan-words or late formations by the exiles operating under Thingol's ban (a word like *Maeth-or* 'warrior' is unlikely to have been a usage in Aman before such things as duels occurred. *Bachor* is another, as there is little evidence of commerce in Valinor). There is *Bëor*, where in Noldorin might be expected *Bioron. Further, some personal names may be loan-words going the other way. *Gald-or* may be one such name, as his House is given as *Nos Galdon*.[3] Certainly the Doriathrin *Gald* + *-or* is more likely than a Noldorin *Galad* + *-or* which yields *Galadhor*; even the description of Galdor's followers' dress and weapons in *The Fall of Gondolin* is more suggestive of the Sindar than of the Noldor.

Fifth is the contextual evidence of the mixture of races and tongues going back to the earliest stories, such as *The Fall of Gondolin* in *BoLT2*, where Ilkorin Elves make up a part of the whole people referred to as Gnomes. This is later clarified and emphasized in *The Silmarillion*, where it is stated that more than half of Turgon's following was made up of the Sindar of Nevrast.

It would be interesting to know if the reading of *Thavron*, *Thavon* is certain, or if the entry predates the removal of *Elboron*, for *Thavor* would not be unlikely, in light of other evidence.

What all this leads to here is that *Maglor* might be seen as a Doriathrin/Ilkorin *epessë* (*GL Magli*, Noldorin *Magl* 'sword') meaning 'great sword one' or 'sword one' = the anachronistic 'Longswordsman'; for it is said in *The Silmarillion* that "Fëanor … tempered fell swords for himself and his sons …" (p. 69).

In the formation of new coinages, one should attempt to follow the appropriate dialect. For example: *pengon* or *pengron* (Noldorin) *vs.* *cwingor* (Doriathrin) 'archer' < **KWIG-**; *cf.* *pethron*, *cwindor* < **KWET-**.

Letters

From Arden Smith:

Has anybody done any work on the etymology of *Aragorn* lately? I can't think of anything more recent than *Letters* (1981), in which the questionable notion that *-(g)orn* meant 'tree' was shattered: "'Tree-King' would have no special fitness for him, and it was already used by an ancestor. The names in the line of Arthedain are peculiar in several ways; and several, though S. in form, are not readily interpretable" (p. 426).

---

[2] Hypothetically, it might be expected that *gadr* yield *gadron*, meaning 'prisoner' or perhaps 'jailer', in Noldorin.

[3] *Nos Galdon* is amended to *Nos nan Alwen* (*BoLT2*, pp. 215, 340). Perhaps even then there was a dialectic distinction in the languages, and *Gald-on* would have been an inappropriate combination of the two dialects.

Bearing in mind that the *g* is most likely a lenited *c* (*cf.* **Argeleb**, **Arvedui**, **Aravir**), the second element would then be **corn*. Noldorin *corn* in the *Etymologies* (*The Lost Road*, p. 365) is derived from **KOR-** 'round', though no specific gloss for the word is given. Supposing that *corn* refers to a sphere (as most of the words in the **KOR-** entry seem to do) and knowing that Aragorn's mother "had in a measure the foresight of her people" (*The Return of the King*, pp. 339-40), we would have 'Globe-King', and Aragorn *did* become the most powerful ruler in Middle-earth.

If that reading makes the name too presumptuous, I have another option. Although we have the root **RIN-** meaning 'circle', it is clear that **KOR-** need not mean 'sphere', as Quenya *corma* 'ring' and *Coron Oiolairë* demonstrate. If this is the case (and I actually prefer this interpretation), then *Aragorn* means 'Ring-King', and the connection here is obvious.

Arden's analysis of **Aragorn** *is well thought out and I tend to agree with 'Ring-king' or 'World-king'. I feel the Noldorin* **corn**, **coron** *of the* Etymologies *shows a strong influence of Doriathrin/Ilkorin. First, because of the presence of Ilkorin* **basgorn**. *Secondly, there is a prevalent distinction in two syllable bases in the* Etymologies *for these to break down into a compressed form of one syllable in Doriathrin/Ilkorin and remain two in Noldorin; cf.:*

Base	Doriathrin/Ilkorin	Noldorin
ERÉD-	*erdh*	*eredh*
ERÉK-	*region*	*eregion*
GALAD-	*gald*	*galadh*
ÑGOLOD-	*(n)gold*	*golodh*
ÑGOROTH-	*ngorth*	*goroth*
SALÁK-WE	*salch*	*salab*
THOR-, THORON-	*thorn, Thorntor*	*thoron, Thorondor*
KYELEP, TELEP-	*telf*	*celeb*

It would be interesting to see if there was a correlation between the use of **Ar-** *to Noldorin and* **Ara-** *to Doriathrin/Ilkorin words from the* Etymologies *as in* **Ara-thorn** *(Doriathrin/Ilkorin but in Noldorin* **Ardhoron** *or* **Arthoron***) and* **Ar-geleb** *(Noldorin but in Doriathrin/Ilkorin* **Aradelf** *or* **Arathelf***).*

From Craig Marnock:

I enjoyed the latest *Essitalmar* (as of course I always do) but, as you said about the three-fold Elvish naming-system "maybe it was devised later". The vaguely Germanic name-giving system and cognomens seem to be well established from the start, but the system has an air of codification after the fact. Certainly the lack of an entry in the *Etymologies* for ep- or *apa-* (I don't think *Apanónar* was one of the names of Men at this time, though I could be wrong) indicates that the essay was written in the post-*LotR* period.

I am rather doubtful about trying to 'regain' "lost" *essi* by this method. *Isfin* and *Finda-(-o-)bar* show the kind of familial related names well-evidenced in Elvish; to say that they are the 'father-names' of Aredhel and Gil-galad is either superfluous or an assertion that could only be confirmed by reference to writings related to the essay on naming-customs that gave the father-names of these two. Either way I don't feel it's particularly relevant.

You say *Dior* is problematic, because you're trying to relate it to *Beren*. But Beren wasn't an Elf, remember, but a man, and the purpose of the father-name seems to have been similar to the Western surname, to indicate relation. Considering that Dior's children were named *Eluréd*, *Elurín* and *Elwing*, he was probably named (his patronymic, that is) for his *grand*-father; reappearance of the *el-* theme at two removes would be even more unusual. *Aranel* 'Elf-king' would be, as you suggest, Lúthien's name for him; and *Dior*, the name by which

— *continued on page 20.*

Transitions in Translations

A column edited by Arden R. Smith

The purpose of this column is to examine peculiarities in translations of Tolkien's works: mistranslations, unusual translations, interesting solutions to the problems of translation, and other curiosities in foreign editions. Ideas and contributions are encouraged: send them to "Transitions," c/o Arden R. Smith, P.O. Box 4395, Berkeley, CA 94704-0395, USA.

The *Hobbit* Γλωσσαρι

Greek Tolkien readers have a little bonus in their version of *The Hobbit* (Χομπιτ. Translated by A. Gabrielides and Ch. Delegiannes. Kedros, 1978. pp. 9-10), namely a glossary of words and names in the book. The glossary has fifteen entries: ῎Αρκος (Beorn), Βάργκ (Warg), Γκάνταλφ (Gandalf), Γκόλφιμπουλ (Golfimbul), θόριν (Thorin), θρέην (Thrain), Μπίλμπο (Bilbo), Νοσφιστής (Smaug), Ντουάλιν (Dwalin), ῎Οιν (Oin), ῎Ορι (Ori), ρουνικά (runes), τρόλ (troll), Φούντιν (Fundin), and χόμπιτ (hobbit).

Two of the names in the glossary have been completely changed in the Greek, those for Beorn and Smaug. The glossary entries explain the translations. The entry for ῎Αρκος reads: "from the Ancient Greek ἄρκος and ἄρκτος, where it means ἀρκούδα [bear]. The author calls him *Beorn*, from the Danish and Swedish *Bjorn*, where it has the same meaning" (my translation). Although this Danish/Swedish word is certainly a cognate, it is quite unlikely that it is the direct source, Douglas Anderson giving a much better etymology: "The name Beorn is actually an Old English word for 'man, warrior,' but originally meant 'bear'" (*The Annotated Hobbit*, p. 125).

The situation is similar with the entry for Νοσφιστής: "In the Ancient Greek, *the plunderer, the usurper.* The author calls him *Smaug*, from the Norwegian *Smyge*, where it has the same meaning" (my translation again). Professor Tolkien himself, however, explains the origin of the word thus: "The dragon bears as name — a pseudonym — the past tense of the primitive Germanic verb *Smugan*, to squeeze through a hole: a low philological jest" (*Letters*, p. 31).

Where, then, did the Greek translators get these etymologies? The answer lies in the bibliography at the end of the glossary: Ruth S. Noel's *The Mythology of Middle-earth* (Boston: Houghton Mifflin, 1977). In Noel's glossary, the entry for *Beorn* reads, "OE 'man, hero'; Dan. Swed. Icel. *bjorn* 'bear'" (p. 178); the Greek translators evidently just ignored the (important) Old English reference. Noel's entry for *Smaug* is also similar to the Greek: "Norwegian, form of *smyge* 'slip, sneak, steal' (p. 189).

Other features of Noel's glossary are reflected in the Greek glossary, as well. For example, only six dwarf-names are listed in the Greek glossary. The only other dwarf-names listed in Noel's glossary are Dain, Durin, Gimli, Náin, and Nár, none of which are major characters in *The Hobbit*.

A couple of Greek entries do not quite accurately reflect the real meaning of Noel's etymologies. Noel's entry for *Golfimbul*, "Icel. *fimbul* 'unearthly'" (p. 184) is transformed into the Greek entry, "in the Icelandic, *extraterrestrial*", referring to the whole name *Golfimbul*. Noel's entry states that *Bilbo* is an archaic term for a type of sword (p. 178); the Greek glossary calls it an *Old English* (στά ἀρχαῖα ἀγγλικά) word, using ἀρχαῖα (ancient, old) instead of ἀρχαϊκα (archaic).

The Greek translators, then, give some slightly inaccurate information in their glossary, but it's not entirely their fault.

About Russian Translations of Tolkien's Works (Part One)
by Nathalie Kotowski

The Hobbit

Hobbit Ili Tuda I Obratno, translated from English by N. Rakhmanova, 2nd corrected edition, published by Detskaya Literatura, Leningrad, 1989. Illustrations by M. Belomlinsky. 300,000 copies printed.

A fine translation! No real problems except sometimes wrong transcription in Russian of names in English (*e.g. Moraya* for *Moria*) but no attempts at translation of names. A good level of Russian language. Very beautiful translations of verses: the translations are verses too, with rhyme and metre and nicely put down. They are by I. Komarova and G. Oussova.

Smith of Wootton Major

Kuznetz Iz Bolchogo Vuttona. Published by Detskaya Literatura, Moscow, 1988. Translated by Youri Naguibine and Elena Gippius. Illustrated by C. Ostrov. A fine foreword by Youri Naguibine ending with the following words: the little book of the English storyteller is surprisingly rich in meaning and I envy those who will understand it full deep.

A beautiful translation very true to the original text and at the same time has something of the old Russian fairy tales.

[In the letter accompanying this article, she adds:]

I saw in the last *VT* questions from Gary Hunnewell about the Russian translation of *The Lord of the Rings*. That question I can answer, Russian being my mother tongue. I can only say to Gary that '*Noro lim, noro lim, Asfaloth*' is perhaps the only correct Elvish in the whole book.

Appendices Can Grow Back!

Wayne Hammond writes:

"You note in *Vinyar Tengwar #9* that no French translation of *The Lord of the Rings* contains appendices except the 'Tale of Aragorn and Arwen.'

"This was true only until 1986, when Christian Bourgois published a 'Presses-pocket' edition in three volumes with Appendices B, C, and D, as well as 'Aragorn and Arwen.' Then in 1988 Bourgois published another edition ('Collection folio junior'), in six volumes, illustrated by Philippe Munch, with Appendices A, B, C, and F part 1 (as 'D').

"As far as I know it's still true that no edition of *LotR* in Spanish contains appendices except 'Aragorn and Arwen,' but Ediciones Minotauro, Barcelona, in 1987 (?) published a separate edition of the Appendices, translated by Rubén Masera.

"Ask me no more about these! I've collected only the information, not the books themselves. As interesting as translations are, I've made room for only one in my Tolkien collection, the 1988 *Smith of Wootton Major* in Russian (*Kuznets iz Bol'shogo Vuttona*) because it's so beautifully illustrated."

Trivia Question

Q: What are the trolls' names in the Danish *Hobbit*?

A: Tom, Bert, and William *Hugger* (*Hobbitten*. Translated by Ida Nyrop Ludvigsen. [København:] Gyldendal, 1980).

Next Issue: More about Russian translations by Nathalie Kotowski and "The If and When of the Dominion of Men".

Two Problematic Quenya Noun Cases   *— continued from page 7.*

Galadriel. It occurs in the phrase yuldar lisse miruvóreva, meaning "swift draughts of miruvor" (yuldar = "draughts"; lisse = "swift (pl) miruvóreva = "of miruvóre"). There was already a genitive in -o, so ItE took a guess and labelled the -va case the "compositive", since miruvóreva means in this case "composed of miruvóreva *[sic —CFH]*". However, we now have two more examples: Mindon Eldaliéva "Tower of the Eldalie" and Nurtale Valinóreva "the Hiding of Valinor" (S 341 & S 102 respectively). As David Doughan says, "[the compositive] would make little or no sense of Nurtale Valinóreva, while Mindon Eldaliéva would be positively gruesome!". He has had a few ideas (a "descriptive" gen.; an archaic form) but is not happy with any of them.

Elerrína (Michael Poxon) also had some ideas, but also could not be very happy with them. However, he does say: "The -va of Quenya is surely related to the -wa of hwesta Sindarinwa and so on, and it seems also to be a form of the past participle as in Sí vanwa ná ("lost") whereas the genitive proper can be traced to a conjunction with the ablative case, and can even be semantically equivalent: Oiolosseo = "from Ever-white"."

Ornendil *[Steve Pillinger —CFH]* agrees that -va and -wa are related, and suggests that they are an adjectival suffix, -va after vowels, -wa after consonants.

I (Nólendil) *[Julian Bradfield —CFH]* played with the idea of subjective and objective genitives, but that's not much good either. The one conclusion that we can safely draw is that it isn't compositive, so I suggest we invent another name. Any suggestions? Otherwise, it is as shadowy as ever. Hope for more data!

Over five years later, Christopher Gilson responded in *Quettar* #28 (August, 1987, p. 15):

> The discussion in *Quettar* 13 of the case suffix *-va* covers all the relevant data and the problems that arise from various interpretations are alluded. Certainly Jim Allan's suggestion of "compositive" is now inadequate. Your [JCB's] idea of subjective vs. objective genitive still seems to hold the most promise....

Chris continues with an explanation too long to include here without proper permission *[Chris adds some detail to Steve's and Julian's surmise that **-va** and **-wa** are related, and suggests a mechanism by which the genitive in **–ō** may in fact arise from the regular phonetic mutation of **–va/–wa** to **–ō** —CFH].*

Two years later, Nancy Martsch offered her comments regarding the *V case* in the July, 1989 issue of *Beyond Bree* (p. 8):

> "ASSOCIATIVE" CASE: This case has been termed "compositive", "partitive", "associative". It is given in the Plotz noun declension without a name. We have two examples:[2] yuldar...lisse-miruvóreva, "draughts...of sweet mead" (Galadriel's Lament), where the draughts are composed of, made of, mead; and the name Mindon Eldaliéva "Lofty Tower of the Eldalië" (S 341), where the tower is definitely made by, not of, Elves. For this reason "associative" seems the best name.

---

[2] There are in fact at least four known examples. Including the two Nancy mentions, there are still ***Nurtalë Valinóreva*** "the Hiding of Valinor" (*S* 102) and ***Mar Vanwa Tyaliéva*** "The Cottage of Lost Play" (*BoLTI* 14).

Use the associative to indicate composed of, made by; and very closely associated with, identified with. The usual translation is "of".

...[T]he associative has only two forms, singular –<u>va</u> and multiple plural –<u>líva</u>.

Paul Nolan Hyde also offered a similarly simple solution in the Summer, 1989 issue of *Mythlore* (#58, pp. 28-30):

Of the synthetic languages, Finnish has one of the most complex noun declension systems. In order to have an idea as to the nature of inflection and the degree to which they can represent semantic function in a sentence, Table 2 is offered below.... If the italicized English words and phrases were rendered into Finnish, they would be in the indicated case with a suffixed ending. The starred words in hard brackets are my invented Anglo-Finnish words to demonstrate the inflection principle.

Table 2 / Finnish Case System

...

partitive   The object receives part of a continual action of the verb: "I am eating *bagels* [*bagel-a]"

...

The Partitive Case in Quenya

In the interlinear translation of Namarie *[in* The Road Goes Ever On *— CFH] ve linte yuldar lisse-miruvore-va* is rendered "like swift (pl.) draughts sweet-nectar-of" (R-58). In Finnish terms, this is a perfect example of a partitive. There appears to be a similar form in *Mindon Eldalieva [in* The Book of Lost Tales *— CFH]*, "Lofty Tower of the Eldalie" (S-341), and equally so in *Mar Vanwa Tyalieva*, "The Cottage of Lost Play" (*tyalie*, "play"; LT-260, LT-287). How the partitive would work in the dual and the plural forms is difficult to say. It might be possible to think of the General Plural as all of the parts of the whole, but the dual partitive and the simple plural partitive would not make much sense. Table 8 reflects this speculation.

Table 8 / Partitive Case

Singular	Dual	Plural	Gen. Plural
Eldaliéva	—	—	*Eldalielíva*

That's about all that's been said of the *Vcase*. Now I turn to what little has been said of the *Scase*. Nancy Martsch in *Beyond Bree* (July 1989, p. 8) tells about the *Scase*:[3]

THE MYSTERY CASE: J.R.R. Tolkien's letter to Dick Plotz gives two cases in parentheses, one under the allative and one under the locative. They are not named. From the Oath of Cirion (Unfinished Tales, Houghton Mifflin, p 305, 317) we know that the case under the allative is the dative (indirect object). What is the other case? Unfortunately there are no clear-cut examples of it in use. There is a sentence in the poem "Nieninque" (The Monsters and the Critics and Other Essays, Houghton Mifflin, pp 215-16) which might contain this case: <u>yar i vilya anta miqilis</u>, "to whom the air gives <u>kisses</u>". But this is an earlier form of Quenya, which differs in subject matter and noun forms from the time of the Plotz letter, so we cannot be sure. The relationship of the mystery case to the locative is probably like that of the dative to the allative.

---

[3] My thanks to Nancy for sending me a slightly expanded version of her discussion.

Christopher Gilson suggests "What we are 'looking for' then is some function related to locative in sense but less objective in function, capable of marking the subject of an idea or a subjective participant, the way the dative can mark either recipient of a gift or subject of an intransitive, in short the reference to participant in an event to whom the action is directed as opposed to a nonparticipant goal of the action. The parallel to the locative would be a participant located at the action as opposed to nonparticipant location."

Tom Loback speculates "perhaps… it's used to express adverbials like: whereon, whereby, whereof, wherein eg. <u>Círyas</u> <u>círalve</u>… 'The ship <u>whereon</u> we sail' …. A title might be 'circumstantive'."

Nancy Martsch wonders "if, since the dative represents movement of both the action of the noun and the direct object to the indirect object (dative), perhaps the mystery case represents focus of both action and object at a location, eg. "Fingolfin strikes a blow <u>at</u> <u>Morgoth</u>" (Morgoth receives both strike and blow)."

Other theories have been proposed. (Send your suggestions!) The mystery case has three forms, singular –<u>s</u>, plural –<u>is</u>, multiple plural –<u>lis</u>. There is no dual.

falma<u>s</u>	falma<u>is</u>	falma<u>lis</u>
lóte<u>s</u>	lót<u>is</u>	lóte<u>lis</u>
*elene<u>s</u>	*elen<u>is</u>	*elene<u>lis</u>

Note that in the Second Declension plural, the –<u>i</u>– of –<u>is</u> replaces final –ë.

So I conclude my brief survey of the two remaining problematic cases in Quenya. I hope this will serve as an impetus for the beginnings of a discussion to remove the remaining obstacles to a full understanding of Quenya's system of noun declension.

Essitalmar

— continued from page 15.

he was mostly known, would be his after-name. Mind you, he is called Dior Thingol's Heir, so perhaps those two are the other way around.

I think we've gone over context *vs.* linguistics before, but I can't let your discussion of ***Aredhel*** pass without comment. "The linguistic factors"? You can say that with a straight face and split the digraph ***dh*** into a lenited ***et-*** and suddenly-spirantised (eh? — I don't think that's a word) ***kel-*** just like that? And expect me not to double-take? Please.

By the way — I liked the way you slipped in that gloss on ***Finduilas*** with a nicely-disguised coinage for 'ivy'. Very slick.

I do not understand Craig's comments on the relevancy of 'father-names'. Does he mean to say that unless Tolkien expressly states something no attempt should be made to figure it out? Isn't it relevant to know whether Fingon had one son or two? The circumstantial evidence suggests he had only one. The rules of names indicating **Findabar** *is an* atáressë *tend to support this. I would suggest that this is the case until a genealogy shows there were two sons.*

Concerning the "splitting of the digraph": this was the point of the essay; to make a linguistically based assumption that **dh** *is an unsplittable digraph is wrong in the first place. Making the assumption that* **Aredhel** *was an* amilessë *requiring insight or foresight led to 'Lady' (***ar-***)'Went' (***kel*** > ***gel*** > ***hel***, see LR, p. 298) 'forth' (***ET-*** prefix, Noldorin ***ed-***, LR, p. 356). From the contextual point of view* **Aredhel** *cannot be simply 'High-elf' as this is a given as the high-born daughter of Fingolfin; therefore, it must have been something else, digraph or no digraph — just like that.*

I was quite proud of my translation of **uilas** *as 'ivy', thank you.*

What's a digraph, you're all asking? A single sound written as two letters.

Publications of Interest

*** BIAOR = Back issues available on request ***

Beyond Bree: Newsletter of the American Mensa Tolkien SIG. Published monthly.
    Editor: Nancy Martsch. *Subscriptions to*: the editor at P.O. Box 55372, Sherman Oaks, CA 91413. Annual subscription: $7.00; Overseas $10.00. *BIAOR*.
    April 1990: Continuing Nancy Martsch's excellent "Teach Yourself Quenya" series. Lesson 20: "Etymology". An exceptional survey of the phonological mutations within the Elvish tongues. Not to be missed.
    May 1990: Lesson 21: "Etymology and Word Formation". Again, not to be missed. Also reprints *I Ngurth Granthira* ('The Death of Caranthir') by Tom Loback, which first appeared on the cover of *VT* #10.

Cirth de Gandalf: Cercle d'études de Tolkien en Belgique. Published bimonthly.
    Editor: Nathalie Kotowski. *Subscriptions to*: the editor at 25 rue Victor Gambier, 1180 Bruxelles, Belgium. Annual subscription: 450 FB; 400 FB in Belgium.
    No. 5, Novembre 1989: Le Quenya: une grammaire: Leçon 5: Les déclinaisons.
    No. 6, Janvier 1990: Leçon 6: Le verbe et les pronoms.
    No. 7, Mars 1990: Leçon 7: Encore sur les noms et les pronoms.

Mythlore: A Journal of J.R.R. Tolkien, C.S. Lewis, Charles Williams, and the Genres of Myth and Fantasy Studies. A refereed journal of the Mythopoeic Society. Published quarterly.
    Editor: Glen GoodKnight. *Subscriptions to*: P.O. Box 6707, Altadena, CA 91003. Annual subscription (includes Society membership): In USA $13.00; Overseas (airmail) to Europe or Latin America $28.00, to Asia or Australia $33.00. *BIAOR*.
    No. LXI, Spring 1990: In his regular *Quenti Lambardillion* column Paul Nolan Hyde presents his analysis of "Fíriel's Song" from *The Lost Road*. This issue also features artwork with Quenya description of "The Wedding of Tuor and Idril" by Tom Loback.

Next Issue

VT #12, our Second Anniversary issue, will feature still more insightful (and inciteful) letters, articles, and columns, perhaps a coup (hint: look for a hitherto unpublished specimen of authentic Elvish to appear in these pages soon!), and just maybe a picture of your editor on the cover! We'll also continue the four-part presentation of Tom Loback's huge "Fifth Battle" mural with the northeast quadrant.

Vinyar Tengwar

The bimonthly 'news-letters' of the Elvish Linguistic Fellowship.
A Special Interest Group of the Mythopoeic Society.

Editor: Carl F. Hostetter, 2509 Ambling Circle, Crofton, MD 21114, USA.

Contributing Editor: Jorge Quiñónez, 3326 Polk Ave., San Diego, CA 92104, USA.

Proofreaders: Jorge Quiñónez and Arden Smith.

Masthead: by Tom Loback.

Tengwar numerals: from Lawrence M. Schoen's *Moroma* PostScript *Tengwar* font for the Mac, available on disk for $6.00 from PsychoGlyph, P.O. Box 74, Lake Bluff, IL 60044.

Subscriptions: Subscriptions are for 1 year (6 issues) and must be paid in US dollars.
$10.00   USA
$12.00   Canada (sent airmail) and Overseas surface mail
$16.00   Overseas airmail

Back issues available: Issues 1 - 7 & 9 - 11 are each $1.75 in the USA, $2.00 overseas surface mail and Canada, $2.75 airmail. Issue 8 includes a large map and costs $4.00 USA, $4.75 surface and Canada, $5.50 airmail. A complete set of back issues is available for $15.00 USA, $17.50 Overseas surface mail, and $20.00 Overseas airmail. *All costs are postpaid.*

Payments: All payments must be in US dollars. It is recommended that overseas members make payments via international postal money order. *Send all payments and make all checks payable to Carl F. Hostetter.*

Submissions: Written material should in some manner deal with Tolkien's invented languages. All submissions must be typed, or must be written unbelievably legibly: if I have to decipher lower-glyphics, the submission is automatically rejected! The editor reserves the right to edit any material (except art) for purposes of brevity and relevance. Ilúvatar smiles upon submissions on 800K (3.5") Macintosh disks in PageMaker, Microsoft Word or MacWrite formats, or as unformatted TEXT files. Artwork should be linguistic, or at least Elvish, in nature. Remember that artwork done in black ink will reproduce the best; I wouldn't harbor great expectations for the quality of reproduction from artwork rendered in pencil, "Flair" pen, chalk, or colored ink.

Send all submissions to Carl F. Hostetter. Direct inquiries to Jorge Quiñónez.

The deadline for VT #12 is June 25, 1990.

Vinyar Tengwar is produced by the editor on an Apple Macintosh II personal computer, using Microsoft Word 4.0 and Aldus PageMaker 3.02. It is printed on an Apple LaserWriter II NTX.

Vinyar Tengwar

Cainen rasta

#12

July, 1990

In This Issue

Editor's Musings

Welcome to *VT* #12, our Second Anniversary issue. *VT* has matured greatly since issue #1, which was edited by Jorge Quiñónez and given away for the cost of postage (thanks to a generous subsidy by Bill Welden). From that first issue, Jorge continuously improved *VT*'s quality, in both content and presentation, and maintained a strict regularity of publication. These are not easy tasks, and it is my extreme good fortune to have been able to build on the foundations laid by Jorge in my own tenure as editor of *VT*.

An unfortunate aspect of *VT*'s maturation, however, appears on the back cover. As you will no doubt be horrified to learn, I've had to raise subscription costs again. While I had hoped to be able to use the rates which Jorge set just before turning production of *VT* over to me (which coincided with *VT*'s new format and increased page count) for at least one year, a widening deficit has shown the previous rate calculation to have been short of the mark. I can only hope that my efforts to continue to improve the quality of *VT* will justify its additional cost.

— Carl F. Hostetter

"We notice in the first place that attempts to reduce grammar to logic, or logic to grammar, have not had the success they should have had if there were a large and important non-rhetorical common factor on which non-literary writing could be built. For a long time the prestige of the discursive reasoning fostered the notion that logic was the formal cause of language, that universal grammars on logical principles were possible, and that the entire resources of linguistic expression could be categorized. We are now more accustomed to think of reasoning as one of many things that man does with words, a specialized function of language. There seems to be no evidence whatever that man learned to speak primarily because he wanted to speak logically."

— Northrop Frye, *Anatomy of Criticism* (Princeton University Press, 1957), pp. 331-2.

E.L.F. News

New Members

The E.L.F. extends a hearty *mae govannen* to:

- Charles Noad   12 Madeley Road, Ealing, London W5 2LH, England.
- Nataliya Prohorova   109180 Moskva, ul. Bol'shaya Polyanka, d. 28, kv. 266, U.S.S.R.

A Tolkien Thesaurus

A Tolkien Thesaurus by Richard E. Blackwelder is available from Garland Publishing (136 Madison Ave., New York, N.Y. 10016). The *Thesaurus* is an alphabetical listing of thousands of words from *The Hobbit* and *The Lord of the Rings* (including the Appendices), each given with the context of the sentence in which the word appears. Write the publisher for price information. A supplement to the *Thesaurus*, entitled "Tolkien Phraseology: a Companion to *A Tolkien Thesaurus*", by Charles Elston and Richard Blackwelder, is available for free from the Tolkien Archives Fund, Marquette University, 1415 W Wisconsin Ave., Milwaukee, WI 53233. *[Reported in* Beyond Bree, *June, 1990, p. 11]*

An Introduction to Elvish *is Still Available*

Jim Allan's required *An Introduction to Elvish* remains available for £6.95 from Bilbo's Bookshop, 3 New Bond St. Bldgs., Bath BA1 2BN. Write for catalogue. *[Reported in* Beyond Bree, *June, 1990, p. 11]*

Foreword to "The Fifth Battle"

by Tom Loback

This issue of *VT* continues the four-part presentation of "The Fifth Battle", or the *Nirnaeth Arnoediad*. It is a black-and-white print which represents the climactic hours of the battle, during which the Elves, Men and Dwarves of the Union of Maedhros were tragically and utterly defeated by the Hosts of Morgoth, led by Gothmog, Lord of Balrogs, and Glaurung, the Father of Dragons.

While the *tengwar* border calligraphy uses a Quenya mode, the descriptions of the battle formations are Sindarin, written in the Mode of Beleriand. This could indicate the origin of the piece was in Eregion during the middle of the Second Age. However, the calligraphic and illustrative style point to a possibly later period.

Anyone interested in acquiring a print of this work should write me at 152 West 26th Street, #36, N.Y. City, N.Y. 10001, USA. The print is limited to 100 copies. Prices vary on the quality of the material: $100.00 for Maplewood veneer, $50.00 for Arches Cover bond (acid-free paper), and $20.00 for heavy white bond. Size: 27" wide by 18" high. Make checks and money orders payable to Tom Loback. Inquiries welcome.

This month's installment reproduces the northeast quadrant of the map. The southeast quadrant will be given next month.

[The second quadrant of "The Fifth Battle" appears as the center spread, pp. 10-11 —CFH]

Letters to VT

• Tom Loback   New York City, New York

VT #11 was quite good. I especially liked Pat's reply and naturally found his comments on Doriathrin enlightening. He sent me an early draft of his translation *[of "Lúthien's Song", which appeared in* VT *#9 — CFH]* many *Moons* ago, querying **lasto dîn**. I suggested it meant 'attend him', but I would agree **dîn** probably means 'silent'. *A* **Hîr Annûn** ... **le linnon im** could also be 'And West-Lord ... to thee I sing' (Sindarin *a* = 'and', see *The Silmarillion*, p. 356). This would, in effect, conjunct the two lines while lessening the title 'Lord of the West' to a more general title. I believe both the Moon and the Sun first arose in the West. I suppose Lúthien would have referred to the Sun similarly as **Hîril Annûn**.

I am curious as to why 'eleven' is given as **cainen minë** as opposed to **minqë** (see *The Lost Road [LR]*, p. 373, and *The Book of Lost Tales, Part One*, p. 260). Is a distinction being drawn between the decimal and duodecimal systems of the Elves? If so, isn't *VT* published on some sort of monthly or lunar system (*Moons* again!) and shouldn't it therefore use the Elven duodecimal?

[The numbering system I am using comes from a handout distributed in conjunction with a talk by Bill Welden at Mythcon XX. Because I did not attend Mythcon XX, I do not know Bill's arguments for or against the systems he presents, and so used the system which Jorge had begun with and recommended (without malice, I hope). The system I am using is indeed labelled "speculative" by Bill, but hey, sparking and discussing controversies is one of the functions of this newsletter, isn't it? Perhaps Bill will be able to provide at least a synopsis of his arguments in these pages. I chose the decimal system simply because I do not have a tengwar font which has the proper duodecimal numerals for 11 and 12. —CFH]

I applaud Jorge's effort to bring all the discussions of the two 'mystery' cases together. I look forward to similar efforts on other discussions and subjects. In the matter of declensions there is a comment by Tolkien in *The Etymologies* (*LR*, p. 360; emphasis mine):

"**ƷŌ**- from, away, from among, out of. This element is found in the old *partitive* in Q[enya] *-on* (ʒō + plural *m*)."

Based on this it would seem that:

1. There being an 'old partitive', there might be a new one.
2. The genitive *-ō*, *-on* became so at the time of *The Etymologies*.
3. Earlier uses of *-ō*, *-on* in the Primary World sense should possibly be seen as partitive also.

Comments, Q(u)enya lovers?

Regarding Edouard's letter: first, as *epessi* exist in Third Age Sindarin I'm inclined to think the custom of the three names is prevalent throughout Elven culture; *e.g.* **Maeglin Lómion** (*ataressë* and *amilessë*), **Beleg Cúthalion** (*epessë* — I would hesitate to say **Beleg** is an *ataressë*, because I suspect, for complex reasons, that he is one of the Elves awakened as a group in Cuiviénen and therefore had no father ("wist no sire"; see *The Lays of Beleriand*, p. 11); *cf.* **Elu Thingol**; evidence for an *ataressë* in Elu's descendants is apparent, and also in **Celebrían**, daughter of Celeborn. Evidence for the *amilessë* is more obscure, but Aragorn's mother called him **Estel** 'hope'.

Finally, whatever my vision of Middle-earth may be, it changes not one word of what Tolkien wrote.

• Paul Nolan Hyde　　　　　　　　　　　　　　　Simi Valley, California

Dear Charlin & Co.

The above salutation must have some other significance other than a blatant corruption of *Thorin & Co.*, but for the life of me I can't pre-call what it is. I will have to *sic* the grand apologist, J.E.C. Kelson on the matter. It undoubtedly has something to do with another of the transtemporal paradoxes which occur whenever I take pen in hand, or keyboard in tip.

First of all, I read with some amusement the editorial disclaimer printed in *VT #8 [Well, #9 really; or is this just another of those pesky transtemporal effects? —CFH]* with regard to any extant typographical "errors" in future issues of the "news-letters" *[That's right, folks! I'm off the hook for this issue! Thanks for writing, Paul —CFH].* While I have no serious objection to being credited with these egregious *faux pas* (I have a series of alter egos who are perfectly willing to leap into the breach in my defence), I find it just a little disconcerting to be denominated the Oliver North of the E.L.F. simply because I have no serious objection to being credited with these egregious *faux pas* (I have a series of alter .... {*oops! another transtemporal verbal wormhole (Ouroboros class) running amok in my prose, beginning to swallow its own tail*}..... Free at last, free at last!

Thirdly {*don't ask!, some verbal wormholes extract sacrifices of ordinal proportions*}, I was somewhat taken by Jorge (sans *tilde*, sans *grave*) Quinonez's description of my *Mythlore* 58 discussion of the Quenya noun declensions (p. 19), as "simple". No doubt, Jorge was groping for the linguistic term "elegant" (which, I think was originally a philosophical term with reference to logic). *Elegance*, of course, is that quality of a presentation which most tersely and adequately accounts for all of the given evidence in the least convoluted manner. Since my presentation was *simply* a presentation of data and a conservative speculation as to what the evidence might suggest about what I chose to call the "partitive" case, *elegant* might indeed be an appropriate adjective to describe my little work. In a more expansive view of Jorge's remarks, my solution was "similarly simple" to that of Nancy Martsch's. I happen to like Nancy very much and if she would accept the term "elegant" as applying to her work in *Beyond Bree*, I have no serious objection to Jorge being credited with having said so.

With regard to the "partitive case" itself, I think that the Finnish partitive helps us understand what is going on in the Quenya declension, but is not necessarily a cognate of it. According to my view, in Quenya only a part of an object receives the action of the verb. My example cited by Jorge, "I am eating bagels [*bagel-a]", means that the bagels are being eaten progressively one at a time. Their non-partitive counterpart would be something to the effect "I am eating all of the bagels in the world at the same time and in a moment there will not be one bagel anywhere on this planet" (that is a mouthful in anybody's parlance). The partitive simply means that only a portion of the whole, or a representation of the whole is receiving the action of the verb. So like-wise in *Namárië*, the phrase *ve linte yuldar* ... *lisse-miruvóre-va* means "like swift (pl.) draughts [portions of all that there is] ... sweet-nectar-of". In this case, not all sweet-nectar has been made into draughts, but representative draughts have been taken from the whole. In an oblique fashion, this has a correspondence with the "neuter noun" form in Old English from whence we have such relics as "sheep (sg.)" and "sheep (pl.)" where one has formally come to represent the whole. *Mindon Eldaliéva*, following this line of reasoning, would mean something like "Lofty Tower of [some, but not all of] the Eldalië", which seems to describe in nomenclature one of the basic aspects of the storyline of the Three Kindreds of the Elves. In *Mar Vanwa Tyaliéva*, a similar aspect may be indicated, "The Cottage of [some, but not all] Lost Play" or "The Cottage of Lost [some, but not all] Play". I think, too, that the adjectival aspect of *–va* is more than fortuitous since the basic nature of adjectives is partitive from the outset. One still may be a little perplexed by **Nurtalë Valinóreva**, but when it is remembered that Valinor is not completely hidden, but only the eastern portions (see *The Silmarillion*, p. 102 and *The Book of Lost Tales, Part One*, p. 223-224) and also that Númenor is not hidden from everyone, the partitive makes sense.

I have grave reservations about the so-called "Dative" and "Scase" additions that Jorge and others have suggested, primarily due to a lack of concrete evidence as to their existence at all. My initial question has to do with Tolkien's conventions in the Dick Plotz letter. Are we to assume that parenthetical forms, of necessity, have to indicate a whole new class of declension? In the Allative, Locative, and Ablative Plural 2 column, we are confronted with parenthetical letters, (r) and (n). Does this mean that for these particular cases there is a Plural 3?... Or does it mean that the declension form has two written manifestations? I think that almost everyone assumes the latter. Could we not take the same approach with the parenthetical forms as additional shortened forms used for the Allative and the Locative cases? I suspect this to be the case *[pun, no doubt, intended —CFH]*. The historical thing to keep in mind is that the Dative case has typically been the compost pile for degenerating declension systems in real languages. As a result, it is one of the most common of the cases in natural language. Isn't it odd that Tolkien would label, albeit briefly, the Nominative, Accusative, Genitive, and Instrumental cases (the other frequently used cases) and not label the Dative, at least with a "D"? It is more than odd; it is almost unthinkable. Could it not be that the Allative, Locative, and Ablative cases, all listed under "(b)", are actually the three-fold Quenya expression of the Dative? I suspect that is the fact of the matter.

Well, that will do for now. I must be off to fire up the "barbie" *[Does Ken know about this? —CFH]*. Leo and Bob Malaise are flying in for the weekend and they are bringing their widowed mother, Melba, from Fosston, Minnesota. Patrick Wynne's bachelor uncle, Einer, has been dating Melba now on a regular basis and everyone wants to give it a rest. Jack Kelson figures to be in attendance since Einer's not coming. He is a little sweet on Melba himself.

• Nathalie Kotowski   Bruxelles, Belgium

Thank you for *VT* #11. It is really a fine issue (as all are) and all your contributors are so clever! I really feel very unqualified to express opinions about Elvish, but after translating and adapting Nancy Martsch's Quenya course, I dare to do so. And it is such fun!

This time, it is about the Vcase:

It seems on first sight quite impossible to see the similarity of the four known cases of the Vcase, in French or English anyway. So I have tried to see it via Russian (which Tolkien knew). In Russian you have the normal genitive, but there is also another way to express the relation of belonging between two nouns. In French it is called the "*adjectif d'appartenance*". You can form an adjective from any noun with the endings *–ov*, *–ine*, and *–sky*. That is the way surnames are formed, such as my own ("Kotowski" comes from the stem *kot* which means 'cat'. There was first a tribe whose symbol was a cat, which gave the surname *Kot–ov*. Those with close relations to this tribe were called *Kotov-sky*).

Let us take the example of Pushkin's novel *The Captain's Daughter*. In Russian this is rendered *Kapitanskaja Dotchka*, not *Dotch Kapitana*, which uses the simple genitive. The distinction in meaning is that the heroine is important *because* she is the Captain's daughter. If she were the daughter of someone else, it would have been no novel at all.

Let us apply this to Elvish:

Yuldar ... **lisse-miruvóreva** — the important thing here is not the draught but that it is *miruvórë*. Had it been tea, ale or champagne, it would not be interesting at all. It is interesting

— *continued on page 15.*

Nólë i Meneldilo

Lore of the Astronomer
by Jorge Quiñonez and Ned Raggett

FOREWORD — The following is a paper which was completed early in 1988, and read at Mythcon XX in Vancouver, Canada in July, 1989. While *The History of Middle-earth* series had reached only *The Lost Road* when the authors drafted this paper, and while the subsequent publication of two volumes in *The History of The Lord of the Rings* series has added some information, it was decided that it would be best to present the paper unrevised, due to numerous requests for the paper to appear just as presented at Mythcon. The authors will leave it to others to answer the unanswered questions.

INTRODUCTION — One can imagine at the turn of the century, young Ronald Tolkien looking at the unfamiliar and unpolluted skies of the southern hemisphere in Bloemfontein, Orange Free State (later South Africa). He must have witnessed a spectacular panorama of stars in the night sky.

Although, by the time J. R. R. Tolkien wrote *The Lord of the Rings* (*LotR*) they became but distant and faint memories, the night sky must have left a permanent impression in the mind of a very young child, and would later become, as reflected by his writings, a lifelong interest.

Priscilla Tolkien, the daughter of Tolkien, once said her father "had a general interest in" astronomy. The article in which this appeared came to the conclusion that Tolkien had enough interest in and knowledge of astronomy to use it convincingly and to lend believability to his stories. The attempt of this article is to explore the *Nólë i Meneldilo* (in Quenya), or Lore of the Astronomer, which he invented in his mythos. Besides using previous studies on the same topic to aid our research, we employ several unpublished sources.

COSMOLOGY — Cosmology can be taken to mean the study of the physical layout of the cosmos, in the same way that geography involves the similar kind of study, but concerning only the Earth. In its own way, cosmology has existed for a long time; every attempt to describe the actual structure of the physical universe, from the earliest known mythic tales onward, is an expression of cosmology in some form. Tolkien was well aware of this tradition of attempting to place the universe into some recognizable form; he therefore did it himself for his own mythology, incorporating some elements from other mythic cycles, as was his wont, in order to produce a final form uniquely his. Of all the elements of his mythology, the cosmological shape of the universe remained among the most unchanged; the majority of the revisions found in the later works involve a simplifying of various concepts he had initially included.

As he and the inhabitants of Middle-earth perceived their universe, the only established physical location in the whole of the universe was *Eä*, the globed world brought forth by the will of Eru. As first conceived in *The Book of Lost Tales* (*BoLT*), the flat, circular level named *Arda* was the area where all creatures and species, from the Valar to the lowest of animals, had their abode. Arda itself floated on an ocean named *Vai*, while above it arced three levels of atmosphere: *Vilna*, called "grey", where "birds may fly safely", the air which we all breathe; *Ilwë*, "blue and clear", where the stars were found; then *Vaitya*, "wrapped dark and sluggish" over everything else. In the "*Ambarkanta*", *Vaitya* and *Vai* are now amalgamated into *Vaiya*, meaning "envelope"; it is a strange thing, described as being like "sea below the Earth and...air above" it; the clear layer above it is given the apt name of *Vista*. A layer called

Ilmen, "clear and pure", is over Vista, but can mingle with it. In *The Silmarillion* (*Silm*), the idea of an ocean is lost, while Ilmen becomes the name for the layer of atmosphere where the stars are found; an unnamed layer of air separates Ilmen and the ground.

Outside of the atmosphere is the barrier between Eä and all else, a structure consistently described as some form of wall. Originally it was called the "Wall of Things" in *BoLT*, vast and of a "deep-blue" color. "*Ambarkanta*" names it *Ilurambar*, or "Walls of the World", "above all imagination" of any living in Arda, "cold, transparent, and hard". *Silm* simply terms them the "Walls of the Night", dark and foreboding. The only openings in the barrier are a pair of gates or doors that permit the sun to pass from west to east in its travails. *BoLT* has the "Door of Night", "utterly black and huge", in the west, while the "Gates of Morn", an arch "of shining gold...with silver gates", is found in the east. Only the Door of Night appears in "*Ambarkanta*"; the sun and moon pass below Arda through Vaiya. Outside of the walls surrounding Eä is the Void or the Abyss, a pit of nonexistence where nothing physical exists; the only area of light in the infinite waste of the Void are the Halls of Eru.

As far as similarities to other cosmologies go, there are several to a number of widespread sources, which testifies more to Tolkien's sense of knowing archetypal images rather than having had direct contact with all the various sources. The idea of the physical universe being surrounded by a limitless void is very widespread, appearing in Judeo-Christian tradition (a very obvious source for Tolkien to draw upon), along with Egyptian, Greco-Roman, Mesopotamian, and other mythologies. The early conception of Arda floating on a vast ocean reflects diverse conceptions of the Earth floating on a sea: Hindu tradition placed the world on four elephants who stood on a turtle who swam a celestial sea, while several Amerind [or American Indian] stories, among them Iroquois traditions, had the world upon (again) a turtle in an ocean. The division of the atmosphere into layers and the Walls and the doors in them, however, appear to be of Tolkien's own creation.

THE SUN AND MOON — In every mythology, in the study of astronomy, the sun and moon hold a notable position. They are the two great lights that human behavior/society has revolved around since early days. The Sun is the source of the light that creates and causes life to grow; its heat sustains us all, its perceived rising and falling from our planet's viewpoint created a basic unit of time, the day. The Moon does not provide life-giving light, but instead creates the supernatural frost that inspires romantics and enables the average person to ward away the night when it shines the strongest; its own pattern of movement created the month. Both these celestial bodies have creative origins in Tolkien's cycle.

Though details have changed, the basic story concerning the creation of the two has remained quite constant throughout Tolkien's developing universe. Soon after Arda's creation, two great lamps were made by the Valar and were placed on two mountains in order to light the world; through the work of Melkor, however, the lamps were destroyed. In their enclave of Valinor, the Valar tried again to bring forth light; again the results were twofold — a pair of trees, one of which produced golden light, the other silver. However, the machinations of Melkor resulted in the destruction of these lights as well. In one last desperate attempt to save them, the trees produced one fruit each. These the Valar created vessels for, intending them to sail the skies of Arda so as to counter the darkness of Melkor; two of the Maiar piloted them as they journeyed. The Sun was the main challenge to the forces of evil, for its strong light dispelled the dark completely, while the Moon watched to see that no evil took place during the hours of night. The Moon travelled irregularly, but the bright Sun stuck to a strict schedule so that dark should never gain too much time; for it, the Valar made the two gates in the walls about Eä.

Tolkien's conception of the origin of the Sun and Moon is a refreshing new interpretation of their creation; the basic account could have easily been at the root of a human culture's society in the past. He effectively reasons why there are two lights rather than one or none or nine by giving them a heritage of two parents. Astronomically speaking, the theory of their movements is by no means scientific, but it describes their actions from a Endorian viewpoint quite well. None of the complexities that Ptolemy and his followers created for their geocentric universe are apparent, for example.

On a distaff note, the recently released *Annotated Hobbit* (p. 179) indicates that, had Tolkien lived long enough, he would have changed the origin of the Sun and Moon once more, this time having both of them be in existence at least from the birth of the Elves. The revision, printed in 1966, appears only here in the published Tolkien corpus.

THE STARS — Perhaps no element of the astronomical bent in Tolkien's cycle has caused more fascination than the stars — not so much for what they are, but as to which ones they are. Ever since the appearance of a list of star names in *Silm*, every article concerning Middle-earth's astronomy has made a crack at identifying them, along with the other stars mentioned throughout the "definitive" corpus. This article follows in this tradition, and attempts to show the evidence to settle the thorny question definitively. (The claims in this section are based on a combination of comparative and linguistic evidence; the catalog at the end of this article provides further backing for the assertions.) Consideration to star names in the *History of Middle-earth* series will be given solely in this section.

The origins and natures of the stars are various. In the original *BoLT* tales, the stars are created by Varda in two spurts. Initially, when she first enters Arda, she sets a few stars in the sky "in her playing". Later, after the Elves awake, she combines silver sparks from Aulë's forge with molten silver. These stars of the second wave are described as having "a power of slumbers", because the molten silver comes from Lórien's garden of dreams. Tolkien revised and changed his story, and the end result has Varda creating only one wave of stars, with an "innumerable" number of them already in place before she begins. This time it is the imminent coming of the Elves that causes her actions, at Mandos' indirect suggestion. Now using dew from the vats of the silver tree Telperion, she "made new stars and brighter against the coming of the Firstborn".

In the finalized works, eight star names are given: one in *LotR* and seven in *Silm*. The one star in *LotR* is *Borgil*, seen by Frodo, Sam and Pippin as they wait at night with the Elves in the Shire: "Away high in the East swung Remmirath, the Netted Stars, and slowly above the mists red Borgil rose, glowing like a jewel of fire."

Remmirath is the Pleaides, a star group in Taurus, while the constellation following *Borgil* into the sky is *Menelvagor*, or Orion (there will be further discussion of them in the next section). What, then, is *Borgil*, a name which means 'red star' in Elvish? Three identifications have been made: Foster thinks it is Aldebaran, Tyler and Henry say it is Mars, while Allan, Martingell, Stone, and, again, Foster, choose Betelgeuse. In terms of astronomical accuracy and plausibility, all three have their points: Aldebaran is a red star in Taurus; Mars is the "red planet" of lore, and its position in Taurus, a constellation in the Ecliptic, can be easily understood; Betelgeuse is a red giant in Orion. However, the clear choice is Betelgeuse. Mars is disqualified because of another association Tolkien made for it, which will be shown shortly. Aldebaran, while plausible, is not as intense as the comparatively brighter Betelgeuse; Stone also demonstrates in his article that, given the time and location in which the hobbits found themselves, while they were stargazing, Aldebaran would have already been high in the sky rather than just coming over the horizon. Borgil is therefore Betelgeuse, because not only is it the one remaining choice, but is the first bright star of Orion to appear, 'hauling' the rest of the constellation after it.

The other seven star names, those in *Silm*, are of a varying degree of ease to decipher. One, *Helluin*, is positively identified as Sirius in the index. The other six appear in a crucial passage describing Varda's formation of new stars in challenge to Morgoth's darkness, and to signal the awakening of the Eldar: "Carnil and Luinil, Nénar and Lumbar, Alcarinquë and Elemmírë she wrought in that time."

No definite identifications of these stars appear in the index; all that is given or can be deduced offhand are basic linguistic roots: *Alcarinquë* means 'glorious', *carn-* in *Carnil* is 'red', *luin-* in *Luinil* is 'blue'. With that it seems that we have run into a brick wall. However, as they have before, Tolkien's original manuscripts provide the answer to the majority of this mystery. As far as we know, only Taum Santoski has published what we are about to "re-reveal"; along with linguistic evidence, we shall definitively label each of the star names with their correspondent in our skies.

In MS 3/9/36 at the Marquette collection, an original of the above mentioned passage is found. Based on external and internal evidence, the date of the manuscript can be roughly placed between 1939 and the 1953, most probably when *Silm* was rewritten. The star names possess some spelling differences (the '*c*' in *Carnil* and *Alcarinquë* is a '*k*', for example), but no major changes are in evidence. What is important, however, are the letters which appear above a majority of the names:

> *Karnil* > *Carnil* = M
> *Lumbar* = S
> *Luinil* = (no letter)
> *Nénar* = N (crossed out)
> *Alkarinque* > *Alcarinquë* = Jup
> *Elemmire* > *Elemmírë* = M

If nothing else provides a clue, the "Jup" does — the six "star" names correspond to the "wandering stars" of the Greeks, the planets. "Glorious" Alcarinquë is Jupiter, largest of the planets, the brightest after Venus (which is treated at the end of this discussion). Lumbar is logically Saturn — no other planet begins with 's'. The two 'm's' represent Mars and Mercury; Carnil would have to be Mars, the Red Planet, because of the *carn-* root, which leaves Elemmírë to be Mercury. Since Arda is Earth, we are left with three planets (Uranus, Neptune, Pluto) and two star names (Luinil, Nénar).

Pluto we have decided to discard from our consideration. First, it was not discovered until 1933, at which time the mythology had been developed to a large extent. Second, it is doubtful that even the keen-eyed Elves, studying the utterly unpolluted skies of Middle-earth, could have spotted such a miniscule body. However, these two factors no doubt enabled the Elves to observe the other two planets, both of which are very large and closer to the sun than Pluto; the two names therefore belong to them. Both the manuscript list and linguistic evidence allow us to make final matchups. Nénar was identified with Neptune, but the scratching out of the 'N' means that it is perhaps Uranus. This is confirmed by the fact that Luinil is an excellent name for Neptune: Neptune has a distinct blue color, and the root *luin-* means 'blue'.

We therefore present this star list for Middle-earth, excluding Eärendil which is Venus, with real Earth counterparts:

Alcarinquë = Jupiter
Borgil = Betelguese
Carnil = Mars
Elemmírë = Mercury
Helluin = Sirius
Luinil = Neptune
Lumbar = Saturn
Nénar = Uranus

An understandable question at this point is: why only the two true stars, when there must have been many brilliant ones in the night sky of Middle-earth? There are three reasonable answers. First, Tolkien was practicing his process of sub-creation by establishing a few links between our sky and that of Middle-earth — not many, but enough to help the reader's acceptance of his world (the same principle applies to the way he worked with constellations, as shall be shown). Second, the moving planets attract more attention than the relatively stationary stars, and thus hold a more prominent place in the sky. Third, both of his choices make sense within the story's framework — Sirius is the brightest star in the sky, aside from the sun, while Betelgeuse, as was shown, is to be expected when Orion is around.

Eärendil is the most important astronomical object in Tolkien's works. The extent of its significance is far too great to be treated in this paper, but a brief overview can be given. He was a mighty warrior of the Elves who became immortal and piloted a ship, a Silmaril on his brow, through the heavens. Besides the Sun and Moon, he is the only living being who becomes a permanent part of the heavens as a heavenly body; this concept of personification appears in a great number of cultures, beginning with the Egyptians. He is clearly identified with Venus as the Morning and Evening Stars, traditional names given to the brightest of planets.

In the *History of Middle-earth* sequence, some more star names are mentioned. Sirius is originally named *Nielluin* ("the Bee of Azure, Nielluin whom still may all men see..."); alternate names are *Gil* or *Ingil*. Arcturus, meanwhile, has been named *Morwinyon*, "who blazes above the world's edge in the west". A rejected name for Jupiter appears in *BoLT1: Morwen*, "daughter of the dark"; at this early point in the development of Tolkien's work, this name was not given to Turin's mother.

Constellations — Constellations are man's way of gathering a maddening chaos of similar items into easily definable bunches, celestially speaking. Even those not inclined to stargazing know the names of twelve if they're astrology buffs. In Middle-earth, the constellations are again the same as in our world, and serve the same functions: besides regulating the heavens, they represent events and persons in the beliefs of the native cultures. As with the stars, some constellations are directly identified, while others have obscure meanings; unlike our attempts with the stars, we were not able to identify every known constellation.

As with the stars, the constellations were also created by Varda. This element of the story didn't change at all through the years. In *Silm*, she "gathered (the stars) together and set (them) as signs in the heavens of Arda." Calling constellations "*signs*" is a good touch on Tolkien's part, since they do symbolize the power of the Valar, especially as opposed to Melkor and his lot. This is reinforced with such constellations as 'The Swordsman of the Sky', variously named throughout the corpus, who is an 'image' of a watchful Vala in the sky (Tulkas' son *Telimektar* in *BoLT*) and "forebodes the Last Battle" with Melkor, and

— continued on page 12.

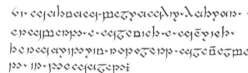

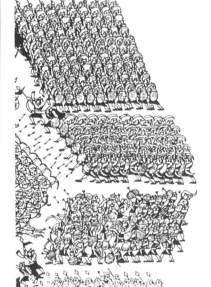

Northeast quadrant of Tom Loback's "The Fifth Battle".

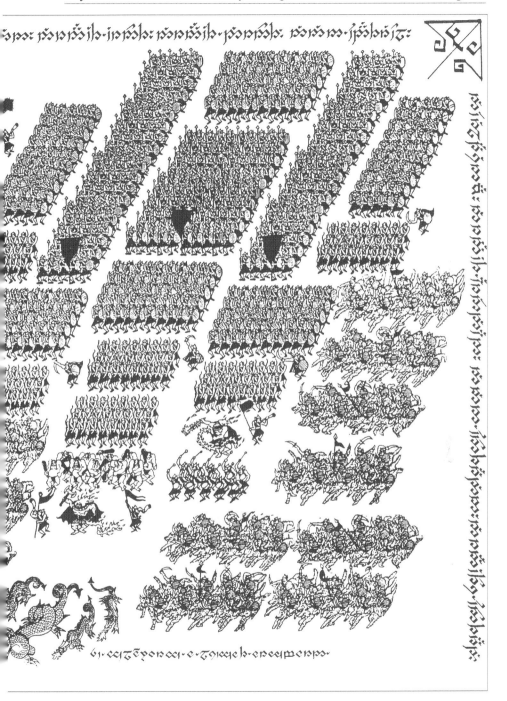

See page 1 for further information on this work.

Nólë i Meneldilo — *continued from page 9.*

Valacirca, "sign of doom" for evil. Such signs provide one of the many reasons for both Melkor's and Sauron's taste for blackening the sky with clouds: obscuring them should boost the evil forces' morale, while weakening those who serve good.

There seem to be a total of seven separate constellations identified in the published writings, with one star group thrown in for good measure. The six positively identified to be constellations are all mentioned in the *Silm* passage describing their creation: *Anarríma*, *Menelmacar*, *Soronúmë*, *Telumendil*, *Valacirca*, and *Wilwarin*. The one star group is the *Remmirath*, mentioned in *LotR*. Also in *LotR* is a reference at one point to Durin's Crown, the formation of seven stars seen in the Mirrormere by Frodo. This could be a separate constellation, another star group, the same group as the *Remmirath*, or simply nonexistent (by our standards).

Menelmacar, also called *Menelvagor*, *Telumehtar*, and *Telimektar*, is one of the two star groups with positive identifications; with his "shining belt" and "diamond sheath", along with the name 'Swordsman of the Sky', he can only be Orion, the legendary fighter of Greek mythology. As noted, he has great symbolic status as a foreboding of the Dagor Dagorath, the Armageddon of Eä. He is also noted for being one of, if not the, most impressive constellations in the sky. A line in *LotR* describes this well: "...there leaned up, as he climbed over the rim of the world,...Menelvagor with his shining belt."

Valacirca is the other defined constellation; its names of 'Sickle of the Valar', the 'Seven Stars', and the 'Sickle', along with the footnote in *LotR* equating it with the Plough or Great Bear, identify it as the Big Dipper. An interesting name given to the group is the 'Burning Briar', found in *The Lays of Beleriand*. [One point must be made clear: though identified as a whole separate group in Middle-earth terms, the Big Dipper is not an official constellation as recognized by the International Astronomers' Union. It is part of the group called the Great Bear (thus Tolkien's identification), but is known as an asterism, rather than a true constellation.]

Of the four remaining constellations, only two have definite counterparts in our heavens. The first is *Wilwarin*, a word which means 'butterfly' in Quenya. Christopher Tolkien identifies it as Cassiopeia. Cassiopeia is known because of its distinctive 'w' shape. This could easily resemble a pair of wings, so we see no reason to disagree with Wilwarin being identified with Cassiopeia. The second is *Soronúmë*, which almost certainly means 'eagle of the west' in Quenya. More than likely, this is a representation of Thorondor, the famed leader of the Eagles. Our identification is Aquila, a constellation whose name is, happily enough, the Eagle, and which is shaped very much like one in flight. However, there are some reservations about this choice. First, simply because a constellation is an eagle in the Greco-Roman tradition does not automatically make it one in the Endorian mind. Second, while Aquila can be seen easily during the summer months (its brightest star, Altair, forms with two others a noted asterism, the Summer Triangle), it is not a dominant group in the sky, whereas one would think that such a constellation should hold an honored place in the sky.

As for the remaining constellations, *Anarríma* and *Telumendil*, no one constellation seems to match well with their translations; the former has the intriguing name 'edge of the sun', while the latter is 'sky-lover'. We have chosen to refrain from any attempt at identification because of this dearth of choices.

Remmirath is the only star cluster mentioned by Tolkien; it can be easily identified as the Pleiades. In a previously mentioned passage, the hobbits observe the group "high in the East". The constellation Taurus, in which the Pleiades is located, would be a good ways up in the eastern sky as Orion appears over the horizon, while the Pleiades itself is a distinctive little group, much more so than the Hyades, another cluster in Taurus.

Durin's Crown remains the greatest enigma among the constellations, as was mentioned. Most identifications have matched it with the Big Dipper — an understandable choice, since the Crown is said to have seven stars, the same number as the Valacirca — but when the shape of the Dipper is considered if used as a crown, the result is a hat with half its brim missing, while the other half bends out, then up in two strange angles. In the earlier manuscripts, the two drafts of the West-gate of Moria show the same basic star pattern as in the final version. Even though the events of Middle-earth are supposed to have taken place some six thousand years ago, the positions of the stars would not have changed significantly. In a letter to the authors of this essay, Patrick Wynne has suggested that the constellation Corona Borealis could be identified with the Crown. Both groups have seven stars, with the middle star being the brightest; the names, meanwhile, have a strong similarity — Corona Borealis means 'the northern crown'. The strongest reservation with this choice is, as with Aquila earlier, that Greco-Roman names do not automatically fit Middle-earth constellations. Another choice is the Pleiades, interestingly enough, since their common name is the 'Seven Sisters' (an appellation that appears in Greco-Roman as well as other traditions), while the group could be seen as forming a very attractive circlet. If this was the case, however, then surely Tolkien would have indicated the connection in his writings, as he does have a tendency to compare and connect two or more different names or descriptions for the same object (for example, the passage in *Silm* where he tosses around a bunch of Elvish and Khuzdul names for Belegost and Nogrod).

When we discover by means of science that Eärendil is not a half-elf in a ship with a Silmaril traversing the night sky, but a planet called Venus, and that the Sun is not an angelic being traversing the sky in a vessel with a fruit, but a very close star, the willing suspension of belief needed is lost. Although J.R.R. Tolkien was masterful enough in his writings to take away our disbelief about either Eärendil or the Sun being something other than what he told us in the text, perhaps Tolkien succeeds in this because his world is our world: Endor is Terra or more simply put Middle-earth is our own Earth. As for the stars and the constellations outside of Middle-earth or Earth and beyond, it is there (to borrow an ending) where the real Story begins for all of us.

Appendix — *An Astronomical Catalog with English translations of the Elvish names*

Taum Santoski's "Star Catalogue", Christopher Gilson's "High-elven Glossary", and especially Tolkien's own *Etymologies* were all very useful in preparing this astronomical catalog. *Key*: Q = Quenya; S = Sindarin; *FotR* = *The Fellowship of the Ring*; *RotK* = *The Return of the King*; *RGEO* = *The Road Goes Ever On* (2nd ed.); *Silm* = *The Silmarillion*; *UT* = *Unfinished Tales*; *L* = *The Letters of J. R. R. Tolkien*; *BoLT1* = *The Book of Lost Tales, Part One*; *LR* = *The Lost Road*; *cf.* = compare; ID = (Primary World) identification.

I. STARS

1) ***Alcarinquë*** (Q 'Glorious'): *Silm*:314 (CJRT); *cf. alkarinqa* 'radiant, glorious' *LR*:348. ID = JUPITER.

2) ***Borgil*** (S 'hot-star' or 'red-star'): *bor(n)-* 'hot, red' *L*:427; *gil* 'star' *RGEO*:72, *LR*:358, *L*:427. ID = BETELGUESE.

3) ***Carnil*** (Q 'red-star'): *karne* 'red' *LR*:362, *Silm*:357; *el* 'star' *RGEO*:73, *LR*:355; *cf.* (*Il*)*men*, *Silm*:99. ID = MARS.

4) **Eärendil** (Q 'sea-lover'): *eär* 'sea' *RGEO*:73; *-(n)dil* 'devotion, disinterested love' *Silm*:362; 'describing the attitude of one to a person, thing, course or occupation to which one is devoted for its own sake' *L*:386. ID = Venus.

5) **Elemmírë** (Q 'star-jewel'): *elen* 'star' *RGEO*:73, *LR*:355; cf. *(Elem)makil*, *UT*:45-50; *mírë* 'jewel' *Silm*:361. ID = Mercury.

6) **Helluin** (Q 'sky-blue'): *helle* 'sky' *LR*:360; *luini* 'blue' *RGEO*:66. ID=Sirius.

7) **Luinil** (Q 'blue-star'). ID = Neptune

8) **Lumbar** (Q 'shadows'): *lumbe* 'gloom, shadow' *LR*:370; *lumbule* 'heavy shadow', *RGEO*:67; *-r* plural. ID = Saturn.

9) **Nénar** (Q 'flame of adamant' *[conjectural; from C. Gilson's "A High-elven Glossary"]*; another meaning could be 'water-high'): *cf. nen* 'water' *LR*:376; *cf. Nenya* 'Ring of Water' and ''Ring of Adamant', *Silm*:288, 298; *nár* 'fire' *Silm*:362, *LR*:374. ID = Uranus.

II. Constellations

1) **Anarríma** (Q 'sun-edge'): *anar* 'sun' *Silm*:99, *LR*:348; *ríma* 'edge, hem, border' *LR*:383. ID = ?

2) **Menelmacar** (Q 'sky-swordsman'): *RotK*:391; *menel* 'firmament, high heaven, the region of the stars' *RGEO*:72; *makil* 'sword' *LR*:371. Known also as: *Telumehtar, Menelvagor*, Swordsman of the Sky, and the Warrior of the Sky. ID = Orion.

3) **Menelvagor** (S 'Swordsman of the Sky'): *FotR*:91. ID = same as number 2.

4) **Soronúmë** (Q 'eagle-west'): *soron* 'eagle' *Silm*:365, *LR*:392; *númen* 'west' *RotK*:401. *["A High-elven Glossary" gives another conjectural meaning: 'eagle descending']* ID = Aquila.

5) **Telumehtar** (Q 'sky-warrior' or 'Warrior of the Sky'): *LR*:391. *telume* 'dome, dome of heaven' *LR*:391; *ohta* 'war' *LR*:379; *cf. Ohtar* 'warrior, soldier' *UT*:282. In *BoLT1*, it is referred to as *Telimektar* (*BoLT1*:268). ID = same as number 2.

6) **Telumendil** (Q 'sky-lover'): ID = ?

7) **Valacirca** (Q 'vala-sickle' or 'Sickle of the Valar'): *Silm*:48, *LR*:365; *kirka* 'sickle' *LR*:365; 'Sickle of the Gods = Great Bear' *LR*:365. Known also as: 'The Sickle' and 'The Wain' (by Hobbits; *The Hobbit*, p.164) and the 'Seven Stars' (Q *Otselen*; S or Noldorin *Edegil* [*LR*:379]). ID = Big Dipper (asterism).

8) **Wilwarin** (Q 'butterfly'): *Silm*:354 (CJRT); *wilwarin* 'butterfly' *LR*:398. ID=Cassiopeia.

9) **Remmirath** (S 'netted-jewel-collective plural'): *rem*, Q *rembe* 'mesh' *RotK*:393; *-ath* collective plural suffix, *cf. elenath, Periannath, RGEO*:75. Known also as: 'The Netted Stars'. ID = Pleiades (star group).

Bibliography

I. General

Allan, James, ed. *An Introduction to Elvish.* Bran's Head Books, Somerset, UK, 1978.

Carpenter, Humphrey. *Tolkien: A Biography.* Houghton Mifflin (hereafter HM), Boston, 1977.

Foster, Robert. *The Complete Guide to Middle-earth.* Ballantine Books, New York. 1978.

Gilson, Christopher. "A High-elven Glossary", *Parma Eldalamberon* #6, 1983, p. 15-28.

Noel, Ruth S. *The Languages of Tolkien's Middle-earth.* HM, Boston, 1980.

Swann, Donald and J. R. R. Tolkien. *The Road Goes Ever On* (2nd ed, rev). HM, Boston, 1978.

Tolkien, J. R. R. *The Lord of the Rings*, Collecter's Edition. HM, Boston. 1982, 1983. *[This volume contains the "Note on the Text" by Douglas Anderson. This particular edition of LotR is the most up to date]*

---------- *The Silmarillion*. HM, Boston. 1977.

---------- *Unfinished Tales*. HM, Boston. 1980.

---------- *The Letters of J. R. R. Tolkien*. HM, Boston. 1981.

---------- *The Book of Lost Tales, Part One*. HM, Boston. 1983.

---------- *The Book of Lost Tales, Part Two*. HM, Boston. 1984.

---------- *The Shaping of Middle-earth*. HM, Boston. 1986.

---------- *The Lost Road*. HM, Boston. 1987.

---------- *The Annotated Hobbit*, annotated by Douglas Anderson. HM, Boston, 1988.

Tyler, J. E. A. *The New Tolkien Companion*. Avon Books, New York. 1979.

II. ASTRONOMICAL

Foster, Robert. "A Glossary of Middle-earth; the Astronomy of Middle-earth", *Niekas* #16, 1966, pp. 15-17.

Getty, Naomi. "Stargazing in Middle-earth: Stars and Constellations in the Work of Tolkien", *Beyond Bree*, April 1984, pp. 1-3. — Readers' comments printed in *BB*, June 1984, p. 8.

Henry, Emma. "A Star on His Brow: the Role of Astronomy in 'The Lord of the Rings'", *The Southern Star* #2, September 1985, pp. 14-16.

Martingell, Scott. "Stars of Middle-earth", *The York Shire Post*, #8, Winter 1982-83, pp. 6-8. — Readers' comments printed in *The York Shire Post* #9, Spring, p. 3.

Poxon, Michael: see Wilson, James and Michael Poxon.

Santoski, Taum. "Star-catalogue", *Lendarin & Danian*, #2, 1981, p. 18.

Stone, Ian J. T. "Will the Real Carnil Go Supernova, Please?", *Quettar* #21, pp. 5-8.

Tolkien, J. R. R. Two fragments from *The Silmarillion* holograph, Series 3, Box 9, Folder 36. From the Tolkien collection at Marquette University Memorial Library, Dept. of Special Collections and Univ. Archives.

---------- Drawings of the West-gate of Moria, Holograph, Series 3, Box 4, Folder 15. *Ibid.*

Wilson, James and Michael Poxon. "Hail, Elentari in the Firmament!", *Quettar* #17-18, Jan.-Feb. 1983, pp. 7-10. — Readers' comments printed in *Quettar* #19, p. 2.

ACKNOWLEDGEMENTS — We would like to thank Gary Hunnewell for providing us with copies of practically every known Middle-earth astronomical article ever published; without his assistance there would be no bibliography for the article and therefore no article. We are additionally indebted to Chris Gilson for providing us with copies of some of his notes (those pertaining to astronomy) from the Marquette Library Tolkien manuscripts.

Letters to *VT* — *continued from page 4.*

to note that if you translate the phrase into Russian, treating **miruvórë** as a Russian word, it would be *miruvórev glotok* — virtually the same ending, which might be significant.

Mindon Eldaliéva — we can apply the same reasoning. The tower is important because it was made by the Elves *and belongs to* the Elves. So you use the "*adjectif d'appartenance*".

Nurtalë Valinóreva — just the same. The hiding is dreadful and impressive because it is Valinor's.

So I would say the V case is more than associative and more than partitive. Can it be labelled something like *possessive*? (as case name, of course, not to be confounded with possessive pronouns or adjectives). I would like to know what all our specialists think.

"Narqelion"

A translation by Paul Nolan Hyde

Synopsis by Jorge Quiñónez

The following text of Paul Nolan Hyde's translation of "Narqelion" *is reprinted with the author's permission from his column* Quenti Lambardillion *which appeared in* Mythlore *LX, pp.48-53. For convenience of comparison, the text of* "Narqelion" *is reprinted here. This text is © Copyright 1989 The Tolkien Trust.*

Narqelion

N•alalmino lalantila	
Ne•súme lasser pínea	
Ve sangar voro úmeai	
Oikta rámavoite malinai.	
Ai lintuilind(ov)a Lasselanta	
Piliningeve súyer nalla qanta	
Kuluvai ya karnevalinar	
V'ematte sinq' Eldamar.	*sinqe*
San rotser simpetalla pinqe,	*rotser:s?*
Súlimarya sildai, hiswa timpe	
San sirilla ter i•aldar:	
Lilta lie noldorinwa	
Ómalingwe lir' amaldar	
Sinqitalla laiqaninwa.	*-álar*
N•alalmino ??á lanta lasse	*lasser*
Torwa pior má tarasse:	
Tukalia sangar úmeai	
Oïkta rámavoite karneambarai	*malinai*
Ai lindórea Lasselanta	
Nierme mintya nára qanta	

In the analysis which prefaces his translation of "*Narqelion*", Paul Nolan Hyde reaches several conclusions about the poem. First, that it was written at around the same time as "Kortirion Among the Trees". Second, that both poems were probably written in the same notebook. With this in mind, Paul focuses on the time period when both poems were written, from Fall 1915 to Spring 1916. He finds that Tolkien had written many poems at this time. The reader should reference *The Book of Lost Tales, Part One (BoLT1)*, pp. 91-92, 108-10, 139; and *BoLT2* pp. 295-8 for these poems. Having read these, Paul notes:

> By now the thematic echoes ought to be apparent even to the most avid poetry despiser. The faded land, the spectral people, the great melancholy, the persistent longing for a time long since past pervades Tolkien's writings in the period of time just prior to leaving for France and the War. All of these are manifest and find their full expression in "Kortirion Among the Trees"....
> Christopher Tolkien gives three versions of Kortirion in *The Book of Lost Tales*: the first, dating from late November 1915; the second, a considerable reworking

of the poem dating from 1937; the third, a version dating from the early 1960's. It is the earliest working which should attract our attention, begun as it was in November 1915, dedicated to Warwick, and entitled (in one of the early copies) "*Narquelion la..tu y aldalin Kortirionwen*" (translated by Christopher as "Autumn (among) the trees of Kortirion").

The last line of "Kortirion Among the Trees" (*BoLT1*, p.33-36) reads "singing a song of faded longing to themselves." Paul Nolan Hyde says of this: "I believe that song of faded longing, sung by Elvish hearts to Elvish hearts, is '*Narqelion*'.... We stand upon the brink of a precipice overlooking the boundary between the Waters and the Land with a single shell held to our ear, hoping to hear the voice of the sea...."

Autumn

Under the spreading Elms
Falling leaves heap up in a sheltered place
Like throngs, never drifting away,
But always stirring with yellow golden wings.
Behold the swift singing flight of Autumn
Pale blue arrows blown down from the vales of the overflowing
Golden clouds which once in ages past made glad;
The leaves and rain, like hands wrung together, sigh for Eldamar.
Then faint pipings from the piper dwindle, fade;
Pale, fallow winds gleaming in the grey, misty rain;
Then up from the cool, sparkling stream through the trees
Musical voices singing up through the trees
From sighings of the blue-green waters.
From the spreading Elm trees every leaf falls
Brothers, of one kin, clustered by a hand beyond the heights
Thick-twined throngs, never to drift away
But forever stirring, with leafy wings, surrendering to Fate.
Behold the Autumn of the Singing Land
Telling forth my foremost sorrow completely.

Transitions in Translations

A column edited by Arden R. Smith

The purpose of this column is to examine peculiarities in translations of Tolkien's works: mistranslations, unusual translations, interesting solutions to the problems of translation, and other curiosities in foreign editions. Ideas and contributions are encouraged: send them to "Transitions," c/o Arden R. Smith, P.O. Box 4395, Berkeley, CA 94704-0395, USA.

The If and When of the Dominion of Men

Sometimes a wealth of information can be contained within a single conjunction. The conjunctions *if* and *when* in a conversation between Legolas and Gimli give a great deal of insight into the characters of Elves and Dwarves. Gimli, examining the stone-work in Minas Tirith, says: "When Aragorn comes into his own, I shall offer him the service of stonewrights of the Mountain, and we will make this a town to be proud of." Legolas, however, says, "*If* Aragorn comes into his own, the people of the Wood shall bring him birds that sing and trees that do not die" (*The Return of the King [RotK]*, p. 148, italics mine).

I believe that Tolkien made this distinction to show a difference between Elves and Dwarves. The use of *when* seems to show a Dwarvish confidence in the defeat of the Enemy. The *if*, however, seems to indicate an Elvish tendency to be non-committal, which Frodo noted elsewhere: "Go not to the Elves for counsel, for they will say both no and yes" (*The Fellowship of the Ring*, p. 93).

Whether or not Tolkien meant to imply these particular traits, it is unlikely that the *if/when* distinction is merely fortuitous. Whatever message the distinction is meant to convey, however, is lacking in the German translation. Here both Legolas *and* Gimli say, "*Wenn Aragorn zu seinem Recht kommt ...*" (*Der Herr der Ringe*. Translated by Margaret Carroux. Stuttgart: Hobbit Presse/Klett-Cotta, 1983. 3 vol. pbk. edition, III, p. 165).

Why is there no *if/when* distinction here? It is not a case of mistranslation; *wenn* may be used to translate both *if* and *when*, as the Lederer/Schulz/Griesbach *Reference Grammar of the German Language* (New York: Scribners, 1969), pp. 460-61, explains: "[G571] *Wenn* is used for PRESENT events, FUTURE events, and REPEATED PAST events.... [G574] The conjunction *wenn* also introduces CONDITIONAL SUBORDINATE CLAUSES, which state the circumstances on which the action of the main clause depends."

Does German lack the means to make this distinction? Lederer/Schulz/Griesbach state further (p. 461 [G574, note 1]): "Theoretically, an ambiguity exists between the conditional and temporal use of *wenn*. If the context does not make the meaning clear, a synonym for *wenn* may be used." These "synonyms" (*falls; unter der Bedingung, daß; im Falle, daß; vorausgesetzt, daß*), however, seem stronger than *wenn* and would be more suitably used to translate expressions like *in case* and *under the condition that* rather than *if*. *Wenn* is therefore properly used as a translation of both *if* and *when*, but the German version thus lacks a fine nuance found in the English original.

About Russian Translations of Tolkien's Works (Part Two)

by Nathalie Kotowski

The Lord of the Rings — The Fellowship of the Ring
    Khraniteli — Letopis Pervaya iz Epopei "Vlastelin Koletz" (*The Guardians — First Chronicle of the Epic* The Lord of the Rings). Translated into Russian by V. Muraviev (Book

I) and A. Kistiakovsky (Book II and all verses). Foreword by V. Muraviev. Published by Radouga, Moscow, 1989. 200,000 ex.

1. *Foreword* — This discusses the life of J.R.R. Tolkien, taken mostly from Humphrey Carpenter's biography. Most important is the statement concerning the significance of the book: "It were best to say that this book is about the nature of power, about those who seek power over Man, an amoral power, a power that enslaves, which is founded on lies and violence. A spiritual surrender before such a power and any compromise with it destroys Man. The common moral laws of the existence of Men are intangible. Human dignity is the most valuable human right and one has to defend it at any price and in any circumstances."

Ten years ago, such a statement would be an open door to the Gulag! One can see now why the first Russian edition of *LotR* was "shortened", and why a new edition comes out now: that is one of the aspects of *Perestroïka*!

2. *Translation of Book I by V. Muraviev* — Muraviev adopts an interesting approach to translation. It strays relatively far from the English text but is still well done. By reading this translation, one has the impression that the original was written in Russian. The only reproach I can make is that sometimes the choice of vocabulary (in the scenes in Bree, for instance) is more appropriate for brawlers in a pub than for the future King of Gondor.

3. *Translation of Book II by A. Kistiakovsky* — Kistiakovsky adopts the same approach to translation as Muraviev, but takes it too far. This is not a translation but a rewriting. Some sentences are missing, others are added. Explanations are given which are not found in the original text, and are sometimes erroneous. One example (and there are thousands): In "The Council of Elrond", Elrond says that he was the herald of Gil-galad. "I beheld the last combat on the slopes of Orodruin, where Gil-galad died, and Elendil fell, and Narsil broke beneath him." The translation reads: "I fought on the slopes of Orodruin, *which are translated as The Fiery Mountains* — where Gil-galad perished and Elendil fell *breaking his sword on the helms of his foes*" (italics mine).

Another example, also from "The Council of Elrond": the name *Minas Tirith* is said to signify 'The Tower of the Last Hope' (and not 'The Tower of Guard'). Some "additions" sound completely wrong: for instance, in "The Council of Elrond" again, Gandalf, speaking about Isildur, says: "After the victory, Isildur went back to Gondor and did not 'go away to perish without glory', as was said in the North."

I personally find that the translator has no right to alter the original text so much. It is a problem of deontology of translators.

4. *Names* — The eternal problem of names! The Hobbitish names are translated, and not too badly (though in the Russian *Hobbit* they are not translated at all). There is no Russian word for 'Shire' (there is nothing similar in the Russian reality), so it is called *Hobbitania*. Some Hobbit names are translated with relish, though I do not understand why the Took family name becomes *Krol*. Perhaps it is because the Russian word *tuki* (pl.) means 'chemical fertilizers'. For the Brandybucks, they understood the element 'buck' as signifying 'hare' and knocked out a name using the Russian root for 'hare'. Gollum is cleverly called *Gorlum* (from Russian *gorlo* meaning 'throat').

Things are far worse with Elvish names. The translators obviously had no idea of the name formation techniques used by Tolkien. Where they thought to have found a stem of English or Latin origin, they fabricated a name in Russian, such as for *Glorfindel* (on the stem 'glory') or *Eregion* (on 'region'!!). This does not explain why the trees of Eregion are oak and not holly. Some modifications are understandable: *Andúril* becomes *Andril*, because phonetically, in Russian, *Anduril* means 'he acted like a fool'!!! There is also a problem in the transcription of English. The famous 'th' sound is transcribed in six different ways, so poor Lúthien's name in Russian is pronounced like the Italian *Santa Lucia* — awful! *Athelas* becomes *aselas* and *Arathorn* becomes *Arahorn*. The translators also don't know that the letter 'c' is pronounced 'k', so *Celeborn* is given as *Seleborn*!

5. *Elvish* — A Russian reader will never be able to pick up Elvish words from the Russian version. The Elvish verses are full of typographical and transcription errors.

A final astonishing fact: the book is illustrated with drawings made in imitation of Tolkien's drawings, but most of them are taken from *The Father Christmas Letters*! Only one illustration is appropriate, an imitation of the drawing from *The Hobbit* depicting The Hill. But the road is now a river, and on the river is a very modern steamship...

And even more about Russian translations(!), in a letter from David Doughan:

"I was interested to see what Nathalie Kotowski had to say about the Russian translations *[in* VT *#10]*. I find the Russian *Fellowship of the Ring* [*FotR*] exasperating and seriously (perhaps fundamentally) flawed, for reasons I state in the next issue of *Quettar* (if Julian accepts my article). I also share Nathalie's enthusiasm for the *Hobbit* translation; on the point of transliteration, I think the translator has taken many of the names to have a specifically English pronunciation, so that *Moria* follows the analogy of *Maria* (as in 'Black Maria', 'They called the wind Maria' — *not* as in 'West Side Story' or '*Ave Maria*').

"However, I am much less happy about the Russian *Smith of Wootton Major* [*SWM*]. It is indeed a very elegant translation (it should be; Nagibin is a short story writer of high and long-established reputation). However, there is a strong tendency to paraphrase in such a way as to distort very slightly the meaning (and more markedly the style — for example, paragraphing and even sentence division is often altered, sometimes quite drastically). I find that these paraphrases have a cumulative effect which takes the translation further from the original than it needs to.

"One interesting detail: while the name 'Tolkien' is transliterated in the *Hobbit* with two syllables (Толкин *Tolkin*), in *SWM* and *FotR* it has three (Толкиен *Tolkiyen*).

"Finally, I thought you might be interested in the Russian publisher's blurb for *FotR*:

> The famous British writer, in his philosophical tale which constitutes the first book of the epic *The Lord of the Rings*, vindicates the ideas of humanity, of readiness for heroism and self-sacrifice in the name of one's native land, and of the cultural unification of nations.
>
> In the language of images created from the material of Welsh legends, Irish and Icelandic sagas, Scandinavian mythology and ancient Germanic epic, the author unambiguously asserts that the victory of good in the world and in the human soul depends on man himself.

Absolutely no comment!"

All I can really add to this is to express my joy at receiving so much about the Russian translations, especially since my own knowledge of Russian is virtually nil. As long as I am on the subject of Slavic translations, I received the following from Christina Scull:

"On the subject of foreign editions some Polish members [of the Tolkien Society] who cannot get money out of the country for subscriptions or [for the Tolkien Centenary Conference in] 1992 have asked if we might be able to sell any editions of Tolkien they can post out (most likely Polish or Russian) and use the money for subscriptions, etc. I do know several people who might be interested. Perhaps you could think of others. In such a case I think it would be fair to allow a price equivalent to the same book in our countries, plus a little extra for postage. Books are generally cheap in Eastern Europe, given the exchange rate, but are not cheap for citizens of the country who earn much less in comparison."

Interested parties can write Christina at 1A Colestown St., London SW11 3EH, England.

Next issue: "Edition Shifting in the German *Hobbit*", and more!

Publications of Interest

**** BIAOR = Back issues available on request ****

Beyond Bree: Newsletter of the American Mensa Tolkien SIG. Published monthly.
   Editor: Nancy Martsch. *Subscriptions to*: the editor at P.O. Box 55372, Sherman Oaks,
   CA 91413. Annual subscription: $7.00; Overseas $10.00. *BIAOR.*
   June 1990: Concludes Nancy Martsch's excellent "Teach Yourself Quenya" series.
   Lesson 22: "The Tengwar", with supplements "Sindarin Tengwar", "English Tengwar",
   and "Black Speech Tengwar". Not to be missed.

The following appeared in the Washington Post Book World *section for Sunday, June 24,
1990 (p. 8). The reviewer is Vic Sussman. What is particularly striking is Mr. Sussman's
sensitivity to the complexity and enormity of Tolkien's linguistic creations, unusual among
reviewers.*

"Speaking of classics, Recorded Books, which also rents and sells, has scored a coup, being
the only audio book publisher to offer an unabridged reading of J.R.R. Tolkien's *The Lord
of the Rings*. This is the first time, says Recorded Books, that every word of this beloved
trilogy has been done on tape, complete with the 35 songs Tolkien sprinkled throughout the
three books. The production was also authorized by the Tolkien family.

"While not children's literature, *The Lord of the Rings* is certainly a remarkable work
whose drama and layered complexity cut neatly across age distinctions. This recording of
the trilogy consists of 53 hours spread over 38 cassettes: *The Fellowship of the Ring* (15
cassettes, $99.95); *The Two Towers* (12 cassettes, $84.95); and *The Return of the King* (11
cassettes, $79.95).

"This is not a dramatization, but a single-voice narration — possibly the longest such
performance aside from recordings of the Bible — by British stage and screen actor Robert
Inglis. Well-known in Great Britain for his one-man performances of Shakespeare, Chaucer
and Dickens, Inglis — and his rich, versatile voice — and Tolkien are a perfect match.

"But what an actor's challenge is a full-length reading of *The Lord of the Rings*! Tolkien
created hundreds of original names for places and characters, made up two complete
alphabets (Tengwar and Cirth), and fabricated various languages including variants of
Elvish, Dwarvish and Orkish. Performing this masterpiece to the satisfaction of Tolkien fans
and scholars would be an accomplishment in itself, but Recorded Books and Inglis have done
much more. They have made *The Lord of the Rings* accessible to children and families who
might not otherwise pick up the books. And many children exposed to Inglis's performance
will go on to read and reread the originals."

Next Issue

VT #13 will feature more of the same, with the return of *Essitalmar*, and probably the
hitherto unpublished authentic Elvish mentioned last issue. We'll also continue the four-part
presentation of Tom Loback's huge "Fifth Battle" mural with the southeast quadrant.

Vinyar Tengwar

The bimonthly 'news-letters' of the Elvish Linguistic Fellowship.
A Special Interest Group of the Mythopoeic Society.

Editor: Carl F. Hostetter, 2509 Ambling Circle, Crofton, MD 21114, USA.

Contributing Editor: Jorge Quiñónez, 3326 Polk Ave., San Diego, CA 92104, USA.

Masthead: by Tom Loback.

Tengwar numerals: from Lawrence M. Schoen's *Moroma* PostScript *Tengwar* font for the Mac, available on disk for $6.00 from PsychoGlyph, P.O. Box 74, Lake Bluff, IL 60044.

Subscriptions: Subscriptions are for 1 year (6 issues) and must be paid in US dollars.
   $12.00   USA
   $15.00   Canada (sent airmail) and Overseas surface mail
   $18.00   Overseas airmail

NOTE NEW RATES*!!!*

Back issues available: Issues 1 - 7 & 9 - 12 are each $2.00 in the USA, $2.50 overseas surface mail and Canada, $3.00 airmail. Issue 8 includes a large map and costs $4.00 USA, $5.00 surface and Canada, $6.00 airmail. A complete set of back issues is available for $20.00 USA, $25.00 Overseas surface mail, and $30.00 Overseas airmail. *All costs are postpaid.*

Payments: All payments must be in US dollars. It is recommended that overseas members make payments via international postal money order. *Send all payments and make all checks payable to Carl F. Hostetter.*

Submissions: Written material should in some manner deal with Tolkien's invented languages. All submissions must be typed, or must be written unbelievably legibly: if I have to decipher lower-glyphics, the submission is automatically rejected! The editor reserves the right to edit any material (except art) for purposes of brevity and relevance. Ilúvatar smiles upon submissions on 800K (3.5") Macintosh disks in PageMaker, Microsoft Word or MacWrite formats, or as unformatted TEXT files. Artwork should be linguistic, or at least Elvish, in nature. Remember that artwork done in black ink will reproduce the best; I wouldn't harbor great expectations for the quality of reproduction from artwork rendered in pencil, "Flair" pen, chalk, or colored ink.

Send all submissions to Carl F. Hostetter. Direct inquiries to Jorge Quiñónez.

The deadline for VT #13 is August 20, 1990.

Vinyar Tengwar is produced by the editor on an Apple Macintosh II personal computer, using Microsoft Word 4.0 and Aldus PageMaker 3.02. It is printed on an Apple LaserWriter II NTX.

Vinyar Tengwar

Cainen neldë

#13

September, 1990

In This Issue

Editor's Musings

Welcome to *VT* #13! Despite the impressive table-of-contents above, this issue was nearly a slimmer one (by four pages) than ususal; only a few (very-) last-minute submissions saved the day. This was in part due to several unusual factors: a slim *Essitalmar* and the fact that Mythcon XXI delayed several projects and commanded much attention from our regular writers. However, it is *clear* that an expanded circle of participation is in order. You don't have to be a bearded scholar or write a dissertation: brief letters of comment or query are quite acceptable, and indeed highly sought-after: after all, *VT* is first and foremost a forum for dialogue, in which people can air their own opinions and seek the opinions of others. Surely if you're interested enough in Tolkienian linguistics to subscribe to *VT*, you must have something to add to this discourse, or at least have some questions to pose of others. It is exactly this process which will keep Tolkienian linguistics (as with any scholarly pursuit) alive and well. *So please write!*

— Carl F. Hostetter

"... Even the lapses that are noticed are customarily ignored in polite society. There are, to be sure, some persons whose attention is abnormally fixed upon the words rather than upon the topic under discussion, and they sometimes make a nuisance of themselves by pointing out the error and getting it laughed at or recorded before the business in hand is allowed to proceed. One should be kind to these people; they are either fools or linguists!"

— E.H. Sturtevant, *An Introduction to Linguistic Science* (Yale, 1947), p. 38.

E.L.F. News

In Memoriam

VT and the E.L.F. extend their deepest sympathy to Miss Vera Chapman (Belladonna Took), founder of the Tolkien Society, on the loss of her son Denis, who died June 23rd, 1990 after a long illness.

New Member

The E.L.F. extends a hearty *mae govannen* to:

• Jerry D. Peterson   5431 N. East River Rd., #1018, Chicago, IL 60656.

Parma *#9 Available*

Parma Eldalamberon #9 has been published. See the Publications of Interest listing on page 21 of this issue for details.

Unwin Hyman Sold

Unwin Hyman Limited has been sold to Harper Collins (and is now a subsidiary holding of a company owned by Rupert Murdoch[!]). Tolkien's works will now be issued under their own imprint within Grafton Books. Tolkien's new agent is Mary Butler, who can be reached at: Grafton Books, HarperCollins Publishers Ltd., 77-85 Fulham Palace Road, Hammersmith, London, W6 8JB, England; Phone: (081) 741-7070. *[Reported in* Beyond Bree, *August 1990, pp. 2-3]*

Hunnewell Collection to be Microfilmed

Gary Hunnewell's vast collection of publications by and about Tolkien is being microfilmed by Marquette University for inclusion in its Tolkien Archives. Gary invites anyone with unusual Tolkien publications to write him regarding possible inclusion of the material on the microfilm. Gary can be reached at 2030 San Pedro, Arnold, MO 63010, USA. *[Reported in* Beyond Bree, *June 1990, p. 11]*

Letters *in Paperback*

The Letters of J.R.R. Tolkien has been issued in a paperback edition from Unwin Paperbacks. Can a Ballantine edition be far behind?

Letters to VT

• Nancy Martsch   Sherman Oaks, California

I think I can explain to Edouard Kloczko why ***Eldaliéva*** and others have a long vowel. It's a matter of stress. Review the rules for pronunciation in Appendix E of *The Lord of the Rings* — if the next-to-last (penultimate) syllable contains a long vowel or a diphthong, or ends in a vowel followed by two or more consonants (*i.e.* is "closed"), it is stressed. If it contains a short vowel and ends in one or no consonant (*i.e.* is "open"), the stress shifts to the preceding (third-from-end, or antepenultimate) syllable. Try saying ***Eldaliéva*** according to these rules with a short vowel — the stress falls on the ***-i-***. And that, it appears, is not permitted. Observation (and Tolkien's comments on "*Namárië*" in *The Road Goes Ever On* [*RGEO*], among others) indicates that the final vowel could receive a secondary stress in poetry, and that it could receive full stress when followed by a suffix or another word in a compound (for example, ***vanimálion***, *The Return of the King*, p. 320). But for words ending in two vowels, such as ***-ie*** or ***-ea***, there are no examples of the stress ever falling on the short ***-i-*** or ***-e-***, and I don't think that it could. So when such a word takes a suffix, or is part of a compound, it is written in such a way that the reader will not mistakenly stress the short vowel. Some *orthographic* device is added to ensure proper pronunciation, such as the accent mark in ***Eldaliéva*** or the double *l* in ***Altáriello*** ("Galadriel's", in *RGEO*).

I think the same factor accounts for the spelling of some verbs, such as ***untúpa***, and perhaps even the infamous ***antaróta***. If you wonder why an accent (or other odd spelling) is there try saying it aloud. This can be enlightening.

The list of vowels in Donald O'Brien's reproduction of Tolkien's *tengwar* (in *VT* #10) is a cogent argument in favor of standardized (rather than totally phonetic) spelling. Some of the odd forms O'Brien notices might be due to English accent: Englishmen pronounce things differently than Americans or Canadians. And thanks also for explaining the use of trilled *vs.* untrilled *r*: to this Californian the whole *r* business seems utter nonsense.

Why couldn't ***Finduilas*** be 'hair-flowing' (***Fin[d]*** + ***duil*** + ***-as*** [?locative])? Makes more sense than some of the other things proposed.

• Steve Gardner   Milton Keynes, England

The article on Astronomy (*Nólë i Meneldilo*) *[which appeared last issue — CFH]* was of particular interest and has been a subject of my own independent study. Naturally, Jorge and Ned's article is more likely to be correct, especially considering the research that they have based their assumptions on. Perhaps the purpose of my comments is to find out why *I* am wrong, rather than to suggest that Jorge and Ned may be wrong!

First, remember that Tolkien lived in England, not California. Therefore if there is to be a deciding factor between two candidates this should be remembered. Also the more prominent constellations are more feasible even if the Elves did have exceptional eyesight! (I am still not totally convinced that they had good enough eyesight to see Uranus and Neptune! *[Why not? After all, under pristine viewing conditions, and if one knows exactly where to look, Uranus is visible to even unaided human eyes — CFH]*).

Soronúmë — The only prominent star in Aquila is Altair. Yes, it is tempting to suggest that this is the Eagle because the Arabs said so. But would not Cygnus *[the Swan — CFH]* be a better candidate? It's far more prominent in the shape of a bird in flight and has no less than four prominent stars. *[I have had the same thought, though the configuration of the stars suggests a much longer neck-to-body length ratio than is appropriate for eagles (but very much so for swans); but I note this as an observation, not a refutation. After all, can anyone really see a Queen in Cassiopeia? And how many bears have long tails, as Ursa Major does? —CFH].*

Telumehtar — Why is it assumed that this is yet another name for Orion? Boötes is quite feasible and even Cepheus and Gemini cannot be ruled out. *[Well, good point, except that Tolkien explicitly equates Telumehtar with Orion:* The Book of Lost Tales, Part One, *p. 268, entry* **Telimektar***;* The Lost Road, *p. 391, entry* **TEL-, TELU-** *—CFH].*

Durin's Crown — Most people suggest that this would be "The Plough" *[i.e. the Big Dipper —CFH]* for various reasons. I dismiss this for the same reasons that the article suggests. The various dependents are that it must be close to the North Pole to be permanently in the sky (day or night); very prominent (Dwarves and Hobbits saw this in the reflection in the Mirrormere); it would be reasonable to assume that it would be a circular/crescent/crown shape; and it would contain seven prominent stars. The Corona Borealis is certainly not prominent enough although the other criteria are well met. My number one candidate is Auriga, which is prominent, as close to the North Pole as "The Plough" and Corona Borealis, and has a distinct crown shape.

• Jenny Coombs   Nottinghamshire, England

I enjoyed Eli Bar-Yahalom's *Mellírë Métima Híno Fëanáro ["The Love-song of Maglor", in* VT *#11 —CFH]*; it amazes me how he writes rhyming, scanning, grammatical (as far as I can see) Quenya which actually makes sense!

As usual, I have a few minor quibbles. Is there any particular reason for the omission of the definite article in the title? I know Quenya does not use articles quite as English does (indeed languages vary quite a lot in this; even German, usually so close to us, allows the definite article with names, while Greek is another matter altogether [*e.g.* τò νῦν and its possible relevance to That Valediction]); but *Mellírë i•Métima Híno* does not sound impossible to me.

Fírië usually refers to a mortal's death from old age, does it not? Is it used here of the "death from grief" to which the Quendi were subject? This meaning seems possible because *fírië* is literally 'fading'.

I think that *miruvórë quanta* would mean 'fills *miruvor*' rather than 'pours' it. Perhaps this could be overcome by the use of the instrumental: 'fills with *miruvor*'. This however raises the further problem that *mīruvōren Yavānna quānta* (macrons indicate stress) does not have a pleasing rhythm.

To be really nit-picking, I found the hiatus of *rossë ëaro* a little awkward, though aided by the stress: *rōssë ēaro*, with a third-foot dactyl. Would *Ulmo — rossë falmo, yallo* make the line too monotonously trochaic?

This brings me on to *yallo*. I do not think the ablative is anywhere used with other than the literal, spatial "away-from" sense, and, though I'd accept that its field could be extended to the temporal, I think the "by, with or from" sense belongs entirely to Latin, where the ablative covers the locative and instrumental. So I'd prefer to render "from, of" in the phrasal verb "to make from, make out of" by the Quenya instrumental: *...rossë ëaro, yanen....*

I like the genitive in line 11, where the Quenya covers both English 'from', as in *Oiolosseo*, and the possessive 'of': *Nesso lintessë* = 'swiftness from Nessa / the swiftness of Nessa'. Compare the Genitive of Quality in *karmëo aina.*

Given *enyo* 'my, of me' and *elyo* 'your, of you', oughtn't *erya* 'his/her/its, of him/her/it' to be *eryo* in the interests of consistency?

A couple of accents, probably an oversight: surely **nin** for **nín** (line 14) and **métima** for **metima** (line 18)? *[This last at least is an oversight, on my part; I gave* **métima** *in the title, but missed it in the body of the poem. I was unsure what Eli might have in mind with* **nín** *(clearly so in Eli's manuscript), and so left it alone —CFH].*

Úner (unlike οὖτις which it resembles) must mean 'no man', 'no male person', which seems a little inappropriate. Could **úminë** 'not one' replace it?

In line 20, is not a participle **iluvekénala** needed instead of a finite verb? This word also illustrates the inconsistent transliteration of the *tengwa* '*kalma*' — personally I prefer *k*, but one or the other.

In conclusion, I liked this poem very much, particularly the alliterative effects and the remarkable "balancing" of lines and stanzas. "***Pella hísië, penna mar***" was very nice, as was the patterning of lines 8 – 13, with the two *Valiet* in second position in each line and the two *Valat* in first, followed by the genitive *Valië* — accusative noun pattern in line 13. I liked the repetition and alliteration of "***Laurefinda ve Laurelin***", an elegant line enhanced by being only three words long; line 21 has a similar, punning effect: "***Indis, engwa indëo olos***".

The basically AABACC rhyme-scheme was pleasing, and I liked the rhythm: the loose ‾˘˘‾˘˘ of the first four lines giving way to complete trochaic tetrameter (loose‾˘‾˘‾˘˘˘ for the couplet and the second stanza and couplet, but being reinstated for the third and fourth stanzas, with trochaic tetrameter reappearing in the third couplet.

While I was not terribly convinced by Tom Loback's *Essitalmar* (*VT* #10) in general, I shall defend his gloss of **Finduilas** against Craig Marnock's accusations of "slickness": 'ivy' seems as good a "long trailing plant" as any. Perhaps J.R.R.T. had in mind *Paradise Lost* IV 304–7: "[Eve], as a veil down to the slender waist, Her unadornèd golden tresses wore Dishevelled, but in wanton ringlets waved As the vine curls her tendrils…", which is rather more poetic than "hairy leaf".

Foreword to "The Fifth Battle"
by Tom Loback

This issue of *VT* continues the four-part presentation of "The Fifth Battle", or the *Nirnaeth Arnoediad*. It is a black-and-white print which represents the climactic hours of the battle, during which the Elves, Men and Dwarves of the Union of Maedhros were tragically and utterly defeated by the Hosts of Morgoth, led by Gothmog, Lord of Balrogs, and Glaurung, the Father of Dragons.

While the *tengwar* border calligraphy uses a Quenya mode, the descriptions of the battle formations are Sindarin, written in the Mode of Beleriand. This could indicate the origin of the piece was in Eregion during the middle of the Second Age. However, the calligraphic and illustrative style point to a possibly later period.

Anyone interested in acquiring a print of this work should write me at 152 West 26th Street, #36, N.Y. City, N.Y. 10001, USA. The print is limited to 100 copies. Prices vary on the quality of the material: $100.00 for Maplewood veneer, $50.00 for Arches Cover bond (acid-free paper), and $20.00 for heavy white bond. Size: 27" wide by 18" high. Make checks and money orders payable to Tom Loback. Inquiries welcome.

This month's installment reproduces the southeast quadrant of the map. The southwest quadrant will be given next month.

[The third quadrant of "The Fifth Battle" appears as the center spread, pp. 8-9 —CFH]

Mythcon XXI — A Review
by Bruce Leonard

I recently returned from Mythcon XXI: another success for the Mythopoeic Society. The Conference, whose theme was "Aspects of Love in Fantasy", was held August 3–6 at California State University in Long Beach, CA.

The Literary Guest of Honor was Diana Paxson, who is currently enjoying a good deal of success with her fiction. She has successfully published ten novels and a number of short stories. Diana is also a harp player and shared her talent with those in attendance. She was hard-pressed with a very full schedule of various papers and with panels regarding writing and literature. Her Guest of Honor speech at the banquet was well received and appropriately focused on love and its place in fantasy (I suspect this will be published in a future issue of *Mythlore*).

The Artistic Guest of Honor was Patrick Wynne who, with the help of Paula DiSante, put together a retrospective of his artwork. Patrick's art has been seen in many journals and, of course, his articles frequent the pages of *VT*. His retrospective was truly awesome, from the first sketch he related to Tolkien's work to very recent pieces. In all, the retrospective comprised approximately 200 pieces and was well attended. Patrick's collection of humorous sketches was especially enjoyable. Patrick also participated in the Masquerade by reading his *Mortalë Valinóreva*, a Quenya translation of "The Darkening of Valinor" from *The Silmarillion*.

The Mythcon Art Show was also quite successful, featuring artwork by Paula DiSante, Tom Loback, Sarah Beach and Sue Dawe, and needlework by Lisa Cowan. I especially liked Paula DiSante's work "I Have Chosen", depicting Lúthien's choice to live as a mortal with Beren.

The entertainment program this year, which was held on Saturday the 4th, was varied and first-rate all the way, the best I've experienced in the four Mythcons which I've attended. It began with the Masquerade, and all the contestants did a superb job and were appropriately recognized. Next was a performance of *The Road Goes Ever On* song cycle, with lyrics by Tolkien and Donald Swann. It was performed by Bruce Langford, who has a wonderful voice, with keyboard accompaniment by Carol Cooper. Omitted from the performance was "Errantry," due to its length and because it tended to somewhat derail the cycle. Then followed a reading from Diana Paxson's novel *The White Raven*, performed by Lynn Maudlin with the help of Alexei Kondratiev and Christina Lowentrout. Next came *Sam Spadegee and the Case of the Missing Mythcon*, another Not Ready for Mythcon Players production, written and directed by Ellie Farrell. The voice of Sam Spadegee was that of none other than David Bratman, in excellent form. Then came the *Mortalë Valinóreva*, read in Elvish by Patrick Wynne, together with the English version read by Chris Gilson, and with harp and chimes accompaniment by Adam Christensen.

By evening's end, Langford had been "persuaded" by Jorge Quiñónez to reprise the Elvish chant from *The Road Goes Ever On* for Jorge's camcorder.

The first paper I was able to attend, having agreed to help set up Pat Wynne's retrospective, was David Bratman's "After *The Silmarillion*" on Friday afternoon. This was an appraisal of Tolkien's works published since *The Silmarillion*. David placed special emphasis on the insight and entertainment to be found in *The Letters of J.R.R. Tolkien*. He also presented his thoughts on the different ways in which the volumes in *The History of Middle-earth* series could be read for entertainment and profit. Hopefully, something of this can be published either in *Mythprint* or *Mythlore* for those who are unwilling to read each volume of *The History of Middle-earth*; I think David's comments would be quite helpful.

The evenings were populated with meetings of various discussion groups, and of course the Mythic Circle, the video program, and naturally ConSuite and various Hallcons.

Saturday began with the traditional procession and opening ceremony. This year's ceremony was enlivened by a phoned report to the police that we were some kind of anti-nuclear weapons protesters about to confront a group of pro-nuclear activists. The police took this fairly seriously. Paul Nolan Hyde was in a costume that could easily have been interpreted as Moses coming down from the Mount; he had to do some fast talking. Given that this was Paul, this was easily accomplished.

Glen GoodKnight began with a reading from C.S. Lewis' *The Four Loves*. Then Pat Wynne gave a very interesting and humorous presentation on his artistic process. That afternoon I attended a panel moderated by Diana Pavlac on "Aspects of Love in Fantasy" in which a distinguished panel discussed some of the models which various people have discovered regarding love in this fiction. Various people, including Diana Paxson, built on the model presented in *The Four Loves*. Also that afternoon, Chris Gilson and friends of *VT* led the first Elvish language lesson. The next paper I attended was "Emotion with Dignity" by Paul Nolan Hyde. Dr. Hyde's thesis was developed from a letter by Tolkien to his son relating his views on the different ways in which men could relate to women. There was also a conversation with Kathryn Lindskoog, moderated by Joe R. Christopher. That evening I attended the E.L.F. meeting, where the company debated the feasibility of using the Elvish tongues as living languages.

Sunday morning included Elvish language lesson number two. The first paper I attended was a panel on the "Harpers of Middle-earth", which was very interesting. There were many harpists present, all of whom were willing to share their music and thoughts concerning the current state of "folk harping."

In the afternoon I attended a paper by Chris Seeman on "J.R.R. Tolkien's Conception of Evil: An Anthropological Perspective." Chris presented a very well thought-out but densely worded paper which I hope to be able to study at length if it's published. Sadly, I missed Paul Hyde's "Vowel-Mouthed Dwarves and Inconsonant Elves: Phonology in *The Treason of Isengard*." I did make it to a panel moderated by Bonnie Callahan on "Fantasy Art," which revealed the inner lives of artists when they're deep within a project. Also that afternoon was a paper by Joe R. Christopher entitled "Lindskoog *versus* Hooper: Who Tells the Truth about C.S. Lewis?" There was a fairly sedate Society auction, then the banquet at one of the university clubs that provided the only good food we had while at the university.

Monday morning began with a "reprised popular choice paper," which actually turned out to be a paper by Joe R. Christopher, which had been scheduled as the first paper on Friday, but which was missed because Dr. Christopher was *en route* from Texas. There was then a Mythopoeic Society Member's meeting, with the largest attendance of my four Mythcons. There was a very lively discussion about the future of the Society, how it should fund itself and how the money should be used.

The closing ceremonies included the traditional "The Baby and the Baby" by Diana Paxson and the "*Chorea Magna*", and a repeat of last year's "Spamalot". All were well received and, naturally, we finished with "What Do You Do With a Drunken Hobbit?".

Overall, some expressed the opinion that this was a lower "energied" Mythcon than those in Marquette and Vancouver; nevertheless, I found it extremely enjoyable and plan to make it to San Diego for Mythcon XXII.

Hope to see you there!

The Way to "Revived" Elvish: A Cornish Model?
by Alexei Kondratiev

We are all by now aware of a certain dichotomy in the motivations of those who study Tolkien's subcreated languages. On the one hand, there are those who are interested in Elvish only because they see it as a key to Tolkien's creative genius, a way of understanding the æsthetic and philosophical concerns that shaped his work, and are therefore unwilling to consider any statement in Elvish that was not composed by Tolkien himself. And then, on the other hand, there are those who, impressed by certain unique æsthetic qualities of the Elvish tongues, seek to experience them first and foremost as *languages* — *i.e.* as a system of paradigms capable of generating a wide variety of new statements, expressive of thoughts and feelings. To test the flexibility and full expressive range of the Elvish languages by using them in speech and writing is, one can argue, just as fruitful a way of exploring the depth and power of Tolkien's subcreation as any other. But since the full corpus of material in Elvish languages — even in Quenya, the best attested of them — is fairly limited, not approaching anything like a complete grammar and lexicon, anyone attempting to speak Elvish will soon encounter the necessity of extrapolating, guessing and, in the end, inventing material not found in the written sources. Even if, with the recent publication of so much of Tolkien's linguistic writings, it is now possible to base all such invention on elements that Tolkien actually produced himself, there remains the legitimate concern that, indulged in indiscriminately, the practice could lead farther and farther away from Tolkien's original idea of Elvish. There is also the fact that Tolkien's conception of the Elvish languages evolved over time, so that material drawn from early sources does not necessarily reflect the same structural and etymological premises as material in later sources.

Reflecting on this situation, I would like to draw attention to a parallel case in the Primary World, involving an extinct language that was revived as a spoken medium on the basis of a limited corpus of written sources. This is Cornish, a Celtic language which was once spoken over most of southwestern Britain south of Severn's mouth, but which through the Mediæval and Early Modern periods progressively lost ground to the political and economic pressures of English, finally becoming extinct at some point in the 19th century. (Traditionally, the last speaker of Cornish is claimed to have been Dolly Pentreath, who died in December of 1777. However, at least one other fluent native speaker, William Bodener, lived until 1794, and John Davey, who had at least some knowledge of the language from childhood, died as late as 1891!) When, at the turn of the century, social and economic changes in Cornwall prepared the ground for a revival of Cornish national consciousness and made the concept of a Cornish national language attractive again, there were no Cornish-speakers left at all. Pioneers in the Cornish movement, like Henry Jenner, had to rely entirely on written records to revive the language as a viable medium of everyday speech. The available records were not particularly extensive. Moreover, they covered a period of many centuries and represented different stages of the language's development, sometimes giving contradictory information on specific points of grammar and syntax.

The earliest stage of the language attested in documents is known as Old Cornish, and covers material dating from the ninth to the twelfth centuries. Most of it consists of very short glosses in Latin manuscripts, but it also includes a seven-page dictionary, usually referred to as the "Cottonian Vocabulary". So the Old Cornish sources give us a fair amount of lexical information, but virtually nothing of grammar.

The Middle Cornish stage lasts until approximately 1500, or the dawn of the Tudor period. Here the material is far richer. As in many other European communities, the feasts of the Church year were, in parts of Cornwall, marked with the performance of miracle plays dramatizing the portions of Scripture relevant to the occasion. By a happy chance, a manuscript containing a cycle of seven complete plays of this kind (now known as the Cornish *Ordinalia*) has been preserved. This, together with an unrelated but linguistically similar play *Beunans Meriasek* ("The Life of St. Meriadoc") and some fragments of like nature, provides us not only with a great deal of vocabulary but with an extensive sampling of grammatical forms, especially in regard to verb conjugation. The dramatic form of the texts encourages a wide variety of expressive tones — from farcical to tragic — and idiomatic expressions are included that surely reflect the colloquial usage of the time. However, one must bear in mind that all of these texts are in verse, and thus likely contain all the inversions and ellipses commonly used by someone writing under the constraints of metre and rhyme. They may not even come close to reproducing the syntax of everyday speech.

Under the Tudors, linguistic centralism became a government policy and the use of Cornish was discouraged. Lack of official recognition and the quick spread of English in influential circles combined to restrict Cornish to the disadvantaged and illiterate classes of society, with the result that no new texts were produced for close to two centuries. But by 1700 some antiquarians were again taking an interest in Cornish, as a curiosity and a unique local tradition. Texts — including a folktale, proverbs, and biographical accounts — were taken down from the last surviving native speakers in the region of Penzance, and they constitute the corpus of Late Cornish. These are our only examples of ordinary prose in Cornish of any period. However, by this time knowledge of the standardized Middle Cornish orthography had disappeared, so that the writers were forced to create their own spellings, often based impressionistically on English phonetics. This sometimes makes the texts hard to interpret; the later the texts, the more vague and inconsistent the spelling becomes. Some phonological change appears to have occurred since the Middle Cornish period. The verb forms are greatly simplified.

So, how can these three disparate bodies of material be combined into a single viable language? Old Cornish gives lexical information that is not entirely duplicated in later sources, but no grammar. Late Cornish provides irreplaceable data on the syntax of ordinary speech, but its spelling system is muddled and unreliable, and the records are not extensive enough to permit reconstruction of full grammatical paradigms. This leaves Middle Cornish, with its more abundant records and relatively consistent orthography, as the logical basis for a revived language; and it is in fact Middle Cornish that R. Morton Nance, one of the main architects of Modern Cornish, used. Nance's "Unified" Cornish adopts a slightly modified version of Middle Cornish spelling and bases its grammar on Middle Cornish usage, though the syntax is simplified in accord with Late Cornish sources. The lexical material from Old and Late Cornish is integrated with that from Middle Cornish, though respelled according to the new standard. This produces enough vocabulary for simple, everyday conversation, but it is not enough for sophisticated literary discourse. Fortunately, Cornish is not an isolated language, but is quite closely related to Breton, and a little more distantly to Welsh, so that Nance could, where necessary, borrow words from those languages, giving them Cornish forms.

While Unified Cornish (a recent minor orthographic reform has resulted in a form called "Common Cornish") has proven quite serviceable and continues to be learned and used by Cornish enthusiasts (there is, in fact, a new generation of native speakers!), a number of scholars have not been pleased with it. Some of the opposition has a political motivation, but there is also a justifiable concern that revived Cornish is a mishmash of material drawn from incompatible sources, having only a tenuous relationship with historical Cornish, and that it may in fact obscure our knowledge and understanding of the language preserved in the texts. Nance tried to get around this objection by carefully labeling all his lexical items. When his *English-Cornish Dictionary* appeared in 1952, it contained a system of symbols for identifying the sources of all the words he had compiled. Thus words from Middle Cornish were left unmarked, words from Old Cornish had a dagger (†), indicating that they had been respelled, and Late Cornish was identified by two daggers (‡); while an asterisk (*) marked words that had been adapted from Breton or Welsh. So the student who wanted to speak Cornish but who was also concerned about the historical authenticity of the material he was using was provided with a clear and unobtrusive key to the sources.

What has all this got to do with Elvish? It provides a precedent for a spoken language developed by extrapolation from limited written sources, while taking care to remain faithful to the patterns set by the sources, and to provide unambiguous reference for all the material it used. Of the Elvish languages, Quenya is probably represented by a wide enough range of texts to provide the rudiments of a spoken medium; but, as in the case of Cornish, such a "Common Quenya" would have to be cobbled together from different stages of the language. The example of Cornish lexicography could provide a method for labeling all the material adopted into "new" Quenya usage: whether it is "Qenya" or "Quenya", whether it is a new, unattested derivation from an attested root, *etc.* The problems encountered in reconstructing Cornish syntax from Middle Cornish might invite one to reflect on the fact that all our longer Quenya texts are verse, and that our only examples of Quenya prose are brief and show limited variety. How does this affect our understanding of Quenya syntax?

"Sindarin" records remain very fragmentary, but the appearance of the *Etymologies* and of a few longer texts has recently expanded our knowledge of this language (or group of languages) to the point where we can begin to appreciate its expressive possibilities. Still, unless an enormous amount of new material emerges in the future, a viable reconstruction of Sindarin will have to depend very much on imaginative extrapolation. The method by which new Cornish vocabulary has been generated by analogy with sister Celtic languages could provide patterns for devising cognates of Quenya originals, or for developing parallel Noldorin and Doriathrin forms, as our understanding of the interrelationship of the languages improves.

Thus a study of the Cornish revival could indeed contribute to the quest for spoken Elvish, by demonstrating how an immense variety of new forms can be produced from the patterns set in a few written documents, without ever having to violate those patterns.

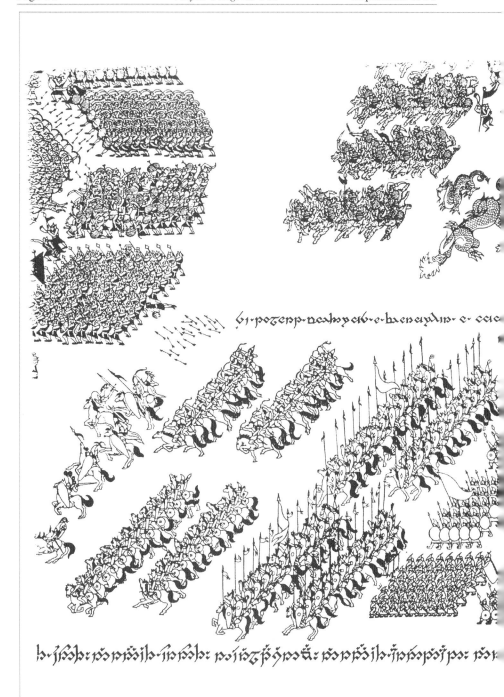

Southeast quadrant of Tom Loback's "The Fifth Battle".

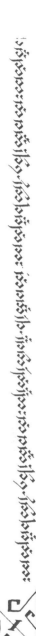

See page 4 for further information on this work.

"The Death of Glorfindel"

by Patrick Wynne

[This month's cover art, and the following notes, transcription and translation, were originally presented in Mythlore LX, pp. 20, 25 and 39. They are reprinted here with kind permission —CFH]

My depiction of "The Death of Glorfindel" closely follows the account given in *The Book of Lost Tales, Part Two*, p. 194. Using a highly stylized approach seemed a good way to echo visually the pseudo-archaic, mannered prose of *BoLT*, and it gave me an opportunity to indulge my love of curvilinear forms. Stylization also made it easier to achieve the sense of space I was after — the sweeping curves of the chasm walls, as though viewed through a fish-eye lens, convey (I hope) a feeling of vast height which would have been difficult to portray with a more realistic technique. The curling plumes of smoke owe more than a little to Tolkien's rendition of the campfire in his illustration "The Trolls" for *The Hobbit* (see *Pictures by J.R.R. Tolkien*, No. 2), and there are other visual references to the work of certain current Tolkien fan-artists (I will let you figure them out for yourselves). I felt there would be a great deal of dramatic potential in depicting not simply the death-plunge of Glorfindel and the Balrog but the death-plunge a split second before its noisy, and no doubt messy, conclusion. My Balrog is a rather corporeal-looking creature, more like a gigantic Orc than the dimly-glimpsed horror of fire and shadow described in "The Bridge of Khazad-dûm", and this is in keeping with the description of these monsters in *BoLT* (cf. Joe Abbott's article in ML 59). My love of the Elvish language led me to include as an integral part of the composition a panel describing the scene in Quenya. The over-all effect of the piece is that of a page from an illuminated Elvish manuscript.

Laurefindil ar i Valarauko sí kostaner tanya aikalesse or i lie. Laurefindilo orme hortane i Malkarauke tildello tildenna, i kallo varna ho uruite latta ar angarakka laurea rembenen. Sí palpanéro onno erekassa, sí aupelektane lattaranko ólemesse. San i Malarauko quanta kaurenen kampe Laurefindilenna i nastane ve leuko rinke, nan er túviéro róma, ar i Valarauke mápe so. San Laurefindilo má hyarya túve sikil i amba nastanéro onno súma terien, ar i ulundo urwa ramne naikenen ar nallante aikalello, mápala ohtaro lokse laurea nu karma; ar yúyo lantier yáwenna. Yé! Lantalto láma haltane ter i ambor ar quante Sornesíreo yáwe.

"Now Glorfindel and the Balrog quarreled upon that peak above the people. The wrath of Glorfindel sent the Balrog flying from point to point, the hero protected from fiery lash and iron claw by golden mail. Now he battered the creature's iron helm, now hewed away its whip-arm at the elbow. Then the Balrog, filled with fear, leaped towards Glorfindel, who stung like the dart of a snake, but he only found a shoulder, and the Balrog seized him. Then Glorfindel's left hand found a dagger, which he thrust upward to pierce the creature's bosom, and the fiery monster roared in pain and fell backwards from the peak, seizing the warrior's golden hair beneath the helm; and both fell into the abyss. Lo! The echo of their fall leaped through the hills and filled the abyss of Thorn Sir."

A Survey of Ring Poem Translations
by Jorge Quiñónez

I am sure everyone is familiar with the Ring Poem (hereafter RP). It is easily the best remembered poem from *The Lord of the Rings*. In this survey article I have included every translation (that I have encountered) of the RP into a Tolkienian language. For reasons of space limitations, I have not been able to include the authors' grammatical notes; the reader is referred to the original publications for these and other details.

We begin with Bill Welden and Chris Gilson who, in 1977, published the first Elvish translation of the RP, in Sindarin, presented in Mode of Beleriand tengwar calligraphy by Paula Marmor as the back cover of *Parma Eldalamberon* #5 (and subsequently represented in Roman transliteration in *Beyond Bree*, Aug. 1982, p.5):

> *Nel cherin di menel nin Erain Edhellath*
> *Os ben rynd sernin Nogothrim ni thûr*
> *Gwent an in Edain, ion amarth na guruth*
> *Min an in Dúhaur, na borod dîn dûr*
> *Be-mBar Mordor, ias caedar Duath.*
> *Min gor i-phain arad, min gor tuwad hain*
> *Min gor i-phain teithad a remmad hain ben Fuin*
> *Be-mBar Mordor, ias caedar Duath!*

Across the Atlantic and four years later, in *Quettar* #11/12 (Dec. 1981, p.3), Ronald Kyrmse and Julian Bradfield published their Quenya translation of the RP:

> *Nelde Cormar Eldaturin nu menel,*
> *otso Naucaturin mi ondomardi,*
> *nelnelde Atanin fírin umbarnen,*
> *ere Morituren morimahalmasse*
> *Morindoresse yass' i lumbuli caitar.*
> *Ere Corma ilye canien, ere Corma túvien,*
> *Ere Corma ilye yalien ar moresse mandien*
> *Morindoresse yass' i lumbuli caitar.*

A few months later, in *Quettar* #14 (May 1982, p. 10), a Quenya version by Michael Poxon was published, a version which, as the author noted, took "liberties with the English version":

> *Nelde cormar hereldarin*
> *Otso cormar herenaukin*
> *Enelde i firatanin*
> *Er corma Herumori morimahalmásse*
> *Noresse yar lumbuli, í morindoresse*
> *Ere corma canatilye ere tuviatilye*
> *Ere yaliatilye ar morinen mandátilye*
> *Noresse yar lumbuli, í Morindoresse.*

Three months later, in *Quettar* #15 (August 1982, p. 8), Richard Trubshaw's translation into his own "'dialect' of Sindarin" appeared:

E Chorlinnod : E Thaurcoriath

Nel coriath n'in Edhilerain nu e menel,
Os n'i Nauhirrim thî hain rend gonion
Neldhel n'Edain fírin amarthen fîr,
Er n'e Thaurvor lim han talan mor
Thî e Mordhoriand îass i lumiath riga.
Er cor gon hain, er cor far hain,
Er cor îal a thî e fuin band hain
Thî e Mordhoriand îass i lumiath riga.

Simultaneously there appeared, in *Beyond Bree,* Aug. 1982 (p.5), an "Unfinished Draft" translation of the RP into Quenya by Patrick Wynne:

Quettalindë i Cormaron

Neldë Cormar i Eldaranin nu i menel,
Otso i Naukatárin ondorondontassen,
Vindë Fírimain yaron ambar ná fírië,
Erë i Herumornan i mornamahalmassë
Mí nórië Mornanórëo, yassë caitar i lumbuli.
Erë Corma ilyë te túrien, Erë Corma te tuvien,
Erë Corma ilyë te yalien ar morniessë te mandien
Mí nórië Mornanórëo, yassë caitar i lumbuli.

In the next issue of *Quettar* (#16, October 1982, pp. 6-7) Julian Bradfield completed the other six lines of J.R.R. Tolkien's two-line Black Speech RP (bracketed below), thus far unique among the RP translations:

Gakh Nazgi … Golug-durub-ûri lata-nût
Udu takob-ishiz gund-ob Gazat-shakh-ûri
Krith Shara-ûri matûrz matat dûmpuga
Ash tug Shakhbûrz-ûr Ulîma-tab-ishi za
Uzg-Mordor-ishi amal fauthut burgûli
[Ash nazg durbatulûk, ash nazg gimbatul
Ash nazg thrakatulûk, agh bûrzum-ishi krimpatul]
Uzg-Mordor-ishi amal fauthut burgûli.

The latest translation of the RP, into Quenya, is that by Chris Gilson and myself, which first appeared in *Parma Eldalamberon #7* (pp. 24-26), and then subsequently in *VT* #1 (p. 6):

Corma Lairë Quenyassë

Neldë Cormar Elda-harnin nu elenarda,
Otso Nauco-héruin toia ondorondossen,
Nertë Atanin fairenen umbartar,
Minë Morna Héren morna mahalmassë
Mí Nórë Mornandor yassë Mordor caitar.
Minë Corma turië te ilyë, Minë Corma hirië te,
Minë Corma tucië te ilyë ar mí mornië nutë te
Mí Nórë Mornandor yassë Mordor caitar.

This translation was the first (and thus far only) to be published after the publication of *The Lost Road*, and so was able to make full use of *The Etymologies*. Thus this version is the first which did not have to coin any new words (for instance, *The Etymologies* contained the first occurrence of the Quenya word for 'nine', **nertë**). Since publishing the original translation, I've adopted several revisions which have been suggested to me by various readers. Thus "**Corma Lairë Quenyassë**" (title) > "**Corma Lairë Quenyanen**"; "**Otso Nauco-héruin toia ondorondossen**" (line 2) > "**Otso Nauco-héruin ondorondoltassen**"; "**Minë Corma hirië te**" (line 6) > "**Minë Corma tuvië te**"; "**mornië nutë te**" (line 7) > "**mornië nutië te**".

Of all the poems written by J.R.R. Tolkien, the Ring Poem is the most often translated. Through this chronological presentation of Ring Poem translations, I hope the reader can gain an appreciation for the development of our understanding of the languages with the increase of the published corpus. Comparing a translation from 1977 to a translation of five years later, we see that the later translation uses fewer words invented by the translator and more words invented by Tolkien himself, the only native speaker of Elvish in this century (however, that may change in the next). The differences among the various translations are testimony to the continuing evolution of our knowledge of, and approaches to, Tolkien's Elvish languages.

[In a timely submission, Nancy Martsch, editor of Beyond Bree*, has sent the following Quenya translation of the Ring Poem, in* tengwar *and Roman transliteration, which is her "answer" to the Graduation Exercise for her recently concluded Quenya Language Lessons.* —CFH]

Nelde cormar an i Eldaheri nu i menel
Otso cormar an i Naukantúri ondomardentassen
Nerte cormar an i Fírimar marte nurun
Er corma an i Mornaher mornamahalmasse
    Mornoro maresse, yasse lómi caitar.
Er corma ilye te turu, er corma te túva,
Er corma ilye te hosta ar morniesse te nuta,
    Mornoro maresse, yasse lómi caitar.

Essitalmar

The Roots of Middle-earth Names and Places

A column edited by Tom Loback

This is a forum for the readers of VT *to submit their ideas and thoughts about names, both of people and places; their meanings and the story that they tell. All are encouraged to submit inquiries, short interpretations and discussions thereof, particularly those names still undefined. Send all correspondence for this column to the editor at 152 West 26th St., #36, N.Y. City, NY 10001, USA.*

Star-struck

I was happy to see Jorge Quiñónez and Ned Raggett's study of stars published *[*Nólë i Meneldilo, VT #12, p.5; originally presented at Mythcon XX, July, 1989 —CFH]. I was somewhat disappointed however to see the short shrift given to the information available in *The Book of Lost Tales, Part One [BoLT I]* and *BoLT II*, particularly as it bears on some of the conclusions made.

I would feel more comfortable about the "easily identified" *Remmirath* as the Pleiades if this constellation were not already named in *BoLT I* as Gnomish *Sithaloth*, Qenya *Sithaloctha* 'fly cluster' (p. 254, entry **Gong**).

BoLT I (p. 262) identifies Sirius as 'the Bee of Azure', Qenya *Nielluin* or *Niellúnë*, *Nierninwa*. *Helluin* likely translates as 'blue-ice' or 'blue-glass', not 'sky-blue' as suggested, and is likely a Noldorin or Doriathrin word. Sirius is also called *Gil* (*BoLT I*, p. 256, entry **Ingil**).

The Qenya Lexicon also identifies Jupiter as *Silindo* (*BoLT I*, p. 265, entry **Silindrin**), perhaps meaning 'small moon' from root **INI** 'small', or 'white-heart' from **ID-** 'heart, mood' (see *The Lost Road [LR]*, p. 361).

I cannot agree with the attributions of the star-names *Carnil, Luinil,* and *Lumbar* as Quenya, which are as likely to be Sindarin (if not more so). I suspect that Jorge's pro-Quenya bias *[Tom has indicated that he is thinking of having Jorge brought up on charges of violating the Ban of Thingol —CFH]* would have led to a Quenya translation for *Borgil*, if it weren't for Tolkien's remarks to the contrary in *The Letters of J.R.R. Tolkien* (pp. 426-7).

Lumbar — 'gloomy-home' or 'cloudy-home' (*LR*, p. 370, entry **LUM-**; p. 372, entry **MBAR-**; *BoLT I*, p. 259, entry **Luvier**). Why try to force the *-r* plural form just to make this a Quenya name? It isn't done with *Nena-r*, which would be as likely as 'waters'.

Luinil — easily read as a Sindarin compound from Doriathrin as *Luin-(g)il* 'blue-star', 'pale-star' (*LR*, p. 370, entry **LUG-**[2]). Could the desire to make these names Quenya account for the complete lack of linguistic citation to back up this attribution to Quenya?

Carnil — 'red-star' in Sindarin by the same reasoning as for *Luinil*, although the syncope of **KARÁN-** (*LR*, p. 362) is puzzling and perhaps points towards Quenya. But *Carn Dûm* is not Quenya, and the syncope is not regular in Sindarin as it is in Quenya, which I take to mean it can go either way.

I have always imagined the *Remmirath* to be the Milky Way, and feel the notion to be supported by the *-ath* general plural ending. But since I know little of astronomy I can't imagine where this could be in the sky relative to the description. *[A quick consultation of a star-chart shows that when Betelgeuse is rising, the Milky Way spans the sky from east to west —CFH]*

Finally, I wonder if any of our E.L.F. star-gazers can identify the constellation in the upper left corner of the painting of Taniquetil in *Pictures by J.R.R. Tolkien*? *[i.e. Plate 31 — This I think is clearly intended to be the Pleaides. However, the configuration of the stars in this representation does not precisely match that of the celebrated asterism; moreover, if we assume we are looking west (or even north across the Bay of Eldamar) to Taniquetil, it is impossible for the Pleiades ever to have the represented orientation. But I think we're not meant to take these details too seriously: note that the Sun and the Moon appear together in the sky to either side of Taniquetil along the horizon, an equally impossible configuration. Worse yet, the lighted crescent of the Moon bows* away *from the Sun! This at any rate is a clear depiction of* Vista, Ilmen, *and* Vaiya *—CFH]* The Big Dipper can be seen in *The Father Christmas Letters* (in the letter for 1927).

Transitions in Translations

A column edited by Arden R. Smith

The purpose of this column is to examine peculiarities in translations of Tolkien's works: mistranslations, unusual translations, interesting solutions to the problems of translation, and other curiosities in foreign editions. Ideas and contributions are encouraged: send them to "Transitions," c/o Arden R. Smith, P.O. Box 4395, Berkeley, CA 94704-0395, USA.

"Edition Shifting" in the German *Hobbit*
— Part One —

Numerous revisions were made to the text of *The Hobbit* for the second and third editions, and the extent of these revisions is beautifully shown in Appendix A (pp. 321-28) of *The Annotated Hobbit*. By examining these revisions, one can determine the source edition from which a foreign edition was translated. As Manfred Zimmerman states in his "'The Hobbit' in Germany" (*Quettar* Special Publication No. 2, pp. 3-7), the 1957 Paulus-Verlag edition was based on the second edition of 1951. He continues: "Probably in 1971 a revision of the translation was undertaken .... The revision was probably done by the original translator Walter Scherf, since no other name is mentioned anywhere. He seems to have taken into account the newest available English edition, the 3rd edition of 1966 .... This revised translation was issued as a paperback in 1974 by dtv in its 'Junior' series ...." This revision is responsible for the phenomenon which I call "edition shifting," since some passages of this German edition reflect the second edition text and others reflect the third edition. In this column, I will discuss where the edition shifting occurs; in part two I hope to be able to discuss why.

According to the listing in Appendix A of *The Annotated Hobbit*, fifty-nine passages were revised for the 1966 edition. In referring to the revised passages, I will be using the numbering given in this listing. Seven of those revised passages are irrelevant as far as the German translation is concerned: I.N (the introductory note is omitted from the translation), I.5 (corrected typo), I.10 (map location varies from edition to edition), II.2 (change of "hadn't" to "had not"), III.5 (corrected typo), and VII.1 and 2 ("lord of the eagles" capitalized — all nouns are capitalized in German).

This leaves fifty-two relevant revisions. Forty-six of these were revised for what Douglas Anderson calls the 1966-A (Ballantine) edition. Eleven of the forty-six were further revised for the 1966-B Allen & Unwin "Third Edition," some of these further revisions being as minor as an added comma. Six revisions were made for the 1966-B edition where the 1966-A text was identical to that of 1951.

It is clear that Scherf used the 1966-B text in revising his German translation. Two of the six B-only revisions correspond to the revised text (page references to the 1974 dtv paperback):

II.9.   "*... ihr Lager hier an Ort und Stelle errichten wollten. Sie zogen zu einer Baumgruppe ....*"(p. 39)

XV.1.   "*... und einen neuen Pfad anlegen, der ins Tal hinabführte.*" (p. 262)

Furthermore, the one passage with both A and B revisions which does not correspond (at least in part) to the second edition corresponds to the 1966-B̲ text: III.7. "*... in irgendeiner Gebirgshöhle gestoßen sind*" (pp. 59-60). The one passage which appears to follow the A-text rather than the B-text (II.1. "… *und dann eine ganze Meile weiter oder mehr*" (p. 36) could just as easily be a blend of 1951 and 1966-B texts, since such mixtures appear elsewhere in the translation. Interpreting this as a mixture, then, we may ignore the 1966-A text and merely consider a second/third edition dichotomy in the German text. The fifty-two relevant passages may be tabulated so:

		2 Follows 2nd ed. (1951)	3 Follows 3rd ed. (1966-B)	2/3 Mix of 2nd & 3rd eds.
A	Revised for 1966-A only	20	8	6
AB	Revised for both 1966-A&B	8	1	2
B	Revised for 1966-B only	3	2	1

A-2	:	I.9, I.14, I.17, I.18, I.19, I.21, II.5, II.11, II.12, II.14, III.3, III.10, V.1, V.2, VIII.1, XIII.1, XIII.2, XV.2, XVII.1, XIX.1
A-3	:	I.1, I.6, I.12, III.2, III.9, IV.1, V.6, XIX.2
A-2/3	:	I.2, I.3, I.13, II.10, II.13, III.1
AB-2	:	I.4, I.7, I.16, I.20, II.3, II.4, III.4, VIII.2
AB-3	:	III.7
AB-2/3	:	I.15, II.1
B-2	:	II.6, II.7, XV.3
B-3	:	II.9, XV.1
B-2/3	:	II.8

    The tables only include fifty-one of the fifty-two passages, since the German translation of passage III.6 follows neither the second nor the third edition text, *nor* any mixture of the two. Here the second edition reads, "They are old swords, very old swords of the elves that are now called Gnomes", and the third edition, "… swords of the High Elves of the West, my kin" (*Annotated Hobbit*, pp. 62 and 324). The German rendering is far from both: "*Es sind alte Elbenschwerter*" (p. 59, "they are old elven-swords").

    Is there any pattern to this edition shifting? Is there any rhyme and reason as to what got revised and what did not? I will examine these questions in my next column and hopefully will find some answers.

*　*　*

More about Appendices

by Nathalie Kotowski

I wanted to give some information about Appendices. First: there is an edition of the Appendices in Spanish. It was issued about two years ago and I have seen it through a friend in Madrid, but I don't remember the publisher. It is a red book, leather-looking. No idea if good or not.

About the French Appendices: it was true that the French edition of *The Lord of the Rings* [*LotR*] at first had no Appendices. Later the Press Pocket edition gave some of them. Two years ago, they were issued as an extra volume. A wholly new edition of *LotR* by Christian Bourgois has the complete work in one volume. It was published a month or so ago. A beautiful book, with some minor errors corrected, the worst left and a few new ones added....

There is a lot to say about the translation of the Appendices. They are done by a different translator (the same who translated *Unfinished Tales*, which is really not bad at all). The real problem is the change of names: they are not the same in the text and in the Appendices, which is very troublesome. There are new difficulties for establishing the Glossary of Tolkien's names of persons and places, the work we do with the Eredain of Switzerland. Not too many great errors but a few "pearls," such as the statement that Hobbits were Half-elven, and this very strange phrase in *The Tale of Years*: "1434 ... *Le Roi Elessar nomme le Thain, le Grand Maître et les Conseillers du Maire du Royaume.*" In French we say of such things, it is a "mic-mac." There is another "mic-mac" in *The Tale of Aragorn and Arwen*, between Arador, Arathorn and Aragorn (it is like the famous story about the man who became his own grandfather).

The general impression is not very good. The translator tried to use an archaic style with inversions and rare words, but the result is only bad French. There are also two translations which, in my opinion, are not legitimate. First, it is said for "a lady fair ..." "*la Dame de Beauté*". La Dame de Beauté was Agnes Sorel, the mistress of King Charles VIII who had a palace in a place named Beauté (a fine pun but you cannot use it in another context). The same can be said about the translation of "Longbeards" as "*à la barbe fleurie*". This expression was used for Charlemagne. *[And William was known as "the Bastard" (before he became "the Conqueror"), but this sobriquet is still freely applied by and to many others —CFH].*

Here you have some points in my private (and ineffective) little war for a better French translation.

* * *

Trivia Question:

    Q: Who is Kalpa Kassinen?
    A: Bilbo Baggins, in the first Finnish translation of *The Hobbit* (*Lohikäärmevuori*. Translated by Risto Pitkänen. Helsinki: Tammi, 1973).

* * *

Next Issue: "Edition Shifting" (Part Two), and more!

Publications of Interest

*** *BIAOR = Back issues available on request* ***

Beyond Bree: Newsletter of the American Mensa Tolkien SIG. Published monthly.
     Editor: Nancy Martsch. *Subscriptions to*: the editor at P.O. Box 55372, Sherman Oaks, CA 91413. Annual subscription: USA $7.00; Overseas $10.00. *BIAOR*.
     July 1990; August 1990: No items of linguistic interest in these issues, but *BB* is always a good read, with interesting letters, reviews and news items. Highly recommended.

Mythlore: A Journal of J.R.R. Tolkien, C.S. Lewis, Charles Williams and the Genres of Myth and Fantasy Studies. Published quarterly.
     Editor: Glen GoodKnight. *Subscriptions to*: P.O. Box 6707, Altadena, CA 91003. Annual subscription: USA $14.50; Overseas Airmail: Europe & Latin America $29.50, Australia & Asia $34.50. *BIAOR*.
     No. LXII, Summer 1990: Cover art "Gandalf at the Library of Minas Tirith" by Patrick Wynne. "Notes Towards a Translation of 'Lúthien's Song'" by Patrick Wynne, reprinted from *VT* #9. Paul Nolan Hyde's *Quenti Lambardillion* column this issue examines the runic writing systems of Middle-earth. Full-page ad for several works by artist Tom Loback. Letter from PNH addressing the phonological development of the Elvish tongues. What are you waiting for? Subscribe!

Parma Eldalamberon: A Journal of Linguistic Studies of Fantasy Literature. Published occasionaly.
     Editor: Chris Gilson. *Parma* #9 is available for $7.00 from the editor at 300 North Civic Drive, #304, Walnut Creek, CA 94596.
     No. 9: An examination of the Quenya past tense markers by Tom Loback. A thorough yet highly readable analysis of "*Narqelion*" by Patrick Wynne and Chris Gilson. An original Quenya poem by our own Jorge Quiñónez. Letters. Lots of artwork from Pat, Tom and Adam Christensen. No one reading *VT* should be without this.

Quettar: Bulletin of the Linguistic Fellowship of The Tolkien Society. Published quarterly.
     Editor: Julian Bradfield. *Subscriptions to*: Christina Scull, 1A Colestown St., London SW11 3EH, UK. Annual subscription: UK £3.00; Europe and surface mail outside Europe £4.00; Airmail outside Europe £7.50. *BIAOR*.
     No. 39, March 1990: Lengthy and rigorous article on "Quenya Morphology" by Craig Marnock. Reader's comments, criticisms and kudos in *Quendillon*. As always, not to be missed.

Next Issue

I've learned I'm a terrible oracle, so I won't mention that imminent unpublished Elvish fragment here. In *VT* #14 we'll have the usual letters and columns and also conclude the four-part presentation of Tom Loback's huge "Fifth Battle" mural with the southwest quadrant, and a description by Tom of the events depicted.

Vinyar Tengwar

The bimonthly 'news-letters' of the Elvish Linguistic Fellowship.
A Special Interest Group of the Mythopoeic Society.

Editor: Carl F. Hostetter, 2509 Ambling Circle, Crofton, MD 21114, USA.

Contributing Editor: Jorge Quiñónez, 3326 Polk Ave., San Diego, CA 92104, USA.

Proofreaders: Jorge Quiñónez and Arden R. Smith.

Masthead: by Tom Loback.

Tengwar numerals: from Lawrence M. Schoen's *Moroma* PostScript *Tengwar* font for the Mac, available on disk for $6.00 from PsychoGlyph, P.O. Box 74, Lake Bluff, IL 60044.

Subscriptions: Subscriptions are for 1 year (6 issues) and must be paid in US dollars.
$12.00   USA
$15.00   Canada (sent airmail) and Overseas surface mail
$18.00   Overseas airmail

Back issues available: Issues 1 - 7 & 9 - 13 are each $2.00 in the USA, $2.50 overseas surface mail and Canada, $3.00 airmail. Issue 8 includes a large map and costs $4.00 USA, $5.00 surface and Canada, $6.00 airmail. A complete set of back issues is available for $20.00 USA, $25.00 Overseas surface mail, and $30.00 Overseas airmail. *All costs are postpaid.*

Payments: All payments must be in US dollars. It is recommended that overseas members make payments via international postal money order.

Make all checks payable to Carl F. Hostetter.

Submissions: Written material should in some manner deal with Tolkien's invented languages. All submissions must be typed, or must be written unbelievably legibly: if I have to decipher lower-glyphics, the submission is automatically rejected! The editor reserves the right to edit any material (except art) for purposes of brevity and relevance. Ilúvatar smiles upon submissions on 800K (3.5") Macintosh disks in PageMaker, Microsoft Word or MacWrite formats, or as unformatted TEXT files. Artwork should be linguistic, or at least Elvish, in nature. Remember that artwork done in black ink will reproduce the best; I wouldn't harbor great expectations for the quality of reproduction from artwork rendered in pencil, "Flair" pen, chalk, or colored ink.

The deadline for **VT #14** *is October 20, 1990.*

Vinyar Tengwar is produced by the editor on an Apple Macintosh II personal computer, using a LaCie Silverscan scanner, Microsoft Word 4.0 and Aldus PageMaker 4.0. VT is mastered for duplication on an Apple LaserWriter II NTX.

Cainen canta

#14

November, 1990

Vinyar Tengwar

In This Issue

Editor's Musings

This issue of *VT* is indeed an auspicious one for Elvish studies. Through the efforts of Patrick Wynne, Chris Gilson, Taum Santoski, and Jorge Quiñónez, and with the gracious permission of the Tolkien Estate, *VT* is privileged to present the Koivienéni Sentence, a hitherto unpublished fragment of Q(u)enya from the Tolkien manuscripts at Marquette University. Chris and Pat have provided a characteristically thorough and fascinating analysis of this new passage; so thorough in fact that I've had to displace Tom Loback's and Arden Smith's regular columns to next issue. Also, this month saw the publication of *The War of the Ring*, the eighth volume of *The History of Middle-earth*; I've provided a brief presentation and discussion of the new linguistic material therein. And this issue also carries an announcement of the first *Colloquium on the Languages of Middle-earth*, a gathering of Elvish scholars who are laboring to produce *I Parma*, The Book, the *magnum opus* of contemporary Tolkienian linguistics.

*   *   *

As this is the last *VT* of 1990, I'd like to take this opportunity to wish our readers around the world a happy and safe holiday season.

— Carl F. Hostetter

"The notion of 'major language' is obviously primarily a social characterisation, and the fact that a language is not included in this volume implies no denigration of its importance as a language in its own right: every human language is a manifestation of our species' linguistic faculty and any human language may provide an important contribution to our understanding of language as a general phenomenon.... When linguists learned in 1970 that the last speaker of Kamassian, a Uralic language originally spoken in Siberia, had kept her language alive for decades in her prayers — God being the only other speaker of the language — they may well have wondered whether, for this person, *the* world's major language was not Kamassian."

— Bernard Comrie, *The World's Major Languages* (Oxford, 1987), pp. ix–x.

E.L.F. News

New Members

The E.L.F. extends a hearty *mae govannen* to:

- Erica Keenan   RD #5, Box 208, Boyertown, PA 19512.
- Taum Santoski   2347 N. Booth St., Riverwest, Milwaukee, WI 53212.
- Galen Tackett   4785 La Mesa Ct., Fremont, CA 94536.

Colloquium on the Languages of Middle-earth

Pursuant to its goal of producing The Book, the ultimate reference work on the imaginary languages of J. R. R. Tolkien's Middle-earth, the Elvish Linguistic Fellowship will sponsor the first annual Colloquium on the Languages of Middle-earth, on February 15–18, 1991. This will be an opportunity for everyone who is interested in this ambitious project to help in making it a reality.

This four day colloquium is intended as the first of three or more annual review sessions for material which will eventually be included in The Book. Each program participant will present one or more monographs on topics such as: "The Grammar of the Quenya Noun", "Writing Systems of Middle-earth", or "Comparative Phonology in *The Etymologies*". These monographs will be collected together in a looseleaf notebook, distributed to all colloquium participants, and reviewed and revised until they provide a definitive source of reference material, from which The Book will be compiled. All members will receive a copy of the proceedings and all updates to it until The Book is published. So even if you attend only one year, you will be able to stay abreast of the project (and participate by mail if you like) in later years.

The following stellar array of Elvish scholars have made a commitment to attend this first meeting: Chris Gilson, Carl Hostetter, Paul Nolan Hyde, Jorge Quiñónez, Arden Smith, Bill Welden, and Patrick Wynne. In addition, several others have indicated a strong interest in attending.

An attending membership is $175. This price does not include room and board, but this first year the hosts, Bill Welden and Jo Alida Wilcox, have agreed to provide room (well, floor space) and board free of charge to all attendees. Membership fees will go toward the costs of holding our meetings and publishing The Book. A full financial statement will be published each year in *Vinyar Tengwar*.

On the evening of Sunday the 17th, from 7:30 on, we will be having an open party as a closing ceremony and celebration. Everyone is welcome and there is no charge, but please call ahead if you plan to attend.

If you are interested in being one of the project authors, and are willing to write several monographs and attend the annual meetings over the next few years (as well as attending most Mythcons, where we will hold a second important meeting each year), we would be excited about having you join us. To register, or for more information, contact

Bill Welden
19419 Valerio St.
Reseda, CA 91335
Phone #: (818) 993-4910.

Letters to VT

• David Bratman   Menlo Park, CA

Alexei Kondratiev's article on Revived Cornish [The Way to "Revived" Elvish — A Cornish Model?, *in* VT *#13 —CFH]* is highly provocative. He describes more clearly than I've seen elsewhere how the language was reconstructed, and offers a model for doing the same with Quenya. It's understandable from Alexei's account why some scholars have scoffed at Revived Cornish as an artificial construct, but there are several appropriate responses that would also be applicable to Quenya. One is to shrug and say "Well, it's the best we can do." Another is to point out that if people actually use it, it's real. And a third is to observe that all languages are human creations and hence in a sense artificial; the question is whether the language breathes and has an inner beauty of its own. Cornish may look a little dim next to other Celtic languages which never died out, but its peculiar character has been caught for the observer, and so has Quenya's.

The advantage of having related tongues available, though, is that they can be used as a crutch to hang reconstruction on, as Alexei describes the other Celtic languages being used for Cornish. I presume that few *VT* readers need to be reminded of Tolkien's own work in reconstructing lost words in Gothic out of Old English and other early Germanic tongues; this task is described in loving detail in T. A. Shippey's *The Road to Middle-earth*. Quenya itself, as Alexei notes, is a useful crutch for reconstructing Sindarin and the other Elven tongues. (But the task may not be as easy as it sounds, if Tom Loback's account in *VT* #10 of the problems in translating Sindarin to Quenya — via English, of all things — is any guide.)

But what most intrigues me in Alexei's article is his opening discussion of the motivations of Elvish Linguistic Fellows. To some, he says, Quenya is "a key to Tolkien's creative genius"; to others, it's a language to study for its own sake, which implies the need to create, or uncover, more of it. This sounds similar to a split among those who study Tolkien's narrative creativity. Some people write *Mythlore* papers exploring how his narrative genius worked. Others prefer to extend the narrative subcreation we've already got. It seems to me, however, that there the similarity ends, for not only is it, in my opinion, a higher calling to write Quenya prose than to write "The Jewel of Arwen", the results lie much more pleasantly on the ear.

I enjoyed Bruce Leonard's Mythcon report [Mythcon XXI — A Review, *in* VT *#13 — CFH]*. One small correction: "After *The Silmarillion*" wasn't a paper I gave, but a panel that included Chris Gilson as well. I guess maybe I did talk too much ....

• Tom Loback   New York City, N.Y.

Each issue of *VT* looks better and better. Of the articles [*in* VT *#13 —CFH]* I most enjoyed Alexei's *The Way to "Revived" Elvish — A Cornish Model?* It seems to echo current "Silmarillionist" and "Ringite" debates precisely. However, I feel it is better to speak or write "incorrect" Elvish than to do neither, as that is one sure way to learn. Each time something is done or tried and then examined and criticized and discussed the range of possible Elvish is broadened. The more people doing it, the merrier. As Jorge's article on Ring Poem variants [A Survey of Ring Poem Translations, *in* VT *#13 —CFH]* aptly demonstrates, Quenya study is advancing smartly and becoming more polished. As the babble of Elvish tongues at Mythcon demonstrated, much enjoyment can be had in such exercise.

— *continued on page 4.*

The War of the Ring
A Linguistic Review
by Carl F. Hostetter

The War of the Ring (*WotR*), the eighth volume in the *History of Middle-earth* (*HoMe*) series, has been published in the United States by Houghton Mifflin. While a thorough literary review is best left to others, there are as usual a few linguistic features which deserve attention here.

Q(U)ENYA:

Alla Earendel Elenion Ankalima (p. 223, note 29) is an early form of Frodo's Quenya cry **Aiya Eärendil Elenion Ancalima!** (*The Two Towers* [*TT*], p. 329), exhibiting the usual *k*/*c* variation and the long-standing form **Earendel**, and the unusual form **alla**, which according to Christopher Tolkien was not changed to **aiya** until after *TT* was in type.

Asea aranaite 'kingsfoil' (p. 394) is the precursor of **asëa aranion** in *The Return of the King* (p. 141).

NOLDORIN/SINDARIN:

The most extensive Elvish passages in *WotR* (p. 218) are the early Noldorin versions of Sam's invocation of Elbereth (*TT*, p. 339). The first version parallels the early version of the chant to Elbereth in Rivendell published in *The Return of the Shadow* (p. 394), except that **lír** appears for **dir** in the third line, and **óriel** and **míriel** here have long vowels indicated:

> *O Elbereth Gilthoniel*
> *sir evrin pennar óriel*
> *lír avos-eithen míriel*

Christopher Tolkien tells us that this was changed on the manuscript to:

> *O Elbereth Gilthoniel*
> *silevrin pennar óriel*
> *hír avas-eithen míriel*
> *a tíro'men Gilthoniel!*

The first two lines of these passages correspond to the first two lines of the chant to Elbereth in *The Fellowship of the Ring* (p. 250): **A Elbereth Gilthoniel, silivren penna míriel**, though **míriel** 'sparkling-like-jewels' (*The Road Goes Ever On* [*RGEO*], p. 72) is found on line 3, and on line 2 we have instead **óriel** (compare the Old Noldorin form **orie** 'rise' found in *The Etymologies* [*The Lost Road*, p. 379, entry **ORO-**]), while the fourth line clearly corresponds to the fourth line of Sam's Invocation in *TT*: **A tiro nin, Fanuilos!** 'O look towards (watch over) me, Fanuilos!' (*RGEO*, p. 72). **Sir evrin > silevrin** can now be seen to definitely correspond to the later **silivren** '(white) glittering', and **pennar** is perhaps a plural form of **penna** 'slants-down' (*ibid.*). The forms **dir avos-eithen > lír avos-eithen > hír avas-eithen** are clearly related to **dir avosaith** 'over the gloomy places' found in the untitled poem given on p. 217 of *The Monsters and the Critics*. A sentence subsequently struck out on the manuscript specifically labels the language of this passage as Noldorin (p. 226, note 50); the term *Sindarin* has yet to arise in the manuscripts treated thus far in *HoMe*.

Another Noldorin passage, obscured on the manuscript but tentatively reconstructed by Christopher Tolkien, is given on page 293, note 23: **Gir.. edlothiand na ngalad melon i ni** [?*sevo*] **ni** [?*edran*]. According to the note in which this passage occurs, this may have something to do with the gates of Minas Tirith, possibly connected with a password (the occurrence here of **melon** ?= 'friend' is perhaps notable).

KHUZDUL:

Gimli's battle-cry ***Baruk Khazâd! Khazâd ai-mênu!*** 'Axes of the Dwarves! The Dwarves are upon you!' (*The Return of the King*, Appendix F, p. 411) appears just so (p. 20), apparently from the first, except that ***ai-mênu*** is hyphenated; ***ai-mênu*** is analyzed as ***aya*** + ***mênu***, with partly illegible meanings which Christopher Tolkien interprets as ***aya*** 'upon' and ***mênu*** 'acc[usative] pl[ural] you'.

ENTISH:

The Ents "short language" is said (pp. 50, 55) to be "an old-fashioned Elvish", as opposed to the full language, which still at this time had the ***Ta-rūta, dūm-da, dūm-da dūm! ta-rāra dūmda dūmda-būm!*** cadence (p. 50).

Finally, we are given yet another tantalizing hint of the linguistic treasures that are in Tolkien's manuscript legacy: on page 20, Christopher Tolkien notes that "after the publication of [*The Lord of the Rings*], my father began an analysis of all fragments of other languages (Quenya, Sindarin, Khuzdul, the Black Speech) found in the book, but unhappily before he had reached the end of [*The Fellowship of the Ring*] the notes, at the outset full and elaborate, had diminished to largely uninterpretable jottings."

[A note to Those Who Are Interested in That Sort of Thing: In his Foreword (pp. x–xi) Christopher Tolkien acknowledges the assistance of Neil Gaiman in explaining the origins of Tolkien's poem *Errantry*. This is surely the noted comic-book writer, author of such acclaimed series as *The Sandman* and the forthcoming *Books of Magic*.]

Letters to *VT*   — *continued from page 2.*

• Jenny Coombs   Nottinghamshire, England

Thank you for another most interesting and well-presented *Vinyar Tengwar*.

I agree with Nancy Martsch's suggestion *[in* VT *#13 — CFH]* that *-ie-* and *-ea-* could not receive stress on the first vowel of the combination, and that this could explain the lengthening in ***Eldaliéva*** *etc.* However, I do not think that the *-ll-* in ***Altáriello*** is due to such a mechanism. Quite a few Quenya words have a "long" form which, in polysyllabic compounds, is usually shortened. The long form, though, is used in the formation of oblique compounds and adjectives, in English as well as in Quenya. Hence ***Silmarillë*** is shortened to ***Silmaril***, but inflections are added to the long form: ***Silmarilli***, ***Silmarillion***; and ***Númenórë*** > ***Númenor***, but the English adjective is *Númenórean*.

I think that the form ***Altáriello*** probably indicates that the name ***Altáriel*** is a short form of ****Altáriellë***, and that the oblique cases are based on this longer form. *-iel* is a common ending in Sindarin women's names: *The Etymologies* gives under the entry **SEL-D-**: "daughter .... Q[enya] *selde*" (*The Lost Road*, p. 385). Hence presumably the meaning 'maiden, woman'. It doesn't seem to be unreasonable that *alata* + *rig-* + *selde* (see *The Silmarillion*, Appendix, entry *kal-*) should end up as ****Altárieldë***, with genitive ****Altárieldo***, but I must say the change *-ld- > -ll-* seems to me less obvious. Any thoughts?

Alexei Kondratiev's article *[*The Way to "Revived" Elvish — A Cornish Model? — CFH]* was fascinating; I entirely agree that The Book, were it ever to appear (*i.e.* a complete dictionary, verb and noun tables, *etc.*), would have to adopt a rigorous system of labelling sources.

Also I enjoyed Pat's Quenya piece *[*The Death of Glorfindel — CFH]*. I thought it read fluently. I was unsure, though, why he switched from the *Silmarillion*'s ***Valarauko*** to the *Book of Lost Tales*' ***Malkarauke*** to combined ***Malarauko***. ***Karma*** 'helm' (line 7) should surely be ***kassa***, as in line 3.

The Elves at Koivienéni

A New Quenya Sentence

Analyzed by Christopher Gilson and Patrick Wynne

The collection of J. R. R. Tolkien's manuscripts at Marquette University in Milwaukee is well known as an abundant source of information for those interested in the study of Tolkien's Elvish languages. One of the more intriguing items to be found there is an unpublished sentence in Quenya, accompanied by an English translation, telling of the coming of Orome to Koivienéni, the Waters of Awakening. This sentence does not occur in connection with the text of any story. According to Taum Santoski it is written on a torn sheet of paper, one side of which bears the sentence and much other linguistic material,[1] the opposite side bearing part of a draft from "The Riders of Rohan."

The sentence and translation are as follows:

> *Eldar ando kakainen loralyar*
> *Koivienenissen mennai Orome tanna*
> *lende i erenekkoitan[n]ie.*

The elves were long lying asleep at
Koivienēni until Orome came thither
that he might awake them.

The Manuscript

Our preliminary study of the Koivienéni sentence was conducted using a transcription provided by Taum. In order that we might verify the transcription and translation of the text before publication, Jorge Quiñónez requested a photocopy of the part of the manuscript containing the sentence, and this was provided by Charles B. Elston, Archivist at Marquette University Library.[2] The photocopy confirmed the essential accuracy of Taum's transcription, but it has also raised three issues regarding the proper interpretation of the manuscript:

1. It looks very much like the final *n* of **Koivienenissen** is a later addition. The *n* is written much smaller than the surrounding letters, and it leaves a significantly narrower space between **Koivienenissen** and **mennai** than the spaces between words elsewhere in the sentence. This could simply be the correction of an oversight, or it could indicate that the final *n* in this inflected form (where it is the plural marker) is redundant, since the *i* in *neni* 'waters' is itself a plural marker. In other words, perhaps the form **Koivienenisse** was grammatically correct in the sentence but Tolkien decided that **Koivienenissen** was "more correct."

2. Tolkien first wrote **erenekkoitanie** as the last word in the Quenya text. The manuscript shows another *n* written beneath the final *e*, and to the immediate left of this *n* is a symbol shaped like an **I**. The vertical stroke of this symbol stands midway between the original *ni* in the word so that its upper horizontal stroke touches the pair of them, while the lower one aligns with the bottom of the additional *n*.

The textual situation suggests two varying interpretations. One is that this **I** is a symbol by which Tolkien meant to indicate that the adjacent **n** should be inserted between the **ni** above it, emending the form of the last word to **erenekkoitannie**. The alternate interpretation we must consider is that we actually have the word **In** here, written on the page *before* Tolkien composed the Koivienéni sentence, and that its juxtaposition is entirely an accident with no further significance for the text.

Any choice between these interpretations requires consideration of the larger context of the manuscript. The English translation is written below (and slightly to the left of) the Quenya sentence. At the end of the third line of this translation, directly below the **In**, there is a word scored through and difficult to read except that it begins with an elaborate capital **D**. We know this word was written before the English text, because in that text the last word "them" was written beneath "awake" in order to avoid running into this deleted word.

This and other aspects of the arrangement of forms on the fairly crowded manuscript page suggest that the Koivienéni sentence and its translation were written after (and fit into the spaces between and to the left side of) a running sequence of lingustic notes each of which Tolkien left incomplete, and two of which began with the words "In" and "D—". For this reason we remain hesitant about the reading of the last word in the sentence and have given the ambivalent spelling **erenekkoitan[n]ie**.

3. Tolkien apparently gives alternate endings for both the sentence and its translation. Beneath the words "that he might" is written "— to —", and beneath that is a symbol resembling that used for proportional variation, i.e. not unlike "∞" with the left side open. If Tolkien intended this as an indication for replacement, then the latter part of the translation would read "... until Orome came thither to awake them." Following the word **erenekkoitan[n]ie** in the third line of the sentence (and separated from it by a space somewhat wider than those within the sentence) is the phrase **na senekkoita**, which has been underlined. Since **na** can mean 'to' in Quenya, there seems to be a logical connection between this phrase and the change in the English. And if we take this to be an alternate form of the Elvish the result would seem to be *... mennai Orome tanna lende na senekkoita*.

It is difficult to say exactly what Tolkien intended by these variant endings; **na senekkoita** and "— to —" may have been emendations of the text, but neither **i erenekkoitan[n]ie** nor "that he might" are crossed out. We do not seem to be dealing with the correction of grammatical errors or a change in Tolkien's conception of Quenya grammar, since **i erenekkoitan[n]ie** 'that he might awake them' and **na senekkoita** 'to awake them' both appear to be grammatically valid but slightly varying means of expressing the same concept in both English and Quenya. Until such time as further information becomes available, we can merely note the existence of alternate endings to the text as first written.

The Text

We now proceed with a discussion of the grammar of the sentence and its relation to the rest of the Quenya corpus. We will use the following abbreviations, with page references to the Houghton Mifflin hardcover editions:

I = *The Fellowship of the Ring*	MC = *The Monsters and the Critics*
III = *The Return of the King*	OM1, OM2, OM3 = versions of
L = *The Letters of J.R.R. Tolkien*	*Oilima Markirya* (MC-220f, 213f, 221f)
LR = *The Lost Road*	S = *The Silmarillion*
LT = *The Book of Lost Tales*, Part One	U = *Unfinished Tales*

Line 1

Eldar : "The elves", nominative plural of *elda* 'elf'. The definite article does not occur in the Quenya. Compare *laurie lantar lassi súrinen* 'like gold fall *the* leaves in the wind', from Galadriel's Lament.

ando : "long". This is an adverb meaning 'for a long time'. Compare *Andave laituvalmet* 'Long we will praise them' (III-231, L-308).[3] Quenya temporal adverbs ending in *-o* can be found throughout the the corpus, beginning with *voro* 'ever'[4] in the Qenya Lexicon (1915). We find the adverbs *ento* 'next' and *rato* 'soon' in the sentence of Arctic (a form of Quenya) appearing in the Appendix to *The Father Christmas Letters* (c.1931-1933), and finally *oio* 'ever, everlastingly' is given in the notes to *Namárie* in *The Road Goes Ever On* (1967).

Ando may be the genitive or partitive[5] form of the adjective *anda* 'long', representing ellipsis of a longer original phrase, such as *lúme ando*[6] 'from/of a long time'. Therefore *ando* would literally mean 'from long' or 'of long', and this latter phrase actually occurs in English. According to the *OED, of long* is an obsolete expression meaning 'since a remote period, for a long time past'.

This pattern of derivation of adverbs in *-o* from adjectives in *-a* also fits two of the other examples. *Ento* 'next' seems to derive from *enta* 'that yonder' (< base **EN-**) in the sense 'at that future time' (cf. LR-399: "whereas *en* yonder [**EN**] of time points to the future"), and *oio* 'everlastingly' derives from *oia* 'everlasting' (LR-379).

kakainen : "were . . . lying". The element *kai-* at the heart of this word derives from the base **KAY-** 'lie down' given in *The Etymologies*. The verb forms *kaire* 'lay' in the earliest version of *Oilima Markirya* and *caita* 'lies' in *Namárie* must also be closely related. Reduplication of the initial consonant and vowel of a verb stem was one of the means by which Quenya formed frequentatives (cf. *fifíru-* 'slowly fade away' < *fir-* 'die, fade', MC-223), and one of the functions of the frequentative is to indicate an action taking place over an extended period of time.[7] This seems to be the application in *kakainen,* and the reason it is translated by the *progressive* past tense 'were lying' rather than the simple past 'lay'. This extended or progressive sense is further specified by the adverb *ando* 'long'.

The suffix *-ne* is used in Quenya to mark the past tense of certain verbs, e.g. *ortane* '(she) lifted up', past tense of *orta-* 'to rise, raise' or *merne* pa.t. of *mere* < **MER-** 'wish' (LR-373). The past tense of *kakai-* 'to be lying' could then be *kakaine* 'was lying'[8] with plural form *kakainen* 'were lying'. The use of *-n* as a plural marker in verbs is not unknown in Quenya. We have *ondolin ninqanéron* 'the rocks lay white' in *OM1,* and *wingildin . . . alkantaméren* 'the foam-maidens . . . made it shine' and *tyulmin . . . aiqalin kautáron* 'the tall masts bent' in *Earendel.* In each of these the plural *-n* is preceded by *-re* or *-ro* and the subject noun is in the dative, characteristics which do not apply to *eldar . . . kakainen.* But the use of plural *-n* also occurs in certain cases of the noun, such as genitive *elenion* 'of stars', *aldaron* 'of trees', or locative *mahalmassen* '(upon) thrones'. And the ablative case shows both *-n* in the Book Quenya declension *ciryallon, lassellon* and also *-r* in *elenillor pella* '[from] beyond the stars' in *OM3.* So we are not surprised that the verb, like the noun, has more than one mark of plurality, nor should we try to anticipate the range of application of variant endings.

There are past-tense forms where the marker *-ne* is assimilated to the final consonant of the base, and these have plurals in *-r.* Thus *ulle,* intransitive past tense of *ulya-* 'pour' (LR-396), apparently from original **ul-ne,* has plural *ullier* in LR-47. Likewise note *elle* 'came' (< **el-ne*), plural *eller,* both in *Nieninque.* But there are as yet no published examples of past tense plural verbs where the suffix *-ne* remains unassimilated and readily evident as the

— *continued on page 12.*

The Fifth Battle
by Tom Loback

This illustration incorporates the demographic studies in the two *Mythlore* articles titled "Kindreds, Houses and Population of the Elves" from issue #51 and "Orc Hosts, Armies and Legions" in the current issue, #62. The conclusions drawn in these articles can be followed in this depiction of the great defeat of the Elves. Generally speaking, each figure represents 100 beings, with the following exceptions: the leaders, the Balrogs and the Dragons. These represent only that person, or Balrog; Glaurung is the large Dragon, and the other Dragons represent an undetermined number of Dragons that is probably less than fifty.

The northwest quadrant *[presented as the center spread in* VT *#11 —CFH]* shows the northern half of the encirclement of Fingon's Army of Hithlum and his allies. Bottom center shows Fingon with his white banner and his Guard directing the battle. To the left, under the square banners, is Círdan's contingent; three of his four groups can be seen. To the right are the Sindar of Annael launching flights of arrows. Topmost are the various Noldorin Houses under Fingon's command with a *Gwanur* of lance-armed cavalry engaging a block of Orcs. Charging into the fray behind them are Fingon's horse archers dismounted. The Orc armies can be counted by their black standards. A fully deployed Orc army can be made out on the eastern side of Fingon's circle, next to the block of *tengwar* writing. North to south it has: 2,500 auxiliary archers; 5,000 Orcs with swords flanking the main force of 10,000 Orcs with spears whose southern flank is also supported by 5,000 Orcs with swords.

The northeast quadrant *[presented as the center spread in* VT *#12 —CFH]* shows the emptying of Angband. The Orc reserve of 100,000 are here accounted as 75,000 foot soldiers in three armies with 25,000 auxiliary wolf-riders. It may be that at this stage Orcs did not ride wolves and that they should be under Glaurung's command of the beasts of Angband. Balrogs can be seen leading and lashing their troops forward. Also, Gothmog's Troll Guard can be made out, front and center of the infantry.

The southeast quadrant *[presented as the center spread in* VT *#13 —CFH]* pictures Maedhros' advance, spearheaded by the seven sons of Fëanor leading the horse archers of Amrod and Amras, who are followed by the *Rochon Fëanorim* (see the Sept. 1989 issue of *Beyond Bree*), in turn followed by the infantry contingents. The infantry, in blocks from west to east and north to south are: Bor's faithful Easterlings — two blocks with one of Ulfang's to their rear; the Noldorin infantry of Caranthir in three blocks with the Dwarves of Nogrod to their rear; Azaghâl's *Belegosthrim* followed by a block of Uldor's with a contingent of Green-elves to their rear.

The southwest quadrant *[presented as the center spread this issue —CFH]* depicts Turgon's arrival on the field with the 10,000 Elves of Gondolin as he breaks through the Orc line to join Húrin's command. Húrin's Men of Dor-Lómin can be made out in three groups bearing round shields, one of which is armed with axes that they raise in celebration of Turgon's arrival. Each House and Kindred of Turgon can be made out by the symbol atop their standard pole. Nowhere are the Men of Brethil, some 3,000 to 5,000, as they are destroyed earlier in the battle.

It can be seen from this illustration that although Fingon is surrounded and sorely pressed by parts of three Orc-hosts (five armies plus), the arrival of Turgon and the approach of Maedhros takes two of the Orc-armies in the rear and surely would have re-established the Elven line. Alas for the Elven cause, Maedhros' headlong advance leaves his flank, uncovered by his cavalry, open to Glaurung's assault; it also presents Uldor with an opportunity for a most effective treachery once the battle is joined. *The Book of Lost Tales, Part One* (p. 241) states that "nearly half the Gnomes and Men who fought there were slain", probably over 50,000.* Most of these casualties are undoubtedly from Fingon's contingent, as Maedhros' troops are for the most part routed, not slain. Although one must imagine, from later history, that somehow Círdan's force managed to cut its way out along with Beleg and Mablung.

*An estimated casualty breakdown would be:

Men of Brethil	2,000 - 3,000
Men of Dor-Lómin	8,000 - 10,000
Noldor of Hithlum	15,000
Sindar of Hithlum	3,000 - 5,000
Círdan	3,000+
Turgon	1,000+
Fëanorians	3,000 - 5,000
Bor's Men	3,000 - 5,000
Uldor's Men	2,000+
Belegost	3,000+
Nogrod	2,000+
Nargothrond	500
Green Elves	500
TOTAL	46,000 - 54,000

*   *   *

This issue of *VT* concludes the four-part presentation of "The Fifth Battle", or the *Nirnaeth Arnoediad*. It is a black-and-white print which represents the climactic hours of the battle, during which the Elves, Men and Dwarves of the Union of Maedhros were tragically and utterly defeated by the Hosts of Morgoth, led by Gothmog, Lord of Balrogs, and Glaurung, the Father of Dragons.

While the *tengwar* border calligraphy uses a Quenya mode, the descriptions of the battle formations are Sindarin, written in the Mode of Beleriand. This could indicate the origin of the piece was in Eregion during the middle of the Second Age. However, the calligraphic and illustrative style point to a possibly later period.

Anyone interested in acquiring a print of this work should write me at 152 West 26th Street, #36, N.Y. City, N.Y. 10001, USA. The print is limited to 100 copies. Prices vary on the quality of the material: $100.00 for Maplewood veneer, $50.00 for Arches Cover bond (acid-free paper), and $20.00 for heavy white bond. Size: 27" wide by 18" high. Make checks and money orders payable to Tom Loback. Inquiries welcome.

This final installment reproduces the southwest quadrant of the map.

[The fourth quadrant of "The Fifth Battle" appears as the center spread, pp. 10-11 —CFH]

Correction: On the bottom of page 6 of *VT* #13, "The Baby and the Baby" should of course read "The Baby and the Bird". Your editor is suitably crimson-visaged.

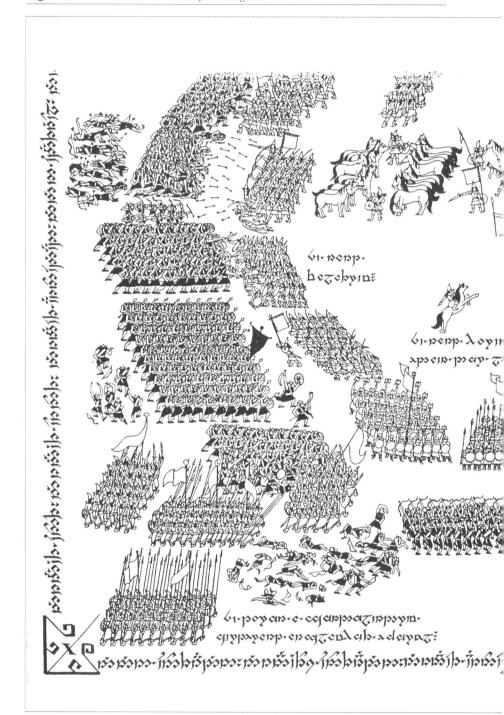

Southwest quadrant of Tom Loback's "The Fifth Battle".

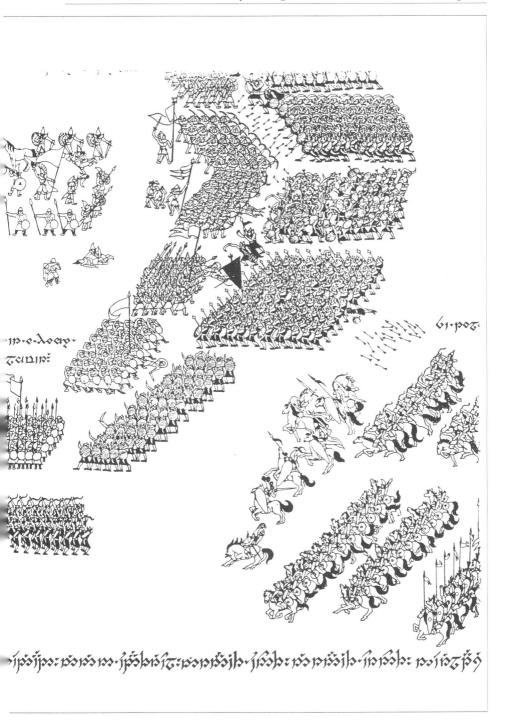

See pages 8-9 for further information on this work.

The Elves at Koivienéni

— continued from page 7.

suffix. Ironically there are past tense singular forms that end in *-r*, e.g. *i lunte linganer* 'the boat hummed like a harp-string' (in *Earendel*). Whatever the explanation of these[9] the resulting ambiguity between singular and plural might account for a distinctive plural **lingane-n* modelled after **lingane-ro-n*, **lingane-re-n*. We must await publication of further examples to confirm or refute this.

Another possible interpretation of *kakainen* is worth looking at. Quenya uses the bare stem of a verb as an infinitive after "see" or "hear". (See MC-223, note to line 23.) In *OM2* we have examples of verb forms ending in *-ne* used in such positions, e.g. *Man tenuva súru laustane . . . ondoli losse karkane* 'Who shall hear the wind roaring . . . the white rocks snarling'. Since these forms are identical to past-tense stems, it seems likely that they function here as past infinitives, literally meaning 'who shall hear the wind *to have roared* . . . the white rocks *having snarled*'. This usage may indicate that the "roaring" and "snarling" are actions which precede the time of hearing, although this temporal distinction is not readily apparent in Tolkien's translation.[10]

Tolkien's notes on Cirion's Oath explain how the Quenya infinitive *enyalie* 'recalling' is put in the dative case *enyalien* 'for the recalling, to recall or commemorate' in *Vanda sina termaruva . . . alcar enyalien* "This oath shall stand in memory of the glory" (U-305, 317). This use of the dative infinitive to express purpose is comparable to one of the uses of dative nouns, as in *Eldain en kárier Isil, nan hildin Úr-anar* 'For Elves they made the Moon, but for Men the red Sun' (LR-72), the *purpose* of making the Moon and Sun being for (the benefit of) Elves and Men.

But the dative of a noun can also be used to express the *means* by which an action is accomplished, as in *eller . . . losselie telerinwa, tálin paptalasselindeen* 'came [*action*] . . . the white people of the shores of Elfland, with feet [*means*] like the music of falling leaves' in *Nieninque*. (Here *tálin* 'with feet' is dative plural of *tál* 'foot', LR-390.) It follows that when one action is accomplished by means of *another* action the latter might be expressed by the dative of an infinitive. And it seems a natural possibility for the dative of a *past* infinitive to be used, signifying that the action providing the means *preceded* the time of the action accomplished. Under this interpretation then **kakaine* 'to have lain' occurs here in the dative *kakainen* 'in lying, having lain'[11] to express the means whereby the Elves were *loralyar* 'asleep', their repose being a precondition of their sleep.

loralyar "asleep", plural of **loralya*. This derives from the base **LOS-** 'sleep', whence also *lóre* 'slumber' and *lorna* 'asleep' (LR-370), or root **LORO** 'slumber', whence *lor-* 'to slumber' (LT-259). The suffix *-ya* is a common adjectival ending,[12] so *loralyar* may be an adjective modifying *Eldar*. A closely comparable form is *pinilya* 'small' (MC-220). For the syntax of *Eldar ando kakainen loralyar* 'elves long were lying asleep', with adjective following the verb but modifying the subject, cf. *lassi lantar laurie* 'leaves fall golden', in the version of Galadriel's Lament with "more normal" word-order in Tolkien's notes for *The Road Goes Ever On*.

If *kakainen* is the case form of an infinitive, then *loralyar* would be the predicate of the sentence, i.e. *loralyar* 'are asleep'. For use of an adjective this way note *Toi írimar* 'which are beautiful' (punctuated as a complete sentence) and *Ilu vanya* 'The world is fair' (LR-72) showing that the verb 'to be' is optional with a predicate adjective. But note that *-ya* is also a common verb ending, and another form closely comparable to *loralyar* is the verb *mirilya-* 'glitter' (LR-372). Indeed we cannot insist on a strict distinction between adjective and verb in every context in Quenya as pairs like *verya-* 'to dare', *verya* 'bold' demonstrate.

Line 2

Koivienenissen : "at Koivienéni", i.e. 'at the Waters of Awakening', the lake in the northeast of Middle-earth where the first Elves awoke. ***Koivienéni*** is a plural form and occurs here with the locative plural suffix *-ssen*. The initial element *koivie* 'awakening' is given in QL as a derivative of the root **KOYO** 'have life' (LT-257), and the suffix *-ie* identifies it as a gerund. The second element *néni* 'waters' is the plural of *nén* (*nen-*) 'water' (cf. *The Etymologies* s.v. **NEN-**).

The form ***Koivienéni*** presents us with a chronological conundrum. It only appears in *The Book of Lost Tales, Part One*,[13] and in all subsequent versions of the First-Age material, from the "Sketch of the Mythology" (1926) onward, the name appears as ***Cuiviénen*** or ***Kuiviénen*** 'Water of Awakening'. It is remarkable then to see the form unique to *Lost Tales* (c. 1916-17) used in a sentence apparently written during the composition of the chapter "The Riders of Rohan" (c. 1941-42) in *The Lord of the Rings*. At that time, with paper in short supply, Tolkien was in the habit of reusing sheets already written on one side, so it is tempting to suppose that here he has made use of a sheet bearing notes made back in the days of the *Lost Tales*. The difficulty with this hypothesis is that among the other linguistic notes on the manuscript page is a cluster of words which appear to be preliminary workings for the name ***Dagor-nui-nGiliath*** or ***Dagor-nuin-Giliath***, the "Battle-under-Stars", which first appears as an emendation of ***Dagor-os-Giliath*** in the Later Annals, and in a marginal note in the *Quenta Silmarillion*, all dated to c. 1930-37.[14] (The concept that the First Battle was "the Battle under Stars" emerges as an addition in the *Qenta Noldorinwa* of 1930, where the form ***Cuiviénen, Kuiviénen*** is already firmly established, cf. *The Shaping of Middle-earth*, pp. 76, 84, 103.)

The retention of long vowel in ***Koivienéni*** beside short vowel in the locative ***Koivienenissen*** is due to a regular rule in Quenya such that unstressed long vowels were shortened. Primary stress occurs on the second-to-last (or *penultimate*) syllable if that syllable is long (as *-né-*) or closed (as *-nis-*), but occurs on the third-to-last syllable if the penultimate is short. Tolkien's examples include *I-sil-dur*, *E-len-tá-ri* vs. *Q-ro-me*, *E-res-se-a*, *An-ca-li-ma* (III-App. E I). There is also "some degree of stress" on the first syllable of the word, according to the notes on Galadriel's Lament. It appears that initial syllable and primary-stressed syllable are the positions where inherited long vowels are retained, and this leads to variation in the length of cognate syllables in longer words and names. Thus *Al-tá-ri-el* (U-266) beside genitive *Al-ta-ri-el-lo* in the Elvish subtitle of the Lament; *En-dor, En-dó-re* 'Middle-earth' beside allative *En-do-ren-na* (III-245, 393); *tye-me-lá-ne* 'I love you' beside *inye tye-mé-la* 'I too love you' (LR-61).

Note that this rule can also account for the differences between ***Kuiviénen*** and ***Koivienéni*** (except for the variation **ui/oi**) if we suppose original singular **kuivē-nēn* beside plural **koivie-nēn-ī*. In *The Silmarillion* (p. 99) there is an allusion to "the Avari that remained by the waters of their awakening", so that the existence of a singular *kuiviénen* implies plural **kuivienéni* with essentially the same meaning. And such late forms as *coire* 'stirring' and *coimas* 'life-bread', derived from the same root (S-357) with variation **ui/oi**, point to the continued existence of a variation **koiviénen* pl. *koivienéni*, with perhaps a slightly different connotation like 'water(s) of stirring' or 'water(s) of coming to life', but meaning basically the same thing as ***Kuiviénen*** in reference to the history and geography of Middle-earth.

mennai: "until". *The Etymologies* s.v. **MEN-** gives the noun *men* 'place, spot'. *Mennai* appears to be the allative inflection of this noun, *menna* 'toward the place', contracted with the conjunction *i* 'that' (cf. *nai* 'maybe, be it that' < *nā-i*). Thus *mennai* literally means 'toward the place (in time) that', and it is used in the sentence as a conjunction that introduces the clause ***Orome tanna lende i erenekkoitan[n]ie.***

Orome : The Koivienéni Sentence presents a unique version of the story of the coming of Orome to the Waters of Awakening, in which it is said that he went there with the purpose of awakening the Elves. The closest of the published versions is that in *The Book of Lost Tales*. There Orome is present at the time of the event: "Behold the woods of the Great Lands . . . are full of a strange noise. There did I wander, and lo! 'twas as if folk arose betimes beneath the latest stars." (LT-114.) Again on the next page it says: "There had Orome heard the awaking of the Eldar, and all songs name that place Koivie-néni or the Waters of Awakening." It is clear in that version, however, that Orome's presence at the Waters was by chance not design, and it is said that Ilúvatar himself awoke the Elves. In all subsequent versions the Elves are said to awake before the arrival of Orome. In *The Silmarillion* the Elves "began to make speech and to give names to all things" before Orome came upon them "as it were by chance", and what he first heard was "afar off many voices singing" (p. 49).

We can rectify these discrepancies only so far. The version in which Orome was nearby to hear the Elves awaking agrees literally with their being asleep until he arrived. And the phrasing "that he might awake them" expresses his *intention* rather than stating whether Orome actually awoke the Elves. The actions of the Valar may serve Ilúvatar's ends in ways they do not anticipate, and the qualifying phrase "as it were by chance" in the *Silmarillion* account implies that Orome's discovery may have been "intentional" on a deeper level.[15] The tales and annals say little about Orome's motives in journeying to the Waters of Awakening, only that he "would ride too at whiles in the darkness of the unlit forests . . . pursuing to the death the monsters and fell creatures of the kingdom of Melkor" (S-41), presumably to decrease some of the dangers there for the coming of Elves and Men. We might infer that Orome harbored a hidden wish to find and awaken the Elves, but only the present text actually suggests this.

tanna : "thither". The pronoun *ta* 'that, it' is given in *The Etymologies* as a derivative of the demonstrative stem **TA-** 'that', and *tanna* must be the allative inflection of *ta*, literally 'toward that' or 'toward it'. Two other Quenya words for 'thither' occur in the corpus, each derived from this same stem with a suffix indicating location or direction. The entry **TA-** gives *tar* 'thither' (and its earlier, hypothetical form **tad*). A comparable suffix *-r* occurs in several words such as *mir* 'to the inside, into' (LR-373), *yar* 'to whom' (in *Nieninque*), and *vear* 'in the sea' (in *OM2*). The form *tande* 'thither' is found in *Nieninque,* and the ending *-nde* must be related to that seen in such Quenya place-names as *Elende* 'Elfland' (LR-223), *Ingolonde* 'Land of the Gnomes' (LR-377), and *Kalakiryan(de),* the region in and near the entrance to the ravine of Calacirya in Eldamar (mentioned in Tolkien's notes on *Namárie*).

This adverb precedes the verb in what is probably normal word-order in Quenya *tanna lende*. In English *Orome thither came* would be less normal than *Orome came thither,* though both are grammatical. Because of this difference in usage Tolkien's translation does not match up precisely line for line with the Quenya.

Line 3

lende : "came". 3rd person singular verb, past tense of *linna* 'go' (LR-368 s.v. **LED-** 'go, fare, travel') or *lesta-* 'to leave' (LR-356). The latter form was apparently abandoned, when its base **ELED-** 'go, depart, leave' was changed to a base **ELED-** 'Star-folk, Elf', though *lesta-* could still derive from **led-ta-* with change of *dt* > Q *st* as in **wed-tā* > *vesta* 'contract' (LR-397). Under base **LED-** the past tense form *lende* is rendered 'went, departed', and the form *linna* 'go' is given after this parenthetically, possibly to suggest that it is not a regular development from this base, but comes from some other source.[16]

The past tense *lende* is formed directly from the base **LED-** plus the past ending *-ne* with change of *dn* > Q *nd* as in *adnō > *ando* 'gate' (LR-348). So *lende* (for *led-ne) and parallel *rende* (for *red-ne) pa.t. of *rerin* 'I sow' < **RED-** (LR-383) have the same construction as *tir-ne* pa.t. of *tirin* 'I watch', or *tam-ne* pa.t. of *tamin* 'I tap'. And the same past tense formation, with derived stem in the position of the root, explains *onta-ne* < *onta-* 'beget, create' (LR-379), *sinta-ne* < *sinta-* 'fade' (LR-392), etc.

Lende is nonspecific with regard to whether the motion referred to is toward or away from the speaker, so it is glossed as both 'came' and 'went, departed'. The same is true of English *go* in its broadest sense 'move'. It means 'move away' only insofar as it is opposed to *come* 'move toward', as in phrases like *come and go*. We also have *Ar Sauron lende númenorenna* 'And Sauron came to-Númenor', in the first version of the Eressean Fragment (LR-56), and *Melko Mardello lende* 'Melko has gone from Earth', in Firiel's Song (LR-72). Note that Melko did not leave the Earth under his own volition, nor did Sauron head in the direction of Númenor so much as allow himself to be transported there. The point of saying *Orome tanna lende* for 'Orome came thither' instead of *Orome tanna túle* may well be that Orome was not specifically heading for Koivie-néni, not knowing before-hand where the Elves would appear, but did "come" there in his wanderings to find there what he wished to find.

i : "that". This is an instance of the article *i* 'the' (derived from the "deictic particle" **I-** 'that', LR-361) used as a relative pronoun introducing *erenekkoitan[n]ie* as a subordinate clause. It is comparable to the use of *i* translated "who" twice in Cirion's Oath: *nai tiruvantes i hárar mahalmassen* 'in the keeping of those (= may they guard it) who sit upon the thrones', and *i Eru i or ilye mahalmar ea* 'the One who is above all thrones' (U-305, 317). We have noted that this also seems to be (etymologically) the second element of the auxiliary verb or adverb *nai* "may" or "maybe" said to be literally 'may it be that, be it that' derived from *nā-i*. This occurs in the Oath and also in Galadriel's Lament. The notes for the latter in *The Road Goes Ever On* contain its derivation and the observation that *nai* "expresses rather a wish than a hope" (p. 68), clarifying the original translation. (Conversely Arctic *ya rato nea* is translated "and I hope it will be soon." This seems to mean literally 'which soon might be', expressing rather a hope than a wish.)

erenekkoitan[n]ie : "he might awake them." This complex verb form requires careful dissection. We can begin with the safe assumption that the element *koi-* derives from the root **KOYO** 'have life' (LT-257), whence *koi, koire* 'life', *koiva* 'awake' and of course *Koivie-néni* 'Waters of Awakening'. This is related to *coire* 'stirring', the name of the Elvish season between *hríve* 'winter' and *tuile* 'spring' (III, App. D), and *coimas* 'life-bread' (= Sind. *lembas*) in *The Silmarillion*. Also note **KUY-** 'come to life, awake' (LR-366) with additional and alternate Q. forms in *kui-* including *kuive* = *kuivie* 'awakening', whence the name *Kuiviénen*.

Of particular interest is the derivation of N *echui(w)* 'awakening' < *et-kuiwē, which shows the use of the prefix *et-* 'out, forth', with little alteration in sense. (Compare English idioms like *wake out of a sound sleep*.) The Noldorin and Sindarin spirant *ch* could result from earlier *kk* (as in N *lhoch* 'ringlet' < *lokko, LR-370, Sind. *roch* 'horse' < *rokkō, L-382), and this suggests that *et-kuiwē > *ekkuiwe before becoming N *echuiw*. *Erenekkoitan[n]ie* shows that this assimilation of *tk* > *kk* took place in Quenya as well, the verb stem *ekkoita-* representing **et-koi-ta-* 'cause to wake up, stir out of sleep'.[17] For other verbs stems in *-ta-* that represent someone affecting the action or status of someone or something else, cf. **usta-** 'burn' (transitive), **vaita-** 'to wrap' (LT-271), **esta-** 'to name', **horta-** 'send flying, speed, urge', **tulta-** 'send for, fetch, summon' (LR-356, 364, 395). The past tense of this stem would be **ekkoitane** 'woke up, awakened'.

We have many verb forms where **-ie-** is part of the inflection, such as **antúlien** 'hath returned', **kalliére** 'shone', **lútier** 'sailed', **utúvienyes** 'I have found it', **enyalien** 'to recall', etc. There are four other examples where the verb form ends in **-ie** without further suffix. We give them with their immediate context for comparison with our present sentence. (LR-56, 72.)

> *Ar Sauron lende númenorenna ... <u>lantie</u> nu huine ... <u>ohtakárie</u>*
> *valannar ... manwe ilu terhante.*
> 'And Sauron came to-Númenor ... fell under shadow ... war-made
> on-Powers ... [Manwe world] broke.'
>
> *Toi aina, mána, meldielto — enga morion: <u>talantie</u>.*
> 'They are holy, blessed, and beloved: save the dark one. He is fallen.'
>
> *Melko Mardello lende: <u>márie</u>.*
> 'Melko has gone from Earth: it is good.'

Each of these five verbs **erenekkoitan[n]ie, lantie, ohtakárie, talantie** and **márie** lacks an explicit subject noun in its own clause, and each is understandable without it because the subject is mentioned or described by the preceding "main" clause. The semantic subject of **erenekkoitan[n]ie** is Orome (the syntactic subject of **lende**); the subjects of **lantie** and **ohtakárie** are possibly both Númenor (which is an adverbial object of **Sauron lende**); the subject of **talantie** is the dark one (the object of the preposition **enga**); while the semantic subject of **márie** is the fact that Melko has gone, i.e. the entire preceding clause.

The ending **-ie** corresponds phonetically to the second element in **man-ie** 'what is it' (LR-59), which is presumably related to the verb **ye** 'is' in Firiel's Song. It also corresponds to the ending of the infinitive **enyalie** which Tolkien mentions in his notes on Cirion's Oath: "**enyalien**: **en-** 'again', **yal-** 'summon', in infinitive (or gerundial) form **en-yalie**, here in dative 'for the re-calling', but governing a direct object, **alcar**: thus 'to recall or "commemorate" the glory'." (U-317.) The term *gerundial* (short for *gerundial infinitive*) means that this Quenya infinitive in **-ie** has certain features like a gerund or verbal noun, such as taking the dative case-ending to distinguish particular functions of the infinitive. The gerundial rendering of **enyalie** would be "recalling" in the sense of the verbal action as an abstract notion, e.g. *Recalling one's successes can be pleasant.* As a noun **enyalie** would be the nominative or accusative to dative **enyalien**.

In this regard we should note that the name **Atalantie** 'Downfall' is mentioned in *The Letters* where a footnote describes "the stem √*talat* used in Q. for 'slipping, sliding, falling down', of which **atalantie** is a normal (in Q.) noun-formation" (L-347, #257). Nothing suggests that this stem is distinct from the base **TALAT-** 'to slope, lean, tip' in *The Etymologies* with verb **talta-** 'to slope, slip, slide down' and other forms, including the later additions "**Atalante** (*a*-prefix = complete) downfall, overthrow, especially as name of the land of Númenor" and **atalta** 'collapse, fall in'. Given the association of occasional noun pairs in **-e** : **-ie** (cf. **kuivie** = **kuive** 'awakening', mentioned above), it seems that we are dealing here with a unified etymology of **atalantie** = **atalante** 'downfall', and that the "normal" abstract noun formation in **-n-ie** is historically identical with the past tense gerundial infinitive. The verbs **talta-** 'slope' and **atalta-** 'collapse' are both from stem *talat-* (the second differing in the prefixed vowel meaning 'complete'), and each has past gerundial **talantie**/**atalantie** (with **-ntie** < **-tnie**), which we could render as 'a fall, a falling, the occurrence of having fallen'. One way of looking at *Toi aina . . . enga morion: talantie* is that it means 'they are holy . . . save the dark one: a falling' = 'whose situation is a falling (in the past)' = 'he is fallen'.

We have Q *mára* < **magra* 'useful, fit, good (of things)' < **MAG-** 'use, handle' given under base **MA3-** 'hand' (LR-371). In Arctic this adjective can be used verbally to mean 'to be good' referring impersonally to the situation, if indeed *Mára mesta an ni véla tye ento* "Goodbye till I see you next" is literally an imperative 'let it be good [with you] till [the time] for me to see you next'. The gerundial to *mára* 'be good' is *márie* 'being good'. Used as in *Mardello Melko lende: márie* to sum up a situation as "being good" it is equivalent to our saying 'and that is good'. We suggest that this Quenya idiom could be extended to descriptions of concrete things "being good" = 'it is good', and thence also applied to personal verbs like *talta-* 'to slip' which can take persons as well as things as subject, **taltie* 'slipping' = 'it is slipping, he is slipping'. Thus with the further distinction of past action *talantie* "having slipped" = 'it is fallen, he is fallen'.

Note that in the past tense gerundial infinitive *talantie* it is the *n* which marks the tense (< **talat-n-ie-*), the ending *-ie* still having the same function it has in the present, that of abstracting the verbal notion. In some verbs the past tense is conveyed by long root vowel, whence our suggestion that *ohtakárie* may be past gerundial infinitive 'having made war'.[18] But with *-n-* as past marker, just as we have *lende* 'went' (< **led-ne*) with metathesis beside *orta-ne* without metathesis, so we seem to have *talantie* (< **talat-nie*) beside *ekkoita-nie* 'having awakened'.[19]

In the Koivienéni sentence the gerundial is introduced by the relative *i* 'that', expressing the wish of Orome in coming. The past tense is used (apparently) because the situation wished for *i ekkoitanie* 'the awakening' is in the past, from the point of view of the speaker of the sentence. Compare the English idiom, where *might* is etymologically the past tense of *may,* and we would say, *He came so that he might awake them* vs. *He will come so that he may awake them.* The word *might* has a life of its own with present and future meaning (but indicating less certainty than *may*), and *He will come so that he might awake them* is also grammatical. But ***He came so that he may awake them* is incorrect, showing that the remnant of a rule requiring past tense "subjunctive" with past tense main verb to express a hypothetical result or purpose in the past, is still in effect in English. A similar rule applies in Latin, and may apply here in Quenya.

Quenya also has a second infinitive form, i.e. "the bare stem of the verb is used (as after 'see' or 'hear') as infinitive." For example: *Men kenuva fáne kirya métima hrestallo kíra* 'Who shall see a white ship leave the last shore'; *Man kenuva lumbor na-hosta* 'Who shall see the clouds gather'. (MC-214, 215, 221-3.) This fact is mentioned by Tolkien off-handedly as part of his explanation of why the latter example has a prefix: "When the bare stem . . . is used . . . as infinitive *na-* is prefixed if the noun is the object not the subject." In other words he implies that while *kirya* 'ship' is subject of *kíra* 'leave', *lumbor* 'clouds' is the object of *hosta* 'gather', and *na-* is used to distinguish this fact. The statement, as part of a conditional ("When the bare stem of the verb is used . . ."), clearly accomodates the description of *enyalie* as "infinitive", implying that in some constructions (including after 'see' and 'hear') the bare stem is used, but in other constructions another infinitive form may be used. Both of these implications are important to our situation, where we have parallel readings *i erenekkoitan[n]ie* 'that he might awake them' and *na senekkoita* 'to awake them', clearly close in meaning, with the latter containing a preposed *na* and the bare stem of our verb *ekkoita* 'awake'. The function of *na* may be to indicate that *sen-* 'them' is the object in this case as well.[20]

This brings us at last to the prefix *eren-* which by process of elimination would mean 'them'. It is clearly related to *sen-* in the alternative form of the sentence, with the phonetic change of **s** > **z** > **r** between vowels. For the etymology of *sen-* we can point to the partly enigmatic information in *Etymologies* under **S-** described as a "demonstrative stem." This entry begins with "*su, so* he (cf. *-so* inflexion of verbs); *si, se* she (cf. *-se* inflexion of verbs)." Various Noldorin pronouns *ho, he, ha,* etc. are given next, but aside from the indication that their vowels can be either short or long, the pronouns *su, so, si, se* are not identified as either Primitive Qendian or Qenya. Perhaps they are both. With shift of **s** > **r** we seem to have *só, so* 'he' in *antaróta* 'he gave it' and *antaváro* 'will he give' (LR-63). In any case it seems likely that *sen-* derives from this *se* 'she' with the addition of the plural marker *-n* mentioned above. And note that object pronouns can be suffixed or prefixed as with *ta* 'that, it' in *antaróta* 'he gave it', but in the same passage *tye-meláne* 'I love thee' and *inye tye-méla* 'I too love thee' (LR-61), with *tye* 'you, thee'.

The precise function of the initial *e-* in *erenekkoitan[n]ie* is not clear. It might be the particle *e* 'indeed' (LR-63). Or it may be that *eren-* is to *sen-* more or less as *elye* 'even thou' is to *-lye* 'thou' in Galadriel's Lament. These may in fact be the same element, since in context in *E man antaváro?* 'What will he give indeed?' it is taken for granted that Ilúvatar will give something to each in the afterlife, and the emphasis of "indeed" is on the doubt about "what" that something will be. There is no suggestion of emphasis like "indeed" or "even" in the Koivienéni translation, however, so it is worth considering another possibility.

In a contrast like *hiruvalye* 'thou shalt find' vs. *elye hiruva* the verb form remains a constant, while the inflection *-lye* 'thou' alters in position. We could suppose a similar contrast of **sen-ekkoitalye* 'thou awakest them' vs. **elye sen-ekkoita* 'even thou awakest them'. But the "bare stem" of the verb can be used like an infinitive with implicit repetition of the subject of the main sentence, as *Orome lende na sen-ekkoita* 'Orome came to awake them' = 'Orome came so that he awakes them'. In effect *sen-ekkoita* by itself means 'he awakes them'. So we have the following analogical pattern when we remove *-lye* from each phrase:

*sen-ekkoita-lye	**e-lye sen-ekkoita*
'thou awakest them'	'even thou awakest them' :
*sen-ekkoita	**e sen-ekkoita*
'he awakes them'	'even he awakes them'.

In other words, since both verb stem and emphatic particle can take explicit pronoun suffix, if a verb stem by itself implicitly refers to a previous subject, then the particle *e* 'indeed' can do the same, so that we have in effect *e* 'even he'.

Such a particle might quite naturally retain stress as a separate word when used to emphasize the subject 'he, she, it'. But it might also be used simply to make the subject explicit, e.g. to say literally 'came so that he awakes them' = **lende i e sen-ekkoita* (contrasting with implicit subject in *lende na sen-ekkoita* 'came to awake them'). Without emphatic meaning there would probably be no separate word stress on the *e* 'he', and it might well merge with the object prefix, yielding *e-sen-* 'he-them'. (Compare compound subject-object pronoun suffixes *-nye-s* 'I-it', *-lme-t* 'we-them'.) And if the construction had emerged early enough in the history of Quenya it would have participated in the shift of **s** > **r** yielding the prefix *eren-* 'he-them'. Thus *eren-ekkoita* would be 'he-them awakes', *eren-ekkoitan[n]ie* = 'he-them having awakened', and *lende i eren-ekkoitan[n]ie* 'came so that [it be] he-them having awakened' = 'came that he might awake them'.

Acknowledgments

We would like to thank the Tolkien Estate for granting permission to publish the Koivienéni sentence, thereby making another valuable example of Quenya available for study by the students of the Elven languages. We are indebted to Taum Santoski for first bringing the existence of the sentence to our attention, and for providing us with a working transcript and much helpful information on the nature of the original manuscript. Thanks also to Charles B. Elston for providing a photocopy of the pertinent portion of the manuscript, to Jorge Quiñónez for acting as our liaison with the Tolkien Estate and the Marquette University Archives, and to Tom Loback for supplying additional insight.

Notes

[1] Taum has also noted that the sentence and other linguistic material are handwritten in black ink, and that this whole side of the manuscript was struck through with three diagonal strokes in pencil.

[2] In the Marquette collection this manuscript is located in Series 3 (*The Lord of the Rings*), Box 9 (Appendices), Folder 13 (Appendix E "Writing and Spelling").

[3] The existence of two adverbs closely parallel in meaning is remarkable but not unusual. English besides *long* as adverb has *longly* (now archaic or dialectal); and Latin besides its normal adverb *longe* 'a long way off, for a long while' has the rarer forms *longiter* and *longum*, all three derived from adjective *longus*. In Quenya *andave* may be an historically newer form than *ando*, since it looks transparently like *anda* 'long' + *ve* 'like, as', and seems to have a more generic meaning, not just 'for a long time' but also 'at great length, greatly'.

[4] *Voro* 'ever, continually' also occurs in *The Etymologies* (s.v. **BOR-**), c. 1937-38.

[5] For the partitive singular *-o*, which in Third Age Quenya had merged with the genitive, cf. *Oiolosseo* 'from Mount Everwhite' in *Namárie*.

[6] For a similar example of a case ending added to an adjective rather than the noun it modifies, cf. *Elendil Vorondo* 'of Elendil the Faithful' in Cirion's Oath, and Tolkien's note about this in U-317.

[7] Cf. our discussion of *lalanti-* in "Bird and Leaf: Image and Structure in *Narqelion*", *Parma Eldalamberon* 9, pg. 19.

[8] The past tense form of *caita* 'lies' may well be *kaine. *The Etymologies* gives examples of verbs where the present tense has root + derivational suffix but the past tense has only root + *-ne* without the other suffix. Thus with suffix *-ya* in the present we have *farya-* 'suffice', pa.t. *farne* (s.v. **PHAR-**) and *vanya-* 'go, depart, disappear', pa.t. *vanne* (s.v. **WAN-**), and with suffix *-ta* in the present *lesta-* 'to leave' (< **led-ta-*), pa.t. *lende* (< *led-ne). This last pair given under base **ELED-** was abandoned when that base (source of Q *Elda*) was changed to connect with **EL-** 'star', but it displays the same principle at work in a derivative similar to *caita* in formation.

The past tense form *kaire* 'lay' does not derive directly from either *caita* 'lies' or *kaine 'lay'. It occurs only in the phrase *Kaire laiqa'ondoisen kirya* 'the white ship lay upon the rocks', in *OM1*. We can note that the suffix *-re* occurs in the same poem also in *kirya kalliére kulukalmalínen* 'the ship shone with golden lights', which may be reflexive in sense, i.e. 'the ship shone with its own lights'. So the literal sense of *kirya kaire ondoisen* may be 'the ship laid itself upon the rocks', distinct from *eldar kakainen Koivienenissen* where the Elves had not lain down of their own accord.

[9] Perhaps *linganer* is a shortened form of *lingane-re parallel to *kalliére, kaire* mentioned above.

[10] Such English constructions as "hear the wind to have roared" are grammatical but somewhat cumbersome, so they are not used very often except in literal translations from

languages like Greek or Latin where past infinitives and participles occur more frequently. The English present infinitive and participle have a broader and more timeless meaning , usually made explicit only by the context.

[11] It is remarkable that the result of this combination *-ne* = past action + *-n* = dative of means, yields a suffix *-nen* identical with the instrumental singular case ending . This is used in Galadriel's Lament in *laurie lantar lassi súrinen* 'like gold fall the leaves in the wind' = 'before the leaves fell there was an action of wind that caused it', past action as means. It seems quite possible that the dative of the past infinitive is the etymological source of the instrumental case.

[12] This is frequently added to one-syllable bases, as *vanya* 'beautiful' (cf. *Vana*, base **BAN**-), *min-ya* 'first', *mer-ya* 'festive', *kot-ya* 'hostile', etc. But *-ya* is also added to longer derivatives, as *herenya* 'fortunate' < *heren* 'fortune' (base **KHER-** 'govern'), *númenya* 'western' < *númen* 'west', etc.

[13] It is punctuated there as *Koivie-néni*. On the "World-Ship" drawing (LT-84) it appears as *Koivieneni* with a short *e* in *neni*, although transcribed as *Koivienéni* in the accompanying list of names. The *e* is also short in *Neni Erùmear* 'Outermost Waters' on the drawing. Perhaps these are examples of the "consistent system of accentuation for Elvish names" that Christopher Tolkien "adopted, though hesitantly" (LT-11) , e.g. always using *Palúrien* although Tolkien wrote *Palúrien, Palúrien, Palurien* erratically.

[14] See LR-107, 249 and the commentary on §88, p. 255.

[15] One is reminded of Gandalf's comment on the finding of the One Ring: "Behind that there was something else at work, beyond any design of the Ring-maker. I can put it no plainer than by saying that Bilbo was *meant* to find the Ring, and *not* by its maker." (I-65.)

[16] For examples of *suppletion* (the combination of unrelated forms into a single paradigm) in the same semantic area as *linna* vs. *lende*, cf. English *go* pa.t. *went;* Greek ερχομαι 'come, go' pa.t. ηλυθον; Welsh *myned* 'to go', *â* 'goes' pa.t. *aeth*. English *went* was originally the past tense of the verb *wend* (cf. *send* pa.t. *sent*). The etymology of *linna* is unclear, but perhaps compare the plural adjective *linte* 'swift' in *Namárie*.

[17] The development of original *tk* into Q *kk* and N, Sind. *ch* is not universal. Contrast *et-kelē 'issue of water, spring', which led to a metathesized form *ektele and thence to Q *ehtele* (not **ekkele) and N *eithel* (not **echel), Sind. *eithel* 'well', LR-363, S-358, 360.

[18] Note that the gerundial **(u)túlie* 'having come' with its idiomatic usage to mean 'he is come, he is finished coming' with previously mentioned subject, might have led by analogy to use with other personal subjects 'I, we, you, they' by the addition of personal endings. Thus we have Aragorn's *utúlien* "I am come" = 'I have come' (III-245f).

[19] If the correct reading of the verb form is *erenekkoitannie* then we have an extra *n* to account for in the structure. Perhaps a past gerundial such as *ekkoita-n-nie was remodelled on *ekkoita-n-ie. We saw that the gerundial ending *-ie* is phonetically the same as the compound form of *ye* 'is' in such words as *man-ie* 'what is it', and perhaps this points to the origin of the ending. But we also have Quenya forms of the verb 'to be' which begin with *n*, as *ná* 'is', *nai* 'be it that', *nea* 'I hope it will be', coexisting beside forms without *n,* such as *ea* 'is, it is, let it be' (S-325, U-305). It seems possible then that a form *nye or *nie was modelled on *ye* by analogy, and thus that *-nie* was substituted for *-ie* in the past gerundial ending, *-n-ie* > *-n-nie*. This is speculative, of course.

[20] In English we use word order to distinguish the pronominal subject of an infinitive from the object, e.g. *He wanted them to awake* vs. *He wanted to awake them*, but a similar sort of Quenya device such as pronoun prefix vs. suffix would not be available here since the bare-stem infinitive is by definition suffixless.

Publications of Interest

Due to space limitations, the editor cannot thoroughly review all publications received; the following reviews emphasize those publications and items which the editor feels would be of special interest to members of the Elvish Linguistic Fellowship. BIAOR = *Back Issues Available On Request.*

Beyond Bree: Newsletter of the American Mensa Tolkien SIG. Published monthly.
> *Editor*: Nancy Martsch. *Subscriptions to*: the editor at P.O. Box 55372, Sherman Oaks, CA 91413. Annual subscription: USA $7.00; Overseas $10.00. *BIAOR.*
> *September 1990*: Mythcon XXI report, with pictures; review of R.E. Blackwelder's *A Tolkien Thesaurus.*
> *October 1990*: Announcement of the 1991 *Beyond Bree* Tolkien Calendar, to be edited by yours truly; listing of Tolkien-related groups.
> *November 1990*: Substantial list of forthcoming Tolkienian publications, provided by Rayner Unwin; review by Nathalie Kotowski of the Russian translation of *The Fellowship of the Ring.*

Mythlore: A Journal of J.R.R. Tolkien, C.S. Lewis, Charles Williams and the Genres of Myth and Fantasy Studies. Published quarterly.
> *Editor*: Glen GoodKnight. *Subscriptions to*: P.O. Box 6707, Altadena, CA 91003. Annual subscription: $14.50, add $7.00 for USA or $8.00 for Canadian First Class delivery; Overseas Airmail: Europe & Latin America $29.50, Australia & Asia $34.50. *BIAOR.*
> *No. LXIII, Autumn 1990*: Various papers from Mythcon XXI, consonant with the theme "Aspects of Love in Fantasy"; an intriguing look at ancient English mining in "The Mines of Mendip and of Moria" by J.S. Ryan.

Mythprint: The Monthly Bulletin of the Mythopoeic Society.
> *Editor*: David Bratman. *Subscriptions to*: Mythopoeic Society Orders Dept., 1008 N. Monterey, Alhambra, CA 91801. Annual subscription: USA $7.00, add $3.00 for First Class or Canadian delivery; Overseas surface $10.00; Overseas Airmail $14.00.
> *No. 123, Vol. 27, No. 9, September 1990*: Mythcon XXI report, part I, with pictures.
> *No. 124, Vol. 27, No. 10, October 1990*: Mythcon XXI report, part II, with pictures.

Quettar: Bulletin of the Linguistic Fellowship of The Tolkien Society. Published occasionally.
> *Editor*: Julian Bradfield. *Subscriptions to*: Christina Scull, 1A Colestown St., London SW11 3EH, UK. Four-issue subscription: UK £3.00; Europe and surface mail outside Europe £4.00; Airmail outside Europe £7.50. *BIAOR.*
> *No. 40, June 1990*: In "On 'legitimacy' in Elvish studies" Chris Gilson argues for the admissibility of pre-*LotR* Elvish forms not demonstrably rejected; Ronald Kyrmse sends a brief discussion on the 'Appendix on Runes' in *The Treason of Isengard*; David Doughan reviews the Russian translation of *The Fellowship of the Ring*; brief reviews of *VT* nos. 5–8.

Next Issue

Our columnists return, with Tom Loback's *Essitalmar* discussing "'Misplaced Anger' or Plurals in the Sindarin Dialects", and the conclusion of Arden Smith's "'Edition Shifting' in the German *Hobbit*" in *Transitions in Translations* . Plus lots of letters and articles from our readers … right?

Vinyar Tengwar

The bimonthly 'news-letters' of the Elvish Linguistic Fellowship.
A Special Interest Group of the Mythopoeic Society.

Editor: Carl F. Hostetter, 2509 Ambling Circle, Crofton, MD 21114, USA.

Proofreaders: Jorge Quiñónez and Arden R. Smith.

Masthead: by Tom Loback.

Tengwar numerals: from Lawrence M. Schoen's *Moroma* PostScript *Tengwar* font for the Mac, available on disk for $6.00 from PsychoGlyph, P.O. Box 74, Lake Bluff, IL 60044.

Subscriptions: Subscriptions are for 1 year (6 issues) and must be paid in US dollars.
$12.00   USA
$15.00   Canada (sent airmail) and Overseas surface mail
$18.00   Overseas airmail

Back issues available: Issues 1 - 7 & 9 - 14 are each $2.00 in the USA, $2.50 overseas surface mail and Canada, $3.00 airmail. Issue 8 includes a large map and costs $4.00 USA, $5.00 surface and Canada, $6.00 airmail. A complete set of back issues is available for $20.00 USA, $25.00 Overseas surface mail, and $30.00 Overseas airmail. *All costs are postpaid.*

Payments: All payments must be in US dollars. It is recommended that overseas members make payments via international postal money order.

Make all checks payable to Carl F. Hostetter.

Submissions: Written material should in some manner deal with Tolkien's invented languages. All submissions must be typed, or must be written unbelievably legibly: if I have to decipher lower-glyphics, the submission is automatically rejected! The editor reserves the right to edit any material (except art) for purposes of brevity and relevance. Ilúvatar smiles upon submissions on 800K (3.5") Macintosh disks in PageMaker, Microsoft Word or MacWrite formats, or as unformatted TEXT files. Artwork should be linguistic, or at least Elvish, in nature. Remember that artwork done in black ink will reproduce the best; I wouldn't harbor great expectations for the quality of reproduction from artwork rendered in pencil, "Flair" pen, chalk, or colored ink.

The deadline for **VT #15** *is* ***January 1, 1991.***

Vinyar Tengwar is produced by the editor on an Apple Macintosh II personal computer, using a LaCie Silverscan scanner, Microsoft Word 4.0 and Aldus PageMaker 4.0. VT is mastered for duplication on an Apple LaserWriter II NTX.

ISSN 1054-7606

Cainen lempë

#15

January 1991

Vinyar Tengwar

In This Issue

Editor's Musings

The slimness of this issue will already have made the necessary topic of this month's "Musings" quite apparent: *VT* desperately needs more submissions! Apparently, the hectic holiday season, coupled with the fact that most of *VT*'s usual writers are laboring on *I Parma* in preparation for the Colloquium (see last issue's *E.L.F. News* for details), accounts for the dearth of material in *VT*'s files. I had hoped that the several important articles which *VT* has been privileged to present of late would prompt, if not more articles (though I had hoped that, too), at least a goodly number of letters of comment or query; this was not however the case. Well, the holidays are over, and now is the perfect time for those of you who don't normally do so to submit an article or a letter.

This issue features an interesting compilation of Elvish linguistic terms by Taum Santoski; an important and thought-provoking *Essitalmar* from Tom Loback on the subject of the formation of plurals in Sindarin, Noldorin, Doriathrin, and Ilkorin; a further examination of the German edition of the *Hobbit,* among other topics, in Arden Smith's *Transitions in Translations*; and new artwork *cum* Quenya composition from Tom. All of this, not to mention last issue's presentation of a new sentence of authentic Quenya from the Tolkien manuscripts, should provide more than ample grist for the critical mill. And if all this is still not provocative enough, how about the quote below? Have at it!

— Carl F. Hostetter

"Tolkien's own off-hand remarks about the importance of philology to the creative conception of the trilogy need not be taken too seriously...."

— Neil D. Isaacs, *Tolkien and the Critics* (Univ. of Notre Dame, 1968), p. 7.

E.L.F. News

New Member

The E.L.F. extends a hearty *mae govannen* to:

• Peter Kramer   Berliner Straße 22, 4836 Herzebrock, Clarholz 1, Germany.

International Tolkien Symposium
on the occasion of the centenary
Saturday, 11th January 1992 — Sunday, 12th January 1992

Aachen, August-Pieper-Haus

Call for papers on aspects of Tolkien's work and its reception, 30 minutes length. For each speaker board & lodging free, honorarium and travel expenses within the Federal Republic of Germany. Deadline for papers (in English or in German): 1 October 1991.

Address: Inklings, Erster-Roter-Haag-Weg 31, D-5100 Aachen, F.R.G.

The papers of the symposium are to be published in vol. 10 of Inklings-Jahrbuch 1992.

1991 Beyond Bree J.R.R. Tolkien Calendar

The 1991 *Beyond Bree* J.R.R. Tolkien Calendar, edited and produced by yours truly, is now available. It features Middle-earth and Primary World events, and an international selection of Tolkien-inspired artwork. For Elvish scholars, the names of the months and of the days of the week are given in their Quenya equivalents, and the day of the month is given in both Roman and *tengwar* numerals.

The Calendar costs: U.S.A. $4.00, Overseas Surface Mail $4.50, and Overseas Airmail $6.00. Send orders to: Nancy Martsch, Editor *Beyond Bree*, P.O. Box 55372, Sherman Oaks, CA 91413.

Mallorn Has New Editor

David Doughan, former editor of *Quettar*, *VT*'s British counterpart, is the new editor of *Mallorn*, the annual Journal of the Tolkien Society. This may help to open another outlet for articles on Tolkienian linguistics, especially for general-interest or Primary-world linguistics pieces which may not have been suitable for *VT* or for *Parma Eldalamberon*. For more information, write David Doughan at 120 Kenley Road, London, SW19 3DW.

VT Gets ISSN

Thanks to the suggestion and kind assistance of Lawrence Schoen, *VT* now sports its very own International Standard Serial Number (ISSN), in the upper right-hand corner of the cover. This should get *VT* into a host of computer databases, and may help *VT* get noticed by the major libraries. Of course, *VT*'s readers can help, too, by approaching libraries with the prospect of subscribing to *VT*.

Letters to VT

• Jorge Quiñónez   San Diego, CA.

I've now seen over 220 pages of *VT* printed in the past 14 issues; an amazing labor by all of those who made it possible. As the current editor, Carl has tied me in the total number of issues produced. When I was editor, I tried to make each new issue better than the last. Carl has carried on this tradition in grand fashion. He continues the dream and the vision I began with, of a regular forum for Elvish studies. Chris Gilson, despite being the most brilliant Tolkienian linguist on the planet, has never been able to put out more than one issue of *Parma Eldalamberon* per year. While each issue of *Parma* is a masterpiece in both the artistic and scholarly departments, once per year is not sufficient to maintain a regular forum for Elvish.

I found David Bratman's letter very interesting, especially since he's not actively involved in the linguistic aspect of Tolkien's works, but more in the narrative part of Tolkien's genius. His comment that it takes "… a higher calling to write Quenya prose than to write 'The Jewel of Arwen', the results lie much more pleasantly on the ear", struck a very deep chord in me: true words, indeed, from the editor of *Mythprint*. Writing pastiche of *The Lord of the Rings* is all too simple (as Terry Brooks' works demonstrate) when compared to trying to compose or speak in J.R.R. Tolkien's invented languages. In *Letters* (I can't remember the number) *[and I can't find it either (aren't Humphrey Carpenter's indices frustrating?) — can anyone out there help? —CFH]*, when someone told Tolkien he was trying to write a sequel to *LotR*, Tolkien was furious. Similarly, when people tried to write literary criticisms of his fictional prose, Tolkien was less than enthused. *But*, when someone was interested in his invented languages, he was more than happy to oblige, and to respond with additional information. From this observation, I tend to think that the majority (99%) of the people today trying to study Tolkien go about it all wrong. The only true way to understand Tolkien's magnificent "litera-linguistic" creation (as Paul Nolan Hyde and others know only too well) is to have a firm understanding of his invented languages. I believe, beyond a shadow of a doubt, that this is the only way Tolkien would have even considered positively or have approved of.

I now seriously doubt that I'll be able to attend the Colloquium in February, but there's one thing I must emphasize to the editor(s) of *I Parma*: do *not* make the mistake that Jim Allan made in giving *An Introduction to Elvish* to a small, unknown publisher. Make sure you get a big publisher like Ballantine or Houghton Mifflin. Let us remember that Ruth Noel chose HM and her terrible little red books have probably outsold *ItE* a hundred-fold.

ૐ

Elvish Linguistic Terms
compiled by Taum Santoski

The following is a list of Elvish linguistic terms found in *The Etymologies* (*Et.*) and in *The Lord of the Rings*.

Q. = Q(u)enya, N. = Noldorin, S. = Sindarin; *RotK* = *The Return of the King*.

Q. *amandi*	'vowel'.	(*Et.*, p. 379, base **OM-**)
Q. *amatikse*	dots or points placed above the line of writing.	(*Et.*, p. 393, base **TIK-**)
Q. *andatehta*,	'long-mark'.	(*Et.*, p. 391, base **TEK-**)
N. *andeith*,		
S. *andaith*		
S. *angerthas*	'long rune-rows'; alphabet, long runic.	(*RotK*, Appendix E, p. 397)
Q. *certar*,	'runes'.	(*RotK*, Appendix E, p. 395)
S. *cirth*, *certhas*		
N. *gasdil*	'stopgap', "name of a sign (*Et.*, p. 354, base **DIL-**; *Et.*, p. 357, base **GAS-**) used to indicate that *g* had disappeared".	
Q. *kalmatéma*	*k*-series of *tengwar*, velars	(*RotK*, Appendix E, p. 398)
Q. *lúva*	'bow', semi-circular part of a *tengwa*.	(*RotK*, Appendix E, p. 398)
Q. *nengwea*	'nasal'.	(*Et.*, p. 376, base **NEÑ-WI-**)
Q. *nuntikse*	dots or points placed below the line of writing.	(*Et.*, p. 393, base **TIK-**)
Q. *parmalambe*	"book-language = Qenya".	(*Et.*, p. 380, base **PAR-**)
Q. *parmatéma*	*p*-series of *tengwar*, the labials	(*RotK*, Appendix E, p. 398)
N. *peth*	'word'.	(*Et.*, p. 366, base **KWET-** [and **PET-**])
N. *prestannen*	"'affected', of vowel [i.e. 'mutated']".	(*Et.*, p. 380, base **PERES-**)
N. *prestanneth*	"'affection' of vowels".	(*Et.*, p. 380, base **PERES-**)
Q. *punta*	"a stopped consonant".	(*Et.*, p. 382, base **PUT-** [under entry **PUS-**])
Q. *pusta*	"(noun) stop, in punctuation full stop", a period.	(*Et.*, p. 382, base **PUS-**)
Q. *putta*	"stop (in punctuation)".	(*Et.*, p. 382, base **PUT-** [under entry **PUS-**])
Q. *quessetéma*	*kw*-series of *tengwar*, labialized series.	(*RotK*, Appendix E, p. 398)
Q. *qetil*	'tongue, language'.	(*Et.*, p. 366, base **KWET-** [and **PET-**])
Q. *samnar*	'diphthongs'.	(*Et.*, p. 385, base **SAM-**)
Q. *sundo*	'base, root, root-word'.	(*Et.*, p. 388, base **SUD-**)
Q. *sundokarme*	'base-structure'. (*Et.*, p. 343; *Et.*, p. 362, base **KAR-**; *Et.*, p. 388, base **SUD-**)	
Q. *surya*	'spirant consonant'.	(*Et.*, p. 388, base **SUS-**)

— continued on page 5.

E.L.F. Member Directory

Alper, Renee
Rivendell
730-F Northland Road
Forest Park, OH 45240

Bar-Yahalom, Eli
32/35 Gut-Levin Street
Ramot-Sapir
Haifa 32922
Israel

Bertenstam, Åke
Stabby allé 11B
2 tr.
S-752 29 Uppsala
Sweden

Blackwelder, R.E.
542 So. Spring, Apt. H
Cape Girardeau
Missouri 63701

Bradfield, Julian C.
Dept. of Computer Science
Univ. of Edinburgh
The King's Buildings
Mayfield Road
Edinburgh, EH9 3J2
Scotland

Braiter, Paulina
ul. Kasztelanska 66/3
P-58-314 Walbrzych
Poland

Bratman, David
1354 Crane St.
Menlo Park, CA 94025

Buchs, Peter
Hubäckerweg 1
5610 Wohlen
Switzerland

Christopher, Joe
820 Charlotte
Stephenville, TX 76401

Coombs, Jenny
17 Grange Ave.
Ruddington, Nottinghamshire
NG11 6BD
England

Del Toro, Steve
9010 SW 125 Ave.
Bldg. G, Apt. 105
Miami, FL 33186

Doughan, David
120 Kenley Rd.
London SW19 3DW
England

Ebenreck, Jered
3451 Sixes Rd.
Prince Frederick, MD 20678

Gardner, Steve
12 The Fleet
Springfield
Milton Keynes
England

Gilson, Chris
300 North Civic Dr.
#304
Walnut Creek, CA 94596

Hammond, Wayne
30 Talcott Rd.
Williamstown, MA 01267

Hunnewell, Gary
2030 San Pedro Dr.
Arnold, MO 63010

Hyde, Paul Nolan
2661 E. Lee St.
Simi Valley, CA 93065

Keenan, Erica
RD #5, Box 208
Boyertown, PA 19512

Kloczko, Edouard
22 rue Victor Hugo
78800 Houilles
France

Kondratiev, Alexei
35-21 161st St.
Flushing, NY 11358

Kotowski, Nathalie
Rue V. Gambier 25/7
1180 Bruxelles
Belgium

Kramer, Peter
Berliner Straße 22
4836 Herzebrock, Clarholz 1
Germany

Kyrmse, Ronald E.
Av. S. Luís
86-17º
01046 S. Paolo
Sp-Brazil

Leonard, Bruce
P.O. Box 3849
Littleton, CO 80161-3849

Loback, Tom
152 W. 26th St.
#36
N.Y. City, NY 10001

Martsch, Nancy
P.O. Box 55372
Sherman Oaks, CA 91413

Noad, Charles
12 Madeley Road
Ealing
London W5 2LH
England

O'Brien, Donald
Okanagan College
7000 College Way
Vernon, B.C. V1B 2N5
Canada

Peterson, Jerry D.
5431 N. East River Rd.
#1018
Chicago, IL 60656

Prohorova, Nataliya
109180 Moskva
ul. Bol'shaya Polyanka
d. 28, kv. 266
U.S.S.R

Quiñónez, Jorge
3326 Polk Ave.
San Diego, CA 92104

Raggett, Ned
691 Levering Ave.
#18
Los Angeles, CA 90024

Ritz, Paul S.
P.O. Box 901
Clearwater, FL 24617

Santoski, Taum
2347 N. Booth St.
Riverwest
Milwaukee, WI 53212

Schoen, Lawrence M.
8 Campus Circle
Lake Forest, IL 60045

Scolese, Walter
via Magellano 5
36100 Vicenza
Italy

Scull, Christina
1A Colestown St.
London SW11 3EH
England

Seeman, Christopher J.
P.O. Box 1213
Novato, CA 94948

Smith, Arden
P.O. Box 4395
Berkeley, CA 94704-0395

Stephen, Donn P.
P.O. Box 2024
Manassas, VA 22110

Tackett, Galen
4785 La Mesa Ct.
Fremont, CA 94536

Thomson, Ken
1802 Edgehill
Pasadena, Texas 77502-2756

Welden, Bill
19419 Valerio Street
Reseda, CA 91335

West, Richard
1918 Madison St.
Madison, WI 53711

Wynne, Patrick
410 3rd St. NE
Fosston, MN 56542

Zimmermann, Manfred
Univ. of Cincinnati
Dept. of German
730-742 Old Chemistry Bldg.
Cincinnati, OH 45221-0372

Elvish Linguistic Terms

— *continued from page 3.*

Q. *tarqesta*	'high speech', spoken Q(u)enya.	(*Et.*, p. 389, base **TA-**, **TA3-**)
Q. *tehta*, N. *teith*	"a mark (in writing), sign, diacritic".	(*Et.*, p. 391, base **TEK-**)
Q. *tekko*	"stroke of pen or brush (') when not used as long mark".	(*Et.*, p. 391, base **TEK-**)
Q. *telco*	'stem', vertical line, part of a *tengwa*.	(*RotK*, Appendix E, p. 398)
Q. *téma*, *témar*	'row, series, line'.	(*Et.*, p. 392, base **TEÑ-**)
Q. *tengwa*, *tengwar*; N. *tîw*; S. *têw, *tîw*	'letter'.	(*Et.*, p. 391, base **TEK-**; *RotK*, Appendix E, p. 395)
Q. *tengwanda*	'alphabet'.	(*Et.*, p. 391, base **TEK-**)
Q. *tengwe*	'writing'.	(*Et.*, p. 391, base **TEK-**)
Q. *tengwesta*	'grammar'.	(*Et.*, p. 391, base **TEK-**)
Q. *tenkele*	'writing system, spelling'.	(*Et.*, p. 391, base **TEK-**)
N. *thinnas*	"'shortness', name of mark indicating short quality of vowel".	(*Et.*, p. 388, base **STINTÄ-**)
Q. *tikse*	'dot, tiny mark, point'.	(*Et.*, p. 393, base **TIK-**)
Q. *tincotéma*	*t*-series of *tengwar*, the dentals.	(*RotK*, Appendix E, p. 398)
Q. *tyellë*, *tyeller*	'grades', of the *tengwar*.	(*RotK*, Appendix E, p. 397)
Q. *tyelpetéma*	*ty*-series of the *tengwar*, palatals.	(*RotK*, Appendix E, p. 398)

Thus Spake Fëanor

by Tom Loback

Reprinted with permission from *Mythlore* LXIV, pp. 17, 21.

Yé ea ve inye intyane. Pertorninya mere soi esta nin, sinanen ve ilqainen. Etvanyo-tye ar envanyo mentyanna. Tíro, per-toron! Sina ná aika ala lambe- tya. Kose er lú atta mapa haryanya ar i meles atarinyo ar nai metyava Noldoron mine man mere ná mólaturo.

The scene is that of *The Silmarillion*, p. 70:

> But even as Fingolfin spoke, Fëanor strode into the chamber, and he was fully armed: his high helm upon his head, and at his side a mighty sword. 'So it is, even as I guessed,' he said. 'My half-brother would be before me with my father, in this as in all other matters.' Then turning upon Fingolfin he drew his sword, crying: 'Get thee gone, and take thy due place!'
>
> Fingolfin bowed before Finwë, and without word or glance to Fëanor he went from the chamber. But Fëanor followed him, and at the door of the king's house he stayed him; and the point of his bright sword he set against Fingolfin's breast. 'See, half-brother!' he said. 'This is sharper than thy tongue. Try but once more to usurp my place and the love of my father, and maybe it will rid the Noldor of one who seeks to be the master of thralls.'

Since I wanted the text to be self-contained and pertinent to the drawing, I ended up excerpting only Tolkien's direct quotes of Fëanor. This manuscript page therefore places the viewer in the crowd outside the House of Finwë, with little narrative distance, to judge the event on his own. The attempt to back-translate the quotation into Quenya hopefully furthers the currency of this representation, despite the problematic syntax. "Recorded as it happened" might also be an operative description.

The more or less literal translation of the Quenya is:

> "Lo it is as even I guessed. Half-brother-mine wishes himself to precede me, this-thing-in as everything-in. Out-forth-thee and again-forth place-thy-to. See, half-brother! This is sharp beyond tongue-thy. Strive but a time again to seize place-mine and the love father-mine-of and maybe will end one Noldor-from who wishes to be thrall-master-of."

Essitalmar
The Roots of Middle-earth Names and Places
A column edited by Tom Loback

This is a forum for the readers of VT *to submit their ideas and thoughts about names, both of people and places; their meanings and the story that they tell. All are encouraged to submit inquiries, short interpretations and discussions thereof, particularly those names still undefined. Send all correspondence for this column to the editor at 152 West 26th St., #36, N.Y. City, NY 10001, USA.*

'Misplaced Anger'
or Plurals in the Sindarin Dialects

The April 1990 issue of *Beyond Bree* had an Elven language lesson that dealt, in part, with the formation of plurals in Third Age Sindarin. Nancy Martsch delineated the vowel changes in examples found in *Lord of the Rings* material; these are shown in Chart #1 below. Chart #2 shows the more extensive system derived from the Noldorin in *The Etymologies*. Charts #3 and #4 show formations in the closely related Doriathrin and Ilkorin languages, meagre though they may be. There are also examples of Noldorin using the Quenya *-i* suffix as a plural: *pel, peli*; *rhanc, rhengy* (though perhaps the usual plural is given as *rhenc*).

Chart 1 — Sindarin

Singular	Plural	Singular	Plural	Singular	Plural
a	*e / ai / ei*	*e ... e*	*e ... i*	*o ... o*	*e ... y,*
a ... a	*e ... ai,*	*i*	*i*		*e ... e,*
	e ... ei	*i ... i*	*i ... i*		*oe ... y*
e	*i*	*o*	*e / oe*	*u*	*y / ui*
				u ... u	?

Chart 2 — Noldorin

Words of one syllable:

Singular	Plural	Citation
a	*e*	*alf, elf*
â	*ei*	*dân, dein; pân, pein;*
		mâl, meil (or *mely*[1]); *tâl, teil*
au	*ui*	*thaun, thuin*
e	*i / î*	*fern, firn; telch, tilch; nen, nîn*
ê	*î*	*hên, hîn*
ei	*î*	*feir, fîr; gwein, gwîn; sein, sîn*
i	?	
î	*ei*	*gîl, geil*
io	*y*	*hniof, hnyf*
o	*ý / y*	*bor, býr; orn, yrn; toll, tyll*
ô	*ÿ*	*pôd, pÿd*
oei	*ei*	*rhoein, rhein*
wau	*ui*	*gwaun, guin*

---

[1] From an Old Noldorin plural *malui*.

Words of two syllables in which the vowel repeats:

Singular	Plural	Citation
a … a	*e … i*	*dangen, dengin*
a … a	*e … e*	*adab, edeb; falas, feles*
	e … ei	*habad, hebeid; talaf, teleif*
	e … ai	*aran, erain*
e … e	*e … i*	*ceber, cebir*
	e … ei	*tele, telei*
i … i	?	
o … o	*e … e*	*doron, deren*
	e … ei	*golodh (goeloeidh) geleidh;*
		thoron, therein
u … u	*y … y*	*tulus, tylys*

Words of two syllables in which the second vowel differs

Singular	Plural	Citation
a … e	*e … i*	*angren, engrin; malen, melin*
a … io	*e … y*	*thalion, thelyn*
a … o	*e … ei*	*gwador, gwedeir*
	e … y	*amon, emyn; annon, ennyn*
	e … ui	*amon, emuin*
e … oei	*e … e*	*telloein, tellen*[2]
i … e	*i … i*	*fileg, filig*[3]
ui … o	*ui … y*	*muindor, muindyr*

Words of three syllables

Singular	Plural	Citation
a … a … e	*e … e … i*	*tawaren, tewerin*
a … o … o	*e … e … y*	*alchoron, elcheryn*
i … io	*i … ui*	*mirion, miruin*

Noldorin also has some plural suffixes of specific intent:

-lir 'row'; *-(h)oth* 'host'; *-rim* 'crowd, host'; *-lim* 'many'

In addition to the plurals above is a Noldorin *collective plural, e.g.* **giliath** (sing. **gîl**, pl. **geil**); *cf* **siniath, hithliniath,** and (with no *i*) **danath**. As opposed to the *general plural* in Doriathrin (pl. **regin**, gen. pl. **region**; *cf* **regornion**). This general plural is evident in Ilkorin as well: Ilk. **Dor-thonion** = 'Land of Pines'; **ulion**, sing. **uglon**; sing. **gwath**, pl. **gwethion**. It is interesting to note Nold. **naith** (pl. **natsai**?), *LR* p. 387. A good question indeed, as no other forms for pluralizing **ai** are found.

---

[2] Mighty unwieldy, this later becomes **tellein, tellen**.
[3] Analogical formation by Tolkien, an additional variant, **filigod**, given just to muddle it up some more.

Plurals in Doriathrin and Ilkorin generally end in *-in*: Dor. ***orth, orthin; eld, eldin***; Ilk. ***tôr, tórin; balthor, balthorin***. However, there are vowel-change plurals, sometimes combined with syncopation and the *-in* suffix, *e.g.* Ilk. ***boron, burnin*** = ***boron*** + ***in*** with syncope of the second *o*. Without a larger body of words from these dialects it is difficult to draw many conclusions, and plural formation would best be done by using analogic forms. The chart below lists the plurals found for these dialects. There are also Exilic Noldorin plurals that use the *-in* suffix, presumably a borrowing from the Beleriandic dialects: ***fer, ferin; oel, oelin***.

<table>
<tr><td colspan="2">Chart 3 — Doriathrin</td><td colspan="2">Chart 4 — Ilkorin</td></tr>
<tr><td>Singular</td><td>Plural</td><td>Singular</td><td>Plural</td></tr>
<tr><td>*lalm*</td><td>*lelmin*</td><td>*adar*</td><td>*edrin*</td></tr>
<tr><td>*eld*</td><td>*eldin*</td><td>*aman*</td><td>*emuin*</td></tr>
<tr><td>*orth*</td><td>*orthin*</td><td>*balthor*</td><td>*balthorin*</td></tr>
<tr><td>*urch*</td><td>*urchin*</td><td>*boron*</td><td>*burnin*</td></tr>
<tr><td>*roth*</td><td>*rodhin*</td><td>*gwath*</td><td>*urthin*</td></tr>
<tr><td></td><td></td><td>*gwini*</td><td>*gwine*</td></tr>
<tr><td></td><td></td><td>*mur(i)lind*</td><td>*myr(i)lynd*</td></tr>
<tr><td></td><td></td><td>*tal*</td><td>*tel*</td></tr>
<tr><td></td><td></td><td>*talum*</td><td>*telmin*</td></tr>
<tr><td></td><td></td><td>*thorn*</td><td>*thurin*</td></tr>
<tr><td></td><td></td><td>*tôr*</td><td>*tórin*</td></tr>
</table>

It can be seen that Ilkorin plurals fall between Noldorin and Doriathrin, in that they often use the *-in* suffix of Doriathrin, yet also have vowel changes similar to Noldorin. In addition, Doriathrin and Ilkorin frequently exhibit syncopation,[4] which is nearly absent in Noldorin. It would appear then that syncope is a regular feature of Doriathrin and Ilkorin, the two original Beleriandic dialects, and that this will prove a fertile area in which to search for the meanings of words and names, as well as the parallel formation of words from Noldorin. There is in Ilkorin *gangel, genglin* which, although it is not so noted, must mean 'harp, harps'. If so, this indicates the syncope rule is more general (and likely more prevalent, therefore) with the loss of more than just a repeated second vowel. This is apparently what is indicated by Ilk. *mur(i)lind, myr(i)lind*, from which is derived the Nold. *moerilind, merilin* without the syncope.

If, for example, the sword of Thingol is viewed from this standpoint, with the presumption that *Aranruth* is a Doriathrin word (as would be expected from its secondary-world context), a possible gloss might be: *ar* + *a* (genitive) + *n'rúth* (< *nrúth*, derived from the old root of the Qenya Lexicon, **NURU**, Gnomish Lexicon *nur-* 'growl, grumble') = 'King's Ire', with ire seen as the display of anger which is an interpretation of a growl. While this has nothing to do with plurals, it demonstrates the value of *The Etymologies* to later material, and the value of simply collecting and collating the material and looking to see what's there. Sometimes this is serendipitous.

---

[4] See *The Letters of J.R.R. Tolkien*, Letter #347, p. 426: "The syncope (loss) of second vowel in a sequence of two short vowels of the same quality … occurred in words of length such as *Telperion*.

Transitions in Translations

A column edited by Arden R. Smith

The purpose of this column is to examine peculiarities in translations of Tolkien's works: mistranslations, unusual translations, interesting solutions to the problems of translation, and other curiosities in foreign editions. Ideas and contributions are encouraged: send them to "Transitions," c/o Arden R. Smith, P.O. Box 4395, Berkeley, CA 94704-0395, USA.

"Edition Shifting" in the German Hobbit

Part Two

As I reported in my last column (*VT* 13, pp. 18–19), the German translation of *The Hobbit* (*Der kleine Hobbit*. Translated by Walter Scherf. München: Deutscher Taschenbuch Verlag, 1974) is based on a mixture of the second and third edition texts. Unlike the clear-cut "edition shifting" found in the Spanish *Lord of the Rings* (see *VT* 7, p. 10), the "edition shifting" in the German *Hobbit* is a confusing jumble. When the German translation was revised, third edition readings were introduced sporadically, but in most cases the original second edition readings were retained.

Were the German revisions made where particular types of revisions had been made in the English text? This does not seem to be the case. Where changes were made in the story's time-frame, the German text contains both second (II.5)* and third (III.1) edition readings, as well as an ambivalent reading (II.8). Most of the landscape revisions retain second edition readings (II.4, II.6, II.7, III.4, XIII.2, XV.2, XV.3), if not all of them: I have interpreted II.13 as a mixture of second and third edition readings, since I assumed *Dornbusch* to be a rendering of the third edition "thorn-bush" rather than of the second edition "thorn-tree", but this may not be the case. Furthermore, the translation retains the second edition description of Gollum's physical characteristics. (V.1, V.2).

Revisions due to conceptual changes in the nature of Middle-earth are only sometimes reflected in the German version. The third edition readings of "pickles" rather than "tomatoes" (I.6), of Smaug's diet consisting of "dwarves and men of Dale" rather than "maidens of the valley" (I.12), and of the Longbeards being the "eldest race" rather than "one of the two races" of the Dwarves (III.9) all appear in the German text. Second edition concepts nevertheless abound, such as the Deep-elves being called "Gnomes" (VIII.1), "men or hobbits or what not" inhabiting the "wide respectable country" east of the Shire (II.3), and the Necromancer's defeat being absolute (XIX.1).

Manfred Zimmermann notes that the German title, *Der kleine Hobbit*, "makes it abundantly clear that this is a sweet little book for the sweet little darlings and no adults need consider it seriously" (*Quettar* Special Publication No. 2, p. 5). We should then expect the revisions lessening the book's childish tone to have been ignored in the German revision. At II.11, the condescending narrator's voice *has* been retained, but at III.2 removed. The childish tone has also been removed from I.1, where hobbits are no longer described as "very much larger than lilliputians", but remains in the description of Gandalf as "a little old man" (I.3).

---

* These designations for the revised passages refer to Appendix A of *The Annotated Hobbit*. See *VT* 13, p. 18).

Context, then, does not seem to have determined which revisions were introduced into the German version and which were not. Were the *most obvious* revisions included? Again I would say no. Among the most obvious revisions are those in which a proper name has been added in the third edition (I.9, I.13, I.16, I.18, XIII.1, XVII.1). *All* of these passages, however, retain the less specific second edition readings in the German text. This would seem to rule out a hypothesis that Scherf revised his translation wherever he *noticed* changes in the English version.

I stated in my last column that I would attempt to determine a pattern to this "edition shifting". I must confess that my attempt has failed. Whatever criteria Scherf used in deciding which revisions to incorporate into his translation remain a mystery to me.

* * *

More about *Kalpa Kassinen*

In my last column's trivia question (*VT* 13, p. 20), I stated that Bilbo was named *Kalpa Kassinen* in the first Finnish translation of *The Hobbit* (*Lohikäärmevuori*. Translated by Risto Pitkänen. Helsinki: Tammi, 1973). Since then, I have been able to analyze the name, and the translation is quite interesting.

Tolkien states that the translation of *Baggins* "should contain an element meaning 'sack, bag'" (*A Tolkien Compass*, p. 160). In this the translator followed Tolkien's recommendation. According to Aino Wuolle's *Finnish–English English–Finnish Dictionary* (New York: Hippocrene, 1990), *kassi* has the meaning "string bag, shopping bag".

What about *Kalpa*? Tolkien wanted names like *Bilbo* to be left "*entirely* unchanged" (*A Tolkien Compass*, p. 155). Why, then, was the name changed? It is clear that the change from *Bilbo* to *Kalpa* preserves the alliteration in the name, and *Kalpa* furthermore is similar in form to *Bilbo*: *stop / i / l / (bilabial) stop / back vowel*.

There is yet another relationship between *Bilbo* and *Kalpa*, which I think makes the translation interesting. As Paula Marmor notes in *An Introduction to Elvish* (p. 184), "A *bilbo* is a Spanish sword, from Bilbao, not a likely Hobbit name. But *bil* 'sword' is found in those old Germanic names ...." What is the meaning of *kalpa*? Aino Wuolle defines it as "sword, épée".

* * *

"Something is rotten in the state of Denmark"

In *The Lord of the Rings* and the Danish translation thereof (*Ringenes Herre*. Translated by Ida Nyrop Ludvigsen. København: Gyldendal, 1981), Boromir asks his father, "How many hundreds of years needs it to make a steward (*marsk*) a king (*konge*), if the king (*kongen*) returns not?" Denethor answers, "Few years, maybe, in other places of less royalty" (English II 278, Danish II 290). The Danish translation elsewhere (I 283) describes Denethor, the Lord of Minas Tirith, as "*kongen* af Minas Tirith". Denmark is apparently a "place of less royalty".

* * *

Trivia Question

Q: What is the name of the German counterpart of Sorhed in *Bored of the Rings*?
A: *Sauerkopf*, meaning "sour-head" (*Dschey Ar Tollkühn: Der Herr der Augenringe*. Translated by Margaret Carroux. München: Goldmann, 1983).

* * *

Next Issue: "Elvish is Fin(n)ished" and more!

Publications of Interest

*Due to space limitations, the editor cannot thoroughly review all publications received; the following
reviews emphasize those publications and items which the editor feels would be of special interest to
members of the Elvish Linguistic Fellowship. BIAOR = Back Issues Available On Request.*

Aglared: Magazine of the Eredain (Swiss Tolkien Society). Published bimonthly.
> *Editor*: Peter Buchs. *Subscriptions to*: the editor at Hubäckerweg 1, 5610 Wohlen,
> Switzerland. Write for subscription info.
> *No. 8* (English edition): Reprints Margaret R. Dean's *Conversational Quenya: Hrestassë*
> ('On a Beach') from *VT* #4; discussion of Eddic riddles; more.

Cirth de Gandalf: Cercle d'etudes de Tolkien en Belgique. Published bimonthly.
> *Editor*: Nathalie Kotowski. *Subscriptions to*: the editor at 25, rue Victor Gambier, 1180
> Bruxelles, Belgium. Annual subscription: Belgium 400 FB, 450 FB elsewhere.
> *No. 10, September 1990*: Continues the presentation of Nancy Martsch's Quenya
> Language Lessons from *Beyond Bree,* translated into French: Leçon 10: encore des
> pronoms et des adjectifs déterminatifs; artwork: "Ulmo and Voronwë" by Tom Loback.
> *No. 11, November 1990*: Leçon 11: Les formes verbales.

Mythlore: A Journal of J.R.R. Tolkien, C.S. Lewis, Charles Williams and the Genres of
> Myth and Fantasy Studies. Published quarterly.
> *Editor*: Glen GoodKnight. *Subscriptions to*: P.O. Box 6707, Altadena, CA 91003.
> Annual subscription: $14.50, add $7.00 for USA or $8.00 for Canadian First Class
> delivery; Overseas Airmail: Europe & Latin America $29.50, Australia & Asia $34.50.
> *BIAOR*.
> *No. LXIV, Winter 1990*: Presents Patrick Wynne's Guest of Honor Address from Mythcon
> XXI, a humorous yet revealing look at the artist's creative process (thanks for the kind
> words on *VT*, Pat!); several works illustrating Fëanor's pointed rebuke of Fingolfin —
> of special note are "Sihe halpbruder. diss ist scherpffer dann dein zung", Pat Wynne's
> careful reproduction of a "Woodcut from a 15th century German edition of … *Das
> Silmarillion. die geschicht von den elbischen staynen silmarilli genant,* printed by Peter
> Wagner, Nuremberg, 1493", and Tom Loback's version with accompanying Quenya
> dialogue (reprinted in this issue of *VT*); "*Essë* and *Narn*: Name, Identity, and Narrative
> in the Tale of Túrin Turambar" by Elizabeth Broadwell; "The Face of Janus: A
> Recounting from the Middle of it All", a history of Paul Nolan Hyde's involvement in
> Tolkienian linguistics in his *Quenti Lambardillion* column; "Professor J.R.R. Tolkien:
> A Personal Memoir" by R.E. Havard.

Mythprint: The Monthly Bulletin of the Mythopoeic Society.
> *Editor*: David Bratman. *Subscriptions to*: Mythopoeic Society Orders Dept., 1008 N.
> Monterey, Alhambra, CA 91801. Annual subscription: USA $7.00, add $3.00 for First
> Class or Canadian delivery; Overseas surface $10.00; Overseas Airmail $14.00.
> *No. 125, Vol. 27, No. 11, November 1990*: Review of R.E. Blackwelder's *A Tolkien
> Thesaurus*.
> *No. 126, Vol. 27, No. 12, December 1990*: "Elven Linguistics Lives!": reviews of *Parma
> Eldalamberon* and *VT*; cover photo "Live Tableau of P. Wynne's 'Artist About To Be
> Struck By The Muse' created at Mythcon XXI".

Vinyar Tengwar

The bimonthly 'news-letters' of the Elvish Linguistic Fellowship.
A Special Interest Group of the Mythopoeic Society.

Editor: Carl F. Hostetter, 2509 Ambling Circle, Crofton, MD 21114, USA.

Proofreaders: Jorge Quiñónez and Arden R. Smith.

Masthead: by Tom Loback.

Tengwar numerals: from Lawrence M. Schoen's *Moroma* PostScript *Tengwar* font for the Mac, available on disk for $6.00 from PsychoGlyph, P.O. Box 74, Lake Bluff, IL 60044.

Subscriptions: Subscriptions are for 1 year (6 issues) and must be paid in US dollars.
$12.00   USA
$15.00   Canada (sent airmail) and Overseas surface mail
$18.00   Overseas airmail

Back issues available: Issues 1 - 7 & 9 - 15 are each $2.00 in the USA, $2.50 overseas surface mail and Canada, $3.00 airmail. Issue 8 includes a large map and costs $4.00 USA, $5.00 surface and Canada, $6.00 airmail. A complete set of back issues is available for $25.00 USA, $30.00 Overseas surface mail, and $35.00 Overseas airmail. *All costs are postpaid.*

Payments: All payments must be in US dollars. It is recommended that overseas members make payments via international postal money order.

Make all checks payable to Carl F. Hostetter.

Submissions: Written material should in some manner deal with Tolkien's invented languages. All submissions must be typed, or must be written unbelievably legibly: if I have to decipher lower-glyphics, the submission is automatically rejected! The editor reserves the right to edit any material (except art) for purposes of brevity and relevance. Ilúvatar smiles upon submissions on 400K or 800K (3.5") Macintosh or 720K (3.5") MS-DOS formatted disks in PageMaker, Microsoft Word, Microsoft Works, WordPerfect, MacWrite, DCA, or RTF formats, or as unformatted ASCII text files. Artwork should be linguistic, or at least Elvish, in nature. Remember that artwork done in black ink will reproduce the best; I wouldn't harbor great expectations for the quality of reproduction from artwork rendered in pencil, "Flair" pen, chalk, or colored ink.

The deadline for **VT #16** *is March 1, 1991.*

Vinyar Tengwar is produced by the editor on an Apple Macintosh II personal computer, using a LaCie Silverscan scanner, Microsoft Word 4.0 and Aldus PageMaker 4.0. VT is mastered for duplication on an Apple LaserWriter II NTX.

ISSN 1054-7606

Cainen enquë

#16

March 1991

Vinyar Tengwar

© Patrick Wynne – 1980

In This Issue

Editor's Musings

Another slim issue; it seems that, apart from the furious activity connected with *I Parma* (see *E.L.F. News*), we are in a "meaningful downturn" (to borrow a euphemism from U.S. economic analysts) in Tolkienian scholarship (at least, in *printed* scholarship). This slimmer *VT*, or one only slightly larger, may become the new norm, which is perhaps not so tragic in light of the recent rise in postal rates.

Still, what this issue lacks in page-count, it more than makes up for in content. This issue we present some of the first fruit from work on *I Parma*, a very satisfying explanation of "The Associative Case" by Pat Wynne, excerpted and expanded from a paper presented at the first E.L.F. Colloquium on the Languages of Middle-earth. Also an unusual answering-machine message from Arden Smith, and an interesting look at the Finnish *Hobbit*, among other topics, in Arden's *Transitions in Translations* column.

— Carl F. Hostetter

"We did not always have grammar. In medieval England, people said whatever they wanted, without regard to rules, and as a result they sounded like morons. Take the poet Geoffrey Chaucer, who couldn't even spell his first name right. He wrote a large poem called *Canterbury Tales*, in which people from various professions — knight, monk, miller, reever, riveter, eeler, diver, stevedore, spinnaker, etc. — drone on and on like this:

> *In a somer sesun whon softe was the sunne*
> *I kylled a younge birde ande I ate it on a bunne.*

"When Chaucer's poem was published, everybody read it and said: "My God, we need some grammar around here." So they formed a Grammar Commission, which developed the parts of speech, the main ones being nouns, verbs, predicants, conjectures, particles, proverbs, adjoiners, coordinates, and rebuttals. Then the commission made up hundreds and hundreds of grammar rules, all of which were strictly enforced."

— Dave Barry, from "What Is And Ain't Grammatical", in *Bad Habits,* pp. 149–50.
(Thanks [?] to Patrick Wynne for sending this passage along)

E.L.F. News

New Members

The E.L.F. extends a hearty *mae govannen* to:

- Erin Clark   41 Fuller Street, Walkerville, South Australia 5081.
- Stanley Friesen   5035 Hayter Ave., Lakewood, CA 90712.
- Tsukusu Ito   1363-4 Kanamori, Machida-shi, Tokyo 194, Japan.
- Paula Marmor   4718 Kester Ave., #214, Sherman Oaks, CA 91403.
- Julio Lopez Perez Pº Maria Agustin, 4-6, Casa 4, 7ºA, 50004-Zaragoza, Spain.

The First E.L.F. Colloquium on the Languages of Middle-earth

The first E.L.F. Colloquium on the Languages of Middle-earth was held on Feb. 15–18, 1991 in Reseda, CA at the home of Bill and Jo Welden, with the purpose of presenting work in progress on *I Parma*, a descriptive grammar of Tolkien's invented languages. In attendance were Bill Welden, Chris Gilson, Patrick Wynne, Arden Smith, Tom Loback, Nancy Martsch, Jorge Quiñónez, and Carl Hostetter.

The weekend was a great success, as evidenced by the minimal amounts of sleep most of the participants got. Papers presented included "Phonology and Morphology in the Ancestral Quendian Tongue" by Bill Welden; "It's All the Same in a Relative Way: Notes on the Demonstrative and Relative Pronouns in Quenya" by Carl F. Hostetter; "A Comparative Analysis of the Sindarin Dialects" by Tom Loback; "The Writing Systems of Middle-earth. Part One: The Tengwar" by Arden Smith; "The Quenya Verb: A Survey and Analysis of its Structure and Inflection" by Chris Gilson; and "The Decline and Fall of the Quenya Noun" by Patrick Wynne [*VT* is pleased to present an excerpt from Pat's analysis in this issue, an explanation of "The Associative Case"].

There were of course many hours of discussion by all on these and related topics (and a few very unrelated topics, in the small hours of the morning) throughout the weekend. We also had an at-times surreal experience at a nearby Russian restaurant and lounge, complete with a Gypsy band. A splendid time was had by all.

The attendees of the Colloquium would like to express their gratitude to their most gracious hosts for allowing us to invade their home, and especially to Jo for the fine fare and for near infinite patience.

The next Colloquium will be held in conjunction with Mythcon XXII, to be held in San Diego, CA on July 26–29, 1991 (for further information on Mythcon registration write Mythcon XXII, P.O. Box 17440, San Diego, CA 92117). Those interested in becoming a contributor to *I Parma* should contact the Editor, Paul Nolan Hyde, at 2661 E. Lee Street, Simi Valley, CA 93065; or Bill Welden at 19419 Valerio St., Reseda, CA 91335.

Tolkienian Linguistic Discussion on Bitnet

Julian Bradfield, editor of *Quettar*, has begun a discussion of Tolkienian linguistics on Bitnet, an electronic network for universities and educators. Bitnet account holders can get more information at: tolklang-request@lfcs.ed.ac.uk (Julian Bradfield). Perhaps Julian (or another E.L.F. member with Bitnet access) can keep us posted on the goings-on?

Letters to VT

• Patrick Wynne   Fosston, Minnesota

Jenny Coombs had a couple questions *[see "Letters to VT" in* VT *#14 — CFH]* on my "Death of Glorfindel" text *[in* VT *#13 — CFH]* which I'd like to belatedly answer. She inquired why I "switched from the *Silmarillion*'s **Valarauko** to the *Book of Lost Tales*' **Malkarauke** to combined **Malarauko**." This does require some justification. When composing a new work in Quenya, there are two approaches one can take. One is to attempt to remain faithful to a particular "dialect" or historical stage of development (in Primary World terms), as Chris Gilson did in his Eldarissan poem "*Alqalindele*" (on the back cover of *Parma Eldalamberon #9*). Craig Marnock's prose piece "*Itarille Quete*" in *Parma #8* is another example, remaining as true as possible to *LotR*-vintage Quenya.

The other approach, and the one which I prefer in my own compositions, is to write in a sort of "Common Quenya" (to use Alexei Kondratiev's term) which borrows freely from all dialects and historical stages to equip the author with as complete an array of vocabulary and grammatical devices as possible. Since the only purpose of this Common Quenya is to serve as a literary tool in the Primary World, when one is confronted with two (or more) apparently contradictory forms it becomes a moot point as to which one Tolkien decided was valid within his Secondary World (if he ever decided at all). Thus when writing my text for "The Death of Glorfindel" and finding myself confronted with no less than *four* Quenya words for "Balrog" — **Valkaraukë/Malkaraukë** (LT1-250; ****Valarauke** in line 5 is a typo for **Valkaraukë** *[Oops! But then again, Paul Nolan Hyde's name does appear in that issue… — CFH]*), **malarauko** (LR-384, *s.v.* **RUK-**), and **Valarauko** (S-353) — I felt free to use *all* of these as synonyms. "Shocking, or charming freedom, according to taste", as Tolkien himself once said (L-343).

I should hasten to add that the use of Common Quenya in creating new Elvish compositions is not at all the same thing as "Unifism", which as a serious scholarly approach to the study of Elvish is very *much* concerned with determining which of two or more apparently contradictory forms was valid in Tolkien's final conception of his languages (although a definite determination of such points can rarely be reached).

Jenny was also puzzled by my use of **karma** 'helm'. This word appears on the back of the dust jacket of the Houghton Mifflin hardcover *Unfinished Tales*: "The cover design represents a Numenorean [*sic*] helmet (*karma*), and is taken from the original colored drawing by J.R.R. Tolkien, which he entitled: "Helmet of a captain of the Uinendili, helm made of overlapping plates of metal, the 'fish-crest' of leather embossed and colored."" To my knowledge the word **karma** occurs nowhere else in the corpus. I take it from Jenny's inquiry that it does not occur on the dust jacket of the British edition of *UT*? **Karma** might derive from the same base **KAS-** 'head' as **cassa** 'helmet' < *kas-sa, *kas-ma (LR-362), whence also **kár** (**kas-**) 'head'. But it could also derive from the base **KAR-** "make, build, construct", whence also **Karmë** 'Art' (literally *'Making'), UT-396. Thus **karma** could literally mean '*objet d'art*' — the helmet on the cover of *UT* is quite ornate.

• Arden R. Smith   Berkeley, California

Despite its slimness, *VT* #15 was (as always) an excellent issue. I found Taum Santoski's list of Elvish linguistic terms (pp. 3 and 5) an especially welcome item, since I had thought about compiling a similar sort of list. It did leave me wondering about a few things, though. Why was the *c* of *calmatéma* changed to *k* when the *c* of *certar* was retained? It also seems to me that *óman* should have been included, since the entry in *Etymologies* (LR-379, base **OM-**) reads "*óman, amandi* vowel". *Etymologies* also contains some older forms not given in the list: ON *andatektha* (whence N *andeith*; p. 391, base **TEK-**), PE **tekmē* 'letter, symbol' (whence Q *tengwa*, N *tîw*; *ibid.*), and PE **kwetta* (LR-363, base **KWET-**). The only derivative of **kwetta* listed in *Etymologies* is N *peth* 'word', but the *Silmarillion* appendix (p. 363, entry *quen-*) gives Q *quetta* and S *beth*, the lenited form of **peth* in Gandalf's "*lasto beth lammen*" (I-320).

I thought that the Neil Isaacs epigraph complemented Jorge's letter nicely by showing an opposing viewpoint, an Evil non-linguistic perspective.

Going back several issues to Edouard Kloczko's *tengwar* table on the cover of *VT* #8, no-one has mentioned any translations of the names of the letters of the *tyelpetéma* yet. Using *Etymologies*, most of them are pretty straightforward: *tyelpe* 'silver' (**KYELEP-**); *indyo* 'grandchild, descendant' (**ÑGYŌ-**); *intya* 'guess, supposition, idea' (**INK-**); *nyelle* 'bell' (**NYEL-**); *arya* 'twelve hours, day (**AR¹-**). The only name that is really debatable is *ithtyar*, which I think is probably the same as *istyar* 'scholar, learned man' (**IS-**). The value of *thty* for this letter (ᚺ) still strikes me as very odd, though; I would have expected *thy*.

• David Bratman   Menlo Park, California

The letter in which Tolkien expresses his fury at a proposed sequel to *The Lord of the Rings* is no. 292, to Joy Hill. *[See Jorge Quiñónez's letter in* VT #15; *thanks to Arden Smith and Erica Keenan who also sleuthed this letter out —CFH]* I couldn't find any subject reference to it in the index either, even after I knew the page number. Lousy indexing, I know; but having once indexed a book myself, I know how hard it is. *[Whenever I'm looking for information in either* Letters *or* Biography *I inevitably give up on their indices in disgust and just start turning the pages from front to back; this process is made especially slow (though often also fruitful) because I invariably find myself pausing to re-read especially fascinating if unrelated sections —CFH]*

With all due respect, I think Jorge has drawn the wrong generalization from Tolkien's varied reactions to his readers. It wasn't that he approved of linguistic inquiries and disapproved of literary ones, it was that he welcomed (when he had time) polite, thoughtful questions on any matter, and hated attempts by others to appropriate his inventions. Thus, Tolkien wrote happily to Rhona Beare on matters literary and theological as well as linguistic (see letter #211, for one); and was terribly flattered by a polite request to have his work evoked in a piece of music (letter #260); yet he was just as irritated at inappropriate and unauthorized use of his language (letter #258) as he was at that proposed sequel.

Tolkien's invented languages are not by themselves the key to understanding his work, though they are the single most important key to understanding the forces that drove his creativity. A knowledge of his use of languages — both real and invented ones — is necessary but not sufficient for the full appreciation of his work. T.A. Shippey's *The Road to Middle-earth* struck just the right note here.

• Nancy Martsch   Sherman Oaks, California

We Tolkien lovers and language enthusiasts in the USA do not appreciate how fortunate we are with regard to the books of the Master.

Massimo Borio of Italy writes of the recent publication of *The Letters of J.R.R. Tolkien* in Italian — under the title *La realtà in trasparenza* ("The transparent truth" [!]; see *Beyond Bree*, March 1991).

Nathalie Kotowski, writing in *Cirth de Gandalf* No. 12, January 1991, lists Tolkien's works available in French: *The Hobbit*, *The Lord of the Rings*, *The Silmarillion*, *Unfinished Tales*, *The Adventures of Tom Bombadil*, *The Father Christmas Letters*, *Faërie* (containing *Farmer Giles of Ham*, *Smith of Wootton Major*, *Leaf by Niggle*, "On Fairy Stories"), and Carpenter's *Tolkien: A Biography*. *Letters* has not been translated.

In the same *Cirth* is a letter by Natalyia Prochorova of Russia, describing how she met Tolkien's works: Until recently, *LotR* was not translated into Russian. *LotR* in English was available in the reading rooms of the big libraries in Moscow and Leningrad, but it was not sold in bookstores. Natalyia and her friends discovered it from *photocopies* of the English version — "and not the first nor the second nor even the third, where it is necessary to guess the meaning of the words...."

• Ronald Kyrmse   S. Paulo, SP – Brazil

[A] linguistic matter (in haste, since I must go on with my translation of Humphrey Carpenter's *Biography* of J.R.R. Tolkien into Portuguese [also a linguistic matter, and with a pecuniary compensation attached]): a historical grammar of Taliska is said (by Christopher Tolkien *[LR-192, footnote −CFH]*) to be in existence; shall we campaign for its publication in one of the forthcoming volumes? Would any of us Quendili be willing to miss such a thing?

[I for one would be delighted to see it. Some have dismissed Taliskan as insignificant, since it is not one of Tolkien's Eldarin tongues; however, if (as I believe) Taliskan was created by Tolkien to suggest an influence by his invented Eldarin languages on the Primary World languages of Men, fictitiously "filling in the gaps" of various Indo-European words whose etymologies are obscure, the Taliskan grammar should prove a most interesting document indeed, even to the purists among the Quendili −CFH]

• Steve Gardner   Milton Keynes, England

Linguists may be interested to know that I.C.E. have created a "Middle-earth Adventure Guidebook 2" and this includes an Elvish dictionary and glossary of terms. It is surprisingly accurate and includes a pronunciation guide and notes on grammar for Quenya and Sindarin. There is a Sindarin/Quenya to English and English to Sindarin/Quenya dictionary.

Could anyone translate "concrete cows" into Sindarin or Quenya? The best we have is ***Mundeli Sernieva***.

The Associative
A "Problematic" Quenya Noun Case Explained
by Patrick Wynne

One of the perennial hot topics among students of Elvish has been determining the functions of, and proper label for, the Quenya case marked by the suffix *-va*, which occurs in such familiar phrases as **lintë yuldar ... lisse-miruvóreva** 'swift draughts of the sweet mead' in *Namárië* and **Mindon Eldaliéva** 'Lofty Tower of the Eldalie' (S-314). Jorge Quiñónez has provided an excellent capsule history of the debate over the "Vcase" in his article "Two Problematic Quenya Noun Cases", published in *VT* #11 (May 1990). Thanks to the ever-growing body of new linguistic material being made available by Christopher Tolkien, we now have sufficient examples of the "Vcase" to form a clear picture of its origin, semantic development, and functions, as well as to finally assign it an accurate label. Of the Túrinesque abundance of names that have been proposed for this case — including "compositive", "partitive", "objective genitive", and "associative" — we will see that *associative* is the term which best encompasses the full range of its functions, all of which indicate the *association* of one noun with another, either in a genitival, adjectival, compositive, or objective sense.

On the chart of Book Quenya noun declensions sent by J.R.R. Tolkien to Richard Plotz (reproduced in transcript in Jorge's article in *VT* #11), the associative case appears in its own subgroup, labelled *c*, with singular forms **ciryava**, **lasseva** and general plural forms **ciryalíva**, **lasselíva**. No particular plural or dual forms are given.[1]

The associative was originally partitive in sense, the ending *-va* probably deriving from the base **AWA-** 'away, forth; out', whence also *ava* 'outside' and privative prefixes *au-*, *ava-* (LR-349). The base **AB-**, **ABAR-** 'refuse, deny' (glossed as 'go away, depart' in its entry as first written) must also be closely related (LR-347). This early partitive sense might explain the associative's lack of a particular plural. In Finnish the partitive case can express 'some from'; in the partitive plural the sense is 'some from a whole group', as in *he syövät omenia* 'they are eating <u>apples</u>' (*i.e.* they are eating some of all the apples there are). If the associative was originally used in a similar manner, the general plural would have been the appropriate form since it refers to the whole of a group: **ciryalíva** ***'some of all the ships there are'. Since the particular plural was originally partitive in sense (**ciryar** ***'some ships'), it would not have been used with partitive *-va* as the result would be redundant: 'some of some ships'.

---

[1] "Pl.1" on the Plotz chart is the *partitive* or *particular* plural, marked by *-r* or *-ī*. This originally meant "some": **ciryar** ***"some ships". "Pl. 2" on the chart is the *general plural*, marked by *-lī*. It meant "all" or "the whole of a group": **ciryali** ***"all ships (previously mentioned)". In Spoken Quenya this "some" *vs.* "all", particular *vs.* general distinction became blurred, and the particular plural was often used to refer to "the whole of a group", for example in race names such as **Eldar**, **Atani**, *etc.* For Tolkien's own discussion of particular and general plurals in the Eldarin languages, *cf. Letters*, p. 178.

From this original sense of 'away from' the associative developed a variety of other meanings, including 'made of' (thus *kanu* 'lead' > *kanuva* 'leaden', LT1-268) and in a broader sense 'partaking of the quality of' (thus *koi* 'life' > *koiva* 'awake', LT1-257; and *úr* 'fire' > *úruva* 'fiery', LR-396).[2] A genitival sense also arose, and *-va* was used as the regular genitive singular suffix for nouns ending in *-ie*, as in *Mindon Eldaliéva* 'Lofty Tower of the Eldalie' and *Mar Vanwa Tyaliéva* 'The Cottage of Lost Play'. This semantic development of the associative parallels that of English *of*. In Old English *of* (stressed form *æf*) originally meant 'away, away from' (*cf.* its Latin cognate *ab*, whose resemblance to the base **AB-** is unlikely to be coincidental), but it later developed senses denoting material (*a floor of wood*), quality (*a man of dignity*), and the genitive (*the capital of Minnesota*). The original sense 'away from' became obsolete, both for *of* and the associative case. These semantic and phonetic parallels are striking, and we might think of the associative case as "the *of-* case".

Associatives such as *kanuva* and *úruva* are essentially adjectival in meaning, and it appears that some such forms came to be regarded in Spoken Quenya simply as nominative singular adjectives which, like other adjectives, could be inflected for case and number. And so on the "World-ship" map (LT1-84) we find *I-Tolli Kuruvar* 'The Magic Isles' with particular plural of **kuruva* 'magical' < *kuru* 'magic, wizardry' (LT1-264). Also note the particular plural *kuluvai* 'golden' in *Narqelion*, singular **kuluva* < *kulu*, *kulo* 'gold (metal), gold (substance)' (LR-365). These particular plural forms of adjectives derived from associatives may indicate the demise of the associative's original partitive sense, or they may have been allowable due to the semantic expansion of the particular plural in Spoken Quenya to include the concept 'whole of a group'.

Although the penultimate vowels in the singular associative forms on the Plotz chart are short (*ciryava*, *lasseva*), we have examples in which these vowels are long, *e.g.* *turúva* 'wooden' < *turu* 'wood' (LT1-270) and *urúva* 'like fire' < *uru* 'fire' (LT1-271). This variation may have depended in part on the original length of the final vowel in the noun; so that **uru* > *úr*, assoc. *úruva*; *versus* *urū* > **uru* assoc. *urúva*. We can also note a similar variation in vowel length in the genitive general plural: *ciryalion* and *lasselion* on the Plotz chart *versus* *vanimálion* (III-259) and *malinornélion* (II-70).

The element *-vo-* in the adjectival suffix *-voite* appears to come from associative *-va*. This is best exemplified by the sequence *uru* 'fire' > *urúva* 'like fire' > *uruvoite* 'fiery' (LT1-271). The addition of *-ite* to *-va* seems to result in little if any change in sense. Conversely, the omission of *-vo-* from *-voite* does not alter the sense either; *cf.* *uruite* 'fiery' (LR-396). The shift from *a* > *o* in *-va* > *-voite* is curious. An *o* > *a* shift occurs in *Valarauko*, plural *Valaraukar* (S-353) and *óman*, plural *amandi* 'vowel' (LR-379). Also the form of the base **WŌ-** 'together' with a short vowel "*wŏ* would if stressed > *wa* in Eldarin" (LR-399), by which development Tolkien explains the variant prefixes *gwa-*, *go-* in Noldorin. As a prefix in Quenya the forms

---

[2] The Finnish partitive is also used to express these concepts, *e.g.* *tammi* 'oak', partitive *tammea* 'made of oak, oaken'.

*wō and **wŏ* survive in *ó-, o-* 'together', and may have contributed to the genitive suffix *-o*. Possibly a suffixed form of this element in Eldarin varied between **-wo* and **-wa* depending on the stress pattern of particular words. With the blurring of the partitive sense of the associative **-wa* (< base **AWA-** 'away') there might be a natural blending with the variant **-wa* of **-wo*/**-wa* 'together'. This could lead to a Quenya suffix *-vo* beside *-va*. When the latter became fixed in form independently of stress, the former may have survived only in a distinctive combination like *-vo-ite* (or a distinctive word like *kaivo* 'corpse').

The common adjectival ending *-wa* must be cognate with associative *-va*, and may be a variant form of it. It is often added directly to the final consonant of a root or base, *e.g.* root **KALA** 'shine golden' > *kalwa* 'beautiful' (LT1-254) and base **3EL-** 'sky' > *helwa* '(pale) blue' (LR-360). Nouns having a stem ending in a consonant may have had associative forms ending in *-wa*, added directly to the stem without the insertion of an epenthetic vowel; thus *nár* 'flame' > *narwā* 'fiery red' (LR-374). Also note *hwesta sindarinwa* 'Grey-elven *hw*' (*tengwa* 34), where *sindarinwa* is parallel to *Noldorinwa* 'Gnome' as "adjective" (LT1-262), but could also be seen as the associative inflection of the noun *Sindarin* 'Grey-elven (speech)'.

There follows a list of all extant examples of associative *-va*/*-wa* that can be identified with reasonable certainty, arranged according to use.

Associatives in *-va*

1. a. As the genitive singular of nouns ending in *-ie*:
       Mindon Eldaliéva 'Lofty Tower of the Eldalie' (S-341)
       Mar Vanwa Tyaliéva 'The Cottage of Lost Play' (LT1-14)
   b. As the genitive singular of other nouns:
       I oros valinoriva *'The Mountains of Valinor' (LT1-85; Christopher Tolkien gives the tentative reading *Toros* for *I oros*.)
2. Indicates the logical object of the action of the verbal noun:
       Nurtale Valinóreva 'The Hiding of Valinor' (S-345). *Valinor* receives the action of the verb **nurta-* 'to hide' (probably from stem **NUR-** or **NŬ-** 'down, under, deep' + transitive verb marker *-ta*; hence **nur-ta-* 'to put something under something else; to hide something').
   Perhaps also in:
       yuldar lisse-miruvóreva 'draughts of the sweet mead' (*Namárië*), assuming *yulda* 'draught' (and *yulma* 'cup') derives from a verb stem **yul-* 'to pour', perhaps related to **ULU-** 'pour, flow' (LR-396); the *lisse-miruvóre* is that which is poured in a draught *yulda*. See also Function 3 below.
3. Indicates the material or substance of which something consists:
       turúva 'wooden' < *turu* 'firewood, wood (in general)' (LT1-270 *s.v.* **Turuhalme**)
       kanuva 'leaden' < *kanu* 'lead' (LT1-268 *s.v.* **Tilkal**)
       Perhaps also in *miruvóreva* '(composed) of mead' (*Namárië*).
4. Indicates a quality of which something partakes:
       sarkuva 'corporeal, bodily' < *sarko* 'flesh' (LT2-347 *s.v.* **Sarqindi**)

kuluvai [plural *'golden (-colored)'] (*Narqelion*) < *kulu*, *kulo* 'gold (metal), gold (substance)' (*LR*-365 *s.v.* **KUL-**)

lintuilindova [*'having many swallows'] (*Narqelion*) < *tuilindo* 'swallow' (LR-369 *s.v.* **LIN²-**)

koiva 'awake' < *koi* 'life' (LT1-257 *s.v.* **Koivie-néni**)

urúva 'like fire' < *uru* 'fire' (LT1-271 *s.v.* **Ûr**)

úruva 'fiery' < *úr* 'fire' (LR-396 *s.v.* **UR-**)

huiva 'murky' < *hui* 'fog, dark, murk, night' (LT1-253, *s.v.* **Fui**).

Taure Huinéva 'Forest of Night' < *huine* 'deep shadow' (LR-382 *s.v.* **PHUY-**)

I-Tolli Kuruvar 'The Magic Isles' < *kuru* 'magic, wizardry' (LT1-269 *s.v.* **Tolli Kuruvar**)

karneva ['reddish'] (< *karne* 'red') as in *karnevalinar* [*'many reddish hues'] in *Narqelion*. For the addition of case endings to adjectives rather than nouns *cf.* ***Elendil Vorondo*** 'of Elendil the Faithful' with genitive inflection of *voronda* 'faithful' in Cirion's Oath (UT-305, 317).

tereva 'fine, acute', from earlier **terēwā* 'piercing, keen' (LR-392 *s.v.* **TER-, TERES-**). This might be the associative inflection of *tere, ter* 'through'. For the addition of case endings to prepositions *cf. minna* 'to the inside, into', allative inflection of *mi* 'in, within' (LR-373 *s.v.* **MI-**).

ciryava, general plural *ciryalíva* < *kirya* 'ship' (LR-365 *s.v.* **KIR-**); *lasseva*, general plural *lasselíva* < *lasse* 'leaf' (LR-367 *s.v.* **LAS¹-**). A precise translation and classification according to use are difficult to ascertain for these forms, since they are not glossed on the Plotz chart and do not occur elsewhere in semantic relationship with other nouns. For now we will tentatively propose the general glosses 'of (or like) a ship', 'of ships'; and 'of (or like) a leaf', 'of leaves'.

Associatives in *-wa*

narwā 'fiery red' < *nár* 'flame' (LR-374 *s.v.* **NAR¹-**). Function 4, to indicate a quality.

hwesta sindarinwa 'Grey-elven *hw*' (III-401) < *Sindarin*, language of the **Sindar** 'Grey-elves'. In LT1-259 *s.v.* **Lindelos**, Christopher notes: "GL has *glin* 'sound, voice, utterance' (also *lin* 'sound'), with the note that *-glin*, *-grin* is a suffix in the name of languages, as *Goldogrin* Gnomish." It may be that *-rin* in *Sindarin* is cognate with the Gnomish suffix *-grin*; thus *Sinda-rin* *'Grey-elven-language'. In *hwesta sindarinwa* the associative may serve Function 4, quality, or it may serve Function 1b, the genitive singular, *i.e.* *hwesta sindarinwa* is a letter belonging to the orthographic system of the Grey-elven tongue.

linyenwa 'old, having many years' < *yén* (*yen-*) 'year' (LR-400 *s.v.* **YEN-**). The first element is prefix *lin-* 'many' (*cf.* LR-369 *s.v.* **LI-**). The structure of this word, *lin-yen-wa* 'many-years-having', exactly parallels that of *lin-tuilindo-va* 'many-swallows-having' in *Narqelion*. Function 4, quality.

— *continued on page 9.*

How Do You Say "Answering Machine" in Quenya?
by Arden R. Smith

Anyone who calls my apartment when I'm not there will hear one of two answering machine messages. One is a parody of a TV commercial. The other is in Quenya. Carl suggested that I should write an analysis of it for *VT*. So here is the message:

> **Sinome mára** Arden Smith. **Sí ú-nan marasse. Queta esselya ar nótelya ar nyárelya apa i timpa, ar le enyaluvan. Hantale.**

An ultra-literal translation of this would be:

> "In this place dwelleth Arden Smith. Now not-am-I home-in. Say (imperative) name-thy and number (**nóte**, LR-378)-thy and tale (**nyáre**, LR-374)-thy after (from **Apanónar**, S-316) the hoot (*cf.* Gnomish **timp**, LT1-268) and thee (see *Parma Eldalamberon* #8, pp. 8–12) again-summon (UT-317)-shall-I. Thanks (from **Eruhantale**, UT-436)."

A more idiomatic translation would be:

> "This is the home of Arden Smith. I am not home right now. Say your name, number, and message after the beep, and I will call you back. Thanks."

When I say my name in the message, I put special emphasis (not to mention an American accent) on it, so people will know that they have reached the right number. Most of my friends expect my message to be incomprehensible anyway.

One final point needs to be mentioned. Having worked in a record store for 2 1/2 years, an answering machine without background music would be unthinkable to me. For this I chose the acoustic guitar intro from "Martha's Harbour" by a British band called All About Eve. Although the song does not mention Elves or anything that is specifically Tolkien related, the music and the lyrics seem as Elvish to me as Galadriel's Lament (the first two lines, for example, are "I sit by the harbour/ The sea calls to me").

So if you ever call me and I'm not home, you may get to hear this message. Otherwise you'll have to put up with my Sy Sperling impression.

The Associative Case   — *continued from page 8.*

> *Talka Marwa* 'Smith of the World' (LT1-266 *s.v.* **Talka Marda**), a title of Aulë. *Talka* may be an agentive derived from the base **TAK-** 'fix, make fast' (LR-389), original *Taklā 'He who constructs, makes' >*Talka* with metathesis of *kl to *lk* (*cf.* base **AKLA-R-** with Qenya derivatives *alka* 'ray of light', *alkar(e)* 'radiance, brilliance'; LR-348). Also note the related Ilkorin form *taga* 'he fixes, *constructs, makes*' given under **TAK-**. *Marwa* 'of the World' < *mar* (*mas-*) 'dwelling of men, the Earth, -land' (LT1-251 *s.v.* **Eldamar**) serves Function 2, indicating that *Mar* "the World" is the logical object of the action of the verbal noun *Talka* "Maker".

Acknowledgement

Thanks to Christopher Gilson for providing many ideas incorporated into this article, and for his help in clarifying and expanding some sections.

Transitions in Translations
A column edited by Arden R. Smith

The purpose of this column is to examine peculiarities in translations of Tolkien's works: mistranslations, unusual translations, interesting solutions to the problems of translation, and other curiosities in foreign editions. Ideas and contributions are encouraged: send them to "Transitions," c/o Arden R. Smith, P.O. Box 4395, Berkeley, CA 94704-0395, USA.

Elvish is Fin(n)ished

Regarding the first Finnish translation of *The Hobbit* (*Lohikäärmevuori*. Helsinki: Tammi, 1973), Ellen Pakarinen writes, "The translator, Risto Pitkänen, made one amusing mistake. He translated Beorn's 'clover' as 'clove', using the Finnish word *neilikka*, which means 'clove', 'carnation' or 'pink'" (*Quettar* Special Publication No. 2, p. 24). Now I don't claim to have any expertise in Finnish, but armed with Finnish dictionaries and grammars and a knowledge of Elvish I discovered that Risto Pitkänen made *more* than "one amusing mistake".

As Ellen Pakarinen notes, this Finnish translation "was treated very much as a book for children with all the names finnicized." This finnicization of the Elvish names in the book produced some very interesting results. What?! *Elvish* names *finnicized*?! Yes, it's true — sadly true. In fact, the only Elvish word which was not altered was **Orcrist**. True, the Finnish spelling is actually *Orkrist*, but that of course is acceptable. Furthermore, the only names in the book which were left *completely* unaltered were *Kili* and *Gandalf*, and neither of them is Elvish.

Some alterations were made to make the Elvish words conform to Finnish phonology. So **mithril** becomes *mitril* (Finnish has no interdental fricatives) and **cram** becomes *krami* (*m* cannot appear in final position). Since *g* only occurs after *n* and before a vowel and *d* apparently only occurs prevocalically in native Finnish words, Pitkänen transformed **Girion** into *Kirion* and **Glamdring** into *Klamtrin*, even though the *dr*-cluster and initial *g* appear in numerous loan-words in Finnish (*e.g. draama* and *geometria*). It is interesting to note that he let *Gandalf* retain a non-Finnish form, while making Sindarin names conform to Finnish phonology. That still does not explain why **Moria** became *Moira* on page 272 (= HM 3rd ed. p. 295) and *Mooria* elsewhere.

Gondolin and **Esgaroth** were not only altered to fit the phonology, but were transformed into *Kontola* and *Eskarila*; the suffix -*la*/-*lä* means 'dwelling-place' (*e.g. pappi* 'clergyman', *pappila* 'rectory'). This suffix can also be seen in *Torkviinilä*, Pitkänen's version of **Dorwinion**. This seems to be more than just a phonological alteration, though. *Tork*- seems to refer to sleep (*cf. torkahtaa* 'doze off', *torkkua* 'be drowsy') and *viini* means 'wine'.

This brings us to the last group of finnicized Elvish names: the outright translations. *Orc* is translated as *mörkö* (meaning 'bugbear, bogy') on page 137 (= HM 3rd ed. p. 149), although *goblin* is consistently *peikko*. Three Elvish proper names were also translated outright. **Galion** became *Lunki*; I wish I could figure out why. **Elrond** became *Keijukas*. Since *keiju* means 'fairy, elf, pixie', Pitkänen apparently saw the meaning 'elf' in the root *el-*. Does this mean that he understood that *el-* has the meanings 'star' and 'elf' in Elvish? I seriously doubt it, in light of the translation of **Bladorthin** as *Oikeamiekka*.

The question to ask here is: "What is the meaning of **Bladorthin** in the first place?" Even armed with *The History of Middle-earth*, the E.L.F. has been unable to figure that out (see Tom Loback's first *Essitalmar*, *VT* #4, p. 6). Did Pitkänen have some sort of gifted insight that allowed him to see the meaning of the name? Hardly. Pitkänen evidently interpreted **blad** as 'blade' (hence *miekka* 'sword') and **orthin** as 'ortho-' (hence *oikea* 'right, correct'). *Oikeamiekka* therefore means 'correct sword', a logical translation of **Bladorthin**. Logical, that is, to someone who doesn't know anything about Elvish.

Fortunately, Finnish Tolkien fans do not have to put up with this nonsense anymore. A new Finnish translation by Kersti Juva appeared in the late 1980's with the title *Hobitti* (Porvoo/Helsinki/Juva: WSOY), featuring names with proper Elvish forms like **Orkrist**, **Glamdring**, **Gondolin**, **Elrond**, **Moria**, **Esgaroth**, *etc.* (Thanks to Gary Hunnewell for supplying information from this newer translation).

* * *

A Retranslation from "Лист Работы Мелкина"
(the Russian version of "Leaf by Niggle")
by David Doughan
(*cf.* 1964 ed. pp. 87–88; 1988 ed. pp. 91–92)

One day Niggle was planting a quickset hedge, and Parish was lying on the grass with a yellow flower in his teeth. Long ago Niggle had depicted many such flowers between the roots of the tree. Mr. Parish was smiling blissfully.

"This is grand!" he said. "Thanks for putting in a word for me. I honestly didn't deserve to be sent here."

"Nonsense," replied Niggle. "I didn't say anything. Anyway, my words were of no account."

"Yes they were," said Parish. "Without you I'd never have got here at all. You see, it was that voice … you know. He said you wanted to see me. So I'm in your debt."

"No, you're in his debt. We are both in his debt," said Niggle.

So they lived and worked together. I do not know how long it went on. Sometimes they sang songs together. And the time came when the house in the hollow, the garden, the forest, the lake — everything in the picture was nearly finished, almost as it should be. The Great Tree was in blossom.

"This evening we'll finish it," said Parish, wiping the sweat from his brow. "We'll finish it and have a proper look at everything. Would you like to go for a long walk?"

Translator's comment: the names "Niggle" and "Parish" have been Russified into Мелкин *(Melkin ≈ petty) and* Прихотт *(a distortion of* приход *= parish).*

However, the characters are always referred to as "mister" or "missis", the workhouse is работный дом *(a term only used for the specifically English institution in translations of Dickens, etc.), and when greeting Parish, Niggle is actually made to say* Хэлло! *(Hello!) in English.*

Not only is the concluding pun on "Niggle's Parish" completely ignored (which makes even more nonsense of the Russification), but the Olympian laughter seems to be attributed not to Niggle and Parish but to some "higher instances" to whom this has been reported. —DD.

[David Doughan's letter accompanying the retranslation above reads as follows:]

Natalya Prohorova has sent me a photocopy of the Russian translation of *Leaf by Niggle* which appeared in Химия и жизнь 1980 no. 7, pp. 84–92 — translator: S. Koshelev. The enclosed retranslation of one excerpt will, when compared with the original, give some idea of the degree of abridgement and the "freedom" of translation. The appended note may also be of interest.

Natalya also informs me that Muravyov's translation of *The Two Towers* has at last been published. Apparently it lives down to the standards of vol. 1 — for instance, we learn of the Grand Dukes of Arnor and Gondor, and the fact that Aragorn is on his way to Minas Tirith to claim his Grand Ducal throne .... I'll let you know more when I get to see a copy (which, in the present state of the Soviet Union, may take a little time).

[Those interested in Russian translations should read David's article on the Russian translation of The Fellowship of the Ring, *"Frodo Torbins in Kvetlorien", in* Quettar #40 *(pp. 8–9), and also Nathalie Kotowski's "The Russian* Lord of the Rings*" in the Nov. 1990* Beyond Bree *(p. 4).* —ARS]

* * *

Ludvigsen gets the red out!

When the Three Hunters are discussing the significance of the White Hand on the Orcs' helmets in the Danish translation of *The Two Towers* (*De to Tårne.* Translated by Ida Nyrop Ludvigsen. København: Gyldendal, 1981), Aragorn contradicts himself, saying: "[Sauron] bruger ikke hvidt. Orkerne i Barad-dûrs tjeneste bruger det hvide øjes tegn" (p. 16). This translates as "[Sauron] does not use white. The Orcs in the service of Barad-dûr use the sign of the *White* Eye" (*cf.* II-18). Oops! The Dark Lord must have started using eye drops!

* * *

Q: What is unusual about the runic inscriptions on Thror's map in the second Finnish translation of *The Hobbit* (*Hobitti*. Porvoo/Helsinki/Juva: WSOY)?

A: These, like the runic inscriptions on the title page and in the introductory note, have actually been translated into Finnish! *A laita tárienna* to Panu Pekkanen for giving Finnish Tolkien fans runes that they can decipher without a knowledge of English and for doing it with calligraphy as good as Tolkien's own. (Thanks again to Gary Hunnewell for photocopies of the Finnish runes).

Next Issue: "Who's Afraid of the Big, Bad Gollum?" and more!

Publications of Interest

Due to space limitations, the editor cannot thoroughly review all publications received; the following reviews emphasize those publications and items which the editor feels would be of special interest to members of the Elvish Linguistic Fellowship. BIAOR = *Back Issues Available On Request.*

Beyond Bree: Newsletter of the American Mensa Tolkien SIG. Published monthly.
    Editor: Nancy Martsch. *Subscriptions to*: the editor at P.O. Box 55372, Sherman Oaks, CA 91413. *Annual subscription*: USA $10; Overseas $13. *BIAOR.*
    March 1991: Report on the first E.L.F. Colloquium on the Languages of Middle-earth.

Cirth de Gandalf: Cercle d'etudes de Tolkien en Belgique. Published bimonthly.
    Editor: Nathalie Kotowski. *Subscriptions to*: the editor at 25, rue Victor Gambier, 1180 Bruxelles, Belgium. *Annual subscription*: Belgium 400 FB, 450 FB elsewhere.
    No. 12, January 1991: Continues the presentation of Nancy Martsch's Quenya Language Lessons from *Beyond Bree,* translated into French: Leçon 12: Les trois derniers case; discussion of the sources and origins of the word *hobbit.*

Little Gwaihir: Magazine of the Tolkien Section of the Śląski Klub Fantasyki (English Edition). Published monthly.
    Editor: Paulina Braiter. *Subscriptions to*: the editor at ul. Kasztelanska 66/3, 58-314 Walbrzych, Poland. Write for subscription info.
    No. 16, February 1991: A Tolkienian language crossword puzzle!

    Nancy Martsch tells me that the Polish Edition *Gwaihirze* ('Little Gwaihir' or 'Gwaihirling') has been running her *Quenya Language Lessons* in Polish.

Mythprint: The Monthly Bulletin of the Mythopoeic Society.
    Editor: David Bratman. *Subscriptions to*: Mythopoeic Society Orders Dept., 1008 N. Monterey, Alhambra, CA 91801. *Annual subscription*: USA $7.00, add $3.00 for First Class or Canadian delivery; Overseas surface $10.00; Overseas Airmail $14.00.
    No. 127, Vol. 28, No. 1, January 1991: Review of two books that use the Welsh elegaic poem *Y Gododdin* as their inspiration.

Next Issue

Arden Smith's next *Transitions in Translations* column sounds especially intriguing, asking the musical question, "Who's Afraid of the Big, Bad Gollum?" We'll also see the start of a new column called "Words and Devices", edited by yours truly and Patrick Wynne, which will examine words in Tolkien's Secondary World languages which have Primary World cognates. Plus news, letters, and that article you've been meaning to send in but keep forgetting about....

Vinyar Tengwar

The bimonthly 'news-letters' of the Elvish Linguistic Fellowship.
A Special Interest Group of the Mythopoeic Society.

Editor: Carl F. Hostetter, 2509 Ambling Circle, Crofton, MD 21114, USA.

Proofreaders: Jorge Quiñónez and Arden R. Smith.

Masthead: by Tom Loback.

Tengwar numerals: from Lawrence M. Schoen's *Moroma* PostScript *Tengwar* font for the Mac, available on disk for $6.00 from PsychoGlyph, P.O. Box 74, Lake Bluff, IL 60044.

Subscriptions: Subscriptions are for 1 year (6 issues) and must be paid in US dollars.

$12.00   USA
$15.00   Canada (sent airmail) and Overseas surface mail
$18.00   Overseas airmail

Back issues available: Issues 1 - 7 & 9 - 16 are each $2.00 in the USA, $2.50 overseas surface mail and Canada, $3.00 airmail. Issue 8 includes a large map and costs $4.00 USA, $5.00 surface and Canada, $6.00 airmail. A complete set of back issues is available for $25.00 USA, $30.00 Overseas surface mail, and $35.00 Overseas airmail. *All costs are postpaid.*

Payments: All payments must be in US dollars. It is recommended that overseas members make payments via international postal money order.

Make all checks payable to Carl F. Hostetter.

Submissions: Written material should in some manner deal with Tolkien's invented languages. All submissions must be typed, or must be written unbelievably legibly: if I have to decipher lower-glyphics, the submission is automatically rejected! The editor reserves the right to edit any material (except art) for purposes of brevity and relevance. Ilúvatar smiles upon submissions on 400K or 800K (3.5") Macintosh or 720K (3.5") MS-DOS formatted disks in PageMaker, Microsoft Word, Microsoft Works, WordPerfect, MacWrite, DCA, or RTF formats, or as unformatted ASCII text files. Artwork should be Tolkienian in nature.

The deadline for **VT** *#17 is May 1, 1991.*

Bibliographical Abbreviations

H	The Hobbit	*LT1*	The Book of Lost Tales, Part One
I	The Fellowship of the Ring	*LT2*	The Book of Lost Tales, Part Two
II	The Two Towers	*LB*	The Lays of Beleriand
III	The Return of the King	*SM*	The Shaping of Middle-earth
R	The Road Goes Ever On	*LR*	The Lost Road
S	The Silmarillion	*RS*	The Return of the Shadow
UT	Unfinished Tales	*TI*	The Treason of Isengard
L	The Letters of J.R.R. Tolkien	*WR*	The War of the Ring
MC	The Monsters and the Critics		

Vinyar Tengwar is produced by the editor on an Apple Macintosh II personal computer, using a LaCie Silverscan scanner, Microsoft Word 4.0 and Aldus PageMaker 4.0. VT is mastered for duplication on an Apple LaserWriter II NTX.

ISSN 1054-7606

Vinyar Tengwar

Cainen otso
#17
May 1991

In This Issue

Editor's Musings

Well, now, this is more like it!

Don't let the short contents list above deceive you; from the heft of this issue it is obvious that my repeated pleas for submissions of the last several issues have brought some results. This issue is fairly brimming over with interesting and insightful (not to mention inciteful) commentary on Tolkienian linguistics. Keep up the good work!

For starters, we have several substantial letters and both a *Transitions in Translations* and an *Essitalmar*. This issue also sees the lengthy inaugural installment of a new column by Pat Wynne and myself, which we call *Words and Devices*. Each issue, *W & D* will examine the relationships of Tolkien's invented languages with those of the Primary World. And we have a gorgeous, honest-to-goodness never-before-printed rendering by Pat Wynne gracing the cover. Such a deal!

The scrutinizing reader will notice that *VT*'s quality of reproduction has improved somewhat; this is due to the fact that I have purchased a laser printer of my very own, and so can now directly print each issue myself instead of having it photocopied. I've also decided to continue the use of a larger font size introduced last issue for improved readability. Hope you like the changes.

— Carl F. Hostetter

"It is these two facts, that the relationship between form and meaning in language is an arbitrary one and that languages can only change through a succession of restricted steps, that gave significance to certain discoveries that were made by linguists some two hundred years ago when the Sanskrit language of Ancient India became for the first time fully accessible to European scholarship. Despite differences in geographical location and in the cultural content expressed through them, Sanskrit, Greek and Latin were found to exhibit such remarkable similarities in the phonological form of corresponding morphs and in the rules which govern the combination of these that descent from a common ancestor was clearly the only possible hypothesis that could account for them."

— Theodora Bynon, in *Historical Linguistics*, Cambridge, 1977, p.12.

Letters to VT

• Chris Gilson   Walnut Creek, California

Vinyar Tengwar is looking better and better. I like the larger type size this issue *[#16]*. It seems more comfortable to read, which in a way makes the contents more accessible and comprehensible, even if the word-count is smaller than last issue. *[I agree, and so will continue the practice —CFH]*. I suspect that the "meaningful downturn" in Tolkienian scholarship that you infer is, for *VT* at least, little more than a seasonal lull. *[This issue seems to bear that out; but keep those submissions coming! —CFH]*

I am inclined to agree with Jorge that the only "true way" to understand Tolkien's art "is to have a firm understanding of his invented languages" (*VT* 15:2). David Bratman clarifies what Tolkien would "have approved of" (*VT* 16:3), but with his further point I can only partly agree. Yes, Tolkien's language invention was one of the key "forces that drove his creativity". But no, it is not true that "knowledge of his use of languages — both real and invented" would be insufficient for the "full appreciation of his work". Well, granted, there are his paintings and drawings. But aside from these *all* of Tolkien's work is a "use of language". An English-speaking scholar would normally consider knowledge of an author's use of English to be the substance of appreciating his work rather than a "key" to it. Jorge's point seemed to be that the use of Quenya and Sindarin, between writer and reader who both have mastered them (to the extent we all have mastered English as a language), would function in the same manner. In this sense true understanding can be achieved only if the reader's knowledge of the uses of Elvish be advanced to the state of the author's.

A scholar trying to explain the characterization of Galadriel must appreciate the significance of those English sentences she is depicted as uttering, and *also* the significance of the Quenya poem she recites. The latter sort of understanding is a "key" in the sense that it is an essential piece of the structure which is frequently missing from its analysis. Just as clearly as the English does, the Elvish sentences have precise and evocative meanings, and are deliberately included in the story because of those meanings. My own impression is that the invented languages are integral to all of the most significant parts of the story. But I admit to a personal bias in this area. And ironically interest in Elvish *per se* is a powerful distraction from studying its actual significance as incorporated in Tolkien's stories, though the one activity is a necessary precursor to the other.

That reminds me (rather obliquely) of Arden's remark (*VT* 16:11) about the meaning of the name **Bladorthin** in *The Hobbit*. He alludes to Tom Loback's inconclusive survey (*VT* 4:6) of prior opinion and possibly relevant Doriathrin (***orth*** 'mountain', pl. ***orthin***) and Gnomish forms (*e.g.* **bladwen** 'plain', LT2:244). I wonder if the fact that the name was originally applied to the character of Gandalf is significant. (This is mentioned by Carpenter, *Biography*, p. 178, which reference I found by consulting the index under 'Gandalf'. *[Also, Christopher Tolkien discusses* **Bladorthin** *in his Foreword to the 50th Anniversary edition of* The Hobbit, *pp. iii–iv —CFH]*) As the name of the wizard this seems more likely to be *blador-thin* with *thin* = 'grey' after all. Could *blador*, formally present in *Bladorwen*, *Ivon i-Vladorwen*, names for Yavanna Palúrien, glossed 'the wide earth, the world and its plants and fruits, Mother Earth' (LT1:264, 273), also be an agent noun *blador* 'wanderer, ranger, pilgrim'? This would have the same suffix as *nandor* 'farmer' (*ibid.*:261), *bachor* 'pedlar' (LR:372), *Menelvagor* 'Swordsman of the Sky' (I:91), *etc.*

I cannot see the reason for Tom's protesting Jorge and Ned's view of *Carnil*, *Luinil*, *Nénar* and *Lumbar* (*VT* 13:16, *re VT* 12:13–14, *re* S:48). He makes a joke about Sindarin *Borgil* but fails to notice the obvious discrepancy between it and *Carnil* if they are so closely parallel as he suggests. Surely the fact that we have *borgil* < *born-gil* (L:426-27) means that we would get **cargil* < *carn-gil*. This is reason enough to look for a Quenya explanation of *Carnil* and the possibility that they suggested (allusively) of *carne* 'red' + *il* 'star' still seems possible. Their reason for hypothesizing that these four star-names are Quenya is not "bias", but the simple observation that the next two names in the same list and the constellation names in the same sentence are all unambiguously Quenya and not Sindarin: *Alcarinque*, *Elemmíre*, *Wilwarin*, *Telumendil*, *Soronúme*, *Anarrima*, *Menelmacar* and *Valacirca*. This does not *prove* that *Lumbar*, *etc.* are also Quenya, but surely it is further grounds for such an hypothesis. ("Context, context, context ..." *VT* 6:9.)

Please note by the way that that was "*an* hypothesis". As the *OED* puts it "most writers" use this fuller form of the indefinite article before *h* in an unstressed syllable. This reminds me that someone has systematically altered the title of my Quenya word-list from the correct *An High-elven Glossary* to the colloquial *A High-elven Glossary* (*VT* 12:14). Now I defend everyone's right to use their own favorite colloquialisms irregardless of the chagrin of others, but I find it a little bit irritating (if not inflammatory *[or ritating —CFH]*) to be systematically misquoted, especially after all the trouble I went to to determine what the proper stress-pattern for *high-elven* would be under the rules inferrable from the *OED*.

Getting back to the Elvish I cannot see that Tom's "gloomy-home" (*VT* 13:16) has anything to recommend it *over* "shadows" (*VT* 12:14) as an interpretation of a star name *Lumbar*. (Neither seems especially appropriate.) Tom notes the parallel in the endings of *Lumba̠r* and *Néna̠r* which may be significant, especially considering the analogous pairing of *Carnil* and *Luinil*. *Lumbar* might contain *-nar* if it has *mb* < *bn*. This combination shows sporadic metathesis, so that for example under **STAB-** we have both **stabnē* and **stambē*. The element *-nar* would presumably be Q *nár(e)* 'flame'. If *Lumbar* actually stands for *lub-nar* then the first element may be from **DUB-** 'lie heavy, loom', whence (without metathesis) *lumna* 'lying heavy, burdensome, oppressive, ominous'. With regular *b* > Q *v* this **DUB-** is apparently also the source of *QL* **LUVU** with *luvu-* 'lower, brood', *lumbo* 'dark, lowering cloud', *etc*. This group would naturally blend with original *lum-* in *lumbe* 'gloom, shadow'. But it is the idea of *looming*, or hanging about when one ought to be moving along, which fits the planet Saturn. Its planetary motion is relatively slow and so seemingly ponderous.

Again in the case of *Luinil* it seems more likely to be Quenya than Sindarin. Tolkien's explanation of why we have *Borgil* rather than **Bornil* from *born + gil* is that "in S. initial *g* was retained in composition, where a contact *n* + *g* occurred". This would cover the *luin-(g)il* Tom proposes (*VT* 13:16), and implies that we should have **Luingil* if the name were Sindarin. But I cannot agree with Jorge and Ned that *Luinil* = Neptune. The list of six names follows the description of Varda making "new stars and brighter against the coming of the Firstborn" (S:48), *i.e.* brighter than the stars she created at the beginning, before the time of the Two Trees. The planets Uranus and Neptune just do not fit this, whether visible to keen-sighted Elves or not. I suspect that this is why Tolkien abandoned the tentative identification of *Nénar* as Neptune, not that he was hesitating between Neptune and Uranus.

The simplest hypothesis to consider next (retaining the manuscript identification of *Karnil*, *Lumbar*, *Alkarinque* and *Elemmíre* as planets) is that *Luinil* and *Nénar* are fixed stars with brightness comparable to the brighter planets. The obvious prime contenders based on this criterion (given that Sirius is mentioned explicitly later) are Vega and Capella, respectively. These are both visible in the sky when Orion is rising. The identity of *Nénar* seems to be clinched by the fact that the Latin name *Capella* (diminutive of *Capra*, the feminine of *caper*) means 'she-goat', and in *QL* we have *nyéni* 'she-goat', *nyéna-* 'lament' from either **NYE(NE)** 'bleat' or **NYEHE** 'weep'. The star is also called *signum pluviale* because it rises in the rainy season. And in the form *Capra* it was sometimes identified with Amalthea, a nymph who fed Jupiter with goat's milk, or the goat herself, one of whose horns broken off became the *Cornu Copiae*. How all this relates to Elven mythology, and presumably to the Vala *Nienna*, is far from clear, and may have been merely incipient. We can provide an oblique connection for her, starting with *nainie* 'lament', albeit unsure whether or not base **NAY-** is related to or was somehow blended with **NEI-** 'tear', **NYEHE** 'weep', **NYE(NE)** 'bleat', *nen-* 'water', **NENE** 'flow', *Nienna*, *Nénar*, *Aldudénie* 'Lament for the Two Trees', *etc*. A connection with Latin *naenia*, *nēnia* 'funeral song, song of lamentation, dirge; incantation; lullaby' is certainly evocative. There is also a Roman goddess of funeral songs, *Nenia*, who had a chapel by the Viminal gate on the north-western edge of Rome.

One last lingering bit of controversy to which I must add a little bit of wisdom. Craig and Tom seem to have lost each other in trying to decide what is or is not a reasonable interpretation of *Aredhel* (*VT* 11:15, 20, *re VT* 10:14–15). I admit to being biased by the inadvertent humor of "Lady Wentforth". Still I have to agree with Craig's objection to *dh = d + h*, and so perhaps I can articulate it for him (and for Tom). Tolkien states in App. E I: "**DH** represents the voiced (soft) *th* of English *these clothes*". He gives no qualifications, no exceptions, no caveats. Nor would it make any sense for Tolkien to use this spelling if the sound combination *d + h* occurred regularly in Sindarin. ("Context, context, context …") Sindarin words can end in *d* and begin in *h* so why would the combination not occur in compounds? Clearly the answer is that some phonological rule for compounds alters either the *d* or the *h* into some other sound when they come into contact. Tolkien has not supplied an obvious example, but we may discover one.

Among the Noldorin forms under bases beginning with **KH** (LR:363–4), the following compounds are mentioned. (I indicate where the second element seems to begin by adding a hyphen if Tolkien has not already supplied one and indicate the closest relative in parentheses:) *or-chel* (*hall*); *Borth-andos* (*handos*, see **BOR-**); *i-rass*, *i-chrass*, *Go-chressiel* (*rhass*); *Bara-chir* (*hir*); *Alf-obas* (*hobas*); *Glam-hoth* (*hoth*). There is a clear tendency for primitive **KH** (the major source of initial *h* in Noldorin and Sindarin) to remain as *ch*. It disappears following another voiceless fricative, *th* or *f* (or *s* as *Lossoth* < *loss-hoth* shows, R:70). The reason for this retention of the fricative in general (*Barachir*, *Gochressiel*, *etc.*) is that some compounds were formed in Old Noldorin before the shift of ON *kh* > N *h* at the beginning of words. In these compounds N *ch* is a survival of ON *kh* without change in pronunciation, just a different transliteration. Thus ON *khalla* > N *hall* beside ON *orkhalla* > N *orchall* > *orchel* (LR:363, 379). This led to a rule relating separate words in *h-* to combining forms in *-ch-*, which is generalized to new compounds. Thus a strong possibility to start with is that *-d* + *h-* at the boundary in compounds could produce *-dch-* though further change may have occurred. This is in any case an indication of *why* the sound sequence might never occur, leaving the spelling *dh* available. Note that N *echui*(*w*) is derived from **et-kuiwē* (LR:366), where initial *e-* is cognate with the prefix *ed-* elsewhere in Noldorin. I suspect that similar compounds led by analogy to an apparent rule that *d* + *ch* > *ch*. And there may be one example of this in *Forochel* the "Ice Bay" where the Lossoth live in the North (III:321), so *forod* + *hell* 'frost, ice' > *Foro*(*d*)*chel* seems likely, with the (*c*)*hel-* of *Helluin* 'Sirius'.

Going back to Tom's difficulty with the canonical *Aredhel* 'Noble Elf' which Christopher Tolkien gives in the index to *The Silmarillion*. First he says, "sufficient as far as it goes, but telling little story" (*VT* 10:14). Then when Craig balks at the phonology, Tom says, "From the contextual point of view *Aredhel* cannot be simply 'High-elf' as this is a given as the high-born daughter of Fingolfin" (*VT* 11:20). I think the urgency of the matter has grown in the telling, but this only shows that if you do not look for a story in the words *Noble Elf* you will not find one. (*Went Forth* is pretty general for the name of an Exiled Noldo, too. It really depends on the interpreter supplying the context.)

Aredhel's privileges and problems all center around her position in the family. She is *the* princess of the House of Finwë, until Galadriel comes along. In Gondolin she is the preeminent Lady, since Turgon's queen is dead, and arguably more *noble* than any but he, since Turgon has no son, and she outranks Idril according to the precedent of Maedhros yielding the leadership of the Noldor to Fingolfin as the elder. But she is also in a sense *too* noble to start a house of her own with anyone available, until she leaves Gondolin to find an *aran* of her own. These are only the trappings of *nobility*, though they certainly connect the character of Aredhel with the meaning of her name. But she also performs the ultimate act of *nobility* in laying down her life for the life of another (S:138). That she does this without thinking and the life saved is her son's explains the action but does not diminish the appropriateness of the name **Aredhel** in the accepted sense. The only other Noldo whose self-sacrifice to this degree is recorded, is Finrod, and he was returning a favor.

Of course **Aredhel** cannot be the name given by her mother as such. But it could be a rerendering of the actual name given into the later language. If the interpretation of its "story" given above is correct, it has a sort of ideal qualification of this type of name, a double sense with a twist, perceiving the *noble* bearing and beauty, while forseeing the *noble* action. I think this vindicates Tom's idea of categorizing names by whether they are given names or nicknames. But I think it is becoming clear that one must start from a solid theoretical idea of the possible etymologies of the name before trying to use the circumstances of its giving to arbitrate or refine such theories.

And given that caveat, I would finally admit that the meanings 'beside, outside' for *ar-* (S:356, LR:349) are worth considering. **Aredhel** 'outside elf' makes sense if the prefix is understood as like an adjective, *i.e.* 'elf from the outside' (or 'elf who is outside'). But this makes more sense as an *epessë* given by the Ilkorins, than as a Noldorin reference to her leaving Gondolin. (A name like *Outsider* if understood in meaning but not in significance would hardly catch on.) Possibly as an Ilkorin interpretation of a Noldorin name we can view **Aredhel** both ways. This fits other circumstantial linguistic factors: In the sense 'noble', N *ar-* corresponds to Dor. *gar-* (from **3AR-** *cf.* N *aran* 'king', *ardh* 'realm', Dor. *garth* 'realm', *garon* 'lord', LR:360), but from **AR-** the prefix *ar-* in Quenya and Ilkorin has local sense 'outside', but in Noldorin is privative, *i.e.* 'without' = 'not having'. So it would be natural on hearing the name **Aredhel** for Noldor and Ilkorins to perceive the meaning of the prefix in completely different but appropriate ways.

● Craig Marnock   Kirkcudbrightshire, Scotland

In *VT* #14's letters, Jenny Coombs talks about derivation *vs.* inflexion in the *-ll-* of **Silmarillion** and **Altariello**. Her discussion assumes that the plural morpheme in **Silmarillion** is the *-i* form and not the *-li* form. But, it occurred to me as I read this, the *-i* plural is a partitive form, referring to a specific number of whatever it is. Since there were only ever three Silmarils, if you were talking about more than one of them, you meant either two or three. Two Silmarils would probably be expressed by the dual plural, and three by the general plural, as we are talking about all of them, and not a specific portion thereof (which is what a partitive means). I'm not sure if this has any relevance to Jenny's argument, but it seemed like an interesting grammatical point.

However, it was more her form for *Altariello* that interested me. She suggests that the uninflected form *Altáriel* was derived from *__rig-__ + *selde*, but this would lead to *-ld-* where the form has *-ll-*. There is a further, and I think greater, problem with *selde* being the second element, in that Jenny here suggests that *g + s > Ø*, which doesn't seem very likely for Quenya between two vowels.

Also I would point out that she gives the genitive form of the name as *Altáriello* with a long vowel, but Tolkien actually gives it as *Altariello*, with a short vowel. This shows (*cp.* *vanimálion*) the lengthening due to stress of an originally long vowel (CE *galatā) as Nancy Martsch originally suggested; the vowel is short in the inflected form as that syllable does not receive the primary stress. I think this would support the idea that the doubling of the *-l-* is due to stress.

I have a few comments also on the major article in *VT* #14, "The Elves at Koivienéni", by Chris Gilson and Pat Wynne. The analysis was certainly impressive (to the extent that any comment upon it can't help but appear carping), but for a mere eleven words of Elvish it does seem a trifle excessive.

ando: Adverbs in *-o*. I am not wholly convinced that this is as regular a "pattern of derivation" as is suggested. *Oio* is also translated by Tolkien as 'an endless period', showing that its meaning is not wholly or even primarily adverbial, and in *Oiolossë* it is modifying *lossë* and glossed 'ever'. This is the gloss given to *oi* in *The Etymologies*, from which *oia* is derived — not the other way around as is suggested. Examples from Arctic also are poor evidence; I would hesitate to make a case which drew half of its examples from such a disputed source. (Obviously I'm in a minority here though ....)

kakainen: The *-n* is unusual but I feel that the first suggestion — a plural past tense marker — is much stronger than the second, mainly because the literal 'for to have lain' simply does not make grammatical sense in the sentence. The morpheme *-ne* in *Oilima Markirya 2* (MC:213–14) is surely a present participle marker — every occurrence except *valkane* is translated by a form in *-ing*, and a past infinitive would not make sense in every case ('the pale phantoms in her cold bosom like gulls to have whined'?).

Also *enyalien* is not a good comparison here — *enyalien* is governing a direct object (*alcar*), as Tolkien points out in his own note to himself, and this is not the case here (pun not intended). The inflexion used in the "Secret Vice" poems to "express the *means* by which an action is accomplished" is *-nen*, as in later Quenya. The dative as we know it does not appear, the closest being a kind of partitive in **-n* found in passive formations (*vean falastanéro*), with clearly related forms in **-ën* and **-ndon*.

loralyar: It is suggested that this is either a verb or an adjective, depending on the gloss for *kakainen*. I would suggest that it might also be a noun, *'the sleepers', plural of *loralya, 'one who is asleep'. Thus 'The Elves, the sleepers, were lying long ...'. I was somewhat bemused by the statement that "we cannot insist on a strict distinction between adjective and verb in every context in Quenya". This lends itself to several possible interpretations, and I am not sure which was intended here. But

I would point out that we should not mistake semantic (poetic) ambiguity, that was intended by the author, with a lack of syntactic understanding, which is purely the result of ignorance on our part.

Orome: I was struck by the treatment given to the different accounts of the coming of Orome upon the elves, particularly the statement "We can rectify these discrepancies only so far." Why should we wish to "rectify" any of Tolkien's work at all, much less read things into several chronologically separated conceptions of the same event that presumably weren't intended (since Tolkien did not intend to publish *The Book of Lost Tales*)?

erenekkoitan(n)ie: With *tk > kk* in Quenya, *cp.* *Ekkaia*, the Encircling Sea, which looks like *et + caia* 'fence', cognate of S. *cai*.

The ultimate derivation of **ekkoitan(n)ie* is interesting, but I feel it falls down for the same reason as the second suggestion for *kakainen* — that it does not make sense. It is suggested that it is a past gerundial, in which case its meaning would be 'having awakened', as I understand it. This would mean that the sentence would read "Orome came thither that (he) them having awakened", which is plainly not grammatical.

The evidence given for the identification of **ekkoitan(n)ie* is very weak, based on a doubtful derivation for *Atalantie*: "it seems ... that the 'normal' abstract noun formation in *-n-ie* is historically identical with the past tense gerundial infinitive" .... Really? Where's the citation to back this up? The identification referred to in the above quote appears to have been done on a 'looks like a duck' basis (it's got an *n* in it and it ends in *ie* — past tense plus infinitive/gerundial, right?) — but in this case it fails to quack like a duck. There is an *-s* in *writes* and an *-s* in *writers*, but I have no difficulty in telling them apart, and I presume an Elvish speaker would have a similar lack of difficulty in differentiating the *-ie* in *laurie* from that in *enyalie*, from that in *avánier*, and from that in *sarnie*. A reluctance to accept this pervades the article, and leads to the cavalier redefinition of forms, such as *utúlien*, which is, we are told, now apparently an "idiomatic usage".

The gloss given for **ekkoitan(n)ie* is apparently "might awake". If *-ie* is here marking the past tense, then **-n(n)-* might perhaps be a subjunctive or optative (or similar) marker. Of course, this suggestion requires acceptance of the heretical notion that Tolkien was capable of changing his mind occasionally....

Lastly, the *e-* in the form. A possible gloss in 'he' is given, by a linguistic slight of hand I don't quite follow. But the evidence might be that "he" appears in the text translation but not the alternative, and that a form *e* meaning 'he' appears in the (Sindarin) letter to Sam in the unpublished Epilogue to *LotR*.

As for the quote on the editorial page of *VT #15*: I don't think we need to pay much attention to this, as it is in error. The creative conception of the trilogy has nothing to do with philology, but everything to do with his publisher's desire for a sequel to the successful *Hobbit*. Of course, it has an awful lot of importance to the conception of the mythos that the trilogy came to be based in ... but this is not the same thing.

With regard to Pat Wynne's letter in *VT* #16: Factually, **karma** does indeed appear on the dust-jacket for *UT*, as published by Unwin & Allen, as the hardback was originally, but nowhere else. I have a paperback *UT* and only noticed the word when looking at a friend's hardback copy.

Impertinently, Pat says that 'Unifism' is "concerned with determining which of two … forms was valid in Tolkien's final conception". I have to say, I have yet to notice any validity being bestowed on one form or another, but rather increasingly complicated examinations being offered which would allow both to be valid.

I thought Steve Gardner's suggestion of **Mundoli Sarnieva** for 'concrete cows' rather good (though I presume his handwriting was more problematic *[Oops! Right you are; I should have caught that −CFH]*). There is a word **tarukko**, **tarunko** meaning 'bull' in *LT2*, but I think nothing meaning 'cow' or 'cattle' anywhere in the corpus. Not knowing anything about building, I don't know what would be best for 'concrete' — perhaps **o-sarnië*, **o-zarnië*, after **olassië**.

I enjoyed Pat's article on forms in *-va et al.*, but I really felt it left out the question of what this declension is used for in Quenya.

I think the term *associative* is as good as any (it seems to have a different field of application from language to language, as far as I can tell), but I think the key to understanding its semantic field lies in its not having a partitive or dual form.

Pat suggests that this is due to its having originally been a partitive, but the entry **3Ŏ-** in *Etymologies* has "This element is found in the old partitive in Q *-on*". As Tom Loback said in an earlier *VT*, this implies that Quenya had both an old and a new partitive *[well, not really, any more than the statement "This element is found in the old dual in (Old) English* wit*" implies that (Modern) English has a new dual — CFH]* — and also, I would say, that *-va* was not *originally* a partitive, as suggested.

The question is, I think, that if you can say 'the hiding of Valinor' (**Nurtale Valinóreva**), why not 'the hiding of the ships' (**Nurtale **Ciryavar**) or 'the hiding of my hands' (**Nurtale **Mányavat**)? Only being able to answer these questions would tell us what kind of an inflexion we have here.

On a side note, I would question the derivation of the *Book of Lost Tales* suffix *-voite* as being from *-va/-wa*. There are four forms given: **uruvoite**, **wanwavoite** 'windy', **rámavoite** 'having wings', and **mavoite** 'having hands'. I would suggest that *-voite* means something specific as a suffix to nouns, and is not merely *-va + -ite*, not least because of the phonology — *-a + -i > -oi* would not merely be 'curious' in Q(u)enya, but unique. Pat was perhaps misled by **uruvoite**, **uru** and **urúva** appearing in the same group and reading them as a "sequence".

By the way, sitting with the Plotz declension beside me as I wrote the above, I noticed that no dual plural form is given for the 'S-case' either. I wonder if this might be because this inflexion is an inessive, like **-r* in the early "Secret Vice" poems, where *-sse* is purely locative (*i.e.* 'in, inside' *vs.* 'at, on'). Consequently it wouldn't be possible to be inside a pair of things, as you'd have to be between them (… tho' I notice this fails the 'hands' test, as above). Any thoughts?

• Paul Nolan Hyde Simi Valley, California

Dear Carl,

I have good Vinyar and bad Vinyar. The good Vinyar is that I was delighted to read about the recent E.L.F. Colloquium on the Languages of Middle-earth held in the home of Bill and Jo Welden in February. I think that great progress was made.

The bad Vinyar is that I thought I was there, but (alas) no mention was made of the ubiquitous PNH who, in his unrivaled arrogance and curmudgeonliness could not possibly be mistaken for anyone else. As I went down the list of attendees, I tried to imagine who you might have confused me with.

Could it have been Bill Welden? No, his affable style of directing the affairs of the Colloquium could not possibly be mistaken for my endless egregious punneries and distressing surly remarks.

How about Chris Gilson? How *about* Chris Gilson? Surely at the moment when I went for Chris' jugular vein in the middle of a discussion about the *sublime present tense of the pituitary case*, I could not be mistaken for anyone else; the puncture marks should have been a dead giveaway.

Might it have been Patrick Wynne? I think not. Patrick's cherubic features are unmistakably his own. Besides, the touch of Fosston Frostbite on the end of his cute little nose made him doubly unique.

Well, there is always Arden Smith. Yes, but to equivocate his earnestness with my austere dogmatism would be no great compliment to either party. Besides, Arden was the one carving Thror's Moonrunes into Jo's coffee table; I forgot my pocketknife.

Tom Loback was there. Significantly so, but to mistake his thick eastern accent for my mellifluous tones would be to self-accuse our editor with a bad case of auditorio-sclerosis along with his evident blindness.

And anyone who suggests a confusion with Nancy Martsch gets a brick for lunch, although the Mensa Lady is a charming and a winsome lass.

I might understand a mistaken identity with Jorge Quinonez. I mean, after all, we are both human,.... I guess. Jorge, however, was the one making nacho cheese sauce with the block of Velveeta™ and the BIC Click. I was the one using the soldering iron.

Now we come to the *coup de grace*. If all of the personae are accounted for, it must mean that *you* were not there, notwithstanding the paper supposedly given entitled, "It's All the Same in a Relative Way: Notes on the Demonstrative and Relative Pronouns in Quenya". I know that this was a rip off of *my* paper, "It's all in the Plane in Bodago Bay: Notes on the Monsters and other Relatives in Kenya". Admittedly, my paper didn't mention much about Tolkien except for the part about the wilting eucalyptus tree, but to be completely ignored for my contributions.... Well!

I hope that you print all of this without all of those loopy hard bracket inserts which shunt off precious readership energy dedicated to *my* prose. The least you could do is to allow me to have my own curly brackets inside of your hard bracket remarks. Something like: [Paul Nolan Hyde is full of {light, truth, and wisdom and has no greater joy than to serve CFH his daily bowl of} prunes]. See how much better that works?

The Malaise boys, Leo and Bob, are somewhat miffed as well about not being touted for their attendance. After all, the poet laureate of *VT* cannot be snubbed with impunity. J.E.C. Kelson, another presenter at the conference, is thinking of sending his cousin Louis "The Adjective" Frizetti looking for you.

In all seriousness, I did enjoy the Colloquium and felt that we went a long way towards establishing the basic ground rules for writing about Tolkien's great gift to us.

[Well, Paul, what can I say, except that I'm very sorry and very embarrassed, and that my brain obviously had not yet returned from Los Angeles as I typed that report; for the record, Paul was very much in attendance (obviously more so than were my own addled wits), and his guidance and suggestions as the Editor of I Parma *were indispensable; to have overlooked his presence and his contributions is unconscionable. Mea maxima culpa.*

By the way, has anyone else noticed that Leo and Bob are also the names of two malicious psychopaths on the television show Twin Peaks, *who...what's that? Oh, just a moment, my wife says that someone named Louis is at the door asking for me ....]*

Pat Wynne's
Top 10 Reasons
Why People Study Elvish

---

10. Study of real languages "just too darned hard".
9. Enjoy snickering over "naughty" elf-words like **yurine** and **Teleporno**.
8. Great perks, like always having a cafeteria table all to yourself at Mythcon.
7. Hoping for prestigious appointment to post of U.S. Ambassador to Tol Eressëa.
6. Misunderstood guidance counselor who advised a career in entomology.
5. Tired of watching "Wheel of Fortune" with the other guys in the psych-ward.
4. Babes are really hot for a guy who can explain lenition.
3. Simply obeying orders from space aliens relaying radio messages through dental fillings.
2. He was the greatest rock and roll star of all time (sorry, that's a reason why people study *Elvis*).
1. A fuller understanding of pretend fairy-languages will help balance the Federal budget and bring about world peace.

Words and Devices

A column by Carl F. Hostetter and Patrick Wynne

"It is said also that these Men had long ago had dealings with the Dark Elves east of the mountains, and from them had learned much of their speech; and since all the languages of the Quendi were of one origin, the language of Bëor and his folk resembled the Elven-tongue in many words and devices." (S:141)

Apologia

The purpose of this column is to examine words and other linguistic features of Tolkien's Secondary-World languages that have apparent cognates and analogues in the languages of the Primary World. It is not surprising that such relationships might exist; after all, Tolkien intended Middle-earth to be our own earth, and his mythology originally included the idea that Tol Eressëa would become England, and that it was visited by the Anglo-Saxon mariner Ælfwine, who wrote chronicles in Old English.

In fact, the quote from *The Silmarillion* given above is but one in a long series of similar accounts detailing the Eldarin origins of the languages of Men, beginning with the earliest story of the Awakening of Men in *The Book of Lost Tales*, where the Dark Elf Nuin awakened Ermon and Elmir, the first Men, and "taught them much of the Ilkorin tongue, for which reason he is called Nuin Father of Speech." (LT1:236) Other expressions of this concept are found in the *Sketch of the Mythology*, the *Quenta*, the *Later Annals of Beleriand*, the *Lhammas* and *Lammasethen*, and the *Quenta Silmarillion*. The most detailed and explicit of these accounts is that given in the *Lhammas* (LR:179):

> The languages of Men were from their beginning diverse and various; yet they were for the most part derived remotely from the language of the Valar. For the Dark-elves, various folk of the Lembi, befriended wandering Men in sundry times and places in the most ancient days, and taught them such things as they knew. But other Men learned also wholly or in part of the Orcs and of the Dwarves;* while in the West ere they came into Beleriand the fair houses of the eldest Men learned of the Danas, or Green-elves. But nought is preserved of the most ancient speeches of Men, save of the tongue of the folk of Bëor and Haleth and Hádor. Now the language of these folk was greatly influenced by the Green-elves, and it was of old named *Taliska*, and this tongue was known still to Tuor, son of Huor, son of Gumlin, son of Hádor, and it was in part recorded by the wise men of Gondolin, where Tuor for a while abode. Yet Tuor himself used this tongue no longer, for already even in Gumlin's day Men in Beleriand forsook the daily use of their own tongue and spoke and gave even names unto their children in the language of the Gnomes. Yet other Men there were, it seems, that remained east of Eredlindon, who held to their speech, and from this, closely akin to Taliska, are come after many ages of change languages that live still in the North of the earth.

---

* The assertion here that the languages of Men were influenced by three different races — Elves, Orcs, and Dwarves — is reminiscent of the tripartite division of tongues by Leibniz into Japhetic (Indo-European), Hamitic (Egyptian, Libyco-Berber, and Kushitic), and Semitic, so called after the three sons of Noah (Genesis 10-11).

We learn in this passage that *Taliska* was the name of "the tongue of the folk of Bëor and Haleth and Hádor", heavily influenced by the language of the Danas, or Green-elves. This Mannish speech is also referred to as *Taliskan* in the *Lammasethen* and its accompanying *Tree of Tongues*. Taliskan was clearly an important language to Tolkien, for Christopher Tolkien tells us that his father actually produced "an historical grammar" of this tongue (LR:192, footnote). The nature of Taliskan's importance becomes evident in the following passage from the *Quenta Silmarillion* (c. 1937–1938):

> Felagund drew nigh among the trees to the camp of Bëor and he remained hidden, until all had fallen asleep. Then he went among the sleeping men, and sat beside their dying fire, where none kept watch; and he took a rude harp which Bëor had laid aside, and he played music upon it such as mortal ear had never heard. For Men as yet had no masters in such arts, save only the Dark-elves in the wild lands. Now men awoke and listened to Felagund as he harped and sang; and they marvelled, for wisdom was in that song as well as beauty, so that the heart grew wiser that hearkened to it. Thus it was that Men called King Felagund, whom they met first of all the Noldor, Gnome or Wisdom;* and after him they named his race the Wise, whom we call the Gnomes.
>
> *Footnote to the text:* It is recorded that the word in the ancient speech of these Men, which they afterwards forsook in Beleriand for the tongue of the Gnomes, so that it is now mostly forgotten, was *Widris. Against this is written in the margin:* quoth Pengolod. *Added to this:* & Ælfwine.

Concerning the Taliskan word **Widris**[†] 'Wisdom' Christopher Tolkien notes (LR:279):

> Whereas in *The Silmarillion* the word in the language of the people of Bëor for 'Wisdom' was *Nóm* (see IV.175), here it is *Widris*, and it can hardly be doubted that this is to be related to the Indo-European stem seen, for instance, in Sanskrit *veda* 'I know'; Greek *idein* (from **widein*) 'to see' and *oida* (from **woida*) '(I have seen >) I know'; Latin *vidēre* 'to see'; Old English *witan* 'to know' and *wāt* 'I know' (> archaic *I wot*), and the words that still survive, *wit, wise, wisdom*.

The Indo-European stem referred to by Christopher Tolkien is **weid-** 'to see', and we can also add its derivatives Greek ἴδρις 'knowing, skilfull' and Old Norse *vítr* 'wise' to the list of forms resembling **Widris**. Since Taliskan was greatly influenced by the tongue of the Green-elves, we should also expect to find words similar in form and meaning to **Widris** among the Elvish languages, all of which sprang from a common ancestor. Thus in the *Etymologies* among the derivatives of the base **ID-** we find the Noldorin noun **idher** 'thoughtfulness' (from earlier ***idrē**) with a related adjective **idhren** 'pondering, wise, thoughtful'. It may be worth noting that at the time when the *Etymologies* and *Quenta Silmarillion* were written

---

[†] It is not expressly stated in the published works that **Widris** is a Taliskan word. But this must certainly be the case, since the *Lhammas* account makes it clear that the folk of Bëor began speaking Taliskan prior to their migration into Beleriand, and therefore it would have been their language at the time of their encounter with Felagund.

(*c*. 1937-1938) the Green-elves were conceived as having once been of Noldorin race, in contrast to the later conception seen in *The Silmarillion*, where they are said to have originally been Telerin. The base **IS-** from which Q *ista-* 'to know', *istima* 'wise', and ultimately *istari* 'wizards' are derived may also be related.

It is a telling detail that in the footnote to the passage from QS cited above, the lineage and antiquity of the word **Widris** is not only attested to by Pengolod of Middle-earth but also by Ælfwine, an Anglo-Saxon mariner who visited Tol Eressëa. It is clear from all this that Taliskan was constructed by Tolkien to have an explicit, genetic relationship not only with the Elvish tongues from which it developed but also with the Primary-World languages of Men, particularly Indo-European. Note, however, that Taliskan was *not* the progenitor of the Indo-European languages; rather, Taliskan and the Indo-European languages share a common origin. According to the *Lhammas*, most Men originally spoke languages derived from the speech of the Dark-elves. When "the fair houses of the eldest Men" migrated west, before they entered Beleriand their language was influenced by that of the Danas. This Danian influence was particularly strong in Taliskan, language of the folk of Bëor, Haleth, and Hádor, who eventually crossed over the Eredlindon into Beleriand. It is from the Danian-influenced language of the "fair houses of the eldest Men" who remained *east* of Eredlindon that those Indo-European languages "that live still in the North of the earth" developed. This language is described as "closely akin to Taliska", and evidence suggests that Taliskan itself exerted an influence on its form. This would answer Christopher Tolkien's question of "why a dotted line (representing 'influence') leads from Taliskan to the 'tongues of Western Men'" (LR:196) in the *Tree of Tongues* accompanying the *Lammasethen*, if we think of "Western Men" as referring to those Men who migrated west but did not enter Beleriand (the ancestors of the later Indo-European inhabitants of Europe).

While the exact development is complex, it is clear from the evidence that Tolkien deliberately intended a genetic relationship for his invented languages and Primary-World languages, at least up to the time of the *Etymologies*, the *Lhammas*, and the *Quenta Silmarillion*. However, despite all this we must still deal with the curious case of Tolkien's 1969 draft letter to a "Mr. Rang" (L:379–87) in which he appears to *reject* such a relationship:

> ... I remain puzzled, and indeed sometimes irritated, by many of the guesses at the 'sources' of the nomenclature, and theories or fancies concerning hidden meanings. These seem to me no more than private amusements, and as such I have no right or power to object to them, though they are, I think, valueless for the elucidation or interpretation of my fiction....
>
> It is therefore idle to compare chance-similarities between names made from 'Elvish tongues' and words in exterior 'real' languages, especially if this is supposed to have any bearing on the meaning or ideas in my story. To take a frequent case: there is no linguistic connexion, and therefore no connexion in significance, between *Sauron* a contemporary form of an older **θaurond-* derivative of an adjectival **θaurā* (from a base √THAW) 'detestable', and the Greek σαύρα 'a lizard'....

This leads to the matter of 'external' history: the actual way in which I came to light on or choose certain sequences of sound to use as names, *before* they were given a place inside the story. I think, as I said, this is unimportant: the labour involved in setting out what I know and remember of the process, or in the guess-work of others, would be far greater than the worth of the results. The spoken forms would simply be mere audible forms, and when transferred to the prepared linguistic situation in my story would receive meaning and significance according to that situation, and to the nature of the story told. It would be entirely delusory to refer to the sources of the sound-combinations to discover any meanings overt or hidden. I remember much of this process — the influence of memory of names or words already known, or of 'echoes' in the linguistic memory, and few have been unconscious....

I relate these things because I hope they may interest you, and at the same time reveal how closely linked is linguistic invention and legendary growth and construction. And also possibly convince you that looking around for more or less similar words or names is not in fact very useful as a source of sounds, and not at all as an explanation of inner meanings and significances. The borrowing, when it occurs (not often) is simply of *sounds* that are then integrated in a new construction....

At first glance this would seem to contradict the entire body of evidence we have presented above, not to mention condemning the very purpose of this column as pointless. But a closer examination of the Rang letter and the context in which it was written shows that Tolkien is not here denying a genetic relationship between his languages and "exterior 'real' languages". Rather, he is condemning the supposition that a "real" word might reveal "hidden meanings" or "inner meanings and significances" concealed in an Elvish word of similar form, beyond (or even contradictory to) the actual meaning Tolkien assigned that word in the historical context of Middle-earth. This was the gross offense committed by Mr. Rang, who was apparently unsatisfied with 'Greenleaf' as a translation of **Legolas** and asked Tolkien if the name might not also bear the covert meaning 'Fiery locks', probably on the "evidence" of Anglo-Saxon *līeg* 'flame' (*cf.* AS *lēgelēoht* 'light [of flame']) and *locc* 'hair'. It is no wonder Tolkien found this sort of nonsensical second-guessing of the meaning of his carefully constructed Elvish words to be exasperating in the extreme, and no doubt Mr. Rang richly deserved the "brief (and therefore rather severe) reply" which Tolkien eventually sent him.

Lest anyone think that the authors of this column are self-serving in giving this interpretation to the Rang letter, it should also be pointed out that the very Secondary-World words cited by Tolkien in his effort to dissuade Mr. Rang from further misguided research lead to clear connections with Primary-World forms. For example, in the letter Tolkien says that the name **Sauron** derives from a base THAW 'detestable'. In the *Etymologies* **Sauron** is given as a derivative of a base **THUS**- *'foul, rotten' (via a primitive adjective **thausā* 'foul, evil-smelling, putrid'), which in turn is said to perhaps be related to **THŪ-** 'puff, blow'. The connecting idea between these two bases is probably the bloated appearance of a decaying carcass. There are two IE roots, **pŭ-²** 'to rot, decay' (whence NE *foul*) and **pŭ-¹/phŭ-**'to blow, swell' (whence NE *pustule*), which at least confirm and illuminate the semantic relationship between 'foul' and 'blow' in the Eldarin tongues. Both the Eldarin bases and the IE roots appear to be imitative in origin, mimicking the sound made when blowing or puffing air from the mouth. There also appears to be a genetic relationship between the IE roots and Q *púrëa* 'smeared, discoloured' (MC:223) and *pustane* 'blowing' (MC:213). These sorts of interconnections provide insight into how the Elves may have perceived the character of Sauron; he was not only 'detestable', but also 'foul', 'pustular', and perhaps even 'puffed-up' with pride.

An even more interesting case is that of the Black Speech word *nazg* 'ring', which Tolkien also discussed in the letter to Mr. Rang:

> This was devised to be a vocable as distinct in style and phonetic content from words of the same meaning in Elvish, or in other real languages that are most familiar: English, Latin, Greek, etc. Though actual congruences (of form + sense) occur in unrelated real languages, and it is impossible in constructing imaginary languages from a limited number of component sounds to avoid such resemblances (if one tries to — I do not), it remains remarkable that *nasc* is the word for 'ring' in Gaelic (Irish: in Scottish usually written *nasg*). It also fits well in meaning, since it also means, and prob. originally meant, a *bond*, and can be used for an 'obligation'. Nonetheless, I only became aware, or again aware, of its existence recently looking for something in a Gaelic dictionary.... It is thus probable that *nazg* is actually derived from it, and this short, hard and clear vocable, sticking out from what seems to me (an unloving alien) a mushy language, became lodged in some corner of my linguistic memory....

A little research shows that Irish *nasc* 'ring', *nascim* 'to tie' and *naidm* 'bond'; Sanskrit *nah-* 'bind'; Latin *nōdus* 'knot'; Gothic *nati* 'net' ; English *net;* and Germanic **nat-sk-* (in Anglo-Norman *nouch* 'brooch', whence NE *ouch* 'a setting for a precious stone') all derive from an IE root **ned-** 'to bind, tie'. In the *Etymologies* we find the base **NAT-** 'lace, weave, tie' (> Q *natse* 'web, net'), which is said to be related to **NUT-** 'tie, bind' (> Q *núte* 'bond, knot', *nauta* 'bound, obliged'). There appears to be a clear genetic relationship between Eldarin **NAT-**/ **NUT-** and IE **ned-**, so that the similarity of BS *nazg* with Irish *nasc* is in fact hardly accidental or subconscious, but a systematic result of this genetic relationship. It should be pointed out that the Black Speech was itself an invented language within the context of Middle-earth, being "devised by Sauron in the Dark Years" to be "the language of all those that served him" (III:409). Most of its vocabulary seems to be derived directly from Elvish, *e.g.* BS *uruk* 'great soldier-orc' < Q *orko*, BS *durb-* 'to rule' < Q *tur-* 'to wield, control, govern', BS *-ishi* 'in' < Q *-sse* 'in, at, upon', *etc.* In this light, it seems likely that Black Speech *nazg* was a development of Q *natse* 'web, net' (< **NAT-**); in Sauron's mind, the main function of a ring was to ensnare others. It is important to realize that none of this means that Tolkien took the word *nazg* directly from Irish *nasc*. Rather, *nazg* was a natural, rule-driven development from the base **NAT-**, just as *nasc* is a natural, rule-driven development from the IE root **ned-**. It is at the level of these basic roots that the *deliberate* phonetic and semantic relationships of Tolkien's languages and Primary-World languages are to be found.

A Brief History of "Cross-Etymologizing"

The present authors are hardly the first to point out apparent relationships between Tolkien's Secondary-World languages and those of the Primary World. In the first *Parma Eldalamberon* (1971), for instance, editor Paula Marmor concluded her column *Beth-Luis-Nion* with "Notes on the Name Varda", in which she gave various words and names from Germanic tongues resembling Q *Varda*. For example, the name *Urðr*, the Norn representing the past, "is taken from the pret. pl. of *verða* (*varð*, *urðum*), to become"; and NE *wraith* "was archaically *warth* or *werth*, a Scottish/North of England term for guardian angel, from the Norse *vörthr*, guardian, from *vartha*, to guard". Elsewhere in the issue various linguistic "mathoms" were given, such as "The Gothic word for East was *urruns*" (derived from *urrinnan*, a verbal form indicating 'run out, go up, rise [of sun]'; *cf.* S *rhûn*, *amrûn* 'east') and "Cornwall was once called Belerium" (*cf.* S *Beleriand*). Marmor also sought to demonstrate a *grammatical* relationship between Quenya and Finnish by comparing their respective case endings in "Notes on the Directive Particles in Quenya and Finnish" in *Parma* 2, an attempt which was thoroughly refuted by Chris Gilson in a letter in *Parma* 4.

Parma 2 also featured an article by Laurence Krieg entitled "A New Word in Gothic — on the Joys and Perils of Cross-Etymologizing", an ironically apt title as we shall see. Krieg noted a newly discovered Gothic word *farwa* 'form, appearance' which he admitted was "only vaguely similar in form" to Q *fana* 'veil, raiment', but which he found similar enough in meaning to invite speculation about a connection. He eventually traced *farwa* back to its "real etymology", IE **kwerpós* 'body' (whence also Latin *corpus*), citing Oswald J.L. Szemerényi. Krieg concluded that "We must therefore accept Szemerényi's etymology for *farwa* and the implications it has for our study of Elvish words: that similarity in form and usage of an Elvish word to some word in a real language doesn't show anything beyond coïncidence. There are many similarities between quite unrelated real languages that seem even stranger and more meaningful than this, but are still coïncidences." This is a classic example of a straw man argument — Krieg proposed a correspondence which he knew from the beginning to be false, so of course he had no problem in disproving it. His conclusion, that since *farwa* cannot be linked to *fana* then *all* Secondary-World to Primary-World linguistic similarities are meaningless, is clearly fallacious. Krieg would have to wait for the publication of the *Etymologies* to discover that Q *fána* 'cloud' developed from the base **SPAN-** 'white', and that this base was "confused in N[oldorin]" with **PHAY-** 'radiate, send out rays of light', whence Q *faina-* 'emit light'. However, he was certainly in a position to discover the Indo-European root **bhā-**[1] 'to shine', with an extended and suffixed form **bhan-yo-* seen in Greek *phainein*, "to bring to light," cause to appear, show, and *phainesthai* (passive), "to be brought to light," appear; whence *fantasy*, *phantasm*, *etc.* (Watkins; see also Flieger 45–47.). Had he done so, he might have reached an entirely different conclusion about the likelihood of a relationship of *fana* with the Indo-European tongues.

In *Parma* 4 appeared "Initial Consonant Mutation in Celtic and Sindarin", compiled by Paula Marmor, Larry Krieg, and Dave Strecker. This article featured detailed charts of the initial consonant mutations of Old Irish, Modern Gaelic, Welsh, and Sindarin, as well as listings of the rules for mutations in Welsh and Modern Gaelic reprinted *in toto* from *Teach Yourself Welsh* and *Teach Yourself Irish*. While a little long on diagrams and short on comparative analysis, this article would probably still provide a useful research tool for students of Goldogrin, Noldorin, and Sindarin, languages which have been somewhat neglected by students of Elvish in favor of Quenya.

The next major work to examine the relationships of Tolkien's languages with Primary-World languages was Lise Menn's "Elvish Loanwords in Indo-European: Cultural Implications", a paper first read in 1976 and included in *An Introduction to Elvish* (a book which also contains numerous "cross-etymologies" scattered throughout its Quenya and Sindarin dictionaries). This article was an admirable effort, especially given the limited lexicon at the time. For instance, Menn proposed a plausible connection between Sindarin **craban*, pl. *crebain* 'crow' and various words meaning 'crow' or 'raven' in IE languages, such as Latin *corvus*, Greek *koraks*, Sanskrit *karawa*, and Old English *hræfn*. Unfortunately, Menn's supposed "cultural implications" were generally a bit too clever, for example her assertion that IE words such as Latin *carn-* 'flesh', Sanskrit *kravis-* 'raw flesh', and Greek *kre(w)as* 'meat' originated from the euphemistic use of Sindarin ***car-*** 'red' by the *vegetarian* Elves, who "may have had trouble bringing themselves to speak directly of the haunches of boar and venison being eaten ... by their human hosts." Of course, Menn could not know about words such as Q *apsa* 'cooked food, meat', Q ***helma*** 'skin, fell' and N ***heleth*** 'fur, fur-coat' (all from the *Etymologies*) which paint a less sentimental picture of the Elves' attitude toward the animal kingdom. Still, one wonders what she supposed to be the purpose of the various Elven hunting expeditions mentioned in Chapters VIII and IX of *The Hobbit*.

An article by Ronald Kyrmse, "The Finnish Connection", appeared in *Quettar* 19 (p. 15). This rather slight piece consisted of "a list ... of Finnish words similar to Quenya", and of the 33 words listed most resembled Quenya in form but not in meaning, *e.g.* Finn. *leuka* 'chin' and Q ***leuca*** 'snake'. Another article by Ronald Kyrmse appeared in *Quettar* 32, "New Insights into Elvish from the *Etymologies*", which featured a short list of bases from *The Etymologies* representing "the contamination of Mannish languages by the speech of the Eldar." Kyrmse's position that these correspondences are due to "contamination" is debatable (as is Lise Menn's use of the term "loanwords"). We have shown in the **Apologia** that such correspondences are more likely due to kinship rather than simple borrowing.

Conclusion

As the above history shows, this column is but the most recent effort in a long tradition of cross-etymologizing dating back at least twenty years. In this introductory installment we have attempted to demonstrate that the investigation of cross-etymologies is a legitimate branch of Elvish Studies, and one which can shed light on many important aspects of Tolkien's languages which might otherwise go unnoticed. Most importantly of all, we hope that we have proven that such investigations are not at odds with Tolkien's own intentions in creating his languages, as long as we demonstrate more **Widris** than the hapless Mr. Rang in reaching our conclusions. "Words and Devices" will be a regular feature in *Vinyar Tengwar*, and we look forward to your comments and criticisms.

Bibliography

Allan, Jim, Bill Welden, and Paula Marmor. "Quenya Grammar and Dictionary." In *An Introduction to Elvish*. Ed. Jim Allan. Somerset: Bran's Head Books, 1978. 3–43.

⸻. "Sindarin Grammar and Dictionary." In *An Introduction to Elvish*. Ed. Jim Allan. Somerset: Bran's Head Books, 1978. 47–90.

The American Heritage Dictionary. Second College Edition. Boston: Houghton Mifflin, 1985.

Buck, Carl Darling. *A Dictionary of Selected Synonyms in the Principal Indo-European Languages*. Chicago: University of Chicago Press, 1949.

Flieger, Verlyn. *Splintered Light: Language and Logos in Tolkien's World*. Grand Rapids, Michigan: Wm. B. Eerdmans, 1983.

Krieg, Laurence. "A New Word in Gothic — on the Joys and Perils of Cross-Etymologizing". *Parma Eldalamberon* 2, 1972: 10.

Kyrmse, Ronald. "The Finnish Connection." *Quettar* 19, n.d. [?1983]: 15.

⸻. "New Insights into Elvish from the *Etymologies*." *Quettar* 32, July 1988: 15–16.

Marmor, Paula. "Notes on the Name Varda". *Parma Eldalamberon* 1, Autumn 1971: 2.

⸻. "Notes on Directive Particles in Quenya and Finnish." *Parma Eldalamberon* 2, 1972: 9.

⸻, Laurence Krieg, and David Strecker. "Initial Consonant Mutation in Celtic and Sindarin." *Parma Eldalamberon* 4, March 1974: 12–16.

Menn, Lise. "Elvish Loanwords in Indo-European: Cultural Implications." In *An Introduction to Elvish*. Ed. Jim Allan. Somerset: Bran's Head Books, 1978. 143–51.

The Oxford English Dictionary. 13 vols. Oxford: Clarendon Press, 1933.

Skeat, Walter W. *A Concise Etymological Dictionary of the English Language*. Oxford: Clarendon Press, 1882.

Watkins, Calvert, ed. *The American Heritage Dictionary of Indo-European Roots*. Boston: Houghton Mifflin, 1985.

Essitalmar

The Roots of Middle-earth Names and Places
A column by Tom Loback

This is a forum for the readers of VT *to submit their ideas and thoughts about names, both of people and places; their meanings and the story that they tell. All are encouraged to submit inquiries, short interpretations and discussions thereof, particularly those names still undefined. Send all correspondence for this column to the editor at 152 West 26th St., #36, N.Y. City, NY 10001, USA.*

Quenya Rag

[The following is from a letter from Craig Marnock, in response to the past several columns]

"Star-struck" *[VT #13]*: You may say that you "cannot agree with the attributions of the star-names **Carnil**, **Luinil** and **Lumbar** as Quenya, which are as likely to be Sindarin (if not more so)". The ban of Thingol was there for good reasons. These three names are part of a list of six stars followed by a list of six constellations (S:55–6), all of which are Quenya. Context (remember what you told me about the importance of context?) alone would lead us to expect High-Elvish, and both **Carnil** and **Lumbar** would be unusual in Sindarin (we would expect internal vowel affection to *e* … *i* in the first place, and *mm* in the second) whereas they are perfectly regular for Quenya. **Luinil** could, as you say, be Sindarin as easily as Quenya, but it appears in a list of twelve Quenya names and Q. **luinë** means 'blue'. If **Carnil** is from **carnë** then **Luinil** can equally be from **luinë**. As for **Lumbar**, the gloss for **DUB-** in *Etymologies* is 'lie, lie heavy, loom, hang over oppressively (of clouds)' and the first derivative given for earlier Qenya **LUVU** is *luvu-* 'lower, brood', so the sense of 'cloud' or 'gloom' appears to be a secondary one. A form *dub + *nar* '(the) lowering fire' might be appropriate for a star which did not rise much above the horizon; not being a *meneldil* I can't suggest which one this might be. (PS — As for **Sithaloctha** — can't a man change his mind occasionally? *E.g.* once in 30 years?)

"Misplaced Anger" *[VT #15]*: I think misplaced ingenuity might be a bit closer. **Aranrúth** is an unusual form (we might have expected ****Aradhrúth**), but this is no reason to go redefining it just because we feel like it. Christopher Tolkien specifically gives us "*rúth* 'anger' in *Aranrúth*" in the Appendix to *The Silmarillion*. If we are going to ignore things just because it is convenient then we may as well all go home now.

Your argument in favour of your derivation seems to have something to do with syncopation (exactly what isn't clear). I don't know about its use in pre-*LotR* conceptions of Elvish, but the later rules appear to be: in Quenya (Vanyarin and Noldorin) the second vowel in a disyllabic base is always syncopated (**tyelpe** from **kyelep-**; **carca** from **karak-**); but in Telerin (and hence Sindarin: CE > PT > [PS] >

S) the second vowel is only syncopated if it does not receive primary stress (*telepi* and *celeb* from **kyelep-**; but *carch* from **karak-**). This appears to be what the acute accents mark on the bases in *Etymologies* (that is, the location of the stress). Obviously the position of the stress in a word will be affected by its length (hence the note you quoted, which incidentally referred specifically to Telerin) so slightly different rules would operate in longer word-formations. I haven't quite worked out what these are to my own satisfaction, but hope to publish a piece on this at some point in the future (this was originally intended to form the second half of an article on lexical derivation in Quenya, of which the first half was published independently in *Quettar* #39).

In any case your derivation for **Aranrúth** elided the first vowel and not the second, something which is very unusual and only happens in one or two places in *Etymologies* as far as I remember.

* * *

In response to Craig's comments on "Star-struck" I would say my object was not to reattribute the star names but to poke a hole in Jorge's pro-Quenya bias (a long-term project) and the blithe assumptions he and Ned made about the names [see "Nólë i Meneldilo", VT *12:5–9, 12–15 —CFH*]. Their purpose was to write the "definitive" piece on Elven star names. Their debatable attributions and arbitrary dismissals struck me as being undefinitive, so I thought I would mention some viable alternatives. I agree that context suggests they are High Elven.

As far as Tolkien changing his mind once in a while, I'm sure he did quite often. I'm equally certain that he never threw anything away. A good example is the name *Caranthir*, originally *Cranthir*. I think he changed his mind on this name because the unsyncopated *Caranthir* was more Noldorin in form than the early *Cranthir* [*C(a)ranthir*]. However, I don't think that *Cranthir* is then necessarily cast out of Elvish entirely. It may be shifted to a dialect where the syncope is appropriate.*

It can be seen in *Etymologies* that syncope is a frequent feature in Doriathrin and Ilkorin but comparatively infrequent in Noldorin. In Doriathrin and Ilkorin both the first or second vowel can be elided, usually determined by the accent in the base. It is not unusual or rare that the first vowel is elided:

BERÉTH-	Ilk. *breth*
BIRÍT-	Ilk. *brith*
DARÁK-	Dor. *drôg*
ERÉK-	Dor. *regorn*
TURÚM-	Ilk. *trumb, trum*

Interesting to note is Tolkien's own change in the base **GALAD-** to **GÁLAD-** which then yields Dor. *gald* but N. *galadh*.

---

* Looking over the evidence, the Ilkorin and Doriathrin forms of *Carnil* would probably elide the first vowel and perhaps retain *gil* > **Crangil* or, if the second vowel is lost, **Cargil* (*cf. Borgil*). The Noldorin form might be **Caranil* if the notion of non-syncopation is accepted.

Unaccented forms show the syncope in Doriathrin and Ilkorin of the first vowel: **MBIRIL-** Ilk. *bril*. In contrast, one can find a plethora of words in Noldorin with the retention of the unaccented vowel, as in **NÉTER-** N. *neder*.

A comparison of words derived from the same base in the three dialects accentuates the basic division in the use of syncopation:

DÓRON-	N. *doron*	Dor., Ilk. *dorn*
ERÉD-	N. *eredh*	Ilk. *erdh**
ERÉK-	N. *Eregion*	Dor. *Region*
GÁLAD-	N. *galadh*	Dor. *gald*
3ARAM-	N. *araf*	Dor. *garm*
KYELEP-,		
TELEP-	N. *celeb*	Ilk. *telf*
ÑGAR(A)M-	N. *garaf*	Dor. *garm*
ÑGOLOD-	N. *golodh*	Dor. *ngold*
ÑGOROTH-	N. *goroth*	Dor. *ngorth*
ÓROT-	N. *orod*	Dor. *orth*
SALÁK-(WĒ)	N. *salab*	Dor. *salch**
TÁRAG-	N. *tara*	Ilk. *targ*
ÚLUG-	N. *ulund*	Ilk. *olg*

* note these rare losses of the accented second vowel

All this leads to a defense of my "misplaced ingenuity". *Aranrúth* would be an unusual form, if Sindarin were simply a modified form of the Noldorin of *Etymologies*. And we would all expect *Aradhrúth* from *Aran* + *rûth* as found in *Caradhras* (*caran* + *ras*, a very nice Noldorin compound, I might add). But Sindarin is not just modified Noldorin, but a language group. Further, context suggests we ought to expect a very Doriathrin name for the sword of a very Doriathrin king. *Etymologies* supports this notion. Compare *Nauglamîr*, "strictly Doriathric in which the genitive in *-a(n)* preceded" *vs.* the N. *mîr na Nauglin, Nauglvir > Nauglavir* (LR:375 s.v. **NAUK-**). Important here is the unlenited *m* in Doriathrin, seen also in *Goldamir vs.* N. *Golovir* (*ibid.*:377 *s.v.* **ÑGOLOD-**). Perhaps the *n* in *Aranrúth* is just the *-a(n)* of the genitive and *-rúth* derives from some as yet unpublished base, but to me at this point it the *û > ú* seems related to the development of **DARÁK-** > Dor. *drôg* and the *n'rúth* similar to what occurs in **TURÚM-** Ilk. *t'rum*. Perhaps *rúth* derives from **RUS-** or √**URU** instead of √**NURU**, but I would not find the existence of a base ***NURÚS-** yielding a Dor. *n'rúth* entirely shocking. However, it is unclear to me from the published material available how Christopher Tolkien came up with *rûth* as 'anger'. I have long ago given up the Appendix to *The Silmarillion* as a source because as he himself stated: "they are necessarily compressed, giving an air of certainty and finality that is not altogether justified". Are we to continue to accept the attributions of the Appendix of *Silm.* such as *fin-* = 'hair' as in *Fingon* when *Etymologies* obviously contradicts this gloss and provides a better and more reasonable one?

My own position is that Sindarin describes a group of more or less similar dialects which may even be mixed at times (see *Etym. s.v.* **THŌN-**). And that by approaching the 'Sindarin' fragments by this method we may come to a clearer understanding of this branch of the Elven language tree. There is evidence to show this approach is viable. Earlier versions show the gate inscription to be a slight modification of the classical Noldorin of *Etymologies*, and *Letters* suggests that Tolkien's modifications to it were not made because of a basic change in the language. (See p. 426 "I thought people would feel *dh* uncouth, and so wrote *d* (for ð & *dh*)…". So too Christopher Tolkien edited out the *c* in **cHîn Húrin** [LR:322, note on §25].) The inscription on Thrór's map *[see Parma Eldalamberon #6 —CFH]* is wholly Noldorin and should be when we consider its context: written by the Dwarves that lived in Moria who dealt extensively with the Noldor of Eregion. The inscription on Túrin's stone by Mablung of Doriath should be Doriathrin and in fact shows the Doriathrin genitive in **Dagnir Glaurunga**. Place-names also show the influence of the appropriate dialect, particularly around northern Mirkwood where the Doriathrin influence was strong. And, as pointed out earlier, replacement place-names can often be shown to be one dialect supplanting another, not a change in Tolkien's conception of the language itself (*e.g.* N. **Aelin-Uial** *vs.* Dor. **Umboth Muilin**).

Another 'more Noldorin' change which may have affected the language from the period of *Etymologies* to the *LotR* period is pertinent to this discussion of syncopation. The word **cirith**, like **Cranthir/Caranthir** moves to the unsyncopated form from the **cris/criss** of the *Gnomish Lexicon* and *Etymologies*. A quick survey of the bases in *Etymologies* shows that some two-thirds result in unsyncopated derivatives in Noldorin, and that in fifteen samples of unaccented first vowels, seven are unelided (two begin with vowels) and eight elide the first vowel, of which only two have Doriathrin and Ilkorin comparisons: **DARÁK-** N. **draug**, Dor. **drôg**; **MORÓK-** N. **brôg**, Ilk. **broga**. Without seeing the original manuscript it is difficult to say whether Tolkien made this change as he went along and expanded on it or if it was there from the start. It is certain and significant that nearly every derivative for the Doriathrin and Ilkorin forms are syncopated with the accented vowel retained. This is not the rule that Tolkien describes in *Letters* for Telerin (although I'm sure that is what he intended for Telerin, I do not think your equation of CE > PT > PS > S will hold up). The rules, as you define them for so-called *LotR* conceptions of Elvish are misleading. Certainly in Quenya syncope of a disyllabic base is the rule, but it is a rule "early fixed" and can be seen even in the *Qenya Lexicon* and the earliest concept of the language. Your reference to Vanyarin and Noldorin is confusing in respect to Noldorin. Do you mean the Quenya dialect spoken by the Noldor in Aman or the Noldorin of *Etymologies*? If the latter, then the syncope certainly is not as you describe, for that Noldorin is moving deliberately away from syncope, even, to a large extent, in longer words and compounds, even unto *LotR* and beyond.

I predict that any such rule regarding syncope for Sindarin that you devise will be loaded with conditions and exceptions if the dialects of *Etymologies* are not considered.

Transitions in Translations
A column by Arden R. Smith

The purpose of this column is to examine peculiarities in translations of Tolkien's works: mistranslations, unusual translations, interesting solutions to the problems of translation, and other curiosities in foreign editions. Ideas and contributions are encouraged: send them to "Transitions," c/o Arden R. Smith, P.O. Box 4395, Berkeley, CA 94704-0395, USA.

Who's Afraid of the Big, Bad Gollum?

Regardless of how many languages a person speaks, whether one or a hundred, one aspect of the foreign editions of Tolkien which everyone can appreciate (or criticize) is the wonderful variety of styles and interpretations to be found in the illustrations. Indeed, one of the best things about Douglas Anderson's *The Annotated Hobbit* is the inclusion of illustrations from various translations. Anderson specifically avoided some illustrations, though, setting forth his rationale in the preface (p. x):

> Tolkien's comments on the illustrations in the translations were mostly negative: Those in the Swedish (1947) were "frightful" and those in the Portuguese "foul." He complained that the character Gollum was always made into some kind of monster, in complete disregard of the text. The observation is indeed true, and for this reason I have included only one illustration of Gollum [from the 1977 Estonian edition, on p. 83].

By weeding out such pictures, however, Anderson deprives the reader of some hilarious renderings of Gollum. I will be discussing three of these, and they all have something in common: Gollum is big. Much too big.

I'll begin with my personal favorite of the three, the "foul" Portuguese version by António Quadros in *O Gnomo* (Porto: Livraria Civilização, 1962). This version is fully clothed and has webbed feet — oh yes, and a beard — a big, bushy, black beard. Taking Bilbo's height to be between 3 and 31/2 feet (L:35), this Gollum's height is about 6 feet.

Next is the Japanese version by Terashima Ryuichi in *Hobito No Bōken* (Tokyo: Iwanami Shoten, 1965). The Japanese Gollum is an unclothed, reptilian sort of creature with froglike fingers and toes. Furthermore, he is approximately 10 feet tall.

Last but certainly not least is the Swedish monstrosity by Tove Jansson in *Bilbo en Hobbits Äventyr* (Stockholm: Raben & Sjogren, 1962), also appearing in the Finnish *Lohikäärmevuori* (Helsinki: Tammi, 1973). This creature is also unclothed, but is otherwise indescribable, apart from something on top of his head that looks like a cross between a laurel wreath and a tossed salad. In the picture in which he appears with Bilbo, he is waist-deep in the water, but assuming bodily proportions as shown in the picture of him in his boat, he seems to be roughly *20 feet tall*!

It is quite apparent that these illustrators had not read *The Lord of the Rings*, where Gollum was revealed to be of "hobbit-kind" (I:62–63), but how did all three illustrators miss the description of Gollum as "a small slimy creature" (H:82)? The answer is quite simple: because the description did not yet exist. Note that all three translations in which these pictures first appeared were published before 1966. They are thus translations from the *second edition*, which makes no mention of Gollum being "a small slimy creature" (see AnnH:324, note V.1).

The King of Araw

Although "the wild kine of Araw" is correctly rendered as "Araws vilde kvæg" on pp. 23–24 of the Danish version of *The Return of the King* (*Kongen vender tilbage*. Translated by Ida Nyrop Ludvigsen. København: Gyldendal, 1981; = English III:27), a word got misinterpreted in the note on p. 330 (= English III:319). Here *den vilde hvide race* ('the wild white race') that lived near the Sea of Rhûn was said to be descended from *kongen af Araw* ('the king of Araw').

Translation Update

Christina Scull has informed me of the existence of Ukrainian and Armenian translations of *The Hobbit*. Can anyone supply additional information on these, *i.e.* actual titles and other bibliographical information? Please send any such information to the "Transitions" address above.

[If someone knows how to get hold of one, I am particularly interested in obtaining a copy of the Armenian translation. —ARS]

Wisdom of the Orient

Though not referring to Tolkien translation in particular, here is a pearl of wisdom from Fung Yu-Lan's *A Short History of Chinese Philosophy* (New York: Macmillan, 1948; p. 15):

> Kumarajiva, of the fifth century A.D., one of the greatest translators of the Buddhist texts into Chinese, said that the work of translation is just like chewing food that is to be fed to others. If one cannot chew the food oneself, one has to be given food that has already been chewed. After such an operation, however, the food is bound to be poorer in taste and flavor than the original.

Trivia Question

Q: The disturbance caused by Bilbo's return is said to have been "a great deal more than a nine days' wonder" (H:314). How bad was the disturbance in the German version?

A: *Schlimmer als ein achtes Weltwunder* 'worse than an eighth wonder of the world' (*Der kleine Hobbit*. Translated by Walter Scherf. München: dtv, 1974; p. 300).

Next Issue

"I'm a Troll Man" and more!

Publications of Interest

Due to space limitations, the editor cannot thoroughly review all publications received; the following reviews emphasize those publications and items which the editor feels would be of special interest to members of the Elvish Linguistic Fellowship. BIAOR = *Back Issues Available On Request.*

Beyond Bree: Newsletter of the American Mensa Tolkien SIG. Published monthly.
 Editor: Nancy Martsch. *Subscriptions to*: the editor at P.O. Box 55372, Sherman Oaks, CA 91413. *Annual subscription*: USA $10; Overseas $13. *BIAOR*.
 April 1991: Tolkien-inspired poetry in Russian, with translation.
 May 1991: "Discography: Tolkien-Inspired Recordings", lists Cædmon's Tolkien recordings and gives Tolkien's tune for "The Stone Troll", among other things.

Cirth de Gandalf: Cercle d'etudes de Tolkien en Belgique. Published bimonthly.
 Editor: Nathalie Kotowski. *Subscriptions to*: the editor at 25, rue Victor Gambier, 1180 Bruxelles, Belgium. *Annual subscription*: Belgium 400 FB, 450 FB elsewhere.
 No. 13, March 1991: Continues the presentation of *Le Quenya: une grammaire*, Nathalie's French translation of Nancy Martsch's Quenya Language Lessons from *Beyond Bree. Leçon 13: L'infinitif et le participe présent*, with the supplement *Les calendriers Quenya*; also *L'Astronomie dans la Terre du Milieu*, a timely topic it seems.

Little Gwaihir: Magazine of the Tolkien Section of the Śląski Klub Fantasyki (English Edition). Published monthly.
 Editor: Paulina Braiter. *Subscriptions to*: the editor at ul. Kasztelanska 66/3, 58-314 Walbrzych, Poland. Write for subscription info.
 No. 17, March 1991: Artwork *cum* Quenya description in "Calacirya ar Túna" by "Frodo Maggot" (Ryszard Derdzinski).
 No. 18, April 1991: Long Quenya translation: "Valaquenta — et Eldaliva Quentallon", again by "Frodo Maggot". Perhaps Ryszard can be persuaded to allow us to reprint this material in *VT*.

 The Polish Edition *Gwaihirze* ('Little Gwaihir' or 'Gwaihirling') has been running Nancy Martsch's *Quenya Language Lessons* in Polish.

Next Issue

VT #18 will feature the start of a regular series of excerpts from Craig Marnock's ongoing Quenya translation of the *Ainulindalë*, while *Words and Devices* continues with "Harping on a Theme". Plus columns from Arden and Tom, letters, news, and whatever else arrives before July 1.

Vinyar Tengwar

The bimonthly 'news-letters' of the Elvish Linguistic Fellowship.
A Special Interest Group of the Mythopoeic Society.

Editor: Carl F. Hostetter, 2509 Ambling Circle, Crofton, MD 21114, USA.

Proofreaders: Jorge Quiñónez and Arden R. Smith.

Masthead: by Tom Loback.

Tengwar numerals: from Lawrence M. Schoen's *Moroma* PostScript *Tengwar* font for the Mac, available on disk for $6.00 from PsychoGlyph, P.O. Box 74, Lake Bluff, IL 60044.

Subscriptions: Subscriptions are for 1 year (6 issues) and must be paid in US dollars.

$12.00   USA
$15.00   Canada (sent airmail) and Overseas surface mail
$18.00   Overseas airmail

Back issues available: Issues 1 - 7 & 9 - 17 are each $2.00 in the USA, $2.50 overseas surface mail and Canada, $3.00 airmail. Issue 8 includes a large map and costs $3.00 USA, $4.00 surface and Canada, $5.00 airmail. A complete set of back issues is available for $25.00 USA, $30.00 Overseas surface mail, and $35.00 Overseas airmail. *All costs are postpaid.*

Payments: All payments must be in US dollars. It is recommended that overseas members make payments via international postal money order.

Make all checks payable to Carl F. Hostetter.

Submissions: Written material should in some manner deal with Tolkien's invented languages. All submissions must be typed, or must be written unbelievably legibly: if I have to decipher lower-glyphics, the submission is automatically rejected! The editor reserves the right to edit any material (except art) for purposes of brevity and relevance. Ilúvatar smiles upon submissions on 400K or 800K (3.5") Macintosh or 720K (3.5") MS-DOS formatted disks in PageMaker, Microsoft Word, Microsoft Works, WordPerfect, MacWrite, DCA, or RTF formats, or as unformatted ASCII text files. Artwork should be Tolkienian in nature.

The deadline for VT #18 is July 1, 1991.

Bibliographical Abbreviations

H	The Hobbit	*LT1*	The Book of Lost Tales, Part One
I	The Fellowship of the Ring	*LT2*	The Book of Lost Tales, Part Two
II	The Two Towers	*LB*	The Lays of Beleriand
III	The Return of the King	*SM*	The Shaping of Middle-earth
R	The Road Goes Ever On	*LR*	The Lost Road
S	The Silmarillion	*RS*	The Return of the Shadow
UT	Unfinished Tales	*TI*	The Treason of Isengard
L	The Letters of J.R.R. Tolkien	*WR*	The War of the Ring
MC	The Monsters and the Critics		

Vinyar Tengwar is produced by the editor on an Apple Macintosh II personal computer, using a LaCie Silverscan scanner, Microsoft Word 4.0 and Aldus PageMaker 4.0. VT is printed on an NEC Silentwriter2 Model 90 laser printer.

ISSN 1054-7606

Vinyar Tengwar

Enquëuna

#18

July 1991

In This Issue

Editor's Musings

Well, a landmark issue in several respects. This issue marks the end of *VT*'s third year of publication, and we've certainly seen some changes in that time: the adoption of laser printing and image scanning, a new column or two, our very own ISSN number, and now inclusion in the Library of Congress. The unprecedentedly large page-count (40!) of this issue is a fitting tribute to this anniversary.

We have another gorgeous cover from Pat Wynne, one which may be familiar to readers of *Mythlore*; anyone interested in what Gandalf is reading should turn to page 11 for Pat Wynne's transcription and prose translation, and Chris Gilson's verse rendering.

We also have the first of a series of articles by Bill Welden dealing with "Counting Numbers"; perhaps we'll now get an explanation for Bill's Quenya number-words, which *VT* has been using since the first issue, and in particular for the very odd-seeming word for *eighteen*.

— Carl F. Hostetter

"From this account, some may begin to think that in treating of grammar we are dealing with something too various and changeable for the understanding to grasp; a dodging Proteus of the imagination, who is ever ready to assume some new shape, and elude the vigilance of the inquirer. But let the reader or student do his part; and, if he please, follow us with attention. We will endeavour, with welded links, to bind this Proteus, in such a manner that he shall neither escape from our hold, nor fail to give to the consulter an intelligible and satisfactory response...."

— Goold Brown (1791–1857). "Of the Science of Grammar". In *English Linguistics: An Introductory Reader*. Scott, Foresman & Co., 1970, p.43.

E.L.F. News

New Member

The E.L.F. extends a hearty *mae govannen* to:

• François Schopphoven   26, rue des mondettes, 51160 Champillon, France.

VT in the Library of Congress

At their request, *VT* has now been added to the holdings of the Library of Congress. Now, any hapless, unsuspecting Congressmen who wander into the Library just might stumble over an issue and discover the joys of consonant mutation in Sindarin or the mysteries of Quenya's associative case. This could have profound ramifications for Western democracy. At any rate, anyone researching Tolkien at the Library is now sure to encounter *VT*.

Priscilla Tolkien to Speak in D.C.

Priscilla Tolkien will speak on "J.R.R. Tolkien: Scholar and Storyteller" at the Martin Luther King Memorial Library in Washington, D.C. at 10 a.m. on August 3, 1991. For further information, or to make reservations, call (202) 727-1151. (Hmmm; first *VT* is added to the Library of Congress, then Priscilla Tolkien speaks at a library in D.C. Mere coincidence? I don't think so!)

Centenary Publications

Houghton Mifflin has sent advance notice of forthcoming publications in honor of the Tolkien Centenary. There will be two versions of a Centenary Edition of *The Lord of the Rings*, featuring 50 full-color illustrations by Alan Lee. The first version sports a foil-laminated jacket with the Centenary seal on the back and a ribbon place-marker; it will retail for $60.00 (ISBN 0-395-59511-8). The second version is a boxed edition of the same, signed by the artist, retailing for $250.00 (ISBN 0-395-60423-0). Both are due in November.

November will also see the publication of a revised paperback edition of Karen Wynn Fonstad's *Atlas of Middle-earth* ($15.95; ISBN 0-395-53516-6) that incorporates material from the *History of Middle-earth* series, and of a paperback third edition of *The Father Christmas Letters* ($10.95; ISBN 0-395-59698-X). And January 3, 1992, the 100th Anniversary of Tolkien's birth, is the publication date for *A Tolkien Family Album* ($29.95; ISBN 0-395-59938-5) by John and Priscilla Tolkien, which "weaves together family reminiscences with personal, informal family photographs, most of them never before published."

Finally, Volume 9 of the *History of Middle-earth* series, titled *Sauron Defeated*, is due out in the States by year's end.

Orders can be placed by calling the HM warehouse at (800) 225-3362.

Letters to VT

• *Chris Gilson*   *Walnut Creek, California*

It was great to see Craig's comments in *VT* #17 about Patrick's and my analysis of the *Koivienéni Sentence*. They may show where we were not entirely lucid. A subtle example of this seems to be the fact that the sentence predates *The Lord of the Rings*. This follows from the fact that the sheet containing the sentence was lined through and the back used in drafting "The Riders of Rohan" (*VT* 14:5, 19 n. 1). This is the reason we had to compare its components with *all* of the available evidence to find the likeliest grammatical connections. To ignore the evidence of Arctic, for instance, might be to bypass the most closely related text in the external chronology.

There is really no controversy about adverbs in *-o*. Craig is "not wholly convinced that this is as regular a 'pattern of derivation' as is suggested" (*VT* 17:6). But Patrick and I simply pointed out the pattern itself, five Elvish words ***ando, voro, oio, ento, rato,*** all conveying a meaning corresponding to an adverb of time in English, a series for which coincidence is out of the question. Of these words ***ando*** itself is the most clearly adverbial in context and the most clearly related to a corresponding adjective, namely ***anda*** 'long' (LR:348). So we were *not* making a "case," but simply pointing out significant parallels. My own personal hunch is that ***piliningeve*** (*Narqelion* line 6; see *Parma* 9: 24-5) and ***andave*** represent the "regular" formation of adverbs of manner. As we mentioned (*VT* 14:19 n. 3), this ending *-ve* seems to derive from *ve* 'like, as', which would parallel the etymology of the regular English adverb ending *-ly* (related to *like*).

On the matter of ***oio*** Craig is correct to note that Tolkien seems to imply that *oi, oio* 'ever, everlastingly' (R:69), used adverbally in ***Oiolosse*** 'Ever-snow-white' (p. 70), and *oio* 'an endless period' (UT:317), used as substantive in ***tennoio*** 'for ever', existed side by side. Thus it is true that *oio* is not "wholly" an adverb, but the adverbial function could still predominate. It does with the English word *ever,* which is a noun only in the phrase *for ever,* but is an adverb in all other contexts.

In the text of the new sentence we can deduce that ***ando kakainen loralyar*** = *were long lying asleep*. A basic qestion here is which of ***kakainen*** or ***loralyar*** is the main predicate and which is subordinate. In considering the syntactic possibilities, we must not assume that a dative of the past tense infinitive in Quenya grammar would function in exactly the same way as a corresponding English paraphrase. What Patrick and I actually suggested is that ***kakainen*** might be the dative of means of a past infinitive (*VT* 14:12). Perhaps dative of *occasion* would have been a better explanation of this idea. Some simple examples with present tense infinitive in English would be: *I am happy **to see** you* or *he was proud **to bear** that name*. Putting the infinitive in the past tense we get: *I am happy **to have seen** you* or *he was proud **to have borne** that name*. (Notice that the corresponding pairs could describe identical situations.) The English sentence *they were asleep **to have lain** there long* would tend to be taken as implying something like: *they must have been asleep to have lain there for very long*. This is because the idea of *occasion* tends to be viewed as pointing to the *cause* of the main idea. While this further implication may not have developed in Quenya, the idea of the dative of occasion is appropriate here.

Craig suggests that in *Oilima Markirya 2* (MC:213-15) the Quenya suffix *-ne* is a present participle marker because "every occurrence except *valkane* is translated by a form in *-ing*" (*VT* 17:6). This is true for the following 7 examples: *qaine* 'wailing' (line 4); *falastane* 'surging' (9); *pustane* 'blowing' (10); *histane* 'fading' (12); *laustane* 'roaring' (13); *karkane* 'snarling' (15); *lungane* 'bending' (23). But what about *sangane* 'gather' in line 22? The contrast of line 13 and line 22 is informative: *man tenuva súru laustane* 'who shall hear the wind roaring' *vs.* *man kiluva lómi sangane* 'who shall see the clouds gather'. This shows that the ending *-ne* is used in a context where English can employ either participle or infinitive. There is no difference in meaning if we translate line 13 as *who shall hear the wind roar*. And indeed the reader can check that in 6 out of the 7 examples of *-ne* cited above, we can replace the English participle by a bare infinitive.

A consistent theory of the infinitives, participles and gerunds in *OM2* must also account for the following parallels to the forms in *-ne*.

tíne	'shining' (line 11)	*yáme*	'yawning' (26)
ulmula	'mumbling' (20)	*lante*	'falling' (28)
túma	'moving' (21)	*píke*	'blinking' (33)
qalume	'heaving' (25)	*silde*	'gleaming' (33)

If more than one Quenya suffix can be used in the same context, just as more than one English construction can, then it is not surprising that Tolkien experimented with rendering the same English poem in several ways in Quenya. *OM2* and *OM3* (MC:221-23) warrant further examination from this point of view. And it seems that a useful approach to sorting out the myriad possibilities for Quenya is to look for a relation between the occurences of phonetically similar suffixes. The *-la* in *ulmula* 'mumbling' could very well be related to that in *lalantila* (*Narq.* line 1), and almost certainly to that in *falastala* 'surging', *etc.* in *OM3*. The *-me* in *qalume* 'heaving' could be related to that in *kelume* 'flowing, flood (tide), stream' (*OM3* n. 8). What this means for the grammar of *OM2* is not something we should decide *before* considering all the logical possibilities.

The grammar of *enyalien* 'for recalling, to recall', as used in *Cirion's Oath* (UT:305) needs clarification. The fact that it can govern a direct object (*alcar* 'glory' and *voronwe* 'faith') is characteristic of being verbal and the particular verb *yal-* 'summon' being transitive. The fact that it is dative is what connects *enyalien* as a substantive to the main sentence. Specifically *termaruva* 'shall stand' takes an indirect object of the thing symbolized or "stood for" = 'shall stand *for recalling, shall stand to recall*'. These two features of the grammar of the gerundial are independent of each other. (Presumably any infinitive of a transitive verb could take a direct object. And probably *termar-* could take a dative noun as indirect object, just as well as taking a dative gerundial infinitive.) We cited this example merely to show that verbal forms used as substantives can be datives, not intending to suggest that the dative functions in **kakainen** and **enyalien** are identical.

Craig says (*VT* 17:6) that the "dative as we know it does not appear" in the "Secret Vice" poems. This ignores **tálin** 'with feet' (*Nieninque,* MC:215–16, line 8; *VT* 14:12), but allowing for this oversight, what does he really mean by the dative *as we know it*? The only dative published in Tolkien's lifetime was **nin** 'for me' in *Namárie.* How else does Craig decide which *unpublished* datives are consistent with this, except by a theoretical attempt to "rectify" one with the other? That is what we do also, because that is what looking for *consistency* is all about.

In trying to understand **erenekkoitanie** (= *he might awake them*), we must continue to appreciate that translating the grammatical markers into English one by one will not automatically "make sense". In fact, to me *Orome came thither that (he) them having awakened* does certainly make sense, even though I know it is not grammatical. If an alien uttered this I would deduce that he was intelligent and knew more about my language than I about his. We should not mistake ungrammaticalness in English with ungrammaticalness in any other language, including Quenya. Anyone familiar with two or more languages will know that grammar does not translate mechanically in every situation.

There is an interesting example from *The Lord of the Rings* of Tolkien's creative use of translation, in the case of **avánier** 'have passed away' *vs.* **utúlien** 'I am come' (*Namárië*, I:394, line 3; III: 245-6). Tolkien describes **avánier** as a "perfect" form (R:66), and in English grammar *have passed* is usually described as the present perfect of the indicative active of the verb *to pass*. It was observed long ago that starting from roots **van-** and **tul-** we could formulate a single rule to yield stems **avánie-** and **utúlie-**, and that *I have come* has essentially the same meaning as *I am come*. It has long been the "accepted" view, therefore, that **utúlien** is also a Quenya perfect, and that its idiomatic translation by copula + perfect participle is a deliberate literary device. It does lend an archaic flavor to Aragorn's English here, since the construction was more popular in English several hundred years ago. But it seems like a glaringly obvious *possibility* that the archaic translation of **utúlien** as 'I am come' might be a deliberate clue to the etymology of the ending in these two forms: **utúl-ie-n** < 'come-am-I', **aván-ie-r** 'passed away-are-they', since this ending *could* be related to certain forms of the verb 'to be' in pre-*LotR* Quenya. This suggestion requires acceptance of the *heretical* notion that Tolkien may not have started from scratch in devising the Elvish sentences for his greatest work.

Finally Craig is right to see in the unpublished Sindarin epilogue to *LotR* a possible corroboration of our hypothesis that **erenekkoitanie** 'he might awake them' = **e-ren-ek-koita-nie**, with **e-** = 'he' and **-ren-** = 'them'. This would also corroborate the straightforward formal inference from contrasting **senekkoita** 'awake them' = **sen-ek-koita**. In fact there is a chicken-and-egg problem with the Sindarin text, whose interpretation is just as speculative as that of our Quenya sentence, even though snippets have been mentioned and repeated frequently enough to become gospel. We felt that the proper time to discuss this Sindarin evidence would be after it is published in a few months, rather than as a cursory support for our hypothesis, which still required some sort of *etymological* explanation. I did find it ironic that this Sindarin is adduced as "evidence" even though Tolkien definitely chose *not* to publish it, but I will not press the point since I do not take the *intent to publish* criterion (*VT* 17:7) to be well thought out or significant. I prefer to stick to a criterion we *know* had relevance for Tolkien, namely logical consistency.

• *Patrick Wynne*   *Fosston, Minnesota*

Craig Marnock raised several interesting points in his comments about my article on the associative. I was puzzled, however, by his assertion that the article "left out the question of what this declension is used for in Quenya". The final three pages of the piece were devoted to a complete listing of all examples of the associative, sorted and arranged *according to use*, with explanations of the classification given when necessary. How could I give a more thorough picture of the use of the associative than this?

Craig expressed doubt that the associative was originally partitive in sense because of the reference in the *Etymologies s.v.* **3Ŏ-** to "the old partitive in Q *-on*". This reference does not necessarily imply "that Quenya had both an old and a new partitive", as Craig and Tom Loback have asserted. Granted, the adjective *old* can mean "designating the earlier or earliest of two or more"; thus the *Old* Testament is referred to as such because there is a *New* Testament. But *old* has other meanings, one of which is "former", *i.e.* "existing long ago but not presently". This strikes me as the likelier meaning in the phrase "the old partitive". *Teach Yourself Finnish* refers to an "old dative case", examples of which survive in a few expressions such as *Jumalan kiitos* 'Thanks be to God', whereas modern Finnish lacks a dative case.

If, however, Craig's and Tom's theory is correct, then which case is the "new partitive"? There are only three possible candidates on the Plotz declension chart, cases to which a label was not assigned: the parenthetical cases in *-n* (*ciryan, lassen*) and *-s* (*ciryas, lasses*) and the case in *-va*. The *-n* and *-s* cases are clearly akin etymologically and semantically to the allative (*-nna*) and locative (*-sse*) cases under which they are placed. This leaves us with *-va* as the only candidate for a new Quenya partitive, which confirms rather than refutes my suppositions.

Craig stated that the reference to "the old partitive in Q *-on*" suggests "that *-va* was not *originally* a partitive". Craig's emphasis on the word "originally" implies that he is indeed assuming that the *-va* case is a new Quenya partitive. If this is so, we are left to wonder: What was the original meaning of the *-va* case if it was not partitive? What root or base did it come from? And how did it acquire its later partitive sense? Unfortunately, Craig did not answer these questions.

Of course, I do not think Craig is right in assuming that *-va* was not originally a partitive. If I correctly understand his objections, he feels that early Quenya would not have allowed the redundancy of two partitive inflections, *-on* and *-va*. However, it is a key characteristic of the Quenya noun-declension system that many of the cases duplicate in whole or in part the functions of other cases. An excellent example of this is the busy little inflection *-r* (very likely a rhotacized version of the "short locative" *-s* case on the Plotz chart), which duplicates the functions of three other cases: locative *-sse* (cf. *ringa ambar* 'in [her] cold bosom', MC:213; *ambar* is replaced by *súmaryasse* in the later version of *Oilima Markirya* [MC:222]), dative *-n* (cf. *yar i vilya anta miqilis* 'to whom the air gives kisses', MC:215), and allative *-nna* (cf. *mir*, explicitly equated with *minna* 'to the inside, into' in *Etymologies s.v.* **MI-**). So *-r* managed to peaceably coexist with other cases which duplicated its functions exactly (in fact, *-r* seems to have lacked any functions unique to itself). Similarly, Quenya also had no less than *three* genitive inflections (*-va*, *-o*, and *-n;* simple apposition was also used to indicate the genitive, as in *Kópas Algalunte* 'Haven of the Swanships', LT1:285). Given the fact that Quenya had two locatives, two datives, two allatives, and three (or four) genitives, there seems no reason to object to the theory that early Quenya had both a partitive case in *-on* and another in *-va*. There may have been some subtle distinction in meaning and usage between the two, although what this distinction may have been is difficult to determine.

Craig also wrote that "the key to understanding [the associative's] semantic field lies in its not having a partitive or dual form" and wondered why, if one can say *Nurtale Valinóreva* 'the hiding of Valinor', it is impossible to say *Nurtale **Ciryavar* 'the hiding of the ships' or *Nurtale **Mányavat* 'the hiding of my hands', adding that "being able to answer these questions would tell us what kind of an inflexion we have here." These very points were covered in some detail in my article. To reiterate: the associative case did not have a particular plural form (the *particular* plural, marked by *-r* or *-i*, is also known as the *partitive* plural) because the associative was originally partitive in sense; a partitive inflection of a partitive plural form would thus be redundant (partitive plural *ciryar* 'some ships' > nonsensical ***ciryavar* 'some of some ships'). I did not account for the lack of a dual associative in my article, although I should have. A dual partitive form such as ***ciryavat* would never have been used since 'some of two ships' is equivalent to saying 'a ship', and so the singular *ciryava* would be used instead. One would probably have used the associative *general-plural* forms to say 'the hiding of the ships' and 'the hiding of my hands'. The general plural did not simply mean 'many' (as many suppose), but referred to 'all' or 'the whole of a group (previously mentioned)', regardless of whether that group consisted of a multitude of items or only two. Thus *Nurtale Ciryalíva* means 'the hiding of the ships' (*i.e.* 'the hiding of the whole group of ships being discussed'), and *Nurtale Mányalíva* is 'the hiding of my hands', an entire set of hands consisting of only two, unless one happens to live near Three Mile Island or Chernobyl. An example of the general plural used with reference to two hands occurs in the early draft of *Namárie* in *The Treason of Isengard*, pp. 284-85: *Tintallen māli* *'the hands of the Kindler'.

The suffix *-voite* is not exclusive to *The Book of Lost Tales* as Craig contends. One example occurs in the *Etymologies s.v.* **INI-** 'female': *hanuvoite*, not translated but clearly meaning something like *'male, masculine, manly' (*cf.* cognates **hanwa** 'male' [also *s.v.* **INI-**] and **hanu** 'a male (of Men or Elves), male animal' [*s.v.* **3AN-**]). In refuting my proposal that *-voite* derives from associative *-va* plus the adjectival ending *-ite*, Craig cited the "curious" and "unique" phonological formula "*-a* + *-i* > *-oi* ". Curious indeed, since I never proposed such a formula in my article; "*-a* + *-i* > *-oi* " is purely Craig's construction, and it implies that the *a* > *o* shift seen in *-va* + *-ite* > *-voite* is due to the juxtaposition of the vowels. This is not at all the case; the *a* > *o* shift in *-va* + *-ite* > *-voite* appears to be attributable to a change in stress patterns, a phenomenon which is not at all unique in the corpus. *The Book of Lost Tales* tells of **Amillo**, the youngest of the great Valar, "who is named **Ómar**, whose voice is the best of all voices, who knoweth all songs in all speeches..." (LT1:75). The names **Ómar/Amillo** appear to be agentives derived from the same root, one not given in the *Lost Tales* but occurring in the *Etymologies:* **OM-**, whence also Q *óma* 'voice'. Thus both **Ómar** and **Amillo** probably mean *'He who speaks or sings with voice', or *'The Vocalizer' (*cf.* a similar pair of names in the *Lost Tales*: **Tamar/ Tamildo**, epithets of Aulë which are clearly agentives—*'The Smelter' or *'The Forger'—both derived from the root **TAMA** 'smelt, forge', LT1:250). The variation between **Óm-** and **Am-** is due to stress; **Óm-** is the stressed form, **Am-** the unstressed form. The same pattern occurs in another derivative of **OM-**: *óman* 'vowel' (with stressed *óm-*), pl. *amandi* (with unstressed *am-*). Similarly, the variation between *-vo-* and *-va* in *uruvoite/urúva* may be due to stress, *-vo-* occurring in a syllable receiving the primary stress and *-va* occurring in an unstressed final syllable.

To answer Craig's question as to why no dual form is given for the "S-case" (or *short locative*) on the Plotz declension chart, perhaps this is because the only possible forms, ***-ts** or *-st*, were unallowable final consonant groups in the final conception of Quenya. Final *-st* does occur at least once in *Qenya Lexicon:* **raust** 'hunting, preying' from root **RAVA** (LT1:260).

• *Nancy Martsch*   *Sherman Oaks, California*

VT *#17*: Beautiful cover by Pat Wynne. (Derived from his '89 Christmas card.)

Re. Paul Nolan Hyde's attendance at Elfcon: Whatever became of that group photo? *[Good question. Bill? —CFH]*

Stars: Sometimes it seems that people get so involved in the words by themselves that they forget the texts from which the words come. Context. **Borgil** comes from a Sindarin list of star-names, stars viewed by (the Sindarin-speaking) Gildor and company and the Hobbits. **Luinil** *et. al.* come from a Quenya series of star-names in a "high" section of *The Silmarillion*. Incidentally, none of these names are used in any of the descriptions of star-making found in any of the *Silmarillion* material written prior to *The Lord of the Rings*. (The only asterism named is the Sickle of the Valar, with various names.) Christopher Tolkien informs us that Tolkien wrote several "Annals" on the *Silmarillion* material after *The Lord of the Rings*. The names first appear in the published *Silmarillion*, and are found in a

Silmarillion manuscript mixed in with *LotR* papers at Marquette University. Pretty good circumstantial evidence for post-*LotR* composition. Also a strong reason why the language would be post-*LotR* in form. Context. I think they're post-*LotR* Quenya.

To the best of my knowledge the first publication of the association of **Luinil** *et al.* with the planets comes from "Star-catalogue" by Taum Santoski in *Lendarin and Danian* No. 2, Winter 1981-2, p. 18, where he cites the Marquette material. The first published association of **Luinil** with Varda's new stars that I know of is "Varda's Stars" by Nancy Martsch, *Beyond Bree*, Oct. '89, p. 7. The only evidence that I know for the association with the planets is the Marquette manuscript. Chris Gilson states that "Tolkien abandoned the tentative identification of **Nénar** with Neptune...." Could he please cite his source?

From Taum's description it appears that either Tolkien himself, or Christopher Tolkien making a note on his father's writing, made the identification with the planets. The usual argument against this is that Neptune and Uranus are too far away to see, and hence couldn't be known. (Quite forgetting that, when asked to name the planets, a person is likely to rattle off the entire list, not solely the naked-eye ones. Or forgetting the non-realistic world of *The Ambarkanta*.) *[Moreover, while there is no textual evidence for it, surely a telescope would be a small achievement for a race that can make* palantíri*? And what's more, Uranus is in fact visible to even human eyes, so long as the night is very dark and one knows exactly where to look.* —*CFH]* I'm quite willing to accept Tolkien's association as fact, at least as fact at the time he wrote it. Gilson's appeal to Classical mythology can be applied to the planets, too. Mercury is **Elemmírë** 'star-jewel', a bright jewel-like planet (and a variable one; hence our word *Mercurial* 'changeable'). Venus is Eärendil bearing the Silmaril with the light of the Two Trees; the brightest planet, and an association with fertility, if one really wants to stretch connections. *[Though perhaps we don't have to stretch connections too far; see my discussion "Over Middle-earth Sent Unto Men: On the Philological Origins of Tolkien's* Eärendil *Myth" in* Mythlore *LXV, Spring 1991, pp. 5–10, esp. note 6.* —*CFH]* Mars is **Carnil** 'red-star', a good description. Jupiter is **Alcarinquë** 'The Glorious (One)'; a description not only of its appearance but perhaps also as king of the gods. Saturn is **Lumbar**, variously translated but always with connotations of "shadow", "gloom". Saturn, as you well recall, is the bringer of old age. He's also the fellow who ate his children (*cf.* Goya's horrific picture). A suitable association. Both Neptune and Uranus are blue, so the name **Luinil** 'blue-star' is suitable for either one. However, **Nénar** clearly contains the word for water, and one of these planets is Neptune, named for the god of the sea. (Is Neptune associated with the rainy season? Does anyone know? *[Not to my knowledge; and I don't see how it could be, since Neptune's rising changes with its position relative to the Sun and Earth.* —*CFH]*) So an equation of **Nénar** with Neptune seems to me the most probable. Anyway, I've no particular reason to ascribe it to anything else—until someone can produce a text by Tolkien that says so.

When J.R.R. Tolkien perceived that he would be unable to complete *The Silmarillion* he asked Christopher, his son most interested in the Matter of Arda, to complete the task. Presumably he discussed his mythology with Christopher as well. Also Christopher has his father's manuscripts, including many not yet published. From what has been published we can see what an awful jumble those manuscripts were (and how bad the handwriting!). Christopher, by his own word, endeavored to be as faithful to his father's writing as possible. He also, in composing *The Silmarillion*, tried to use the latest coherent manuscripts on the subject. In *The Shaping of Middle-earth* Christopher names two works on the *Silmarillion* material composed after *The Lord of the Rings*: "The Grey Annals" and "The Annals of Aman" (composed 1951–2). As more and more of the Matter of Arda is published we can see where changes have taken place. There are "discrepancies" between the pre-*LotR* and *Silmarillion* material that must have an explanation in the late- and post-*LotR* writings. (For instance, we can see that "Sindarin" emerged late in *LotR*. Another reason why *LotR* makes a good dividing point.) To dismiss as unreliable the material in the Appendix to *The Silmarillion* simply because one does not understand or agree with it, as does the unnamed rebutter to Craig Marnock (is that you, Carl? *[Heavens, no! That was in Tom's column, so why you'd think it was anyone other than Tom is beyond me. Whenever I intrude on someone else's writing, I set it in square brackets and italics, just like this note, and end it with my initials, thusly: −CFH]*) is *the height of arrogance*. Do not be so quick to ascribe to error that which you do not understand, for your understanding may be lacking. Also, it is unjust to score Christopher for the "*fin-*" misidentification, considering the amount of paper (and in three different locations!) he has to go through. Could you do so much better? I think we owe Christopher Tolkien a debt of gratitude for all that he has done, instead of this carping and criticizing. Remember, publication might have ceased after *The Lord of the Rings*. And you would have to do the research through the manuscripts yourself.

For what it's worth, **Aranrúth** could be two separate words, **aran** and **rúth**. There are instances of a compound being written together and separately: **Gil-galad** and **Gilgalad**, for example. Craig Marnock overlooked **carag**, also from **KARAK-**.

"*Words and Devices*": Very interesting. Don't forget those awful puns, like **Sahóra**.

[You freely call "fin- = 'hair'" a misidentification (rather than simply ascribing it to an imperfect understanding as you seem to demand of others), which is all that Tom has done. No one feels anything but intense gratitude to Christopher Tolkien for the work he has done, and every issue of VT or Beyond Bree or any other Tolkienian publication is an expression of that gratitude (we certainly aren't in this for the money!); but Christopher is still human, and therefore capable of error, all the more so because of the complexity of the manuscripts. As scholars, it is our duty to question and probe, rather than to simply blindly accept everything as printed. This is how our knowledge advances, and how errors, where they occur, are corrected. −CFH]

• *Jorge Quiñónez*   *San Diego, California*

The artwork in *VT* in the past issues has been outstanding! The two Valar on the covers of *VT*s #15 (Mandos) and #16 (Melkor) and the Maia on the cover of *VT* #17 (Aiwendil) all prove that *VT* is moving up in the world: It has become a publication of Valinorean stature. Since *VT* #9, Pat Wynne has had five covers, Tom Loback three, and Adam Christensen one. I think Pat's artwork, despite most of it being very old, was quite impressive. Laurefindel killing the Valarauko in *VT* #13; Mandos greeting the dead in Quenya (and not in that bombastically Beleriandic babble-Sindarin); the magnificent Melkor descending to claim what was properly his; or even the foolish bird-brain Aiwendil; it was all very good. Keep the Great Ones of Valinor coming, Pat.

On another matter, I have to apologize to Chris Gilson for incorrectly citing his "<u>An</u> High-elven Glossary" as "<u>A</u> High-elven Glossary". It was an oversight on my part (Ned had nothing to do with it).

I was glad to see Craig Marnock back after a long hiatus with a letter of comment. His remark on Chris and Pat's article in *VT* #14 that "... for a mere eleven words of Elvish it does seem a trifle excessive ..." seemed to me a bit excessively trifling, especially when he should look at the length of many of his own letters of comment. I've read biblical commentaries of over 100 pages on some of the shorter *Tehillim*.

Craig's remark on Pat's article on the Associative case, that he "really felt it left out the question of what this declension is used for in Quenya", shows that he misunderstood Pat's purpose behind the article: it was meant as a descriptive study of the Associative case, rather than a prescriptive study; *i.e.* it was an article *describing* how the case was used in Tolkien's works, rather than *prescribing* how to use it in your own Quenya. (It is important to note that we agreed at the Colloquium that *I Parma* would be descriptive in nature, which is a bit more conservative and therefore "safe".)

I fear people are getting the impression that *VT* is becoming a newsletter only for columns, especially now that there are three columns, and more on the way. (I read on the last page of *VT* #17 that Craig will be doing a series on his own translation of the *Ainulindalë*; additionally, Eli Bar-Yahalom tells me that he's going to write a bilingual column in Quenya and English!) Don't you think that this is going to rob space from other people who want to do regular articles?

[Well, of course not! You assume that VT *has a fixed page count; this is not so. I'd be deliriously happy to have a 64-page* VT *(of course, I'd have to raise subscription rates to cover the increased postage costs if this happened, but it would [I think] be worth it!). It's true that the last issue of* VT *was dominated by letters and columns, but I can only print what people send me. Craig's translation of the* Ainulindalë *isn't really a column, since it has a definite end (though this will be some time in arriving); rather, it is a series of articles. —CFH]*

I would like to see someone do a review of the Elvish content of ICE's *Middle-earth Adventure Guidebook 2*. Any takers out there?

The Death of Glaurung
by Patrick Wynne
[based on The Silmarillion, *pg. 222]*

San Turambar tultane finie ar verie ar rastane i-ollo ar túle nonna i-urulóke. San ettunkiéro Urdolwen ar ranko ilya-tuonen teviéva, nastanéro maksakumba lókenna. Nan íre Laurundo sinte nurunaike, ramniéro, ar taura-angayassenen rumniéro ar hante sar kilya ar entasse kaire palpala palúre unqualenen. Ar ustanéro ilqua entasse mennai úr mi so quéle.

Prose translation

"Then Túrin summoned his cunning and boldness and climbed the cliff, and came beneath the dragon. Then he drew Gurthang, and with all the might of his arm and of his hate, he stabbed the soft-bellied worm. But when Glaurung knew his death-pang, he roared, and in his great misery he heaved himself up and hurled himself across the chasm, and there lay beating the ground in his agony. And he burned everything there, until the fire within him died."

Verse translation
by Christopher Gilson
Reprinted with permission from Mythlore *LXII, Summer 1990*

Then Master-fate did manly fetch
His cunning, clomb that cliff beneath
The drake and drew his death wand out.
Then with arm all strength of anger stung
That hero the soft, hord-heaping snake.
When Golden-girt with pangs of pain
In mighty misery mounted up,
He coiled across and clove the gorge
To lay along it, bosom beating,
Until his flames unfurl and fires slake.

Ainulindalë
"The Great Music of the Ainur"
by Craig Marnock

— Part One —

Introduction

This is the first part of what I hope will eventually be a complete translation of *Ainulindalë*, "The Great Music of the Ainur", as published in *The Silmarillion*. I have the first of four pages drafted, and a third of this revised. I hope (but cannot promise) to present a paragraph or two every issue of *VT*, which should provide an impetus to get the whole finished.

It is the first paragraph I present here, with a few notes on some of the forms used. Funnily enough, the first paragraph is one of the hardest of all to translate; some of the phrases here have been through half a dozen different renderings. For this version I have tried to follow the English as closely as possible. I have translated some idioms exactly, but have not tried to be consistent in this.

Alternative suggestions, comments, and other feedback are actively encouraged. I hope one day to publish a revised version in a single edition.

However, suggestions must follow the rules of the "game": this rendering is written, as far as is humanly possible, in the so-called "final-form" Quenya of *The Lord of the Rings* and after. This is partly the fun of the exercise, and alternative readings should ideally follow this. (Words not found in this corpus tend to be supplied by morphological manipulation [see my article in *Quettar #39*] or by translation from Sindarin.)

Translation
The Silmarillion, p. 15

1   *Eä Eru, yo essë ná Ilúvatar Ardassë;*
      ar tanerwë[1] i Ainur minyavë, i ner i órerwo híni,
      ar nentë va[2] su i lúmenna tanerwë ilyë natï[3].

4   *Ar queterwë tenna, ánala lindëo lini tenna;*
      ar lindentë sun, ar nerw' alassëa.[4]

6   *Nán[5] anda lúmessë lindentë ilya[6] eressessë, ecar[7] hostiessen,*
      ar nossenta hlaster;
      an ilya nolë Ilúvatáro óreo i men eryavë yallo tules,
      ar lolóëntë[8] nossë' onólenna.[9]

10 *Nán onólenta loë andavë ter hlastienta oialë,*
      ar erelamma ar olinienta[10] loër.

Notes

1. Pronouns. Aliens have a tendency to notice what you want them to. My own personal alien pointed out to me the extreme regularity of the "Plotz" declension (so regular that Tolkien even missed out half of one of only two declensions required for an entire inflexionally rich language), and wondered if this might not reflect some underlying æsthetic in what was, after all, a personal project.

   I must say I found this quite reasonable, and it seemed to apply to the examples of the pronouns we find in "final-form" Quenya in much the same way as the declensions we find in the text and which appear in the chart.

   My reasoning here runs (very) briefly like this: **-rwa* is to *-rya* as *-ro* is to *-re*. Consequently **-rwë* is to **-rwa* as *-nyë* is to *-nya*, and *-lmë* is to *-lma*.

   Concerned readers should feel free to mentally replace my forms with their own favourite hypothetical final-form 3 masc. sing. pronouns where relevant.

2. Based on CE *gwa-* as seen in ***Legolas*** (Letter #211). For the sense here I have assumed it is the successor of **ngua* in LT2 (App. *s.v.* **Golosbrindi**) and **WŌ-** in *Etymologies*. The most logical meanings are either prepositional ('with') or adverbial ('together') — in which case the following **su* ('him') should be omitted.

3. "... before aught else was made" is probably the hardest phrase to render I've so far come across. Alternative suggestions are welcome. *Nat* ('thing') is from *Etymologies*, and is a very handy word. Another attempt at glossing 'before' is ***tenn' i lúmë yassë***. Also some form of √*khil* 'follow' might be better than *ilyë*.

4. Why are there so few words for 'happy'? I'm sure there is a word meaning 'joyful' in Sindarin somewhere, but cannot find it. ('Glory' is *Gelw* in the letter to Sam, but I don't know if this is what I was thinking of.) Rather than use a lengthy paraphrase each time (*e.g. **órerwa quantë cálenen***) this is based on *Etymologies* **GALÁS-**.

5. Just about every main clause in the *Ainulindalë* begins with either 'and' or 'but', so using this seemed unavoidable (< **NDAN-**).

6. This should perhaps be omitted but does sit nicely in the text; it is assumed to mean 'each'.

7. A blind "phonological translation" of *egor* in the unpublished Epilogue to *LotR*.

8. A frequentative of a hypothesised verb 'to grow', based on *loa*. Perhaps read forms of **al-* (from √*gal* 'to grow' intr.) or maybe **anda-* 'to wax' (*cp. **cúna-***) where appropriate.

9. Uses *gwa-* as noted above — perhaps instead stressed **va-*, possibly also **-ngólë*. Alternatively read ***nossen*(g)*ólë*** here.

10. The best I can do for 'harmony' (a coinage, of course). Perhaps a more musically minded E.L.F. member can supply a better one.

Counting Limits
by Bill Welden

It is easiest to think of time in terms of space. The future lies ahead of us, the past behind. History is a vast continent and each ancient civilization thrives in some remote valley (though the mountains are perhaps impassable). The present is only a small part of the totality of history.

The reality, however, is that the past only exists to the extent that it is reflected in the present. Alexander is a name in some books that still exist; is Greek architecture in Egypt; is a few broken statues scattered around the Mediterranean. Any past-Alexander is a fiction, designed to explain the remnants that carry his name. Far from being a small part of history, the present is everything; and history is completely contained within it.

Language reflects reality in miniature, in this as in so many other ways. Like fragments of ancient statues, words tell stories. The word calculate, for example, tells of a time when arithmetic was done with pebbles (Latin *calculi*, ultimately from Greek *khalix* 'limestone', the source also of *chalk* and *calcium*) on counting boards.

When a sequence of words is learned by many people and survives for generations, it captures and preserves history just like an individual word. The word *helpmate* 'helper' found its origin in the King James translation of Genesis 2:18 "I will make an help meet for him". This sentence continued to be recited long after the Anglo-Saxon *meet* was abandoned in general use in favor of the equivalent Latin word *appropriate*. Knowing *meet* only in the context of this verse, people were free to assume it to be a noun, modified by 'help'. Thus *help-meet* 'helper'. Obviously archaic (context!) it needed only to be modernized as *helpmate*.[1]

The longest sequence of words which everybody learns (and everyone has learned for generations uncounted) are the cardinal numbers; and every language reveals something of its history through the sequence of its number words.

Consider English *eleven* and *twelve*. Comparison with other Germanic languages (but particularly with the ancient Gothic *áinlif, twalif*) shows that these words are not root-words, but metaphors meaning 'one left over' and 'two left over'. The implication seems to be that at one time the counting sequence stopped at ten. If you needed to count eleven things, you would have 'one left over' when you got done.

Now it is easy to assume that we are talking about people who did not understand numbers beyond ten; but this was not the case. The counting sequence could be used directly on small collections of objects. Large collections could be counted by dividing them into groups of countable size, and then counting the groups:

---

[1] Had Chris Gilson been there, of course, he would have explained that the use of the word 'an' indicated that 'help' was not accented, and therefore could not be the first element of a nominal compound.

The old man's flat face and dark eyes showed nothing, but his voice was sullen with displeasure. "Wild Men are wild, free, but not children," he answered ... "I count many things: stars in sky, leaves on trees, men in the dark. You have a score of scores counted ten times and five. They have more. Big fight, and who will win?" (III:106)

A short counting sequence is quite analogous to a measuring stick: as long as it does the job most of the time, we are quite satisfied with the occasional need to juggle it around to measure something longer.

The Germans who added the numbers *áinlif* and *twalif* were not satisfied with just ten numbers, but seemed to be happy with twelve, since there is no evidence of a **thrilif*. Our number system appears to have been built up in layers, at one point going no farther than ten, and later stopping at twelve. Such counting limits can be seen in virtually every language.

An interesting parallel occurs in the Greek language, where *eleven* and *twelve* are *hénteka* and *dódeka* (literally 'one-ten' and 'two-ten'), but *thirteen* is *dekatreís* 'ten-three', *fourteen* is *dekatésseres* 'ten-four' and so forth. Using a similar line of reasoning, we would explain this discontinuity in the Greek counting sequence by hypothesizing an ancient counting limit at twelve. In fact, Ancient Greek (which, unlike Common Germanic, is very well documented) has words for *eleven* and *twelve*, *héndeka* and *dódeka*, but no words for *thirteen* through *nineteen*. When they needed to say 'thirteen', they used the metaphor *treís kai deka* 'three and ten'.

There are indications of even older counting limits in the Indo-European number sequence. First, note that *oktō*, the reconstructed IE word for 'eight', can be explained as a dual form, containing the root **kwet-* for 'four'. The root for 'nine', **newn-* has been explained as a derivative of **newo-* 'new', being a new number after a counting limit at eight; or alternatively as containing **oino-* 'one' (the first *n*) and having a meaning like 'one from ten'.

The Indo-European words for 'one' through 'seven' do not yield so readily to analysis, suggesting that they might be older formations than the words for 'eight' and 'nine'. These words are also conspicuously absent from the second decade in Latin: 'eighteen' is *duodēvīginti* 'two from twenty' and 'nineteen' is *undēvīginti* 'one from twenty'.

The variety of metaphors used for the number 'eighteen' in the Indo-European languages suggests strongly that the common ancestor of these languages had no word for this concept. We have Latin *duodēvīginti* 'two from twenty'. Ancient Greek *oktō kai deka* 'eight and ten', German *achtzehn* 'eight-ten', Lithuanian *ashtunolika* 'eight left over' (likely borrowed from Germanic), and from the Celtic branch Irish *ocht-deec* 'eight-two-five', Breton *triouch* 'three-six' and Welsh *deunaw* 'two-nine'.

Here is one sequence of events which could have led to the evidence we see. Perhaps there was a time when number words existed for 'one' through 'seven', as well as 'ten'. Words for 'thirty', 'forty', *etc.* (though not 'twenty', which was a special case) were formed by a straightforward metaphor 'three tens', 'four tens', and so forth. Words for 'eleven' through 'seventeen' were formed by a metaphor which became analytically obscure to the native speakers, so that they no longer saw an obvious connection between, say, 'five' and 'fifteen'.

Now, when words were coined for 'eight' and 'nine' they no longer suggested how to create corresponding words for 'eighteen' and 'nineteen'. Each of the descendent language groups devised its own metaphor for these less-used numbers.

Similar types of speculation and analysis can be done with every language group in the world. With rare exceptions we see that number sequences are not the work of a single individual or even a single culture; but are built up bit by bit over time, driven by different social perspectives and the changing demand to be able to work with higher numbers.

Even though we have only four words for numbers higher than ten in Tolkien's languages, there is still some evidence of counting limits in Eldarin.

The number *minque* 'eleven' (root **MINIK-**), for example, is derived from the root **MINI-** meaning 'stand alone', 'stick out', or secondarily, 'one'. This might refer to the fact that it 'sticks out' beyond the number sequence (which therefore stops at ten); or, noting that roots ending with **-K** often refer to cutting, it may mean 'one (cut) from (twelve)'. In any event, the fact that this number word is derived from a different number root strongly suggests a counting limit at ten.

Similarly, for the material of the *Lost Tales*, the words for 'nine' and 'ten', *olma* and *lempe*, can be seen as derivatives of 'three' and 'five', *ole* and *lemin*; suggesting a limit of counting between five and eight. Perhaps this limit is six: Tolkien tells us that the Elves "preferred to reckon in sixes and twelves" (III:385).

There is more evidence for a counting limit at six in this early material, but presenting it will require a proper analysis of the word *leminkainen*. We are told that this word means 'twenty-three', even though it has as a component the number 'five', *lemin*. I will take this up in my next article.

I have taken much of the material of this article from Karl Menninger's excellent book *Number Words and Number Symbols*, translated from the 1958 revision entitled *Zahlwort und Ziffer*, published by Vandenhoeck and Ruprecht in Göttingen. My translation is by Paul Broneer and was published in 1969 by the M.I.T. Press. I have also made extensive use of Calvert Watkins' *Indo-European and the Indo-Europeans*, published as an appendix to the first edition of the *American Heritage Dictionary*.

Though my credentials are in Eldarin studies and not in European historical linguistics, I have taken significant liberties of interpretation and speculation in presenting this material. If you are interested in this subject, I strongly recommend that you find a copy of Menninger's book and read it. He speaks with more authority and goes into additional detail on the subject of counting limits (as well as many other interesting aspects of written and spoken numbers).

Words and Devices
A column by Patrick Wynne and Carl F. Hostetter

"It is said also that these Men had long ago had dealings with the Dark Elves east of the mountains, and from them had learned much of their speech; and since all the languages of the Quendi were of one origin, the language of Bëor and his folk resembled the Elven-tongue in many words and devices." (S-141)

The purpose of this column is to examine words and other linguistic features in Tolkien's Secondary World languages that have Primary World cognates and analogues. Comments and contributions are encouraged: send them to Carl F. Hostetter, 2509 Ambling Circle, Crofton, MD 21114, USA.

Harping on a Theme

No musical instrument is more evocative of Middle-earth than the harp, with its haunting, Elvish sound and gracefully curved shape. Harps are a recurrent element in Tolkien's mythology and provide a bittersweet accompaniment to the great deeds of the Elder Days. In the earliest version of Tolkien's cosmogonic myth *The Music of the Ainur* (c. 1918-20) harps are present at the very creation of the universe, forming part of the angelic orchestra which played before Ilúvatar:

> "Then the harpists, and the lutanists, the flautists and pipers, the organs and the countless choirs of the Ainur began to fashion the theme of Ilúvatar into great music…" (LT1:53).

The Book of Lost Tales also features a God devoted to harps: "In Valmar too dwelt Noldorin known long ago as Salmar, playing now upon his harps and lyres, now sitting beneath Laurelin and raising sweet music with an instrument of the bow." (LT1:75) Salmar was to survive into *The Silmarillion*, where he was demoted to the rank of Maia but retained his connection with music: "Salmar…who made the horns of Ulmo that none may ever forget who once has heard them…" (S:40)

Harps figure prominently in some memorable events of the First Age. Our previous column cited the tale of Felagund's first meeting with the folk of Bëor, when the Elven-lord "took a rude harp which Bëor had laid aside, and he played music upon it such as mortal ear had never heard." (LR:275) Bëor's "rude harp" was immortalized as an heraldic symbol on Finrod's coat of arms (see plate 47 in *Pictures by J.R.R. Tolkien*). The harp as an Elvish heraldic device also occurs in *The Fall of Gondolin*. One of the eleven houses of the Gondothlim in Gondolin was the People of the Harp, under the lordship of Salgant, and as they marched into battle "a harp of silver shone in their blazonry upon a field of black, but Salgant bore one of gold…" (LT2:173). Another unforgettable image is Fingon's discovery of Maedhros upon the heights of Thangorodrim : "Then in defiance of the Orcs, who cowered still in the dark vaults beneath the earth, he took his harp and sang a song of Valinor that the Noldor made of old…suddenly above him far and faint his song was taken up, and a voice answering called to him. Maedhros it was…" (S:110).

This fascination with harps was evident in later ages as well. In *The Hobbit* Tolkien wryly characterizes the sort of person impervious to the allure of harps, writing that among the treasures the Dwarves found in Smaug's lair were "many golden harps strung with silver...and being magical (and also untouched by the dragon, who had small interest in music) they were still in tune." (H:203) In *The Lord of the Rings*, both Elrond and Galadriel play harps (see I:388 and III:308), and the tragic fate of the last High King of the Noldor in Middle-earth is succinctly yet poignantly encompassed in the opening couplet of *The Fall of Gil-galad* (I:197):

> *Gil-galad was an Elven-king.*
> *Of him the harpers sadly sing:*

Not surprisingly, the Elvish languages also reflect this emphasis on harps. Among the abundance of Elvish words for 'harp', 'harpist', 'harp-music', and related concepts there are several forms which appear to be related to words in the Primary World, and in this installment of "Words and Devices" we will explore some of the more intriguing cross-etymologies to be found in this area of Elvish vocabulary.

In the Appendix to *The Book of Lost Tales, Part One* Christopher Tolkien says of the name *Salmar*: "This name must belong with derivatives of the root SALA [in the *Qenya Lexicon*]: *salma* 'lyre', *salmë* 'harp-playing', etc." (LT1:265) Primary-World forms related to these words might readily suggest themselves to the reader, but to fully appreciate the possible connections of *Salmar*, *salma*, and *salmë* with the later tongues of Men we must first examine their construction purely in terms of the linguistic scenario of the Secondary World presented in the *Lost Tales*.

Although no definition is given for the root SALA, it is probably verbal — 'to play (the harp)' — since the endings *-ma* and *-më* seen in the derivatives *salma* and *salmë* are most often used with verbal roots. *-ma* and *-më* occur frequently in the Qenya vocabulary of the *Lost Tales*. *-ma* forms agent nouns which refer to a thing that performs the action of the root. Examples include *tulma* 'bier', literally *'a thing that bears', < TULU 'fetch, bring, bear' (LT1:270); and *vaima* 'robe', literally *'a thing that enfolds', < VAYA 'enfold' (LT1:271). The literal sense of these words might also be passive rather than active, *i.e.* a *tulma* 'bier' is *'something that is carried', and a *vaima* 'robe' is *'something that is wrapped'. Most often nouns in *-ma* refer to concrete objects, but not always; note *kalma* 'daylight' < KALA 'shine golden' (LT1:254)[1]. From these examples we can see that *salma* 'lyre' is literally *'a thing that plays' or *'something that is played' < SALA *'to play'.

---

[1]　This noun appears with more concrete definitions in later writings. In the second version of *Oilima Markirya* (*c.* 1931) *kalma* is glossed as 'light' in line 12 and as 'candle' in line 19 (MC:213-15). The *Etymologies* (*c.* 1937-38) *s.v.* **KAL-** lists *kalma* 'a light, lamp' beside *kala* 'light'. In Appendix E of *The Lord of the Rings* *calma* 'lamp' is the name of *tengwa* 3. It is difficult to say whether these various glosses of *kalma* as 'daylight', 'light', 'candle', and 'lamp' at different chronological periods represent a change in Tolkien's conception of the word's meaning. On one hand, the entry in the *Etymologies* implies the

The name **Salmar** itself contains **salma** 'lyre'. There are several examples in the *Lost Tales* of an agentive suffix *-(a)r*. This suffix could be applied to a verbal root, as with **vardar** 'king', literally *'ruler, governor', < **vard-** 'rule, govern' (LT1:273). It could also be applied to a noun, as with *falmar* 'wave as it breaks', literally *'foamer', < the noun *falma* 'foam' (< FALA). **Salmar** follows the latter pattern: *'The Harper' or *'The Lyre-player' < **salma** 'lyre' + agentive *-r*.[2]

The suffix *-me* forms nouns referring to a verbal action, much like English verbal nouns in *-ing*. Some of these verbal nouns are used concretely, for example **ormë** 'summit, crest', literally *'a rising', < ORO *'rise' (LT1:256). But far more often verbal nouns in *-më* refer to abstract concepts or intangible things: **qalmë** 'death', literally *'dying', < QALA 'die' (LT1:264); and **númë** 'West', literally *'setting', < NUHU 'bow, bend down, stoop, sink' (LT1:263). And so we have **salmë** 'harp-playing' < SALA *'to play (the harp)'.

The *Lost Tales* vocabulary also features an agentive suffix *-mo*. It appears often in masculine names, such as **Ulmo** *'The Pourer' < ULU 'pour, flow fast' (LT1:270); and **Kalmo** *'Goldgleamer' < KALA 'shine golden" (LT1:254). Although these names are not glossed in the *Lost Tales* (hence the asterisks before our translations), it is clear from numerous similar forms which *are* translated in later writings that these names are agentives—**Ulmo**, for example, is translated as 'The Rainer' or 'The Pourer' in the Index to *The Silmarillion* (S:352).

The three noun endings *-ma*, *-më*, *-mo* in the *Lost Tales* are clearly related in both form and function. In general terms:

> *-ma* Agent (the thing performing an action)
> *-mo* Agent (the person performing an action)
> *-më* Action (usually abstract, sometimes concrete)

---

development of a distinction between 'light' = 'radiance' (**kala**) and 'light' = 'a thing from which light comes' (**kalma**). Yet in *OM2* **kalma** is used in both the abstract and concrete senses, just as English *light* can refer to daylight, light in general, or any object which emits light. The various glosses of **kalma** could represent a clarification of the word's full semantic range rather than indicating a shift in its meaning.

[2] However, it should be noted that *'The Harper' may not be the meaning of the name in the later versions of the mythology. In the other writings published to date Salmar is only mentioned twice, once in the 1930s version of the *Ainulindalë* (*cf.* LR:161) and again in *The Silmarillion*. In both instances no connection is made between Salmar and harps, and all that we are told of him is that he made the great horns of Ulmo, called the Ulumúri in *The Silmarillion*. In the 1930s *Ainulindalë* these horns are referred to simply as "the conches of Ulmo". In the *Etymologies*, also written in the 1930s, there is the following entry:

SYAL- *syalmā : Q *hyalma* shell, conch, horn of Ulmo. N *half* seashell.

It is tempting to suppose from this that in the later versions of the mythology Tolkien intended to connect the name **Salmar** with the base **SYAL-** and its derivatives rather than with **salma** 'lyre', but nothing definite can be said on this matter without further evidence.

In his introduction to the Appendix in *The Book of Lost Tales, Part One* Christopher Tolkien notes that "an old vocalic 'ablaut' (variation, in length or quality, of vowels in series)" (LT1:247) is a characteristic of the Elvish languages during the *Lost Tales* period. An example of this ablaut may be found among the derivatives of the root HELE in QL: *helkë* 'ice', *hilkin* 'it freezes', and *halkin* 'frozen'. It seems possible that the noun endings *-ma*, *-më*, *-mo* also shared a common origin, and the variation of the final vowels is due to the "old vocalic ablaut".

When it came to forming nouns, Indo-European had a healthy selection of derivative suffixes to choose from. One of these suffixes was *-mo-*, which also had the form *-mā*. As with many IE derivative suffixes, the uses of *-mo-/-mā* were sufficiently diverse to make it difficult to characterize them concisely. It is worth noting, however, that among the uses of *-mo-/-mā* (and their resulting Greek and Latin forms) were some that are highly reminiscent of Qenya *-ma*, *-mo*, *-më*. For example, in Greek *-mo-/-mā* led to a suffix *-μη* appearing in a number of abstract verbal nouns which resemble Qenya verbal nouns in *-më*. Examples include φήμη 'saying, speech, report' (< *bhā-ma*, from root **bhā-**[2] 'to speak'), ὀσμή 'odor, fragrance' (< *od-mā-*, from root **od-**[1] 'to smell'), μνήμη 'memory' (< **mnā-**, extended form of the root **men-**[1] 'to think'), and γνώμη 'intelligence, opinion' (< root **gnō-** 'to know'). The Latin cognate of Greek *-μη* was *-ma*, and the form equivalent to φήμη was *fāma* 'talk, reputation, fame'. Other, more concrete examples of Latin nouns in *-ma* which resemble Qenya nouns in *-ma* are the neuter plural *arma* 'fittings, arms, weapons of war' (< *ar(ə)-mo-*, from root **ar-** 'to fit together'), *flamma* 'flame' (< *flag-ma*, from **bhel-**[1] 'to shine, flash, burn'), and *gemma* 'bud, gem' (< *gembh-mā*, from **gembh-** 'tooth, nail'). IE *-mo-/-mā* also led to Greek forms in *-μος* and Latin ones in *-mus*. For example, the IE root **anə-** 'to breathe' in suffixed form *anə-mo-* led to Greek ἄνεμοσ 'wind' and Latin *animus* 'soul' (as well as *anima* 'wind, breath, life').[3]

Another IE derivative suffix with even greater similarities to Qenya *-ma*, *-mo*, *-më* was *-men-*. This led to the Greek masculine suffixes *-μην* and *-μων* as well as Latin *-mō* (genitive *-mōnis*), which appear in agent nouns and action nouns. These Greek and Latin masculine agent nouns recall the Qenya masculine agent nouns in *-mo*.[4] Examples in Greek include ἡγεμών 'leader' (< ἡγέομαι 'lead', from the root **sāg-** 'to seek out') and γνώμων 'a judge, interpreter' (< the root **gnō-** 'to know'). An interesting example in Latin is *pulmō* 'lung' (< *pl[e]u-mon-* 'lung', literally 'floater', from the root **pleu-** 'to flow'), with Greek cognate πλεύμων, πνεύμων 'lung'.

---

[3]   The difference in meaning between the Greek and Latin forms recalls that seen in Q *súle* 'breath' in the *Etymologies s.v.* **THŪ-** 'puff, blow' and Q *súle* (earlier *thúle*) 'spirit', given as the name of *tengwa* 9 in Appendix E of *LotR*.

[4]   The Greek and Latin agent nouns are masculine in the *grammatical* sense and can also refer to things lacking sexual gender, *e.g.* Gk. τελαμών 'strap for carrying', L. *sermō* 'discourse'. On the other hand, Qenya lacked grammatical gender, so Qenya agent nouns in *-mo* are masculine only with reference to sexual gender.

IE -*men*- also yielded neuter suffixes, Greek -μα (genitive -ματοσ) and Latin -*men*. Carl Darling Buck, in his *Comparative Grammar of Greek and Latin*, describes these neuter nouns as "Originally action nouns, but most frequently denoting the result of the action." (pg. 320) The Latin forms in -*men* are thus reminiscent on Qenya forms in -*më*. For example, the verb stem seen in Latin *frangō* 'break' (from the IE root **bhreg-** 'to break') also led to the noun *fragmen*, which according to Buck's statement may have originally been an action noun 'breaking' but came to have the meaning 'fragment', referring to the result of the action rather than to the action itself. In some words the distinction between the action and the result of the action is inconsequential, as in Latin *flūmen* 'stream' < *fluō* 'flow', an etymology which invites comparison with Qenya *kelumë* 'stream' < KELE, KELU 'flow, trickle, ooze' (LT1:257).[5]

Greek -μα is highly suggestive of Qenya -*ma*. According to Buck, -μα is "One of the most productive types in Greek, the number running to several thousands." (*ibid.*) Examples include πρᾶγμα 'act' (< πράσσω 'do'), ποίημα 'a work, poem' (< ποιέω 'make'), and δέρμα 'skin' (< δέρω 'flay'). Note that the concrete/abstract contrast seen in the pair μνῆμα 'monument' *versus* μνήμη 'memory' (both from the root **men-**[1] 'to think') parallels the concrete/abstract contrast which is typical of Qenya nouns in -*ma* versus those in -*më*.

Another Greek noun in -μα is ψάλμα 'a tune for a stringed instrument'. Greek ψαλμός 'the sound of the harp, a song sung to the harp' is a derivative of the same verb stem and was taken into Latin as *psalmus*, which ultimately led to English *psalm*. There seems little doubt that the correlation of form and meaning between Qenya *salma* 'lyre' and *salmë* 'harp-playing' and ψάλμα, ψαλμός, *psalmus*, and *psalm* [6] is deliberate, and that Tolkien meant to imply a genetic relationship which includes both the verb stems SALA and ψαλ- as well as the derivational suffixes -*ma*/ -*më* and -μα/-μος (IE -*men*-/-*mo*-).

Both ψάλμα and ψαλμός derive from the verb ψάλλω, which according to Liddell and Scott's *Intermediate Greek-English Lexicon* had the basic meaning 'to touch sharply, to pluck, pull, twitch', as well as 'to play a stringed instrument with the fingers, not with the plectron', and later 'to sing to a harp'. The ultimate origin of ψάλλω seems unclear. Calvert Watkins, in his *Dictionary of Indo-European Roots*, hesitantly lists ψάλλω as a possible derivative of the IE root **pōl-** 'to touch, feel, shake': "Perhaps suffixed form **psal-yo-* in Greek *psallein* [= ψάλλω], to pluck, play the harp (but more likely of imitative origin)". Watkins also notes that the root **pol-** 'finger' (whence Latin *pollex* 'thumb') may be the same root as **pōl-** 'to touch, feel, shake', which explains the assumption that the latter could be the source of ψάλλω, with its sense of plucking with the fingers.

---

[5] This early item in the High-elven vocabulary occurs with virtually the same form and meaning in the third version of *Oilima Markirya*, written in the last decade of Tolkien's life: *kelume* 'flowing, flood (tide), stream' (MC:223).

[6] The Old French form of *psalm* was *salme*, orthographically identical to Qenya *salmë* (though undoubtedly the pronounciation differed).

Tolkien may have intended for SALA and its derivatives to provide the "real" source of ψάλλω and its derivatives. It is unfortunate that not much light can be shed on the literal meaning of SALA or its connections with other Elvish roots. It certainly cannot be connected with **LEP-**, **LEPET** 'finger' (closely akin to **LEP-**, **LEPEN**, **LEPEK** 'five') in the *Etymologies*, bases which probably existed in a similar form at the time of the *Lost Tales* judging by the words **Lemin** 'five' and **Lempe** 'ten' which Christopher Tolkien mentions as being among the original entries in the *Qenya Lexicon* (LT1:246). About the most that can be said is that SALA is semantically (and perhaps phonetically) akin to another root in QL: TYALA, whence *tyalië* 'play, game' (LT1:260). This kinship is emphasized in the *Etymologies*, where we learn under the entry **ÑGAN-**, **ÑGANAD-** that the name **Salgant** of the lord of the People of the Harp was to be replaced by **Talagant** (or **Talagand**) 'Harper', the first element derived from the base **TYAL-** 'play'.

The base **ÑGAN-**, **ÑGANAD-** cited above is translated in the *Etymologies* as 'play (on stringed instrument)',[7] and not surprisingly the derivatives listed in its entry are exclusively concerned with harps. The Quenya forms given are *ñande* 'a harp', *ñandelle* 'little harp', *ñandele* 'harping', *ñanda-* 'to harp', and *ñandaro* 'harper'. Other derivatives include Noldorin **gandel, gannel** 'a harp' and Ilkorin **gangel, genglin**. The Ilkorin forms are not translated, but **gangel** is obviously 'a harp' and **genglin** the plural form 'harps' (compare Ilk. **talum** 'ground, floor', pl. **telmin**, LR:390). Both N **gandel, gannel** and Ilk. **gangel** 'harp' are apparently cognate with Q *ñandelle* 'little harp'[8] rather than *ñande* 'a harp', implying that small harps were the norm in Middle-earth.

Readers of the *Kalevala* will recall that the Finnish word for harp is *kantele*. Runo 40 of the epic describes the making of a *kantele* by the archetypal shaman Väinämöinen, a passage which we quote here from the translation by Francis Peabody Magoun, Jr. (pg. 274):

> He made a pikebone instrument, produced an instrument of eternal joy.
> From what was the harp's frame? From the great pike's jawbone.
> From what are the harp's pegs? They are from the pike's teeth.
> From what are the harps's strings? From the hairs of the Demon's gelding.
> Now the intrument was produced, the harp got ready,
> the great pikebone instrument, the fishbone harp.

Of course, the *kantele* was more conventionally made from wood. In an appendix to his translation, Magoun gives the following description, with an accompanying illustration: "*kantele*, an ancient Finnish five-stringed instrument, held on the knees and plucked with fingers, is probably most conveniently rendered by "harp," though it might be thought of as an unsophisticated zither" (p. 383).

---

[7] This base is probably onomatopoeic, with an echoic element *ÑGA- also seen in the bases **ÑGAL-**, **ÑGALAM-** 'talk loud or incoherently' and **ÑGAW-** 'howl'.

[8] The diminutive suffix *-lle* also occurs in **Telellë** 'little elf', an early vocabulary item in the *Qenya Lexicon* (see LT1:267). The feminine ending *-lle* seen in **Tintalle** 'Kindler' (< *tinta-* 'to kindle, make to spark'; *cf.* LR:394) may be the same suffix.

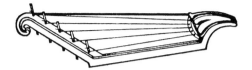

Kantele also has an alternate (Biblical) form *kannel*.[9] According to Y.H. Toivonen's *Suomen Kielen Etymologinen Sanakirja* ('Etymological Dictionary of the Finnish Language' — and we would like to offer our thanks to Arden Smith for his invaluable help in providing us with translated transcriptions of numerous entries from this work), *kannel* and *kantele* have a host of cognate forms in Baltic and Balto-Finnic languages, including Karelian-Aunus *kandeleh*, Norwegian Lappish *gan'del*, and Russian гусли < *gȯslĭ* < **gandtli*. Toivonen only tentatively assigns a Baltic (and thus Indo-European) origin for these words, citing Lithuanian *kañklės* and Latvian *kuõkle* (< **kantlē*), but M.A. Branch is not so hesitant in his Introduction to W.F. Kirby's translation of the *Kalevala*, stating flatly that "the Baltic-Finnish *kantele* and the names of several god-figures derive from ancient Balt words" (p. xix).

Finnish *kantele*, *kannel* (with their various Balto-Finnic cognates) and the Elvish derivatives of **ÑGAN-**, **ÑGANAD-** are remarkably similar in form and meaning. We can compare Finnish *kantele* and Karelian-Aunus *kandeleh* with Q *ñandelle* 'little harp' as well as *ñandele* 'harping', and Norwegian Lappish *gan'del* is virtually identical to N *gandel* 'a harp'. Equally striking is the similarity between Finnish *kannel* and N *gannel* 'a harp'. As a rule, Finnish words do not begin with *g-*,[10] and foreign words with initial *g-* imported into Finnish were modified to fit Finnish pronunciation, so that *giraffe* > Finn. *kirahvi* and *galosh* > Finn. *kalossi*. N *gannel* > Finn. *kannel* fits this pattern perfectly. The over-all pattern of correspondences here is pervasive and demonstrates that Tolkien intended these Secondary-World words to be the common ancestors of the Primary-World forms.

Q *ñandaro* 'harper' has an apparent cognate in Greek: πανδοῦρα, which led to English *banjo*, *bandore*, and *mandolin*. Watkins lists **pandoura** in his *Dictionary* (though it is not strictly speaking an Indo-European root, since it only appears in one branch of the family), describing it as a Greek noun of "obscure origin" indicating a three-stringed lute. The *OED* notes that the ancient Greeks associated the word with the god Pan, but this was mere folk-etymology, for the word is almost certainly not Greek in origin. Indeed, various sources speculate that the word is ultimately Egyptian or Oriental. Perhaps Tolkien intended Q *ñandaro* to clear up the mystery and provide us with *pandoura*'s original source.[11]

---

[9] According to Aino Wuolle's *Suomalais Englantilainen Koulusanakirja*. 10th ed. Helsinki: Werner Söderström Osakeyhtiö, 1966.

[10] There are in fact a handful of Finnish words beginning with *g-*, but most of these appear to be loanwords of recent vintage, *e.g. geeni* 'gene' and *galvanoida* 'galvanize'.

[11] There might also be an etymological relationship between *pandoura* and *kantele*. The only real phonological difficulty is the relationship between *p* and *k*; and it may be significant that IE **kʷ-** became Gk. π- under certain conditions.

The harp, for all its grace of form, would be a mere ornament without its strings. In the *Etymologies* under the base **TUG-** we find the proto-form **tungā*, which led to Q *tunga* 'taut, tight (of strings, resonant)'. We see from this that *tunga*, when applied to strings, refers to their sonic quality under tension, such as the sound produced by plucking the strings of a harp or by the release of a bow string. Our own word *tight* comes from IE **tenk-²** 'to become firm, curdle, thicken' (quite similar to **tungā*), which is itself an extended form of **ten-** 'to stretch', whence English *tense*, *etc*. **Ten-** also has derivatives meaning 'something stretched or capable of being stretched, string', such as *tendon* and Greek τόνος 'string, hence sound, pitch', which entered English as *tone*. Similarly, from a suffixed form **ten-tro-* comes the Persian word *tār* 'string' as in *sitar*, "a Hindu stringed instrument…having a track of 20 metal frets with 6 or 7 main playing strings above and 13 sympathetic resonating strings below" (*American Heritage Dictionary*). Although undefined in the *Etymologies*, **TUG-** probably means ***'to pull (tight)', being closely related to the base **TUK-** 'draw, bring'. Among the derivatives of **TUG-** are words meaning 'muscle, sinew' (Q *tuo*, N *tû*, etc.). The derivation of Q *tunga* from this same base may imply that the resonant strings referred to were produced from sinew, historically the material of choice in the many cultures that produce bows (and another piece of evidence against the sentimental insistence that Elves were vegetarian animal-rights activists).

TUK- 'draw, bring' is probably intended to be related to IE **deuk-** 'to lead', which has various Germanic descendants indicating 'to pull, draw, lead' or 'to draw, drag', such as English *tug*, *tow*, and *tie*. **Deuk-** also led to words indicating 'to lead' (via Latin *dūcere*) such as English *duct*, and it also occurs in *educate*, from Latin *ēducāre*, literally 'to lead out'. The base **TULUK-**, whence Q *tulka* 'firm, strong, immoveable, steadfast', appears to be an extended form of **TUK-** and is thus also related to **TUG-**, from which its meanings are probably derived by a semantic process similar to that which gave rise to both *string* and *strong* (and *strangle*) from the IE **strenk-** 'tight, narrow'.

Finally, in line 7 of the poem *Earendel* (MC:216) we find Q *linganer*, 'hummed like a harp-string'. Here again there is an explicit connection between the form and function of a string and its resonant sound, for *linganer* seems to derive from the base **LING-** 'hang', source of the Quenya verb stem *linga-* 'hang, dangle' and the second element in *Laurelin*, genitive singular *Laurelingen*, 'hanging gold' (see LR:369). **LING-** itself is related to **LIN²-** 'sing'. There is an Indo-European root **leig-¹** 'to bind', with a zero-grade form **lig-ā* which gave rise to Latin *ligāre* 'to bind'; and which can be found in our own word *rely* (which interestingly is synonymous with *depend*, literally 'to hang down from'). These IE forms give us some insight into the possible etymological connections of **LING-** within Elvish itself. The base **SLIG-**, with derivatives Q *lia* 'fine thread, spider filament' and *líne* 'cobweb' (both of which a spider uses *to bind* its prey, recalling IE **leig-¹**), is probably akin to the base **SLIN-**, whence N *thlinn*, *thlind* 'fine, slender'. In the *Qenya Lexicon* roots are formulated according to Qenya phonology, rather than that of Primitive Qendian as in the *Etymologies*,[12] and the base **SLIG-** appears in QL in the suffixed form LI + *ya* 'entwine', since original **sl-* became *l-* in Qenya and intervocalic **g* disappeared. LI + *ya* produced Q *lia* 'twine', *liantë* 'tendril' (this is the second element in the name of the monstrous spider *Ungwe Lianti*, *Ungweliantë* in the *Lost Tales*), and *liantassë* 'vine' (LT1:271). We can see from these roots/ bases and their derivatives that the original sense underlying **LING-** 'hang' was *** 'to dangle from a slender thread', as the slender strings of a harp hang down from the instrument's harmonic curve to join the soundboard, or a spider dangles from its line of silk, or the clustered blossoms of Laurelin hung from their delicate stems.

And with this image of Laurelin's "long swaying clusters of gold flowers like a myriad hanging lamps of flame", we come at last to the end of our cross-etymological exploration of the harps of Middle-earth. We have shown that Tolkien carefully crafted many of the roots, derivative suffixes, and words connected with harps in the Elvish tongues to provide the ancient predecessors of forms in the later languages of Men. Through these words, we—like Fíriel in the poem "The Last Ship"—can still hear distant echoes of the music of a fair folk who long ago passed away:

> A sudden music to her came,
> as she stood there gleaming
> with free hair in the morning's flame
> on her shoulders streaming.
> Flutes there were, and harps were wrung,
> and there was sound of singing,
> like wind-voices keen and young
> and far bells ringing.

Bibliography

The American Heritage Dictionary. Second College Edition. Boston: Houghton Mifflin, 1985.

Buck, Carl Darling. *Comparative Grammar of Greek and Latin*. Chicago & London: The University of Chicago Press, 1933.

_____. *A Dictionary of Selected Synonyms in the Principal Indo-European Languages*. Chicago: University of Chicago Press, 1949.

Liddell, Henry George and Robert Scott. *A Greek-English Lexicon*. Revised by Henry Stuart Jones and Roderick McKenzie. Oxford: Clarendon Press, 1940.

_____. *An Intermediate Greek-English Lexicon*. Oxford, 1889. Oxford University Press, 1986.

---

[12] For a more detailed discussion of the important distinction between the 'roots' of QL and the 'bases' of the *Etymologies*, see *Bird and Leaf: Image and Structure in **Narqelion*** by Christopher Gilson and Patrick Wynne in *Parma Eldalamberon 9*, note 3, pp. 7-8.

Lönnrot, Elias. *Kalevala.* Trans. W.F. Kirby. Everyman's Library, 1907; rpt. with additional
    material London: Athlone Press, 1985.

_____. *The Kalevala, or Poems of the Kaleva District.* Trans. Francis Peabody Magoun,
    Jr. Cambridge: Harvard University Press, 1963.

The Oxford English Dictionary. 13 vols. Oxford: Clarendon Press, 1933.

Skeat, Walter W. *A Concise Etymological Dictionary of the English Language.* Oxford:
    Clarendon Press, 1882.

Toivonen, Y.H. *Suomen Kielen Etymologinen Sanakirja.* Lexica Societatis Fenno-Ugricae
    XII, vol. 1. Helsinki: Suomalais-Ugrilainen Seura, 1955.

The Khazâd: Custodians of Hidden Hoards
by Arden R. Smith

The English word *hoard* (OE *hord*; OHG *hort*, ON *hodd*, Goth. *huzd*) comes
from Gmc. **huzdam* (Watkins 60), **huzdō-* (de Vries 246, Drosdowski/Grebe 273)
or **huzdo-* (Skeat 242) with the original meaning 'thing hidden away'. Is it merely
coincidental that the Khuzdul root KʰZD referring to the secretive and avaricious
Dwarves, seen in **Khazad-dûm**, **Khazâd** (early version **Khuzûd**, LR:274, 278), and
Khuzdul, should be so similar in form?

The Germanic word supposedly comes from an Indo-European suffixed form
meaning 'a thing hidden': **kudh-tó- > *kud-dhó-*, **kudᶻdhó-* (Prokosch 84); **kudh-
to-* (Watkins 60); **kudh-dho-* (Buck 778, Skeat 242); or **kus-dho-* (Buck 778,
Watkins 60), whence also Gk. κύσθος 'concealed place, female organ' and Lat.
custos 'guardian', lit. 'hider'. Like the verb *hide*, it derives ultimately from an Indo-
European root meaning 'to cover': **(s)keu-* (Buck 778, de Vries 246, Drosdowski/
Grebe 273, Watkins 60) or √KEUDH (Skeat 242).

Accepting the derivation of *hoard* and its Germanic cognates from this Indo-
European root as fact (though this etymology could theoretically be inaccurate), the
derivation of the Germanic words from Khuzdul would have to be by way of Indo-
European. This is, however, considerably more problematic phonetically than a
loan from Khuzdul directly into Germanic. Perhaps a merging of the Dwarvish and
Indo-European roots can be assumed. Whether or not Tolkien intended a linguistic
relationship between **Khuzûd/Khuzdul** and *huzd*, it seems likely that this was his
inspiration for the KʰZD root.

Bibliography

Buck, Carl Darling. *A Dictionary of Selected Synonyms in the Principal Indo-European
    Languages.* Chicago: University of Chicago Press, 1949.

de Vries, Jan. *Altnordisches etymologisches Wörterbuch.* Second ed. Leiden: E.J. Brill, 1962.

Drosdowski, Günther, Paul Grebe, *et al. Duden Etymologie: Herkunftswörterbuch der
    deutschen Sprache.* Mannheim/Wien/Zürich: Bibliographisches Institut, 1963.

Prokosch, E. *A Comparative Germanic Grammar.* Philadelphia: Linguistic Society of
    America, 1939.

Skeat, Walter W. *A Concise Etymological Dictionary of the English Language.* Oxford:
    Clarendon Press, 1882.

Watkins, Calvert, ed. *The American Heritage Dictionary of Indo-European Roots.* Boston:
    Houghton Mifflin, 1985.

Letters to W & D

• *Tom Loback*

The following quotations are Tolkien's, mostly from *Letters*, that bear directly on the matters discussed in the new *VT* column "Words and Devices". They will be referred to in the argument that follows by the number they are assigned here.

1. "Nobody believes me when I say that my long book is an attempt to create a world in which a form of language agreeable to my personal aesthetic might seem real." (L:264)
2. "Of course the book was written to please myself (at different levels), and as an experiment in the arts of long narrative, and of inducing 'Secondary Belief'." (L:412)
3. "…looking around for more or less similar words or names is not in fact very useful even as a source of sounds, and not at all as an explanation of inner meanings and significances. The borrowing, when it occurs (not often) is simply of *sounds* that are then integrated in a new construction; and only in one case *Eärendil* will reference to its source cast any light on the legends or their 'meaning' — and even in this case the light is little." (L:387)
4. "Though actual congruences (of form + sense) occur in unrelated real languages, and it is impossible in constructing imaginary languages from a limited number of component sounds to avoid such resemblances (if one tries — I do not)…". (L:384-85)
5. "There is *no* 'symbolism' or conscious allegory in my story." (L:262)
6. "I utterly repudiate any such significances and symbolisms." (L:383)
7. "There is *no* 'allegory', moral, political or contemporary in the work at all …. So something of the teller's own reflections and 'values' will inevitably get worked in. This is not the same as allegory. We all, in groups or as individuals, *exemplify* general principles; but we do not *represent* them." (L:232-33)
8. "I would also exclude, or rule out of order, any story that uses the machinery of Dream, the dreaming of actual human sleep, to explain the apparent occurrence of its marvels …. I would condemn the whole as gravely defective: like a good picture in a disfiguring frame …. It is at any rate essential to a genuine fairy-story, as distinct from the employment of this form for lesser or debased purposes, that it should be presented as 'true'…it cannot tolerate any frame or machinery suggesting that the whole story in which they occur is a figment or illusion." (MC:116–17)

What Pat and Carl have done is to put a new spin on the Allegorian position that so infuriated Tolkien. They maintain that, because their perceived connection to Indo-European roots is in their minds demonstrably correct, this distinguishes it from previous "incorrect" attempts to do essentially the same, albeit on a different level of linguistic investigation in terms of temporal location and ultimate source. They extend this to a radical (perhaps *reactionary* would be a more apt designation) interpretation of the entire corpus of the Secondary World's relationship to the Primary World. Theirs is not the simplistic, overt charge like the usual "contemporary" allegory, linguistic and otherwise, found in *Letters*, but an insidious suggestion that attempts to show that the very thing attempted by Mr. Rang and others, while vehemently denied by Tolkien himself, is exactly what Tolkien is doing at the root level of language. That he does not specifically deny this in *Letters* is just a result of his never being asked. Quotes 3 and 4 make this amply clear. By a sleight of hand, using an IE root that serves their purpose, they manage to obfuscate Tolkien's clear rejection of Mr. Rang's position by suggesting it is only Mr. Rang's *result* that is wrong rather than his Allegorian approach. They maintain, coyly, that "these sorts of interconnections provide insight into how the Elves [!] may have perceived the character of Sauron...." How does this differ essentially with Mr. Rang, since they all claim Primary World in the meaning of a Secondary-World name; one mistakenly at the fruit; the others, equally mistakenly, at the root. Finally, there is an attempt to buy off (okay, promote compromise and acceptance with) the other Unifists (Conceptionists and Ringites, except as they are Allegorians, need not apply) and Silmarillionists (such as myself—I note the widening schism with Unifism as it becomes more apparent) with the sop of promoting interest in *Etymologies* through this misguided approach.

I would not deny that there *might* be a vague connection between *Etymologies* and Primary-World IE roots at the time of writing, just as there is a clear attempt to connect Tol Eressëa with England at the time of writing *Lost Tales*. But this demonstrates clearly Tolkien's gradual abandonment of a trite literary device used to achieve the "suspension of disbelief" as quotes 2 and 8 above show he understands quite well. Why he never completely abandoned it is still open to debate. I think he concluded that the frame set off the picture well.

[Tom accuses us of constructing etymological "allegories"—that is, he feels that we are seeking hidden, inner meanings in Tolkien's words, meanings other than (and contrary to) those which Tolkien himself provides. To be sure, this is exactly what Mr. Rang was attempting in his "etymology" of **Legolas** *as 'Fiery-locks', when Tolkien makes it clear that it means 'Green-leaf'. And to be equally sure, this is antithetical to our own approach, which discovers and accepts Tolkien's own explanations, and then notes where striking similarities exist between Tolkien's given forms and meanings and those of the Indo-European languages, particularly among IE roots. Quite the opposite of proposing "hidden" meanings in the word* **Sauron***, we detailed Tolkien's own stated meanings and demonstrated that exactly the same relationship exists between Tolkien's* **THUS-** *'foul, rotten', whence* **Sauron***, and* **THŪ-** *'puff, blow', as between IE* **pŭ-²** *'to rot, decay' and* **pŭ-¹/phŭ-** *'to blow, swell'. The meanings that Tom objects to are in fact all provided by* Etymologies; *our example served only to confirm and explain semantic relationships which were plainly intended by Tolkien.*

As for the validity of our central position— that Tolkien specifically constructed his Secondary-World languages to be seen as the ancestor of the Primary-World (particularly the IE) languages—we can only hope, if Tolkien's own elaborate and explicit explanation of the Eldarin descent of the Tongues of Men, <u>as confirmed by an Anglo-Saxon mariner</u>, is insufficient, that it will be amply demonstrated by the progress of this column, as it continues to present correspondences of form and meaning so numerous and precise that they cannot be mere coincidence. —CFH & PW]

Essitalmar

The Roots of Middle-earth Names and Places

A column by Tom Loback

This is a forum for the readers of VT *to submit their ideas and thoughts about names, both of people and places; their meanings and the story that they tell. All are encouraged to submit inquiries, short interpretations and discussions thereof, particularly those names still undefined. Send all correspondence for this column to the editor at 152 West 26th St., #36, N.Y. City, NY 10001, USA.*

The horror, the horror...

Deep in the heart of darkness of Elven linguistic studies the lone Sindarin scholar labors, attempting to blaze a trail through entangled vines of data, dimensional overlaps and densities of time and space, beset on all sides by the predatory philological beasties quick to pounce on the slightest misstep.

When first criticizing Ned and Jorge's linguistic attributions, the world, Middle-earth, seemed a simpler place with not much more than Quenya and Sindarin involved. Since then the idea that Sindarin might be a group of languages has demonstrably gained viability. At that time, Noldorin seemed to be the operative source for Sindarin, based on the Gate Inscription and Thrór's Map, so the assumption was made that some star names might be Sindarin, meaning Noldorin.

In Noldorin, or Exilic Noldorin to be exact, there is a phenomenon described by Christopher Tolkien as Initial Variation of Consonants (IVC); see LR:298–99. The rules for this are:

1. "a consonant at the beginning of the second element of a compounded word"; or
2. "of the second word in two words standing in a very close syntactic relation, as noun and article";

"underwent the same change as it would when standing in ordinary medial position."

Examples given are: $p > b$, $t > d$, $k > g$, demonstrated in *tâl* 'foot' but *i•dâl* 'the foot', ***Thorondor*** (< ***Thoron*** + ***taur***). Further,

> "medially, original voiced stop -*g*- became 'opened' to -ʒ-, which then weakened and disappeared; in this case therefore the 'initial variation' is between *g* and nil, the lost consonant being represented by a sign called *gasdil* ('stopgap, see the *Etymologies*, stem DIL), transcribed as '. Thus *galaδ* 'tree', *i•alaδ* 'the tree'; *Gorgoroth, Ered-'orgoroth*."

At the time, it seemed possible under the IVC that ***Carnil*** and ***Luinil*** were Sindarin from ***Carn*** + ***gil*** and ***Luin*** + ***gil*** with the medial ***g*** varying to nil. ***Borgil*** was mentioned to demonstrate that stars could and did have names in Sindarin, not just Quenya. After all, if the night sky of Middle-earth is as exact a parallel as they suggest, the parallel might extend to the use of two languages, Sindarin and Quenya, as in the primary world the planets are in Latin and constellations in Greek. *[Well, actually almost all constellation names are Latin:* e.g. *Ursa Major and Ursa Minor; "Earth" is of course a Germanic name; and more than a few star names are Arabic,* e.g. *Betelguese. —CFH]* Be that as it may, the contradiction of **Carnil** and **Borgil** was overlooked, partly because it seemed to come into direct collision with IVC.

However, since that time, as the differences of Noldorin and Doriathrin/Ilkorin became better understood, the apparent relationship of Noldorin to Sindarin was modified. Many words in what may be classified as "later Sindarin" are decidedly un-Noldorin, **Borgil** and **Aranrúth** among them. The collision between IVC and the maintenance of the "absence of mutation" in Sindarin, described in L:426–7, will here be examined by cataloging words in Noldorin and Doriathrin/Ilkorin and subjecting them to the rules laid out in *Letters* to see what, if anything, is revealed about the relationship of these languages to Sindarin.

According to *Letters*, the lenition or "mutations" (presumably IVC) of Sindarin do not occur in the following circumstances:

1. When the second noun functions as an uninflected genitive, as in **ost-giliath**, **ennyn Durin**.
2. a. in compounds, and

    b. when a noun is virtually an adjective, as in **Gil-galad** 'Star (of) brilliance'.
Tolkien goes on to say that in Sindarin "initial *g* was retained in composition, where a contact *n* + *g* occurred. So *born* 'hot, red' + *gil* to *borñgil*; *morn* 'black' + *dor* to *morñdor*; the triconsonantal group then being reduced to *rg, rd*."

It was noted previously that the Doriathrin compound **Nauglamír** was unlenited as compared with N. **Nauglavir**, confirmed by D. **Goldamir**, N. **Golovir**. From these examples alone, it can be seen that what is described in 2a above does not apply to Noldorin, but does apply to Doriathrin. In fact, as the following list shows, in Doriathrin/Ilkorin only one compound word can be found that does mutate, while in Noldorin mutation is widespread.

D. **Dol-med**

D. **Dun(n)-(n)gorthin**

D. **Dur-gul, Mor-(n)gul**

D. **Eglador**

D. **Egla-mar** (*vs.* N. **Gondobar**)

D. **Gal(d)-breth**

D. **Thin(d)-gol**

D. **Thruin-gwethil** (*vs.* N. **Dol-(g)wethil**)

D. **Umboth**, from **ub** + **moth** by metathesis

I. **Ar-gador**

I. **Ar-ros** to **Aros**, *cf.* **Eglorest**

I. **Ascar** (*vs.* N. **asgar, ascar**)

I. **Bas(t)-gorn** (*vs.* N. **Basgorn** from **Bas** + **corn**)

I. **Bel-thron(d)-ding**

I. **Bril-thor**

I. **Duil-(g)wen**

I. **El-bereth, El-boron > Eldun, Elrun**

I. **Er-mabrin** (*vs.* N. **Erchamron**)

I. **Esgal-duin**

I. **Gar-thurien**

I. **Taig-lin**

I. **Thar-gelion**

I. **Thorn-tor** (*vs.* N. **Thorondor**)

I. **Tin-dum** (*vs.* N. **Tinnu**)

I. **U-dov-on**

I. **Ulgund, ulgon** (*vs.* N. **Ulund, ulun**)

As seen in the next list of Noldorin compounds there is no maintaining of the lack of mutation in compounds (case 2a), but rather the exercise of IVC is in full fly.

P > B

ambenn, dadbenn (*-penn*)
cambant (*-pant*)
cirban (*-pann*)
gobel (*-pel*)

T > D

Cirdan (*-tan*) [but *Barthan*?]
Daedelu (*-telu*)
Gwador (*-tor*)
Heledirn (*-tirn*)
Mindon (*-tonn*)
Rhamdal (*-tal*)
Thorondor (*-taur*)

K > G

Forgam (*-cam*)
Morgoth (*-coth*)
Turgon (*-caun*), *cf.* *Fingon*

G > nil

Awarth, ulwarth (*-gwarth*)
Brolas (*-glas*)
Celegorn (*celeg-gor*)
Edegil (*edeg-gil*)
Eredwethion (*-gwethion*)
Forodweith (*-gwaith*)
Iarwath (*-gwath*)
Rathloriel (*-gloriel*)
Taragaer (*tarag-gaer*)
Tauros (*-gos*)

MB > M

Ammarth (*-mbarth*)
Gothmog (*-mbauk*)

Interestingly, in Noldorin compounds when *ng* is present the *g* is retained: *gorgoroth* (*gor-ngoroth*), *ingem, Inglor* (*Id + glor*).

Case 2b, "when the noun is actually virtually an adjective", seems a further modification of 2a, perhaps in respect to Noldorin as the example *Gil-galad* shows that the variant base in Noldorin would yield *galad* and that the *-galad* in the name is not from the N. *calad*. It is unclear, at this point, how to take 2b. Perhaps it refers to the hyphenated form as a reverse of normal word order in which the second noun will then function as an adjective to differentiate from a possible *Galadil* 'Brilliant Star'.

Case 1, when the second noun functions as an uninflected genitive, seems to indicate a noun that does not have a genitive inflection but functions as a genitive because of word order, or perhaps any inflection (although *gil-iath* would seem to be a collective plural inflection). Comparing Noldorin and Doriathrin/Ilkorin forms shows two different results, Noldorin mutating along IVC lines, and Doriathrin/Ilkorin not mutating: N. *Aran Dinnu* (*tinnu*) [*cf. Aran Chithlum*] 'King (of) Twilight' *vs.* D. *Tor Tinduma* 'King Twilight-of'.

Curiously, N. *Tinnu* 'Twilight' is uninflected and mutates while D. *Tinduma* (from *Tindum* 'Twilight') is the inflected genitive (*cf. Dagnir Glaurunga*) which does not mutate.

The horror comes in, appropriately enough, with *Ered Gorgoroth*, which shows retention of medial *-g-* with *rng* reduction, but shows *gasdil* pre-eminent in *Ered-'orgoroth* at times with Tolkien himself vacillating between *Ered-'orgoroth* and ***Ered Gorgoroth*** even after *The Lord of the Rings* (*cf.* **Amon Uilos**, **Nan Dungoroth**, **Nann'Orothvor**) as told in the note in LR:298–99. Happily, Doriathrin/ Ilkorin is a model of compliance here with **Nan Dungorthin** and **Dorthonion**.

The situation becomes more horrifying when, as it is now apparent, another factor is involved with lenition—"anglicization". It was mentioned in the previous column that one reason for the difference in the Noldorin of the Gate Inscription with that of "Classical" Noldorin of *Etymologies* might be seen in *Letters*, p. 426: "I thought people would feel *dh* uncouth, and so wrote *d* (for ð and *dh*) in names." This pops up in *Etymologies* also: "**MAD-**...*Maidhros* (anglicized *Maidros*)" (LR:371); *cf.* **Caradras**, later changed to **Caradhras**. The opinion here is that anglicizing came first, but then led to the idea which changes the "Classical" Noldorin of the version of the Gate Inscription seen in *Biography* (Plate 12) and *TI* (p. 182), and in *RS* (p. 450). Looking at the earlier Noldorin version in *Biography* and *TI* it can be seen to be the "Classical" Noldorin of *Etymologies*:

Ennyn Ðurin Aran Vória...i•ndíw thin > i•thíw thin

The *tengwar* letters show *D* or *Dh* for Ð, while *i•ndíw > i•thíw* shows a correction and modification of IVC 2 above, because the noun does not undergo the same mutation as it would in ordinary medial position (compare **andeith**) but the nasal mutation described later on in *Letters* (p. 427). At the same time **Caradhras** is being used in its anglicized form, **Caradras**.

It would seem that the final version of the Gate Inscription can be seen as what its interior history says it is: a Second Age form of Noldorin that was modified to comply with Thingol's Ban. The reasoning is this: the rules in *Letters* describe when mutation does not occur, implying that these are exceptions to a normal occurence of mutation. As we see from the lists above, there is practically *no* mutation in Doriathrin/Ilkorin except that which has already occurred earlier near the level of bases (*e.g.* **basgorn** in Ilkorin comes from **bast + gorn**, the *c > g* in **gorn** having occurred long before the compounding with **bast-**; whereas, in Noldorin, **corn** has not mutated and does not unless IVC conditions are met). Therefore, the rules in *Letters* are not rules *per se* for Doriathrin/Ilkorin, but simply describe what is the state in Doriathrin/Ilkorin and then provide a function or rule to bring Noldorin into line with it as per Thingol's Ban.

One side benefit to all this is that when Chris Gilson's suggestion that ***Aredhel*** can be seen to be interpretable differently and appropriately in Noldorin and Ilkorin, this can be applied to other much-debated names too, with surprising results. ***Turgon*** in the Noldorin of *Etymologies* is ***Tur + caun***, but in Ilkorin it would be ***Tur + gon*** 'Master of Stone', as the ***-g*** is retained, not mutated, thereby accomodating the old Qenya name ***Turondo***.

Finally, never let it be said that *Essitalmar* is afraid to admit being wrong or to eat its words, in this case ***Carnil*** and ***Luinil***—and tasty words they are, too; everyone should try some. OK, they are Quenya, although there is ***Illuin*** (*cf.* ***Helluin***)....

Transitions in Translations

A column by Arden R. Smith

The purpose of this column is to examine peculiarities in translations of Tolkien's works: mistranslations, unusual translations, interesting solutions to the problems of translation, and other curiosities in foreign editions. Ideas and contributions are encouraged: send them to "Transitions," c/o Arden R. Smith, P.O. Box 4395, Berkeley, CA 94704-0395, USA.

I'm a Troll Man

I make no secret of my interest in Tolkien's invented languages and have as a result had to put up with a considerable amount of good-natured (?) ribbing. One of my friends at the record store where I used to work, for example, called me "Troll Man". I can't really complain; Gandalf is called essentially the same thing in the Danish translations of *The Hobbit* (*Hobbitten*) and *The Lord of the Rings* (*Ringenes Herre*), both translated by Ida Nyrop Ludvigsen and published by Gyldendal.

The Danish word for 'troll', namely *trold*, actually appears in many places in the Danish translations where 'troll' does not appear in the corresponding English text. The word *trold* is (as it should be) consistently used as the translation of 'troll' (H:36/43 *etc.**; pl. *trolde*, pl. with def. art. *troldene*), with such expected derivatives as *bjergtrolde* 'hill-trolls' (III:172/168, 352/338) and *Stentroldene* 'the Stone-trolls' (III:415/410). Unfortunately, this same word *trold* is also used as a translation of 'goblin' in both *The Hobbit* and *The Lord of the Rings*. 'Azog the Goblin', for example, is *trolden Azog* (H:28/33) and 'the Goblin-wars' are *troldekrigene* (H:53/62). *Trold* and *nisse* ['pixie, goblin'] are both used as translations of 'goblin' in its rare occurrences in *The Lord of the Rings* (*e.g. nissehyl* for 'goblin-barkers' at I:42/35 and *ond nisse* ['evil goblin'] for 'goblin' at I:212/193). In *The Hobbit*, however, *nisse* is not used and *trold* alternates with *bjergtrold*. *Trold* tends to be used more often before Thorin and Company are captured by the goblins, after which *bjergtrold* becomes more common. The words are still used interchangeably, though, as can be seen in the translation of 'the Great Goblin' as both *Den store Trold* and *Den store Bjergtrold* (H:62–63/73–74). *Bjergtrold* is not an improvement on *trold* in any case, since it is used to translate both 'goblin' and 'hill-troll'. In addition, 'hobgoblins' is rendered as *kæmpebjergtrolde* (H:128/149), but 'orc' fortunately appears as *ork* (pl. *orker*, pl. with def. art. *orkerne*).

Trold also appears in the word *trolddom*, meaning 'magic'. This term is used in reference to the magic practiced by all sorts of evil creatures, *e.g. dragens trolddom* 'dragon spell' (H:203/236), *trolddomstårnet* 'the tower of sorcery', *i.e.* Minas Morgul (I:281/258), *Fjendens trolddomskunster* 'arts of the Enemy' (I:295/270). It is also used to refer to *god trolddom* 'good magic' (H:266/310) as practiced

---

* Page references are to the Danish and English versions (HM H 3rd ed., LotR 2nd ed.) respectively.

by the Istari or the Elves (*elvertrolddom* 'Elf-magic', I:409/376). Of course, the same word should be used to translate 'magic', whether good or evil, as this usage is noted by Galadriel:

> *For dette her er vist, hvad dit folk ville kalde trolddom, selv om jeg ikke*
> *helt forstår, hvad de mener, og de bruger åbenbart det samme ord om*
> *Fjendens forræderiske virksomhed.*

> "For this is what your folk would call magic, I believe; though I do not understand clearly what they mean; and they seem also to use the same word of the deceits of the Enemy." (I:410/377)

Practitioners of magic are similarly endowed with troll-names. Galadriel is called *troldkvinde* ('Sorceress' II:121/118, 'Mistress of Magic' II:287/275). The term *troldkarl* is used in reference to the Wizards (I:23/17) and the Necromancer (H:128/149). 'The Necromancer' is in fact translated variously as *spåmanden* (H:29/34), *besværgeren* (H:266/310), *Åndemaneren* (I:287/263, similarly at H:128/149), and *Troldmanden* (I:9/5). This last term, *troldmand*, is also used as a translation of 'sorcerer' in reference to the Witch-king (I:295/270, III:92/92) and of 'wizard' in reference to the Istari (H:10/13, 266/310, I:39/33, *etc.*). *Gandalf troldmanden*, Gandalf the Troll-Man. At least I'm in good company.

Information from the Russian Front
by David Doughan

The Two Towers in Muravyov's translation has now been published. It continues the various positive and negative precedents set by Хранители. It is still highly readable, and very vivid in style. The orcs speak Russian criminal slang (which worries Natalya Prohorova more than it does me), Sam seems to have swallowed a dictionary of traditional Russian folk-sayings which he regularly regurgitates, and Aragorn turns out to be the Heir of the Grand Dukes of Arnor and Gondor. *[See Nathalie Kotowski's piece on titles below. —ARS]* There are also a number of pointless changes as per Хранители (*e.g.* the birch-woods of Neldoreth). The Muravyov approach is interestingly described by a rival translator with reference to a 19th century story by Leskov about a Russian peasant who tries to shoe an English flea: "and of course a flea with horseshoes on jumps quite a different way".

A *rival* translator? Yes indeed! A complete translation in one volume by Vladimir Grushetskiy and Natalya Grigoryeva is due to appear from the Severo-Zapad (= North West) publishing house (in Leningrad) this summer, and yet another (the one referred to above) is at present seeking a publisher. The possibility of three translations competing for increasingly scarce resources (especially paper) and for non-black market distribution is somewhat worrying, though it does reflect the depth of commitment of Russian Tolkienists. Natalya Prohorova tells of various *samizdat* translations circulating in Russia, especially on disk—one enthusiast apparently got hooked so quickly and so thoroughly that he read the whole work straight from a PC screen rather than delay the experience by printing it out. And in the provincial town of Ivanovo, they were so beset by shortages that they not only could not find a Russian translation—they couldn't even get hold of an English original. The one thing they had was a Polish translation—so they found a Polish speaker, and prevailed upon him to read a translation of the entire work directly into a tape recorder. So whenever somebody wanted to hear "the story of nine-fingered Frodo and the Ring of Doom", they were just handed the appropriate cassette (Natalya vouches for the authenticity of that story). We Westerners don't realise how lucky we are....

About Titles in the Russian *Lord of the Rings*
by Nathalie Kotowski

The only way of testing the validity of a translation is back-translation to the original text. But it sometimes can be dangerous insofar as the deep meaning of the translated word is not fully understood. So I have some remarks about David Doughan's statement about "Grand Dukes of Arnor and Gondor" (in the new Russian translation of *The Two Towers*, but there were hints already in *The Fellowship*).

Of course it is not Grand Duke! The title Grand Duke was bestowed upon the members of the Russian Imperial family in the last three centuries (after Peter I took the title of Emperor) and everybody remembers the great reveling parties of Grand Dukes in Paris or the gigantic hunting parties for buffaloes organized by the American government in the last century for such Grand Dukes who were only bored aristocrats who had nothing better to do and a rather bad reputation, as many aristocratic families have even now.

But the Russian word *Veliki Kniaz*, better translated as Grand Prince, has another, far older meaning. The title "king" was never used in the whole of Russian history. In the beginning, during the dynasty descending from Rurik, who probably was a Scandinavian prince (about VII–VIIIth century), there were only Grand Princes holding first the greatest city, at that time Kiev (simple princes holding the minor ones). The nearest to this concept in Western history is High King. And the most famous of them was Vladimir, who christianized Russia just a millennium ago. The Veliki Kniaz Vladimir, Vladimir the Little Sun, became the chief and the most beloved character of the whole Russian epos, just like Charlemagne in France, and therefore, in all epic stories or fairy stories, one always meets a Veliki Kniaz, never a king. The Russian term for king, *korol*, is used for some foreign and sometimes enemy leader. It probably comes from Polish, from the time of the great wars between Russia and Poland in the XVIth century, when the Rurik dynasty came to an end.

So I think the title *Veliki Kniaz*, Grand Prince of Arnor and Gondor, is absolutely apt and says more to a Russian reader. There is another title sometimes used in the translation; it is that of Tsar. *Tsar* comes from *Caesar* and was taken first by Ivan III, Grand Prince of Moscovia, who became Tsar of All Russia. But the title itself is far older, coming from Byzantium and used even by the Tatarian rulers. It is also used in epic songs and fairy tales. In the Russian *Lord of the Rings*, it is used for Gil-galad (in Sam's song). I have seen it "back-translated" by somebody (I think it was in *Little Gwaihir*) as Emperor. That of course is preposterous, using a modern term to translate an old one. *[Emperor isn't really any more modern than "Tsar", since it comes from the Latin* imperator, *a title held by the commanders of the Roman army and after Julius Caesar a title held by the Roman emperors. —ARS]* The use of the term "tsar" still lives in Russian in the old sense in a lot of expressions, for instance, to say "long, long ago", one would say "in the time of Tsar Pea" (*vo vremena tsaria Gorokha*), and nobody will ever confound it with emperor....

I was most distressed by the quality of the translation of *The Fellowship of the Ring* (*The Two Towers* is far better), so I would like to stress things which are really good but not fully understood.

Armenian/Ukrainian Update

The Armenian and Ukrainian Hobbit translations are apparently not as new as I had thought. Wayne Hammond writes:

"In (partial) answer to your query in VT #17, the Ukrainian Hobbit is *Hobit, abo, Mandrivka za imlysti hory*, Kiev: Veselka, 1985, translated by Oleksandr Mokrovol's'kiy, illustrated by Mikhail Belomlinskiy; and the Armenian Hobbit is *Khobbit, ili, Tuda i obratno*, Yerevan: Sovetakan Groch, 1984, translated by E. Makaryan, illustrated by Mikhail Belomlinskiy. These citations are derived from Åke Bertenstam's bibliography in *Arda*, with refinements after advice to me from David Doughan. I haven't seen the physical books to verify this. Åke got the Armenian edition from the Soviet Union national bibliography, hence the Russian title.

"Belomlinskiy's illustrations get around!"

Trivia Question

Q: Returning to the goblins in the Danish translations, what does the Danish Gollum call the "goblinses"?

A: *Bjergtrolderne*, as opposed to the correct definite plural form *bjergtroldene*. Gollum's version thus has an extra letter—but it's not a sibilant! (*Hobbitten*. Translated by Ida Nyrop Ludvigsen. København: Gyldendal, 1980, p. 82)

Next Issue

"Toppo and Poppo", Nathalie Kotowski's review of the Russian *Two Towers*, and more!

꒰꒱

Publications of Interest

Due to space limitations, the editor cannot thoroughly review all publications received; the following reviews emphasize those publications and items which the editor feels would be of special interest to members of the Elvish Linguistic Fellowship. BIAOR = Back Issues Available On Request.

Cirth de Gandalf: Cercle d'etudes de Tolkien en Belgique. Published bimonthly.
> *Editor*: Nathalie Kotowski. *Subscriptions to*: the editor at 25, rue Victor Gambier, 1180 Bruxelles, Belgium. *Annual subscription*: Belgium 400 FB, 450 FB elsewhere.
> *No. 14, May 1991*: Continues the presentation of *Le Quenya: une grammaire*, Nathalie's French translation of Nancy Martsch's Quenya Language Lessons from *Beyond Bree*. *Leçon 14: Participe passé et adjectif verbal.*

Little Gwaihir: Magazine of the Tolkien Section of the Śląski Klub Fantasyki (English Edition). Published monthly.
> *Editor*: Paulina Braiter. *Subscriptions to*: the editor at ul. Kasztelanska 66/3, 58-314 Walbrzych, Poland. Write for subscription info.
> *No. 19, May 1991*: Ah! Someone's paying attention: artwork by Marjo Took incorporating the *Koivienéni Sentence* in *tengwar*.

Mythlore: A Journal of J.R.R. Tolkien, C.S. Lewis, Charles Williams and the Genres of Myth and Fantasy Studies. Published quarterly.
> *Editor*: Glen GoodKnight. *Subscriptions to*: P.O. Box 6707, Altadena, CA 91003. *Annual subscription*: $20.00, add $8.00 for USA or $8.50 for Canadian First Class delivery; Overseas Airmail: Europe & Latin America $35.00, Australia & Asia $40.00. *BIAOR*.
> *No. LXV, Spring 1991*: An exploration of the philological possibilities behind the name *Earendel* in "Over Middle-earth Sent Unto Men: On the Philological Origins of Tolkien's *Eärendil* Myth" by Carl F. Hostetter; reprints "The Elves at Koivienéni: A New Quenya Sentence" by Christopher Gilson and Patrick Wynne from *VT #14*; Paul Nolan Hyde's *Quenti Lambardillion* column, "Pointing With an Index Finger: 'Five feet high the door and three may walk abreast'", a brief history of his voluminous indices together with "A Comprehensive Index of Proper Names and Phrases in *The Hobbit*".

Next Issue

In addition to the usual offerings, *VT* #19 will feature an original Quenya poem by Chris Gilson, an article on mistakes and changes to Elvish words in *The Lord of the Rings*, and whatever else arrives before September 1.

Vinyar Tengwar

The bimonthly 'news-letters' of the Elvish Linguistic Fellowship.
A Special Interest Group of the Mythopoeic Society.

Editor: Carl F. Hostetter, 2509 Ambling Circle, Crofton, MD 21114, USA.

Proofreaders: Arden R. Smith and Patrick Wynne.

Masthead: by Tom Loback.

Tengwar numerals: from Lawrence M. Schoen's *Moroma* PostScript *Tengwar* font for the Mac, available on disk for $6.00 from PsychoGlyph, P.O. Box 74, Lake Bluff, IL 60044.

Subscriptions: Subscriptions are for 1 year (6 issues) and must be paid in US dollars.

$12.00   USA
$15.00   Canada (sent airmail) and Overseas surface mail
$18.00   Overseas airmail

Back issues available: Individual copies of back issues are available at the current per-issue subscription price: $2.00 USA, $2.50 Canada and Overseas surface mail, $3.00 Overseas airmail. Deduct 25% if ordering a complete set of back issues. *All costs are postpaid.*

Payments: All payments must be in US dollars. It is recommended that overseas members make payments via international postal money order.

Make all checks payable to Carl F. Hostetter.

Submissions: Written material should in some manner deal with Tolkien's invented languages. All submissions must be typed, or must be exquisitely legible: the editor will not decipher lower-glyphics. The editor reserves the right to edit any material (except artwork) for purposes of brevity and relevance. Ilúvatar smiles upon submissions on 400K or 800K (3.5") Macintosh or 720K (3.5") MS-DOS formatted disks in PageMaker, Microsoft Word, Microsoft Works, WordPerfect, MacWrite, DCA, or RTF formats, or as unformatted ASCII text files. Artwork should be Tolkienian in nature.

The deadline for VT #19 is September 1, 1991.

Bibliographical Abbreviations

H	*The Hobbit*	LT2	*The Book of Lost Tales, Part Two*
I	*The Fellowship of the Ring*	LB	*The Lays of Beleriand*
II	*The Two Towers*	SM	*The Shaping of Middle-earth*
III	*The Return of the King*	LR	*The Lost Road*
R	*The Road Goes Ever On*	RS	*The Return of the Shadow*
S	*The Silmarillion*	TI	*The Treason of Isengard*
UT	*Unfinished Tales*	WR	*The War of the Ring*
L	*The Letters of J.R.R. Tolkien*	QL	*The Qenya Lexicon, App.* LT1 & 2
MC	*The Monsters and the Critics*	GL	*The Gnomish Lexicon, App.* LT1 & 2
LT1	*The Book of Lost Tales, Part One*	Et	*The Etymologies, in* LR

Vinyar Tengwar is produced by the editor on an Apple Macintosh II personal computer, using a LaCie Silverscan scanner, Microsoft Word 4.0 and Aldus PageMaker 4.0. VT is printed on an NEC Silentwriter2 Model 90 laser printer.

ISSN 1054-7606

Vinyar Tengwar

Otsóna

#19

September 1991

In This Issue

This issue of Vinyar Tengwar *is dedicated*
to the memory of

TAUM SANTOSKI
1958 – 1991

Sunset and evening star,
    And one clear call for me!
And may there be no moaning of the bar,
    When I put out to sea,

But such a tide as moving seems asleep,
    too full for sound and foam,
When that which drew from out the boundless deep
    Turns again home.

Twilight and evening bell,
    And after that the dark!
And may there be no sadness of farewell,
    When I embark;

For tho' from out our borne of Time and Place
    The flood may bear me far,
I hope to see my Pilot face to face
    When I have crost the bar.

            —Tennyson

In Memoriam

Taum Santoski

On August 19th Taum Santoski, Tolkien scholar and member of the Elvish Linguistic Fellowship, died of cancer. He was 32.

I will leave the presentation of biographical details to those who know them better than I. Taum and I rarely discussed the mundane particulars of our daily lives. As C.S. Lewis wrote of Friendship in *The Four Loves*, "What have these 'unconcerning things, matters of fact' to do with the real question, *Do you see the same truth?* " And that was the most important thing about Taum: *He saw the same truth.* Most people, even ardent Tolkien aficionados, don't comprehend the fascination of Elvish. We feel rather silly trying to explain to them why we devote so much precious time to trying to decipher the obscure grammatical details of languages that never really existed. But Taum was that rarest of rare birds, a kindred spirit who not only was deeply interested in Tolkien's invented languages, but who realized that the languages are *important,* a matter worthy of serious scholarly consideration.

Taum was a prominent figure in Tolkien circles and was well known for his work with Tolkien's manuscripts at the Marquette University Archives in Milwaukee. Besides working on his own book on the writing of *The Hobbit,* Taum invested much time and energy in helping Christopher Tolkien research some of the volumes in *The History of Middle-earth,* a process which could require a remarkable degree of perseverance—he might spend long hours laboriously deciphering the original pencilled text beneath an ink version, only to discover that the two texts were virtually identical. Taum loved to share the linguistic discoveries he made at Marquette, exhibiting a generosity not easily forgotten. His letters were full of fascinating Elvish tidbits, presented with a scholar's eye and a keen wit. We all owe him our thanks for bringing to light the "Koivienéni Sentence", published in *VT #14,* and the remainder of the linguistic material in that manuscript, including another new Quenya sentence, will be published in *VT* early next year. Even Taum's illness could not dampen his enthusiasm for the languages of Middle-earth. During the last year Taum managed to write articles on Elvish for both *VT* and *Parma Eldalamberon.* He also volunteered to write the section on Adûnaic, one of his favorite subjects, for *I·Parma,* the ELF's comprehensive book on Tolkien's languages.

Taum's perseverance, generosity, and enthusiasm are gone now, beyond "the Circles of the World". It is a bitter loss, and one we can ill afford. I can only offer Gandalf's advice on parting: "I will not say: do not weep; for not all tears are an evil." *Namárië Rúmil, nai hiruvalye Valimar.*

—*P. Wynne*

E.L.F. News

New Member

The E.L.F. extends a hearty *mae govannen* to:

- Heike Kubasch   11 Altamont Circle #11, Charlottesville, VA 22901.
- Johan Crister Welin   Vattentornsgatan 36, S–424 37 Angered, Sweden.

Changes of Address

Please make note of the following new addresses:

- Chris Gilson   500 C North Civic Drive, Walnut Creek, CA 94596.
- Ken Thomson   200–A Marion Street, Tryon, NC 28782–2940.
- Bill Welden   961 Lundy Lane, Los Altos, CA 94024–5934.

Second Annual Colloquium on the Languages of Middle-earth

Pursuant to its goal of producing *I•Parma*, 'The Book', the ultimate reference work on the invented languages of J. R. R. Tolkien's Middle-earth, the Elvish Linguistic Fellowship will sponsor the Second Annual Colloquium on the Languages of Middle-earth, on February 14–17, 1992. This will be an opportunity for everyone who is interested in this ambitious project to help in making it a reality.

Each program participant will present one or more monographs on Endorean linguistics. These monographs will be collected together in a looseleaf notebook, distributed to all Colloquium participants, and reviewed and revised until they provide a definitive source of reference material, from which *I•Parma* will be compiled. All members will receive a copy of the proceedings and all updates to it until *I•Parma* is published. So even if you attend only one year, you will be able to stay abreast of the project (and participate by mail if you like) in later years.

An attending membership is $175. This price does not include room and board, but again this year the hosts, Bill Welden and Jo Alida Wilcox, have agreed to provide room (well, floor space) and board free of charge to all attendees. Membership fees will go toward the costs of holding our meetings and publishing *I•Parma*.

If you are interested in being one of the project authors, and are willing to write several monographs and attend the annual meetings over the next few years (as well as attending most Mythcons, where we will hold a second important meeting each year), we would be excited about having you join us. To register, or for more information, contact Bill Welden, 961 Lundy Lane, Los Altos, CA 94024–5934; phone #: (415) 948–2976.

Letters to VT

• *Jenny Coombs* *Ruddington, Nottinghamshire, England*

Thank you very much for *VT*#17; every issue seems to be even more beautifully presented. I liked Pat's lovely rendering of Radagast on the cover.

I was convinced by Chris Gilson's interpretation of **Bladorthin** as equivalent in meaning to **Mithrandir**. (The latter has a more pleasing shape; I'm glad JRRT chose it.) I believe the world needs more pedantry, and therefore appreciated Chris's point about the indefinite article before *h*. To me, *h* is a consonant (despite the poor treatment it receives in Latin and Greek — not only is it completely ignored in elision and in calculating quantity, it is dropped in or out of words quite arbitrarily, as far as I can see: hence *pulcer/pulcher* and so on.) So I use the pre-consonantal form of both articles before *h* (the latter is apparent only in speech; *i.e.* I pronounce *the* before *house* in the same way as before *dog*, rather than with the long vowel as before *apple*.) How does Chris stress "High-elven Glossary"? To me it feels more natural to have two dactyls, *i.e.* with most stress on *high* and *glos-*. I admit I have not consulted the *OED* rules of stress, but I have applied the rules I have subconsciously gathered from learning English. My mother thinks it's the hyphen which makes the difference (*cf.* "High German", where both are stressed but *ger-* gets the primary stress). From Chris's use of "an", I assume he would say "high-élven". An incredibly minor point, but interesting!

I accept Craig Marnock's reservations about my discussion of **Silmarillion** and **Altariello** in *VT* #14; I'm not that convinced myself by my arguments! I'm sorry about getting the quantity wrong in **Altariello** (not **Altáriello**); that was careless.

I, too, was troubled by **riel < rig + selde**; I entirely share Craig's doubts. But we have JRRT's word for it that the name means something like "woman garlanded in radiance"; any other thoughts on what composes **Altáriel**? It would be (a bit) easier if JRRT hadn't abandonded **YEL-** in favour of **SEL-D-**; but apparently he did.

I'm not quite won over by the idea that syllables are lengthened due to stress. I must admit, I find it æsthetically rather unsatisfying, and particularly the apparently arbitrary mixture of vowel-lengthening and consonant-doubling. The argument is, I take it, that **Altariel** receives stress on the **-tar-**, which therefore lengthens to **Altáriel**; but the oblique cases like **Altarielo** would receive stress on the **-i-**, which is felt to be dysphonious, and so the penultimate syllable is lengthened to **Altáriello**. Why not ****Altariélo**? or conversely ****Altarriel**? Perhaps the distinction is that the **-a-** in **Altáriel** is lengthened because it is under stress, whereas the **-l-** in **Altariello** is duplicated to prevent stress falling on the **-i-**. I admit, **Silmarilli** is a general plural.

We know that **Silmaril** is a shortened form of **Silmarille**: *LR*, p. 383, **RIL-** "*Silmarille, Silmaril* (pl. *Silmarilli*)." Although we don't know *which* plural JRRT meant here, I think the **-i** form was the more usual, and JRRT would probably have made some comment or indication had he been referring to the "general plural".

How *would* the general plural of **Silmaril/Silmarille** be formed? If it were based, as I suggest oblique forms are, on the long form of the word, this would give **Silmarilleli**. Haplology could well reduce this to **Silmarilli**, *i.e.* perhaps the general plural is the same as the partitive plural. This would be convenient, as otherwise one of the four numbers will be redundant when referring to any of the three Silmarils. Presumably if a speaker wished to make it clear that he was using the *general* plural of such a word, he would use the form in *-lleli*, complete and unabridged. So I would decline Fëanor's jewel as:

Singular:	*Silmarille, Silmaril*
Dual:	*Silmarillet, ?Silmarillú*
Plural:	*Silmarilli*
General Plural:	*Silmarilleli, Silmarilli*

The alternative view, which Craig suggests, would, I presume, be:

Singular:	*Silmarille, Silmaril*
Dual:	*Silmarilú* (****Silmarilt** being unlikely)
Plural:	*Silmarili*
General Plural:	*Silmarilli*

At the moment I'd go for the first set, since to me the return of the second *-l-* in oblique forms of **Silmaril** does seem to parallel other words, where oblique cases are built on the long form. Thus **Valinor** < **Valinóre**, but **Nurtale Valinóreva**; **Númenor** < **Númenóre**, but JRRT writes **Númenóreans**. **Valatar** but **Valatáren**. I suppose it could be argued that this is due to stress; but then why not ****Kortírion**, *úvánimo* and so on? Neither line of argument really seems to fit all situations.

When I saw the form **mundeli**, I assumed it was a feminine. We have **mundo** = 'bull', and such pairs as **sermo/serme** (**SER-**), **melindo/melisse** (**MEL-**) '*amícus/ amíca*' *[as agentives, these Quenya forms would best be glossed in Latin by* amātor, amātrix *—CFH]*, **YŌ/yēn** 'son/daughter' (**YŌ**), which seem to indicate a tendency for *o* to mark the male and *e* the female. So I was quite happy to accept **munde** as 'cow', though I admit this could be the Quenya equivalent of 'she-bull' or 'bulless'. I am not enough of a purist for this to worry me; 'bullesses of stone' will do for 'concrete cows'.

I enjoyed Pat Wynne's "Top 10 Reasons Why People Study Elvish"! Personally, I'm obeying orders from space aliens.

One question occurs to me, to which I should be interested to learn Quendillion reactions. (That was the genitive general plural, by the way, hence the double *lambe. Or so I hope.*) What if Christopher were to discover, under a pile of second-year exam scripts in an old chest in a forgotten attic, the complete and definitive primers, grammars, and dictionaries of all Secondary-World languages, right down to Taliska and the precise relationship between Legolas's Ilkorin dialect and Goldogrin? We would know exactly which words JRRT abandonded, of which ones he altered the meaning, what the significance was of the *a-* augment he prefixed to **vánier**. Would we be pleased, or horrified? Perhaps it's fortunate that the idea is about as likely as that Physics will be over by the end of the century.

Lirilla Valinorello Noldorinwa

A Song of the Noldor of Valinor
by Christopher Gilson

San tulkaner óre Findekan
kostallon otorni hostien,
ar lomba nu mandulumbule
nilmon yetuváro yárean;
er lendie sangarontion
talmanna, i tarna tápina,
nandellea noldo lírinen
mir tárie óma ortane,
qettar leokarko lámina:

> Toron, linnuvalve ailinen
> ondolinnar undu Eldamar,
> yar i wingerondi tyalinen
> eller elveallo Ambalar.
> Ai nilmo, lendiévan ingo
> falman Ilmarinda fascala,
> nán rankonya rúse ringo
> málya merin málo rahtala.

San qettali qinge Maryarus,
formaite tarasse temnea
haryon Feanáro martanen,
lammar ve pilindi, lasta lús
terhante olóri lindova
ar qentale qerna mir nier;
yondoinen onóru kostane
úy' enyalien; ve yáreo
nandelle ar óma tyálier:

Then Fingon set his heart upon
gathering his brothers out of strife,
and secret under dark clouds from hell
he will look for his friend of old;
but having gone to the thronged mountains'
base, the way across blocked,
the harp-wielding gnome in song
unto the heights his voice uplifted,
words from the shadowy crag echoed:

> Brother, let us go to the pool's
> many rocks underneath Elven-home,
> whither the foam-fays in their play
> came from the starlit East.
> Ah friend, I would have come first
> to the foam under Ilmarin to bathe,
> but my arm weary with cold
> thy hand I wish (my) love to stretch out.

Then Maedhros chanted the many words,
manacled right-handed on high
the heir of Feanor in destiny,
sounds like arrows, at a quiet moment
(he) broke through the dreams of the singer
and the story turns into tears;
for the sons the two brothers having quarrelled
is not a memory; as of old
harp and voice played (together):

Toron, linnuvalve ailinen	Brother, let us go to the pool's
ondolinnar undu Eldamar,	many rocks underneath Elven-home,
yar i wingerondi tyalinen	whither the foam-fays in their play
eller elveallo Ambalar.	came from the starlit East.
Ai nilmo, lendiévan ingo	Ah friend, I would have come first
falman Ilmarinda fascala,	to the foam under Ilmarin to bathe,
nán rankonya rúse ringo	but my arm weary with cold
málya merin málo mahtala.	thy hand I wish (my) love to wield.

San leukane nande Findekan	Then Fingon loosed his harp
kamballo, i qinga mápala,	from his hand, the bow seizing,
ar tunga pilindo tiksenen	and with the arrow's point taut
Manwenna i téra mente mán	to Manwe the right end by his hand
an nilmova kyerme naikele;	for his friend's pain prayed;
súrisse Sorontar ortane	in the wind Thorondor lifted up
vor nilda i noldo tar tea,	the ever friendly gnome in that direction,
ar Maryarus angayassenen	and Maedhros in misery
temnallo i ranko lehtane.	from the manacle his arm released.

Toron, linnuvalve ailinen	Brother, let us go to the pool's
ondolinnar undu Eldamar,	many rocks underneath Elven-home,
yar i wingerondi tyalinen	whither the foam-fays in their play
eller elveallo Ambalar.	came from the starlit East.
Ai nilmo, lendiévan ingo	Ah friend, I would have come first
falman Ilmarinda fascala,	to the foam under Ilmarin to bathe,
nán rankonya rúse ringo	but my arm weary with cold
málya merin málo antala.	thy hand I wish (my) love to give.

— *Cwestlthir Gwession* —

February – March 1991

The preceding poem was imagined as a performance piece, with verses (in the metre of "Earendel") chanted by choir and the refrains sung as duets (to the tune of "Nieninque"). The latter echoes the following "song of Valinor" (S:110) which the poem (to that effect) attributes to the shared memory of Fingon and Maedhros.

Wingerondi

óma 1:

Toron, linnuvalve ailinen
    ondolinnar undu Eldamar,
yar i wingerondi tyalinen
    eller elveallo Ambalar.

óma 2:

Ai nilmo, lendiévan ingo
    falman Ilmarinda fascala.
A nán rankonya rúse ringo :
    málya merin, málo, raktala!

Mermen

voice 1:

Brother, let us go out on the bay
    to the rocks beneath our Elven-home,
where the mermen swim and with their play
    stir up starlight in the eastern foam.

voice 2:

Ah friend, I would have been the first there
    under snow-white slopes to bathe with thee.
Alas my arm is cold and weary :
    Pray thy hand, my love, stretch out to me!

Words and Devices
A column by Patrick Wynne and Carl F. Hostetter

"It is said also that these Men had long ago had dealings with the Dark Elves east of the mountains, and from them had learned much of their speech; and since all the languages of the Quendi were of one origin, the language of Bëor and his folk resembled the Elven-tongue in many words and devices." (S:141)

The purpose of this column is to examine words and other linguistic features in Tolkien's Secondary-World languages that have Primary-World cognates and analogues. Comments and contributions are encouraged: send them to Carl F. Hostetter, 2509 Ambling Circle, Crofton, MD 21114, USA.

Pointed Remarks and Cutting Comments

We devote this installment of "Words and Devices" to addressing two letters that raise some important issues, requiring responses that "grew in the telling" as our research quickly led us into fascinating territories.

• *Jenny Coombs*   *Ruddington, Nottinghamshire, England*

I was most interested by your and Pat's "Words and Devices". I agree that there are certainly some links between Indo-European and invented roots. There seem to me to be essentially three types of link. First, where JRRT is (or may be) trying to indicate an "actual" connection between Primary- and Secondary-World languages. *Widris*, for example, must be meant to recall "wit", "ϝοῖδα" *etc.*, and **PHAY**-φαίνω. Secondly, mere similarity, which may be due to JRRT's subconscious (*e.g.* *nasc*/*nazg*), or to chance—as JRRT points out, if you are stringing a limited set of phonemes together in various combinations (and still more if those combinations are limited by an essentially "European" idea of euphony) then you are going to get a lot of words which happen to sound similar. Thirdly, I think there is JRRT's sense of humor. For instance, Gandalf's name among the Haradrim, *Incánus < Inkā + nūs* 'northern spy', is identical to Latin *incānus* 'white-haired', as CRT points out somewhere. This is, I think, JRRT punning with us: a name which bears an appropriate meaning in a Primary-World language. Another example is *Orthanc*, with its Sindarin and Anglo-Saxon meanings of 'forked height' and 'cunning device'. The difficulty is of course distinguishing the three types of link.

I would have believed your analysis of the links between *nasc* and *nazg*, IE **ned**- and Eldarin **NAT-** and **NUT-**, absolutely, had it not been for JRRT's unequivocal denial. The evidence you present is quite convincing—but in the Rang letter you reproduce, JRRT places *nazg* firmly within the chance/subconscious category, and states that he tried to make it "distinct in style and phonetic content from words of the same meaning in Elvish, or in other real languages." This would seem to rule out the possibility that *nazg* was "a natural, rule-driven development from the base **NAT-**", at least on the conscious level. Are you suggesting that JRRT's subconscious mind applied rules of sound-shift to obtain Black Speech *nazg* from **NAT-** and **NUT-**, while consciously he was aware of no connection?

Another word which struck me is ***Carcharoth*** and its root **KÁRAK-**. I am sure JRRT was glancing at ΚΑ ΡΧΑ ΡΟΣ, which Liddel and Scott give as 'sharp-pointed, jagged, with sharp or jagged teeth'; it is used of the wolf in "κάρχαρον μειδήσας", 'grinning with sharp-pointed teeth'. The big question, again, is what sort of link we are to infer. Either JRRT was deliberately linking Indo-European and Eldarin bases (either because the former developed from the latter, or because the former was influenced by the latter, or because both developed from a common proto-language); or JRRT did not remember Greek κάρχαρος when he sought a name for the great wolf, but was subconsciously influenced by it; or JRRT was fully aware of the resemblance and is joking with us (if ***Carcharoth*** started life as "Red Maw", then there is a pun of the ***Incánus/Orthanc*** variety).

You can get quite paranoid about this sort of thing, spotting puns when probably none exist. For instance, could ***ekkaia*** possibly be a pun on ἐκ-γαια (*sc.* ἐκ-γαιης, only Quenya words cannot end in -*s*): 'outside/beyond Earth'? *[Quenya words can in fact end in -s: "Q. permitted, indeed favoured, the 'dentals' n, l, r, s, t as final consonants", L:425. A handful of earlier Quenya words also end in k: e.g. **helk** 'ice-cold' LR:364. —eds.]* I wouldn't put it past him. And I was recently struck by ***Ilterendi***, as Aulë named the fetters "for they might not be cleft"; could JRRT have been subconsciously influenced by Latin *tero?* In Latin *interendi* would mean something like '(masculine) objects which may not be worn away'. (I have a feeling I have read this suggested somewhere, but my memory may be playing tricks on me. If *I* have been "subconsciously influenced", my apologies.)

In general, even when JRRT isn't actually constructing etymological links, I think he uses phonetic similarities (perhaps subconsciously) to enhance the effect of his languages; as I leaf through *Etymologies*, many of the words seem vaguely familiar, just as Frodo felt when hearing *Nainie* (or *Naenia?*). For instance, although I cannot think of a Primary-World example where *mor-* means 'dark', the sound already has an oppressive feel for me, because of *morior*, mortal, morbid, mordant and so on (even though English *mor* is pronounced differently from Eldarin and Latin *mor*, which adds to its phonetic heaviness), whereas *el*, with its front vowel and liquid, feels uplifting, and recalls *Elysium, elm*, κυριε ελεισον, and so on. H.G. Wells and C.S. Lewis must have felt similarly: *cf.* Eloi, Morlocks, *eldila*, Maleldil. *[Lewis probably based the latter two on Elvish; cf. L:33: "...eldila, in any case, I suspect to be due to the influence of the Eldar in the Silmarillion". —eds.]* Other words sound phonetically appropriate even where there is no connection of sense: *e.g.* ***linta*** 'swift', ***slindi*** 'fine, delicate' (**SLIN-**), ***ndakie*** 'to slay'. JRRT used the web of sense-association he had acquired through his study of many languages, and combined it with his personal sense of euphony and onomatopoeia (as described in "A Secret Vice") to create languages which can also attract us, who share some languages and phonetic taste with JRRT.

Going on to Menn's essay, I agree that there could be an etymological link between Eldarin ***korko***, ***corch*** (**KORKA-**), ***kraban***, *etc.* and IE *corvus*, κόραξ, *etc.* Or equally both groups could be onomatopoetic in origin ("caw"). *Cf.* ****kukūwā***, ***ku***, ***kua*** 'dove'. Similarly, whereas Menn postulates an "actual", Secondary-World link between Eldarin ***el-*** and such words as ἐλεέω ('I have mercy' < 'I behave in accordance with Eldarin teaching' [! Tell that to the Alqualondeans]), I would say, as above, that *el-* had "good" sense-associations for JRRT, and therefore seemed an appropriate sound for 'star', because he was already familiar with its Greek meaning.

I think Lise Menn must have been terribly disappointed by *The Silmarillion.* She appears to have the impression from *LotR* that the Eldar are superhumanly saintly, an understandable though mistaken impression, since the Eldar in *LotR* are a race in senescence, already withdrawn from the world. This aloofness Menn appears to have taken for holiness. It is rather unfair to look back on her essay with the benefit of 1991 hindsight, but it is nevertheless amusing. "Clearly the Sindar…did their best to keep the very existence of iron and steel weapons a secret from their Bronze Age neighbors….when have Humans restrained themselves from trade in armaments?…to have hidden, for several hundred years, the very existence of superior weapons from a war-loving community shows a superhuman restraint and morality which could only have been maintained by Elves." Compare that with the bloodthirsty mob which rampage through the centuries in *QS!*

Editorial Response

Chance and the Subconscious

Jenny's classification of similarities between Primary- and Secondary-World languages into **1)** genuine genetic connections, **2)** subconscious/chance similarities, and **3)** puns is essentially sound. However, Jenny lends too much weight to *chance resemblance* and *subconscious borrowing* as explanations for such similarities. It is an acknowledged phenomenon that "actual congruences (of form + sense) occur in unrelated real languages" (L:384), as Tolkien notes in his letter to Mr. Rang. For example, Italian *donna* and Japanese *onna* are similar in form and both mean 'woman', but they are unrelated words in unrelated languages. However, Mario Pei in *The Story of Language* (pg. 383) notes that "in accordance with the statistical laws of probability" such chance congruences occur "in one word out of a few thousands." So Jenny's statement that pure chance will yield "a lot of words which happen to sound similar" is simply not so, since part of Pei's point is that while chance does produce congruences between unrelated languages, it does not produce them in abundance. Yet even the most casual examination of the *Etymologies* or the *Qenya* and *Gnomish Lexicons* will show that similarities between Elvish and Primary-World words are remarkably common, occuring at a far more frequent rate than merely "one word out of a few thousands", a fact which is all the more striking given that the Elvish vocabularies currently available to us are quite small in comparison to those of real languages.

The statistical probability of chance congruity is lessened by the fact that words consist of two independent variables: sound *and* meaning, "form + sense". Let's say we are glossopoeists setting out to create a new word. We could first devise an aesthetically pleasing sound sequence, say *girtos*. We are now faced with a virtually *infinite* number of meanings which we could assign to this sound sequence. We might through sheer chance select the meaning 'to turn', ignorant of the resemblance between *girtos* and the IE root **kert-** 'to turn, entwine'. If, however, we go on to invent several hundred other words, and a large percentage of these have close sound-and-meaning correspondences with IE roots, then one must conclude that something other than mere chance is at work, for there is no innate correspondence between the sound of a word and the concept it signifies (with a few minor exceptions, such as echoic words). This fundamental fact is the basis of historical linguistics, and it demands that where there are a significant number of sound-and-meaning correspondences between two separate languages, there must be an historical relationship between the two. The unavoidable conclusion is that the majority of the sound-and-meaning correspondences between Elvish and Primary-World languages must be deliberate.

As for some of these correspondences resulting from subconscious borrowing rather than conscious intent, this undeniably happened, since Tolkien himself states in his letter to Mr. Rang that both ***Erech*** and ***nazg*** were probably subconscious "echoes" of Mesopotamian *Erech* and Gaelic *nasc*. Nonetheless, subconscious borrowing must have been a very negligible element in Tolkien's linguistic creativity. Tolkien's careful literary craftsmanship and fastidious attention to detail are well known. He once wrote about *The Lord of the Rings:* "Hardly a word in its 600,000 or more has been unconsidered. And the placing, size, style, and contribution to the whole of all the features, incidents, and chapters has been laboriously pondered." (L:160) How much more "laboriously pondered" were Tolkien's languages? They were already in an elaborate and highly polished state in 1915, and Tolkien continued to refine them for almost another sixty years. It is difficult to imagine that cross-etymological connections that seem obvious to us today — and who among us would put his or her knowledge of linguistics on a par with Tolkien's? — would have remained opaque to Tolkien himself. For example, Jenny points out the similarity between Latin *tero* 'to rub, wear away' and Q *Ilterendi* from the *Lost Tales* (apparently from a root TERE *'bore' in the Qenya Lexicon, with other derivatives *tereva* 'piercing' and *teret* 'auger, gimlet'; also note the later base **TER-**, **TERES-** 'pierce' in the *Etymologies*, whence Q *ter*, *tere* 'through'), and she wonders if Tolkien might have been subconsciously influenced by the Latin verb. *Tero* is related to Latin *terebra* 'a gimlet, borer' and *terebro* 'to bore through, pierce, perforate', all from the IE root **tera-[1]** 'to rub, turn; to bore, pierce', and this root appears cognate with Elvish TERE *'bore' and **TER-**, **TERES-** 'pierce'. The IE root **der-[2]** 'to split, peel, flay' may also be cognate with these Elvish forms. The congruences of form + sense between these Elvish and IE roots and their derivatives are so close and clear-cut that it seems impossible to conclude that they resulted from anything other than Tolkien's *conscious* design.

Even in the case of subconsciously borrowed words such as ***Erech*** and ***nazg***, Tolkien constructed plausible linguistic histories and connections for them within his Secondary World. Thus ***Erech***, for example, is described as "a pre-Númenórean name of long-forgotten meaning", which "of course fits the style of the predominantly Sindarin nomenclature of Gondor (or it would not have been used)" (L:384), and Tolkien even drops a hint about its long-forgotten meaning: "I was probably...influenced by the important element ER (in Elvish) = 'one, single, alone'." (*ibid.*)

Similarly, Black Speech *nazg* was carefully fitted into the linguistic framework of Middle-earth. It is well established in Tolkien's mythology that evil cannot create, only corrupt; thus, for example, it is said that "Morgoth, since he can make no living thing, bred Orcs from various kinds of Men" (UT:385, note 5). It is consonant with this theme that Sauron should corrupt the languages of the Elves to provide a language for his minions, and so we find many instances where a word in the Black Speech was clearly derived from an Elvish form: BS locative *-ishi* < Q locative *-sse*, BS *burzum* 'darkness' < Q *mornie* 'darkness', BS *durb-* 'to rule' < Q *tur-* 'to wield, control, govern', and so on. Of course Tolkien must have been consciously aware of these derivations — they occur too frequently in the tiny extant Black Speech vocabulary to assume otherwise — and so it is equally probable that Tolkien deliberately derived *nazg* from Q *natse* 'web, net', < **NAT-** 'lace, weave, tie'.

Jenny asserts that this is ruled out by Tolkien's comments that *nazg* was subconsciously derived from Gaelic *nasc* and "was devised to be a vocable as distinct in style and phonetic content from words of the same meaning in Elvish, or in other real languages". First of all, let's remember that Q *natse* and the bases **NAT-** and **NUT-** 'tie, bind' occur in the *Etymologies* (c. 1937–38) and had a fixed existence well before Tolkien created *nazg* for *The Lord of the Rings*. The obvious genetic connection between **NAT-** and **NUT-** and IE **ned-** 'to bind, tie' was therefore also in existence before *nazg* and stands independent of any controversy concerning *nazg*. But Jenny is seeing a contradiction between our comments and Tolkien's about the origin of *nazg*, when no contradiction in fact exists. In corrupting *natse* to *nazg*, Tolkien was indeed consciously striving to produce a new word "distinct in style and phonetic content from words of the same meaning in Elvish" — *nazg* is recognizably alien to Eldarin phonology, and bears no resemblance to *corma*, the usual Quenya word for 'ring' (as in *Cormarë* 'Ringday' [III:390]). Note that Tolkien was not saying that *nazg* had to be completley different from other words phonologically, only that it should be "distinct", as befits a word in a language with purposely corrupted phonology. Tolkien's subconscious came into play in choosing the sound-shifts used to corrupt *natse;* with *nasc* "lodged in some corner of [his] linguistic memory" he chose shifts resulting in a BS word similar to the Gaelic one, and the similarity was enhanced by the fact that he had earlier devised a genetic connection between the base **NAT-** (whence *natse*) and IE **ned-** (whence *nasc*), unaware at the time where this would later lead. Thus while the similarity of *nasc* and *nazg* was subconscious, that of *nazg* and *natse* was deliberate, and the similarity of the IE and Eldarin roots from which *nasc* and *nazg*/*natse* derive was deliberate as well.

Missing Links

An important motivation which Tolkien may have had in devising these Primary-/Secondary-World connections was a desire to supply etymological *missing links*. A look through the *OED* or any other etymological dictionary will show that the origins of many words are unclear or entirely unknown. Tolkien often appears to have devised Eldarin forms with the specific purpose of providing the original source — the missing link — in the etymology of such mysterious words.

Jenny mentions Gandalf's name *Incánus*, which brings to mind an example of such a "missing link". Christopher Tolkien discusses in *Unfinished Tales* (pp. 399–400) how his father implied in a note written in 1967 that the name *Incánus* originated from Latin *incānus* 'quite grey, grey-haired' (Latin *cānus* 'whitish-grey' < a suffixed form **kas-no-* of IE **kas-** 'grey'). In making such puns, Tolkien was always careful to make sure that the pun-word also had a plausible etymology within the context of his sub-created world—an important point to remember—though in the case of *Incánus* Tolkien had some difficulty in deciding how the name fit into the linguistic structure of Middle-earth. Besides the attribution to the language of the Haradrim—*Inkā* + *nūs* 'northern spy'—in another note Tolkien says that *Incánus* was a Quenya name, < *in(id)-* 'mind' and *kan-* 'ruler'. The Quenya element *in(id)-* 'mind' appears closely related to a base in the *Etymologies:* **INK-**, **INIK-?** with Quenya derivatives *intya-* 'guess, suppose' and *intyale* 'imagination', as well as N *inc* 'guess, idea, notion'. The base **INK-**, **INIK-?**, with its connotations of intuitive reasoning, is highly evocative of NE *inkling*, one definition of which is "a slight or vague knowledge or notion, a suspicion". *Inkling* derives from a rare verb *inkle*, meaning "to give a hint of, to get an inkling or notion of", and according to the *OED* the origin of this verb is unascertained. It would appear that Tolkien intended for **INK-**, **INIK-?** to solve the mystery of the origin of *inkle* and *inkling*. His personal interest in these words is obvious—during the late '30s when the *Etymologies* was composed, the Inklings were in full swing and formed an important part of Tolkien's life.

Carcharoth

Jenny is probably correct in positing a connection between *Carcharoth* and Greek κάρχαρος 'sharp-pointed, jagged, with sharp or jagged teeth'. But the bewildering history of the name *Carcharoth* is every bit as diabolical as the wolf-ward of Angband himself, and we should examine it more closely before passing judgment. *Carcharoth* did not start life as 'the Red Maw'; *Carcharoth* did not even start life as *Carcharoth*. At its earliest occurrence in *The Tale of Tinúviel* (1917) the name is *Karkaras*, often given as *Karkaras Knife-fang* with 'Knife-fang' clearly intended as the translation. *Karkaras* is a Qenya form, and in the Qenya Lexicon under the root KRKR we find *karkaras* 'row of spikes or teeth', as well as *karka* 'fang, tooth, tusk' (LT2:344). While 'Knife-fang' and 'row of spikes or teeth' provide us with similar images, they remain distinct enough in meaning to require some effort in reconciling them as coexistent translations of *Karkaras*.

The key element in *Karkaras* may appear in *Helkaraksë* 'Icefang', in the *Lost Tales* the name of a narrow icy promontory extending from the western lands (LT1:167). The first element in Helkaraksë is *helkë* 'ice' or *helka* 'ice-cold' (LT1:254). Although a word *karaksë* 'fang' does not occur in the *Lost Tales* lexicons, it appears to derive from KRKR, and this is supported by the *Etymologies*, which gives the latter element in *Helkarakse* as *karakse* 'jagged hedge of spikes' < **KÁRAK-** 'sharp fang, spike, tooth' (= KRKR). In *Karkaras* we see *karaksë* shortened to *karas*. The shortening of a name by dropping the final vowel is characteristic of Qenya, as with **Valinórë** and **Valinor** 'Asgard' in the Qenya Lexicon. Apparently final **-ks** was not allowed and was simplified to **-s**. This is supported by a contemporary example in *The Cottage of Lost Play*, where **Lindeloksë** 'singing cluster', a name of Laurelin, is emended to **Lindelos** (*cf.* LT1:258). The entry for **PEL-** 'revolve on fixed point' in the *Etymologies* demonstrates the same principle; primitive ****pel-takse*** became Q **peltas** 'pivot' with loss of the final vowel, but the plural **peltaksi** retained **-ks-** in internal position, where it was allowable.

Reduplication is common in Quenya, where it serves a variety of functions, such as indicating repetition; *e.g.* compare **fir-** 'die, fade' with its reduplicated, frequentative form **fifíru-** 'slowly fade away', literally *'to fade and fade'. Thus we might suppose **karaksë** 'fang' had a reduplicated form ****kar-karaksë*** (shortened to **karkaras**), with the reduplication indicating the repetition or multiplicity of *'a row of many fangs'. The similarity of **karka** 'fang, tooth, tusk' with the initial syllables of **Karkaras** may have led to a coexistent, alternate interpretation of the name as **karka** 'knife' (if we can accept this as an extension of the meanings 'fang, tooth, tusk') + **karaksë** 'fang'.

In the Gnomish Lexicon the Goldogrin equivalent of **Karkaras** is **Carcaloth**, changed to **Carchaloth** (LT2:344). The first element is **carc** 'jag, point, fang'. Vacillation between **r** and **l** is typical of Gnomish (as with the plural suffixes **-rim**, **-lim**), and the form **Carchaloth** may also have been influenced by Gn. **-loth** 'cluster', as though the name meant *'Fang-cluster' (*cf.* Q **loksë** 'cluster' in **Lindeloksë** and its cognate **-loth** in **Sithaloth** 'fly-cluster', Gnomish name of the Pleiades [LT1:254]). The Gnomish Lexicon also gives the form **Carchamoth** (< **Carcamoth**). Here the initial element is still **carc** 'fang', but the ending appears to be **moth** '1000' (LT1:270), with the full name meaning *'Thousand Fangs' (our thanks to Christopher Gilson for suggesting this interpretation).

After the *Lost Tales* Tolkien continued to niggle with various forms—all of them presumably "Low-elven"—interpreted as 'Knife-fang'. **Carcharoth** first appears in *The Lay of the Children of Húrin* (*c.* 1918–25), where "**Carcharoth** the cruel-fangèd" is an emendation from **Carcharolch**, a form occurring nowhere else (LB:125). In the *Qenta Noldorinwa* (1930) we find "**Carcharas** Knife-fang" (SM:112), though this was emended at all occurrences to **Carcharoth** (SM:115, note 8). "**Carcharos**, the Knife-fang" appears in line 3714 (manuscript A) of *The Lay of Leithian* (1925–31). This was emended to **Carcharas**, then to **Carcharoth**, and in the margin of the manuscript at this point is written "Red Maw", as well as **Caras**, an illegible word beginning **Car-**, and yet another form: **Gargaroth** (LB:292). This may be the very moment at which Tolkien decided to change the meaning of **Carcharoth** from 'Knife-fang' to 'Red Maw'. Concerning a reference to "**Carcharoth** knifefang" in Synopsis III of *The Lay of Leithian*, Christopher Tolkien notes (LB:293-4) that the translation 'Knife-fang' "survived into the A-text of the Lay...but was replaced in B by the translation 'Red Maw'. The words 'red maw' are used of Karkaras in the *Tale*, but not as his name (II.34)." In the first version of the *Earliest Annals of Beleriand* (contemporary with the *Qenta Noldorinwa*) the form **Carcharoth** occurs in the text as first written, and it appears to be the form used exclusively from that point on, as in the *Later Annals of Beleriand* and the *Quenta*

Silmarillion (*c*. 1937–1938). *QS* provided the main text of the Beren and Lúthien story in *The Silmarillion*, where **Carcharoth** is given as 'the Red Maw' (pg. 180).

This semantic shift from 'Knife-fang' to 'Red Maw' requires reinterpreting one of the elements in **Carcharoth** as 'red'. One might conclude that the new etymology is N *caran* 'red' + **caroth* 'maw', the latter a variant of **caraes* 'jagged hedge of spikes' seen in N **Helcharaes**, = Q **Helkarakse** (LR:362). Just as **caloth* in **Carchaloth** seemed influenced by Gn. *-loth* 'cluster', so the form and meaning of **caroth* may have been influenced by Dor. *roth* 'cave' < **ROD-** 'cave' (which appears related to IE **rēd-** 'to scrape, scratch, gnaw'; the O-grade form **rōd-* led to Latin *rōdere* 'to gnaw', whence NE *corrode* and *erode*).

However, the *Etymologies* suggests another interpretation, for under the base **KÁRAK-** *Carcharoth* is given in parentheses after N *carch* 'tooth, fang', implying that it is the *first* element which means 'maw'. If so, the likeliest candidate for the second element is N *rhosc* 'brown' (< **RUSKĀ-**) or some related form. This word also occurs in **Rhosgobel** 'russet enclosure' (UT:461), dwelling-place of Radagast the Brown. NE *russet* does not simply mean 'brown', but rather 'of a <u>reddish</u>-brown colour' (*OED*), ultimately from Latin *russus* 'red' < IE **reudh-1** 'red, ruddy' (whence also NE *red*), and 'reddish-brown' is perhaps a more precise description of the color of a wolf's mouth than 'red'. Tolkien chose the words in his translations with care, and by selecting *russet* to translate *rhosc* in *Rhosgobel* he was not only telling us that the Elvish word had connotations of redness, but he was also hinting at a genetic connection between *rhosc* and IE **reudh-1** 'red, ruddy'.

Obviously there was some waffling about whether **Carcharoth** meant 'Knife-fang' or 'Red Maw', and in the latter instance, about which element meant 'red'. This uncertainty may not be due solely to indecision on Tolkien's part; he may have intended that in Middle-earth itself the situation was confused—*Carcharoth* may have originally been 'Knife-fang' but was later folk-etymologically reinterpreted by Elvish speakers as 'the Red Maw' under the influence of such words as *caran* 'red' and *rhosc* '(reddish-)brown'. This confusion is all the more understandable when one realizes that the Eldarin words for 'fang' and 'red' are etymologically related. The base **SKAR-** 'tear, rend' (> Q *harna-*, N *harno* 'to wound') must be akin to (or the source of) **KÁRAK-** 'sharp fang, spike, tooth'; *i.e.* **SKAR-** 'tear' is the action performed by **KÁRAK-** 'fang' (literally ***'tearer, wounder'). Similarly, **KARÁN-** 'red' describes the *result* of tearing with a fang, and the original sense of the base may have been 'wound-colored'. Examples of this sense connnection may be found in Indo-European as well. The IE root **sker-1** (also **ker-**) 'to cut' — source of NE *shears, sharp, scrape*, and *scar*—has a variant form **kar-* seen in Latin *carō* (gen. *carnis*) 'flesh', and the association between 'flesh' and 'flesh-colored' resulted in a number of derivatives referring to red, including NE *carnation* 'deep red', *carnelian* (a variety of red chalcedony), and *incarnadine* (as in *Macbeth* Act II Sc. II: "No, this my hand will rather the multitudinous seas incarnadine, making the green one red.").

The genetic connection between IE **sker-1**,**ker-** 'cut' and Elvish **SKAR-** 'tear', **KIR-** (> N *critho* 'reap'), and **KIRIS-** 'cut', is unmistakable. There is another, undoubtedly related, IE root **skel-1**,**kel-** 'cut' which is clearly cognate to other Elvish bases with the sense of 'cut', including **KIL-** (also **SKIL**) 'divide', and **SKEL-** (> Q *helta* 'strip'). And yet another IE root of the same meaning, **rei-**[1] 'to scratch, tear, cut', has a clear cognate in the base **RIS-** 'cut, cleave'. It is interesting to note that **sker-**[1] 'cut' is identical to another IE root **sker-**[2] 'to leap, jump about'. The sense 'leap, jump' also seems inherent in Elvish **SKAR-**, which led to a primitive form **askarā*, whence N *Ascar* 'violent, rushing, impetuous', one of the tributaries of Gelion, described in the *Quenta Silmarillion* as "swift and turbulent, falling steeply from the mountains" (LR:263).

As we mentioned at the beginning of this lengthy diatribe—and perhaps it is no coincidence that in *The Tale of Tinúviel* Tinwelint's daughter included "the tail of Karkaras" in her lengthening spell, which listed "the names of all the tallest and longest things upon Earth"—it is very likely that Tolkien intended a genetic connection between Greek κάρχαρος and *Carcharoth* in all its various forms (including one which is identical to the Greek: *Carcharos* in *The Lay of Leithian*). Walde-Pokorny's *Vergleichendes Wörterbuch der indogermanischen Sprachen* [*'Comparative Dictionary of the Indo-European Languages'*] gives an IE root **qhar-** 'sharp, pointed', whence Skt. *khára-* 'hard, rough, sharp' and Modern Persian *xār, xārā* 'rock, thorn'. The relationship here to **KÁRAK-** 'sharp fang, spike, tooth' and **SKAR-** 'tear, rend' is clear. Another likely IE cognate appears in Watkins as **gher-**[4] 'to scrape, scratch', which in the extended zero-grade form **ghr̥(ə)-k-* led to Greek χάραξ 'a pointed stake' (*cf.* Q *karakse* 'fang' or 'jagged hedge of spikes') and χᾰράσσω 'to make sharp or pointed, sharpen or whet; to furnish with notches or teeth (like a saw)'.

Greek κάρχαρος 'pointed, sharp, biting' (a variant of καρχαρέος 'biting') is an onomatopoeic reduplicated form derived from IE **qhar-**. We have previously mentioned that *Karkaras* is a reduplicative form as well, and like κάρχαρος it has a strongly onomatopoeic flavor—in it one can hear the fangs of a wolf clattering together. Other closely related forms include καρχαρόδων 'with sharp teeth' and καρχαρίας 'shark'—fans of the movie "Jaws" may recall that the scientific name of the Great White Shark, a modern-day 'Red Maw', is *Carcharodon carcharias*—as well as καρχαλέος 'rough, cutting, sharp'. This latter word also meant 'fierce' (used of fire) and 'dry, scorching, parched (with thirst)', influenced by καρφαλέος 'dry, parched' < κάρφω 'dry up, wither'. While there is no etymological connection whatsoever between καρχαλέος 'parched with thirst' and *Anfauglir* 'the Jaws of Thirst', another name for Carcharoth (S:180), it is tempting to speculate (especially considering the form *Carchaloth* in the *Lost Tales*) whether this Greek form might have played some small rôle in inspiring the narrative motif of the wolf of Angband's overwhelming thirst caused by the burning of the Silmaril within him (*cf.* S:185–6: "At the foot of the falls [of Esgalduin] Carcharoth drank to ease his consuming thirst…within he was wellnigh all consumed as with a fire").

In all versions of the mythology, *Carcharoth* is portrayed as the unsleeping wolf-ward before the gates of *Angband* 'Hell', literally 'Iron-prison' (LR:371). Tolkien may have intended for Carcharoth to be the actual primeval entity whose baleful existence was dimly remembered by the later Greeks as Κέρβερος, the monstrous multi-headed watch-dog guarding the entrance to Hades. (The etymology of *Κέρβερος* is uncertain; it has been explained as a mere "happy invention", and Austro-asiatic and Mediterranean origins have also been proposed. Walde-Pokorny tentatively connect it with Skt. *karbará-, śárvara-* 'spotted, mottled', from an IE root **ƙerbero-** of the same meaning—imagine *Κέρβερος* as "my dog Spot"!—and compare this root with **ƙer-** 'gray'.) Continuing this line of thought, perhaps we can also postulate a connection between ***Carcharoth*** and Latin *carcer* 'prison' (= Gk. *κάρκαρον*), genitive *carceris* in *carceris custos* 'gaoler'. The origin of *carcer* is unclear; Watkins describes the word as "probably borrowed from an unidentified source…representing reduplicated form **kar-kr-o-*". It would appear that Tolkien identified Watkins' "unidentified source", once again providing the missing link in a mysterious etymology.

Linguistic *déjà vu*

It is hardly due to mere "effect" that Frodo found many of the words of the Eldarin tongues to be "vaguely familiar". Rather it is because his language, Westron, was descended from Adûnaic, and was furthermore "enriched and softened under Elvish influence" (III:406). While it is true that *The Lord of the Rings* as published cites no specific genetic connection between Adûnaic and the Eldarin tongues, it seems most likely that such a connection in fact existed, since Adûnaic plainly takes the place of Taliskan, of known Eldarin descent. There is also the evidence of an explicit statement by Faramir on the matter (WR:159–60) — removed late (certainly *post*–1944; see WR:162) and seemingly only because of compression — which after much emendation (*ibid.* 160, 169 note 31) read:

> "The Common Tongue, as some call it, is derived from the Númenóreans, being but a form changed by time of that speech which the Fathers of the Three Houses spoke of old. This language it is that has spread through the western world amongst all folk and creatures that use words…. But this is not an Elvish speech in my meaning. All speech of men in this world is Elvish in descent; but only if one go back to the beginnings. What I meant was so: many men of the Three Houses long ago learned the High-elven tongue of the Noldor, as it was spoken in Gondolin or by the Sons of Fëanor. And always the Lords of Númenor knew that tongue, and used it among themselves."

In any case, a strong relationship, whether due to common origin or to influence, of Adûnaic with the Eldarin tongues is demonstrated by numerous examples of related words in these langauges. For instance, the name ***Adûnakhôr*** 'Lord of the West', and indeed the very word ***Adûnaic*** itself, clearly contains an element ***adûn(a)-*** either cognate with or borrowed from Q ***Andúnë*** 'the West'; while ***-khôr*** is clearly related to Q ***heru*** 'lord' (< **KHER-** 'rule, govern, possess'). And there is ***Agathurush***, the Adûnaic translation of Sindarin ***Gwathló*** 'the shadowy river from the fens' (UT:263), which clearly exhibits a relationship between S ***gwath*** 'shadow' (*cf.* Q ***avathar*** 'The Shadows' [S:318]) and the initial element ****agathu-***.

Appendix F to *LotR* informs us (III:407) that Westron, the Common Speech, began as a sort of pidgin at the Númenórean haven of Pelargir, where "Adûnaic was spoken, and mingled with many words of the languages of lesser men it became a Common Speech". After the downfall of Númenor, the remnants of the Faithful fled to the North-west of Middle-earth, where they used the Common Speech, and they "enlarged the language and enriched it with many words drawn from the Elven-tongues." It was this language, heavily influenced by and probably cognate with the Elven tongues, that Frodo spoke.

Thus Frodo felt the relatedness of his language with Quenya, just as we can read something in Latin—like Catullus's *Dā mī bāsia mīlle* 'Give me a thousand kisses'—and feel the relatedness, since English is cognate with Latin and enriched by borrowings from that language. For instance, the Westron word for 'Hobbit', *banakil* 'halfling' (III:416) contains the same Quenya element *-kil* 'man' found in *Tarkil* 'High Man', "a Quenya word used in Westron for one of Númenorean descent" (III:409; and see bases **KHIL-** 'follow' and **TĀ-, TA3-** 'high, lofty, noble'). The element *nîn* in Westron *Branda-nîn* 'border-water' (III:416) is clearly related to Q *nén* 'water', while the element *-bas* 'town, -ton' in the Westron village-name *Galabas* (*ibid.*) must be related to Q *-mar* 'dwelling, home'; the *Qenya Lexicon* (LT1:251 *s.v.* **Eldamar**) notes a Qenya ending *-mas* "equivalent to English *-ton*".

By the same token, it is hardly due to mere "effect" that *we*, like Frodo, find many of the words of the Eldarin tongues to be "vaguely familiar", since Tolkien carefully constructed his languages to be seen as cognate with the Indo-European tongues. This is once again demonstrated by the element *mor-* 'black' that Jenny cites. This is clearly cognate with IE **mer-[1]**, which according to Watkins means "To flicker; with derivatives refering to dim states of illumination". Among the derivatives of this root are NE *morn* and OE *mirce* 'darkness', whence NE *murk*. This latter OE element appears in Tolkien's *Mirkwood*, which he notes (L:369–70):

> "is not an invention of mine, but a very ancient name…its ancientness seems indicated by its appearance in very early German (11th c.?) as *mirkiwidu* although the **merkw-* stem 'dark' is not otherwise found in German at all (only in O.E., O.S., and O.N.)…In O.E. *mirce* only survives in poetry, and only with the sense 'dark', or rather 'gloomy', only in *Beowulf* 1405 *ofer myrcan mor ["over the murky moor" —eds.]* : elsewhere only with the sense 'murky' > wicked, hellish. It was never, I think, a mere 'colour' word: 'black', and was from the beginning weighted with the sense of 'gloom' …."

The base **MOR-** has both connotations: Q *more*, N *moru* 'black' *vs.* Q *morna* 'gloomy, sombre', N *maur* 'gloom'. This last form is particularly interesting, since the English word *Moor* for the Northern African people that conquered Spain in the 8th century may (according to the *OED*) ultimately derive from Greek μαυρός 'black', a form of ἀμαυρός 'dark, hardly seen, dim, faint, shadowy; obscure; blind' (Liddell & Scott). These are also clearly related to Gnomish *maur* 'dream, vision' (LT1:261 *s.v.* **Murmuran**).

• *Tom Loback*   *New York, New York*

Let's see if some cross-etymologizing can be accomplished without Indo-European roots. Let's even use the bases from *Etymologies* that were used in the last column.

TUK- 'draw, bring'. Well, sounds familiar, sounds like *tuck*—egads! One of the definitions of *tuck* in the *Oxford Universal Dictionary* (1955) is: 'to draw, pull'. Or *Thugee*, the strangler cult, certainly involves drawing a cord around a neck.

How about **TUG-**, Noldorin *tû* 'muscle, sinew'? Why, there's *thew* 'muscles or tendons' and associated with *sinew*. Good grief, Modern English comes from Noldorin!

Need more proof? Try **TUMPU-** 'hump', N. *tump*. Gadzooks! *OUD* has *tump* 'a hillock, mound; molehill', not to mention *tumescence*, *tumid*, *tumor*, *tumult*, and more, all having to do with swelling or rising like a bulge or hump. Further, *tump* is so close to *thump* (that pesky *t* to *th*). But *thump* is a sound that a lump of a chump with a mump makes when he trips over a hump in the dump with a bump. Humph!

We're not even out of the *t*s and already the correspondences defy coincidence, and we didn't even have to resort to the several hundred other languages descended from Indo-European to make the point.

Sarcasm aside, what appears to be going on is that Tolkien composed an abstract paradigm of IE-type languages as a result of his æsthetic choice (we know that Finnish and Welsh are his models). That this parallels development in real languages is unsurprising and does not prove your central thesis. Why does he not say when asked about the similarity of Sindarin to Welsh that Sindarin is related in the genetic sense that you suggest?

If Salmar the harp-maker becomes Salmar the horn-maker as the evidence suggests, and Ælfwine finally disappears, and the Tol Eressëa = England connection is dropped, **Widris** is changed to **Nóm** and the Valar are no longer gods—what does this suggest? Especially when your strongest IE arguments fall in the period when the concept of immediate and direct connection of Middle-earth to the real Earth is never as close again as it was then. Are any IE connections consistent by language throughout or only a piece here connected to Greek or a piece there to the Baltic tongues? The argument can be made, with the same information you present, that what is being done could be a parallel development of a similar language group only tenuously related to ours. "On Fairy-stories" describes how the suspension of disbelief is achieved. That this is not reducible to a mathematic clarity is the magic of art over science. But to try to get this across, try substituting "bases" and "Indo-European roots" into what Tolkien says about Sindarin and Welsh in *Letters* (p. 426): "[The bases of the *Etymologies* were] deliberately devised to resemble [the roots of Indo-European] in phonetic origin and grammatical use; but are not the *same* in either p[honetic] o[rigin] or g[rammatical] u[se]."

Editorial Response

Well, there he goes again.

The less said about the cut-and-paste quotation with which Tom closes his letter, the better. Mutilating a quote until it says what one wishes it to say hardly constitutes good scholarship, and we might gain an equal amount of insight into Elvish—which is to say none at all—by substituting the words "Tom" and "green cheese" in the same passage.

Turning to the beginning of Tom's letter, we find a salvo of satiric barbs which fall short of their intended target. It is impossible of course to compare Elvish bases with Modern English (NE) words without reference to Indo-European roots, since the form and meaning of NE words reflect the form and meaning of the Indo-European roots from which they derive. If we examine the NE words Tom mentions in the light of Indo-European, the exercise becomes far more instructive:

• Tom is probably correct in connecting **TUK-** 'draw, bring' with NE *tuck*, since the latter (along with NE *tug* and *tow*) derives from IE **deuk-** 'to draw, pull, lead', which appears akin to Elvish **TUK-**.

• NE *Thugee* and *thug* come from Hindi *thag* < Skt. *sthagaḥ* 'a cheat' < *sthagati* 'he conceals' < IE **(s)teg-** 'to cover', and so in fact refer to a secretive nature rather than to "drawing a cord around a neck". IE **(s)teg-** may be akin to Elvish **STAG-** 'press, compress' in the sense that to *conceal* something is to *suppress* it (< Latin *supprimere* 'to press under; to conceal').

• NE *thew* is of uncertain etymology. One theory stipulates that it comes from OE *thēaw* 'usage, custom' (< 'observance'), derived from IE **teu-** 'to pay attention to, turn to'. If so, no connection is apparent between these forms and Elvish **TUG-**, Noldorin *tû* 'muscle, sinew'. However, another possibility is that *thew* derives (either mechanically or by association) from OE *þȳwan, þēowan* 'to press, squeeze, compress', which (though we have been unable to confirm it) must be descended from IE **teuə-** 'to swell', which is clearly related to **TUG-**.

• NE *tumescence, tumid, tumor,* and *tumult* all derive from IE **tūm-*, an extended form of the root **teuə-** 'to swell'. IE **tūm-* 'to swell' is almost identical with the Qenya Lexicon root TUMU 'swell (with idea of hollowness)' (LT1:269), which in turn must be very closely akin to the base **TUMPU-** 'hump'. NE *tump* might belong with **tūm-* and its derivatives, although its precise history is obscure. Welsh has a word *twmp* 'mound, hillock, heap', but this may be a borrowing of NE *tump*. According to the *OED, tump* does not occur before the end of the 16th century and is chiefly a western and west-midland word. Tolkien's love for the early English of the West Midlands is well known—"I am a West-midlander by blood (and took to early west-midland Middle English as a known tongue as soon as I set eyes on it)" (L:213)—and thus it is not inconceivable that with **TUMPU-** 'hump' (> N *tump*) Tolkien was providing his own answer to a linguistic mystery in his beloved west-midland dialect.

Of course, the similarity between N *tump* and NE *tump* does not mean that Modern English comes from Noldorin. Rather, the similarity is the natural result of these languages descending from a common ancestor; for as Tolkien carefully explains in the *Lhammas*, most languages of Men share a common ancestor with the Elvish tongues. Tom attempts to dismiss similarities between Elvish and Primary-World languages by claiming that "Tolkien composed an abstract paradigm of IE-type languages" which merely "parallels development in real languages". This idea of "an abstract paradigm of IE-type languages" *sounds* scholarly enough, but it is little more than a cleverly turned phrase which is devoid of substance and unsupported by even a single citation of evidence. Tom asserts that the strong resemblance in form and meaning between the Elvish tongues and "real languages" is largely coincidental and implies no genetic connection, or at best only a tenuous one; in other words, "If it looks like a duck, and quacks like a duck, it's a geranium." We strongly disagree, for the following reason:

There is no getting around the fact that **at the time of the writing of the** *Etymologies*, **the** *Lhammas*, **and the** *Quenta Silmarillion c.* **1937–38, Tolkien intended and purposely constructed a genetic connection between his languages and those of the Primary World.** Tolkien states this clearly and explicitly in the *Lhammas* (LR:179):

> The languages of Men…were for the most part derived remotely from the language of the Valar. For the Dark-elves…befriended wandering Men in sundry times and places in the most ancient days, and taught them such things as they knew….Now the language of [the folk of Bëor and Haleth and Hádor] was greatly influenced by the Green-elves, and it was of old named *Taliska*…Yet other Men there were, it seems, that remained east of Eredlindon, who held to their speech, and from this, closely akin to Taliska, are come after many ages of change languages that live still in the North of the earth.

For those with some knowledge of Indo-European, the fact of its genetic connection with the tongues of Middle-earth is made equally clear by the overwhelmingly Indo-European structure evident throughout the *Etymologies*, and further evidence is provided by the few items of Taliskan vocabulary currently available to us, such as **Widris** 'Wisdom' appearing in the *Quenta Silmarillion*— Christopher Tolkien notes that "it can hardly be doubted that this is to be related to the Indo-European stem [**weid-** 'to see']" (LR:279), and JRRT himself explains the sense connection in L:270: "I-E words for *see* (as indeed our *see*) often mean, or the same 'bases' may mean, 'know', 'understand'. (This is particularly true of the √WID base [the zero-grade form of **weid-**]: Latin *video* has its exact equivalent in O.E. *witian* 'watch, guard'; but ⨍oᵢ∂a (=Latin *vīdī*) in O.E. *wāt* 'wot', 'I know'.)" Another example of Taliskan occurs in the brief text *The 'Alphabet of Dairon'* (contemporary with *QS* and the *Lhammas*), where we read that "a related [runic] alphabet was early in use among the eastern branch of the Danians, beyond the Blue Mountains, whence it also spread to Men in those regions, becoming the foundation of the Taliskan *skirditaila* or 'runic series'." (TI:455). Christopher Tolkien says of this passage (*ibid.*):

> The reference to Taliska…is very interesting as adumbrating a relationship between the runes of Beleriand and the ancient Germanic runes; *cf.* V.279 on the 'Indo-European' word *widris* 'wisdom' in the ancient tongue of the people of Bëor. It seems clear that the second element of Taliskan *skirditaila* 'runic series' is to be understood as an ancestral cognate of the word seen in Old English *tæl* (with a sense 'number, reckoning, series'; Old Norse *tal*, etc., and cf. Modern English *tale, tell*); the first element may perhaps be connected with the Germanic stem *sker-*, seen in Old Norse *skera* 'cut, carve', Old English *sceran* (Modern English *shear*, cf. ultimately related *shard, potsherd*).

It is clear that the element *skirdi-* is genetically related to the Eldarin bases **SKAR-** 'tear' and **KIRIS-** 'cut', and to IE **sker-¹,ker-** 'cut', the origin of the Germanic stem that Christopher Tolkien cites (see our discussion of **sker-¹,ker-** in our response to

Jenny Coombs above, p. 16). This is made all the more obvious by the Elvish words for runes, Q *certar* and S *cirth*, sg. *certh*; the *certar* were "devised and mostly used only for scratched or incised inscriptions." (III:395, 401) The element *-taila*, in addition to the relationship with OE *tæl* < IE **del-²** 'to recount, count', itself related to **del-¹** 'long', is clearly related to Eldarin **TAY-** 'extend, make long(er)', whence Q *taile* 'lengthening, extension', as a series or reckoning is an extended set of objects.

Since the majority of the etymological information provided in the *Etymologies* remains valid in *The Lord of the Rings*, *The Silmarillion*, and *Unfinished Tales*, then one must conclude that the genetic connection also remains valid in the later corpus. In other words, any base or form from the *Etymologies* that has a demonstrable phonetic and semantic relationship with Primary-World words, and whose etymology remained unchanged, must perforce retain that relationship in the later corpus. Perhaps Tolkien developed a distaste for this feature of his languages later in his life; but if so he could not undo it with a mere nod and a wink. After so many decades of carefully crafting the genetic connections, he could not disconnect his languages from those of the Primary World without scrapping virtually everything he had ever invented and starting again from scratch.

And why should he? Tom seems almost desperate in his efforts to dissociate Middle-earth from our own world. Tolkien may have abandoned Ælfwine and the equation of Tol Eressëa with England, but he never set aside the conception that Middle-earth is our Earth. Despite Tolkien's coyness in the matter (L:347, note), Númenor (Q. *Atalantië*) IS Atlantis, and Eärendil IS the Anglo-Saxon's Earendel. Does the changing of *Widris* to *Nóm* as a name for Finrod really indicate a move *away* from such a connection? On the contrary, the change shows Tolkien making the connection even closer, for *Nóm* 'Wisdom' is a far more obvious "pun" than *Widris*, being instantly evocative of NE *gnome*, used in the early writings (including earlier editions of *The Hobbit*) to translate *Noldor*, the kindred to which Finrod belonged. In a draft of Appendix F of *The Lord of the Rings*, Tolkien wrote: "I have sometimes (not in this book) used 'Gnomes' for *Noldor* and 'Gnomish' for *Noldorin*. This I did, for whatever Paracelsus may have thought…to some 'Gnome' will still suggest knowledge." (LT1:43-44) *Nóm* must be related to the Elvish bases **ÑGOL-** 'wise, wisdom, be wise' and **ÑGOLOD-** 'one of the wise folk, Gnome', as well as to **NOWO-** 'think, form idea, imagine'; and Tolkien obviously devised these forms to imply a genetic connection with IE **gnō-** 'to know', the root which led to Greek γνώμη 'intelligence, thought' and γνώμων 'one that knows or examines, a judge, interpreter', whence NE *gnome*.

Statements explicitly equating Middle-earth with our world can be found in abundance in Tolkien's later writings. For example:

- "'Middle-earth'…is not a name of a never-never land without relation to the world we live in…imaginatively this 'history' is supposed to take place in a period of the actual Old World of this planet." (30 June 1955; L:220)

- "I am historically minded. Middle-earth is not an imaginary world….The theatre of my tale is this earth, the one in which we now live, but the historical period is imaginary." (1956 or later; L:239)

- "...the Shire...is expressly stated to have been in [Europe] (I p. 12) [: 'The regions in which Hobbits then lived were doubtless the same as those in which they still linger: the North-West of the Old World, east of the Sea.']....I hope the...gap in time between the Fall of Barad-dûr and our Days is sufficient for 'literary credibility', even for readers acquainted with what is known or surmised of 'pre-history'. I have, I suppose, constructed an imaginary time, but kept my feet on my own mother-earth for place. I prefer that to the contemporary mode of seeking remote globes in 'space'. However curious, they are not lovable with the love of blood-kin....Many reviewers seem to assume that Middle-earth is another planet!" (14 October, 1958; L:283).

- "[Middle-earth] is an old word, not invented by me...It meant the habitable lands of our world, set amid the surrounding Ocean. The action of the story takes place in the North-west of 'Middle-earth', equivalent in latitude to the coastlands of Europe and the north shores of the Mediterranean....If Hobbiton and Rivendell are taken (as intended) to be at about the latitude of Oxford, then Minas Tirith, 600 miles south, is at about the latitude of Florence. The Mouths of Anduin and the ancient city of Pelargir are at about the latitude of ancient Troy." (8 February 1967; L:375-6)

Given that the languages of the Men of Middle-earth are akin to the languages of the Elves, and that Middle-earth is "the actual Old World of this planet", wouldn't it be astonishing if we could *not* find relationships between the Eldarin tongues and Indo-European? The question we have before us is not whether such relationships exist — Tolkien makes it plain in the *Lhammas* that they do — but rather what the nature and extent of these relationships are. Tom raises a important point when he asks if the connections are systematic or piecemeal. Cross-etymologizing is still a science in its infancy, for all its twenty-plus years of existence, and much research remains to be done. The principles of comparative linguistics need to be applied to the Eldarin and Indo-European languages to determine if Tolkien devised an orderly system of sound shifts and phonetic correspondences between the two groups, and as research progresses on this topic it will be addressed in future installments of our column.

Bibliography

Buck, Carl Darling. *A Dictionary of Selected Synonyms in the Principal Indo-European Languages*. Chicago: University of Chicago Press, 1949.

Frisk, Hjalmar. *Griechisches etymolgisches Wörterbuch*. Zwei Bände. Heidelberg: Carl Winter Universitätverlag, 1960.

Liddell, Henry George and Robert Scott. *A Greek-English Lexicon*. Revised by Henry Stuart Jones and Roderick McKenzie. Oxford: Clarendon Press, 1940.

The Oxford English Dictionary. 13 vols. Oxford: Clarendon Press, 1933.

Pei, Mario. *The Story of Language*. New York: Meridian, 1984.

Walde, Alois. *Vergleichendes Wörterbuch der indogermanischen Sprachen*. Herausgegeben und bearbeitet von Julius Pokorny. Zwei Bände. Berlin: Walter de Gruyter, 1930.

_____. *Lateinisches etymolgisches Wörterbuch*. Vierte Auflage. Zwei Bände. Heidelberg: Carl Winter Universitätverlag, 1965.

Watkins, Calvert, ed. *The American Heritage Dictionary of Indo-European Roots*. Boston: Houghton Mifflin, 1985.

A *Fragment of* Valaquenta

by Ryszard Derdziński

Reprinted with corrections from Little Gwaihir *#17, March 1991*

Valar ar Maiar — *Et Eldalíva Quentallon*

Eru, yo esse Eldalambesse ná Ilúvatar, estasse ontane óretyallo Ainui, yar tyaler ar línder i Melkalindale nu Mahalmatyá. Sina Lindalello ná Ambar, an Ilúvatar ante anwa haimé Ainulindalen ar kenentes kalavye mi morniesse. San nótimar tello emélier Ambaro vanimie ar lúmequentassesya, an ekéniente kuivie ar loasya mi doresse.

San Ilúvatar ante dorentá anwa Amien ar etermaretyes mí Yawesse, ar antetyes Muinaró an uresye tennoio mí Ambar-óresse, yo esse na Ea. San sine Ainullon, yar eyéstier tana er sinya Ambar, utúlier Ambarenna, ar nesye Lúmeo Estasse. Ainur tatánier mi Eo menessen, yon landié óri Atanion ar Eldaron u-istar, tenna tannar Ardá. San Ainur utúlier kemenna yasse amárier mi fanantassen.

Valar

Ainullon antarë Eldar estar Valain, Ardo Melkain, ar Atani ester te eruin. Otso nar Melka Valaron ar otso nar Valieron. Nótuvalmë essinta sina mí ómassë ve estane ner mí Eldaron quenyassë marala mí Valinoressë, nan Eldar mí Endoressë marala ester te mí lambantessen atessin, ar Atani ester te líessen. Sina Valaron essi: Manwë, Ulmo, Aulë, Oromë, Mandos, Lórien ar Tulkas; san Valieron essi nar: Varda, Yávanna, Nienna, Estë, Vairë, Vána ar Nessa.

Si Melkor u-nótalmë Valannar ar mí kemenessë u-quetalmë essento.

Manwë ar Melkor ner Ilúvatarionin. Melkor né antara ilyë Ainullon estassë yar utúlier Ambarenna; nan Manwë, Ilúvataro melda, ista Ero óri san núva Ambaro minya Kementarollon mí mettassë, aranen ily'Ardo ar ilúvi i cuiar esyassë. Manwë melë súrë ar lumbor, ar ilyë vilmeni, et tariellon tenna yawennar, et anpalaneä ilmen menello tenna súlenna nurula mí salquessë. San essetya ná Súlimo. Melatyë ilie linte filiti melka rómanen, yar utúlar ar avanar ilya quettanten.

Indisen Manwo ná Varda, Elentári, ya ista ilyë Eärmeni. Varda-vanimo u-quenuvan mí Quenyassë ar Atan-lambassen an antaryessë cala Ilúvataro alata. Mí cataryasse ná melkarya. Et Eä-yawellon utúlieryë Manwenna. Avánierye et Melcorello, i ú-melatyer. Manwë ar Varda unútane nar ar marar mí Valinoressë; Oromardente caita Oiolossessë, ar oiolossi, antara aikalë antara orotarmo Ambaressë — Taniquetilessë. Mahalmatyo tariello Manwë tira anpalan ilyessen ter hísier an mornier ar eärefalmar. A Varda anmaika hlara ómar rómello tenna númenna, et tumbor ar ambollon ar Melkoro Morniellon, yar ortanetye Ardo ilyë nóriessen. Ainullon marda sina Ambaressë Varda melar ar laitar Eldalië. Estanter Elbereth ar aiantë esseryo umbulessen Endoro, laitanter líressen lindala menel elcalassë.

Transitions in Translations

A column by Arden R. Smith

The purpose of this column is to examine peculiarities in translations of Tolkien's works: mistranslations, unusual translations, interesting solutions to the problems of translation, and other curiosities in foreign editions. Ideas and contributions are encouraged: send them to "Transitions," c/o Arden R. Smith, P.O. Box 4395, Berkeley, CA 94704-0395, USA.

Toppo and *Poppo*

In "Elvish is Fin(n)ished" (VT 16:10-11), I discussed the Finnicization of Elvish words and names in *Lohikäärmevuori*, Risto Pitkänen's Finnish translation of *The Hobbit* (Helsinki: Tammi, 1973). Pitkänen's treatment of the dwarf-names in *The Hobbit* is quite similar: some names are altered to conform to Finnish phonology, some are translated according to incorrect interpretations.

Of the nineteen dwarf-names appearing in *The Hobbit*, only **Kíli** remains unchanged in *Lohikäärmevuori*. Most of the names have been changed because they contain sounds that do not occur in native Finnish words. The letter *f*, for instance, only occurs in loan words, so **Fíli** and **Fundin** become *Vili* and *Vuopo*. The same applies to *b*, so **Balin**, **Bifur**, and **Bombur** appear as *Poppo*, *Pihnu*, and *Puhnu*.

Some restrictions are only due to the position of the letter in the word. Native Finnish words cannot begin with *g*, so **Glóin** becomes *Klontti*. Initial *d* cannot occur either, so **Dwalin** goes to *Toppo*, **Durin** to *Tuurin*, and **Dáin** to *Tanska*. **Dori**, however, becomes *Jorri* (not **Torri*) for some reason unknown to me. Similarly unexplainable is the change of the initial *n* in **Náin** to *v* (*Vanska*).

So far I have only discussed initial letters. In some cases, the remainder of the name is unchanged or only slightly altered: (**K**/**F**)*íli* > (*K*/*V*)*ili*, (**D**/**N**/**-**)*ori* > (*J*/*N*/-)*orri*, (**D**)*urin* > (*T*)*uurin*. Some are substantially changed, for no reason I can find other than to make it sound more Finnish: (**-**/**Gl**)*óin* > (-/*Kl*)*ontti*, (**Dw**/**B**)*alin* > (*T*/*P*)*oppo* with (**Fundin** > *Vuopo*).

In a couple of cases, the alteration of the name seems to be further motivated. For example, **Dáin** becomes *Tanksa*, which is the Finnish name for Denmark. It seems that Pitkänen assumed a connection between **Dáin** and *Dane*, though the actual meaning of the name (Old Icelandic *Dáinn*) is 'deadlike' (Gould 943) or 'the dead one, the one in trance' (Motz 113). **Bifur** and **Bofur** apparently become *Pihnu* and *Puhnu* because **Bombur** is translated as *Kuhnu*: a Finnish word for 'sluggard' is *kuhnus* (Alanne 252; Wuolle 65). This fits well with Bombur's character, though the actual Icelandic name (*Bumburr*, *Bǫmburr*) means either 'the swollen one' (Gould 943) or 'drummer' (Motz 113).

The names of the dwarves of the royal line are altered more than the other dwarf-names in the book: **Thrór**, **Thráin**, and **Thorin** become *Ukko*, *Ukain*, and *Ukonnuoli* respectively. *Ukain* appears to retain the ending of **Thráin**, but has the initial syllable of *Ukko* and *Ukonnuoli*, both of which have meanings in Finnish. *Ukko* is Finnish for 'old man' (Alanne 818; Wuolle 175), perhaps apt for Thorin's grandfather, although *þrór* means 'boar' (Gould 955; Motz 115). Thorin's name is the crucial one in this group. Although *þorinn* means 'bold' (Gould 955), Pitkänen apparently connected the name with that of the thunder-god Thor: *Ukonnuoli* is Finnish for 'thunderbolt' (Alanne 818). *[It is likely that Pitkänen extended this idea in translating* **Thrór** *as* Ukko *(which can mean both 'old man' and 'thunderer': cf the diminutive form* ukkonen *'thunder'), since Ukko is the ancient Finnish thunder-god, the* ylijumala *'god on high', the god of the sky and of the elements in the* Kalevala, *and thus closely parallel to Thor. —CFH]*

Secondary materials cited

Alanne, Severi. *Finnish-English Dictionary*. Superior, WI: Tyomies Society, 1919.

Gould, Chester Nathan. "Dwarf-Names: A Study in Old Icelandic Religion." *PMLA* 44 (December 1929): 939–67.

Motz, Lotte. "New Thoughts on Dwarf-Names in Old Icelandic." *Frühmittelalterliche Studien* 7 (1973): 100–17.

Wuolle, Aino. *Finnish-English English-Finnish Dictionary*. New York: Hippocrene, 1990.

On the Russian Translation of *The Two Towers*
by Nathalie Kotowski

I recently received the long-expected Russian translation of *The Two Towers* (*Dve Tverdyni*. Translated by Vladimir Muraviev. Moscow: Raduga, 1990), thanks (many thanks) to Natalya Prokhorova. I was a little afraid of opening it, after the distressing experience of the translation of the *Fellowship*. But I had a pleasant surprise. It is not only better but sometimes brilliant. Some chapters I read with delight: a marvellously rich Russian language, with archaic tones, just like Tolkien wanted it (remember Letter No. 171). The chapter "The King of the Golden Hall" is flawless, as is the speech of Faramir and the return of Gandalf. In these pages, the translator, Muraviev, has done a really good job. But there are also debatable points. First, the title: it is called *The Two Strongholds*, "stronghold" being taken here practically in an abstract sense (just like "The Lord is my stronghold…"), and I don't think Tolkien had that in mind. Worse, in my mind, is the speech of Sam: Sam is "russified" to excess, with old expressions from the peasant language and proverbs of the old times, making him look stupid. It only gets on one's nerves. Sam does not have to be "russified" in the first place, and all these *soi-disant* peasant-shrewd expressions are out of character and out of place. I will not try to give examples: back-translation would yield nothing to an English-speaking reader. But it is a pity because Sam loses many of his characteristics, and he is one of my favourite characters.

Muraviev also didn't lose his bad habit of giving extra explanations, adding to the text, though there are far fewer than in the *Fellowship*. So we can learn to our astonishment that there is a form of Elvish which is called "Middle-Elvish" (no word about Old Elvish or Modern Elvish). At least he doesn't try anymore to give equivalents from "Númenórean translated in Elvish so-and-so and in Common Speech so-and-so." And Elvish names are left alone.

But I really have to say something in favour of Muraviev, though I have criticized him at full length. Most bad translations are the result of haste or, worse, lack of concern. The French translation is such a one. Muraviev is definitely in love with the text and gives the best effort he can. One can imagine the conditions in which he had to work. The first shortened version he did was at a time when one had to cope with ideological and political problems. He probably had no one to confer with. He obviously did not understand the importance of Elvish in Tolkien's work, hence the impossible "translations" of Elvish names and his clumsy attempts to "explain". He probably knows more now, so *The Two Towers* is far, far better, with a great richness of the Russian language, which may, however, not be to the liking of Russian readers, unfortunately used to simpler speech.

I am looking forward to *The Return of the King*, which is announced with the bizarre title *The King's Suite [Maybe the translator misinterpreted "return" as "retinue" —ARS]*.

I have to add that the mafioso-looking portrait of Tolkien on the cover is still there, there are no illustrations save a representation of the rings, wrongly with five for the Dwarves *[as in the first volume —ARS]*, and the map is, I think, taken from Barbara Strachey's *Journeys of Frodo* (I cannot check — somebody has taken my copy away and has not given it back). But it does have the date of 6 March on it.

The Plight of the Collector

What do 'normal' people think of those of us who collect translations, especially when we collect them in languages that we do not understand? Warren Weaver, expert on and collector of translation of Lewis Caroll's *Alice* books, writes of his experience while searching for *Alice* translations in India:

"When I asked about the possibility of trying to locate secondhand copies of the earlier editions, the dealers quite clearly considered it inexplicable that anyone would want *another* edition of a book he already had and obviously couldn't read. When, in recognition that a twenty- or thirty-cent transaction did not merit a great deal of effort, I offered to pay a few dollars each for any of the missing editions, the dealers promptly concluded — or so it seemed to me — that they were dealing with an insane person, and did their best to get me quietly out of the shop."

> — Warren Weaver, in *Alice in Many Tongues*, Madison: University of Wisconsin Press, 1964, p. 65.

Trivia Question

Q: By the time Mr. Bliss had paid for everything, his adventures cost him a total of three pounds, sixteen shillings, seven and a half pence. How much did his German counterpart, Herr Glück, have to pay?

A: Seventy-six marks, ninety-five pfennigs. (*Herr Glück*. Translated by Anja Hegemann. Stuttgart: Hobbit Presse/Klett-Cotta, 1983, p. 92.)

Next Issue

"How many *Meilen* are in a *Lár*?" and more!

Publications of Interest

Due to space limitations, the editor cannot thoroughly review all publications received; the following reviews emphasize those publications and items which the editor feels would be of special interest to members of the Elvish Linguistic Fellowship. BIA = *Back Issues Available.*

Cirth de Gandalf: Cercle d'etudes de Tolkien en Belgique. Published bimonthly.
   Editor: Nathalie Kotowski. *Subscriptions to:* the editor at 25, rue Victor Gambier,
   1180 Bruxelles, Belgium. *Annual subscription:* Belgium 400 FB, 450 FB
   elsewhere.
   No. 15, July 1991: Continues the presentation of *Le Quenya: une grammaire,*
   Nathalie's French translation of Nancy Martsch's "Quenya Language Lessons"
   from *Beyond Bree. Leçon 15: Adverbes, Adjectifs comparatifs, Nombres et
   Pronoms.*

Little Gwaihir: Magazine of the Tolkien Section of the Śląski Klub Fantasyki
   (English Edition). Published monthly.
   Editor: Paulina Braiter. *Subscriptions to:* the editor at ul. Kasztelanska 66/3,
   58-314 Walbrzych, Poland. Write for subscription info.
   No. 22, August/September 1991: More Quenya prose from Ryszard Derdziński,
   this time paraphrasing the Downfall of Númenor and the arrival of Elendil on
   the shores of Middle-earth.

Mallorn: The Journal of the Tolkien Society. Published annually.
   Editor: David Doughan. *Subscriptions to: Mallorn* and the bimonthly bulletin
   Amon Hen are received in conjunction with membership in the Tolkien
   Society;write Chris Oakey, Flat 5, 357 High Street, Cheltenham, Glos., GL50
   3HT, UK. *Annual subscription:* UK £15, Surface Mail £16, European Airmail
   £17, USA/Canada Airmail £19.50, Australia Airmail £20. *BIA.*
   No. 28, September 1991: Good "where to begin" advice in "How to Learn Elvish"
   by Nancy Martsch.

Quettar: The Bulletin of the Linguistic Fellowship of the Tolkien Society. Published
   occasionally.
   Editor: Julian Bradfield. *Subscriptions to:* Christina Scull, 1A Colestown St.,
   London SW11 3EH, UK. *Four-issue subscription:* UK £3, Europe and Surface
   Mail £4, Airmail £7.50. *BIA.*
   No. 41, August 1991: Article "On Quenya Case Endings" by Andrew Carrick;
   "The Steinborg Tengwar" by Arden Smith demonstrates that the *tengwar*
   caption to Picture No. 27 in fact reads "Steinborg", not "Stanburg"; review of
   Parma Eldalamberon #8; a "Quenya Psalter" (parts of Psalm 7 in Quenya) by
   Jenny Coombs; letter from Chris Gilson on vowel lengthening in Quenya;
   review of *VT* #s 9–15; "*The War of the Ring:* A Linguistic Review" by Carl
   Hostetter, reprinted from *VT #14* .

Vinyar Tengwar

The bimonthly 'news-letters' of the Elvish Linguistic Fellowship, a Special Interest Group of the Mythopoeic Society.

Editor: Carl F. Hostetter, 2509 Ambling Circle, Crofton, MD 21114, USA.

Proofreaders: Arden R. Smith and Patrick Wynne.

Masthead: by Tom Loback.

Tengwar numerals: from Lawrence M. Schoen's *Moroma* PostScript *Tengwar* font for the Mac, available on disk for $6.00 from PsychoGlyph, P.O. Box 74, Lake Bluff, IL 60044.

Subscriptions: Subscriptions are for 1 year (6 issues) and must be paid in US dollars.

$12.00 USA
$15.00 Canada (sent airmail) and Overseas surface mail
$18.00 Overseas airmail

Back issues available: Individual copies of back issues are available at the current per-issue subscription price: $2.00 USA, $2.50 Canada and Overseas surface mail, $3.00 Overseas airmail. Deduct 25% if ordering a complete set of back issues. *All costs are postpaid.*

Payments: All payments must be in US dollars. It is recommended that overseas members make payments via international postal money order.

Make all checks payable to Carl F. Hostetter.

Submissions: Written material should in some manner deal with Tolkien's invented languages. All submissions must be typed, or must be exquisitely legible: the editor will not decipher lower-glyphics. The editor reserves the right to edit any material (except artwork) for purposes of brevity and relevance. Ilúvatar smiles upon submissions on 400K or 800K (3.5") Macintosh or 720K (3.5") MS-DOS formatted disks in PageMaker, Microsoft Word, Microsoft Works, WordPerfect, MacWrite, DCA, or RTF formats, or as unformatted ASCII text files. Artwork should be Tolkienian in nature.

The deadline for **VT #20** *is November 1, 1991.*

Bibliographical Abbreviations

H	*The Hobbit*	LT2	*The Book of Lost Tales, Part Two*
I	*The Fellowship of the Ring*	LB	*The Lays of Beleriand*
II	*The Two Towers*	SM	*The Shaping of Middle-earth*
III	*The Return of the King*	LR	*The Lost Road*
R	*The Road Goes Ever On*	RS	*The Return of the Shadow*
S	*The Silmarillion*	TI	*The Treason of Isengard*
UT	*Unfinished Tales*	WR	*The War of the Ring*
L	*The Letters of J.R.R. Tolkien*	QL	*The Qenya Lexicon, App.* LT1 & 2
MC	*The Monsters and the Critics*	GL	*The Gnomish Lexicon, App.* LT1 & 2
LT1	*The Book of Lost Tales, Part One*	Et	*The Etymologies, in* LR

Vinyar Tengwar is produced by the editor on an Apple Macintosh II personal computer, using a LaCie Silverscan scanner, Microsoft Word 4.0 and Aldus PageMaker 4.0. VT is printed on an NEC Silentwriter2 Model 90 laser printer.

ISSN 1054-7606

Vinyar Tengwar

Attacainen

#20

November 1991

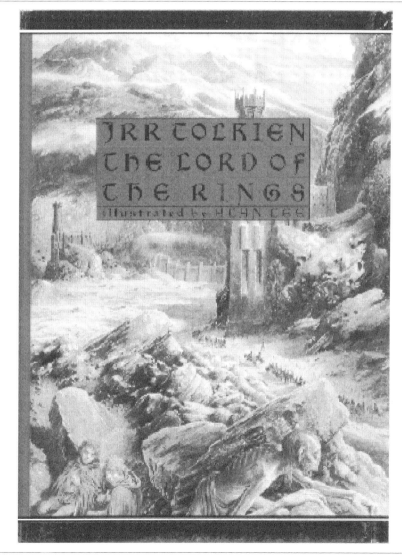

In This Issue

A safe and joyous Holiday Season
and New Year to all.

— Donations *In Memoriam* Taum Santoski —

Donations in Taum's memory may be made to:

The TolkienCollection
c/o Charles, Elston, Archivist
Special Collections and Archives
Marquette University
1415 W. Wisconsin Ave.
Milwaukee, WI 53233

"In the present work, it will be maintained that the only language universals that are of empirical interest are those to which potential counterexamples can be constructed. Putative universals which simply test the ability of linguists to come up with abstract analyses that are consistent with any conceivable set of data may tell us something about linguists, but they do not tell us anything about language."

— Bernard Comrie, in *Language Universals and Linguistic Typology.* 2nd ed. University of Chicago Press, 1989, p.15.

E.L.F. News

New Members

The E.L.F. extends a hearty *mae govannen* to:

- Jeff Brenny   10475 Claudis Ave., Buena Park, CA 90620.
- Kevin Davis   Rt. 2 Box 265, Doerun, GA 31744.
- Gloria Huffman   1027 N. Olive St., Santa Ana, CA 92703.
- Lisa Star   8114 MacArthur Blvd., Bethesda, MD 20818.
- Wendell Wagner   9146 Edmondston Rd., Apt. 201, Greenbelt, MD 20770.

Second Annual Colloquium on the Languages of Middle-earth

Pursuant to its goal of producing *I•Parma*, 'The Book', the ultimate reference work on the invented languages of J. R. R. Tolkien's Middle-earth, the Elvish Linguistic Fellowship will sponsor the Second Annual Colloquium on the Languages of Middle-earth, on February 14–17, 1992. This will be an opportunity for everyone who is interested in this ambitious project to help in making it a reality.

Each program participant will present one or more monographs on Endorean linguistics. These monographs will be collected together in a looseleaf notebook, distributed to all Colloquium participants, and reviewed and revised until they provide a definitive source of reference material, from which *I•Parma* will be compiled. All members will receive a copy of the proceedings and all updates to it until *I•Parma* is published. So even if you attend only one year, you will be able to stay abreast of the project (and participate by mail if you like) in later years.

An attending membership is $175. This price does not include room and board, but again this year the hosts, Bill Welden and Jo Alida Wilcox, have agreed to provide room (well, floor space) and board free of charge to all attendees. Membership fees will go toward the costs of holding our meetings and publishing *I•Parma*.

If you are interested in being one of the project authors, and are willing to write several monographs and attend the annual meetings over the next few years (as well as attending most Mythcons, where we will hold a second important meeting each year), we would be excited about having you join us. To register, or for more information, contact Bill Welden, 961 Lundy Lane, Los Altos, CA 94024–5934; phone #: (415) 948–2976.

The Lord of the Rings — *illustrated by Alan Lee*

Reviewed by Carl F. Hostetter

Boston: Houghton Mifflin Company, 1991. 1200 pp. $60.00. ISBN 0-395-59511-8.

This is a sumptuous one-volume hardcover edition of *The Lord of the Rings,* lavishly illustrated with fifty watercolor paintings by Alan Lee, issued in honor of the Tolkien Centenary. The dust jacket is extremely elaborate, and a real eye-catcher. The front depicts Frodo, Sam, and Gollum before the Morannon, with the title superimposed in gold lettering on a blue background. The spine is blue with the title in gold lettering, with the "JRRT" sigil and an oval cameo from the Battle of the Hornburg. The back depicts the flooding of Orthanc, superimposed with the Tolkien Centenary Seal, with the Ring Inscription in gold *tengwar*. The *cirth* from the title page runs the entire width in a black-on-gold banner at the top and bottom.

The text is that of the one-volume edition that has been available from HarperCollins (*née* Unwin Hyman) in the United Kingdom for some time, and while it features an attractive type font, it has unfortunately not been reset for this edition, but rather reproduced and enlarged. This results in noticeably poor type quality in parts of the book. The maps, too, suffered greatly in reproduction, and in fact are illegible in parts. Also, the pagination does *not* conform with that of the previous Houghton Mifflin hardcover and trade paperback editions, the accepted standard in citation by scholars. And despite its claim to be "an authoritative edition" that "incorporates all corrections and revisions intended by its author", it in fact is missing some corrections and additions that were made to the previous and more truly authoritative HMCo editions: *e.g.* Merry's wife Estella Bolger is missing from the Brandybuck genealogy.

Of course, the star of this new edition is Alan Lee. His watercolors have a "soft" character, sometimes even diaphanous, as in my favorite painting (presented on last issue's cover), depicting Frodo and Gildor near Woodhall. His palette is dominated by pale earth-tones and metallic blues and greys, which is quite appropriate to many scenes, but does create a somewhat "mono-tone-ous" look. Lee's characters are generally well-rendered (considerably more skillfully than those of Ted Nasmith), but he could have done with a little more research *(e.g.* his Elves do *not* have pointed ears, and his Elrond is bearded!). The scenes depicted are for the most part well-chosen and well-placed in the text, and certainly enhance the narrative. A particularly nice contrastive pair (facing pp. 848 and 880) effectively conveys the changing tide of war: the first is a very dark and grim illustration of the defeat at Osgiliath, dominated by Orcs nearly overwhelming a visibly shaken warrior of Minas Tirith (probably Faramir); the second brightly depicts the triumphant Rohirrim driving against the hosts of Mordor and their Mûmakil as the stormclouds break.

On balance, I heartily recommend the illustrated *Lord of the Rings* as a greatly welcome (and frankly long overdue) addition to the Tolkien library, and a fitting tribute to Tolkien on the occasion of the Centenary. It will turn up under a great many Christmas trees this year, and deservedly so; I can think of no better gift for a Tolkien fan, and it is certainly an attractive way to introduce new readers to Tolkien's *magnum opus.*

Source List of the Elvish Languages found in The Letters of J.R.R. Tolkien

by Taum Santoski

Reprinted with permission from Lendarin & Danian *2 (Winter, 1981–2)*

[Pat Wynne sent this index to me shortly after Taum's death, in order to bring it to the wider audience it deserves. It is reprinted here with a few minor and silent emendations. This index will be a greatly-valued tool for those who, like me, are perpetually disgusted at the poor index that Letters *is saddled with, as well as a sobering reminder of the great loss that Taum's untimely death represents. —CFH]*

This is a list of the Elvish vocabulary contained in *The Letters of J.R.R. Tolkien* (ed. Humphrey Carpenter, Boston: Houghton Mifflin, 1981). In these letters Tolkien frequently discussed his invented languages, some in great detail, to publishers, friends, and fans. Examples of five languages (including one dialect) are in these letters.

The translations of Elvish words in this list are mostly those made by Tolkien. In a few instances I have glossed some words, by deduction, without the benefit of authority. One example is the Quenya word **vanimar**. Such glosses have not been noted, but a quick check of references will indicate those so treated.

Tolkien's languages were in a constant state of revision. The meanings of words, their etymologies and even the form were always subject to scrutiny and change. Some of these changes may be seen in a few overly long translations and entries.

The list is not strictly alphabetical. There is no 'C' listing, because that sound was merely a Latinization of the sound /k/; all words beginning with 'c' or 'k' will be found under 'K'. I have included a separate entry for /ch/ (following 'H') and for /th/ (following 'T'). Attached to these lists is a compilation of brief notes from the letters dealing with grammar and etymology. I have not composed an essay, preferring to let them stand alone. An essay would have required introducing explanations, examples, and rules not found in the text.

There are seven sections in this list: Quenya, Sindarin, Telerin, Common (Primitive) Elvish, Woodland (Silvan) Dialect, Elvish Roots and Notes on Grammar. The Quenya and Sindarin lists are the largest of the sections, the Woodland and Telerin sections the smallest. The numbers in each entry refer to a page in *Letters* where can be found the first occurrence of a word, a translation, or an important note.

I would like to make a few linguistic observations. There may be a relationship between the words **Eä** 'It Is' and **iâ** 'void, abyss'. In the *Ainulindalë* frequent mention is made of the Void where Melkor searched for the Secret Flame. Could **Eä** be the opposite of **iâ**? In the Roots and Common Elvish sections we find the C.E. *yagā* 'void, abyss' and √**YAG**. I think perhaps that an early meaning might have been: 'that which is not'. Perhaps the C.E. form of **Eä** was *aya*: 'that which is'. Since Arda was at first mostly water there may be a relationship with the **gaya** 'awe, dread' (S:359) which was the ancestor of the Quenya word **eär** 'sea'.

Quenya

A

Ainur 146.
aiya 'hail!': 385.
alda 'tree': 426.
an- superlative or intensive prefix: 279.
Anar 'Sun': 425.
Anarion 156.
ancalima 'exceedingly bright, brightest': 278, 385.
andave 'long': (308)/448.
Andúril 'Flame of the West (as a region)': 273, 425.
Angamaitë 'Iron-handed': 425.
Aramund 'Kingly bull': 423.
arandil 'king's friend, royalist': 386.
arandur 'king's servant, minister': 386.
Arda 'realm': 283.
arnanóre/arnanor 'royal-land, Arnor': 428.
Atalantie 'Downfall': 347.
atta '2': 427.

E

Eä 'It Is': 284.
Earendel 8.
Eärendil 'Great Mariner, Sea-lover': 149, 150, 282, 385; as **Eârendil**: 153.
Earendur '(professional) mariner': 386.
Elda, pl. **Eldar** 'Elf, Elves': 33, 176, 281.
Eldalië 85, 129.
Eldamar 'Elvenhome': 204.
elen 'a star': (265)/447.
Elendil (**Eled + ndil**) 'Elf-friend': 156, 206, 386.
elenion 'of stars': 385.
Endórë/Endor 'Middle-earth': 224.
Eressëa 150–1, 442.
Eru 'the One': 194, 204.

Eruhîn, pl. **Eruhíni** 'Children of the One God': 189, 194, 345.

H

hēr (**hĕru**) 'master': 282.

I

Ilúvatar 'God, the Father of All': 155, 204.
Isil 'Moon': 425.
Isildur 156.
Istari 'wizards, those who know': 180, 202, 207.

C/K

kălĭma 'shining brilliant': 279.
Calion, Tar- 155.
carnemírie 'with adornment of red jewels': 224.
certar 'runes': 223.
ciriat '2 ships': 427.
Cormacolindor '(the) Ringbearers': (308)/448.
Kortirion 8.

L

laica 'green': 282.
laire 'Summer': 282.
laita 'bless, praise': (308)/448.
laituvalmet 'we will praise them': (308)/448.
lasse, pl. **lassi** 'leaf': 282, 382.
lasse-lanta 'leaf-fall': 382.
lassemista 'leaf-grey': 224.
laure 'gold, not of metal but the colour, golden light': 308.
lin, lind- 'a musical sound': 308.
lóme 'night': 308.
lor 'dream': 308.
lúmenn' 'on the hour': (265)/447.

M

malina 'yellow': 308.
Manwe 'Blessed Being': 259, 283.
Mardil 'devoted to the House, sc. of the Kings': 386.
Melko early form of Melkor: 446.
Melkor 147, 259.

Meneldil 'astronomer': 386.
Meneltarma 'Pillar of Heaven':
194, 204.
more 'dark(ness)': 382.
morna adj. 'dark': 382–3.
mundo 'bull': 422.

N

Namárië (in *tengwar*) 224.
Narsil 425.
Narya 186.
Nenya 186.
Noldor 'Masters of Lore'; "N = ng
as in *ding*": 176.
nórë 'land (as an inhabited country,
area)': 303, 361.
nostari 'parents': (308)/448.
numē-n 'going down, sunset, west,
occident, the direction or
region of the sunset': 303, 361.
Númenórë/Númenor 'West-land,
Westernesse, Land in the
West': 130, 151, 224, 303,
361.

O

Oiolosse 'Mount Uilos': 278.
Olórin 259.
omentielmo This version appeared
in Frodo's original (lost)
manuscript. See *omentielvo*:
265, 447.
omentielvo 'of our meeting': 447.
ondo 'stone': 410.
orne 'tree': 308.
Orofarne 'mountain dwelling':
224.
Oromë 281, 335.
ortani 'raised': 426.

P

palantir, pl. **palantíri** 110, 199,
217.
palantíră 'far gaze' (with
continuative of **TIR**): 427.
Pengolod 130.

Pereldar 'Half-elven': 386.

Q

Quendi 'Elves': 176.
Quenya 'Elvish': 176.

R

Rasmund 'horned bull': 423.
rimbe 'host, horde, people': 178, 382.
rokko 'horse, swift horse for riding': 178,
282, 382.
Rómendacil 425.

S

Sauron 78, 104, 151, 380.
síla 265.
Silmarilli 'radiance of pure light': 26,
148.
Sindar 'Grey-elves': 176.
Sindarin 'Grey-elven': 176.
sorno/þorno 'eagle': 427.

T

Tar- 155.
tárienna 'to the height': (308)/448.
Tarmund 'noble bull': 423.
taure 'forest': 308.
te 'them': (308)/448.
Teleri 426.
telpe 'silver'. This became the usual form
in Valinor instead of *tyelpe* because
of the Teleri: 426.
tengwa, pl. **tengwar** 'letter(s)': 223.
tol 'isle': 442.
tumba 'deep valley': 308.
Turambar 150.
Turcomund 'chief of bulls': 423.
tyelpe 'silver': 426. See *telpe*.

U

Undómiel 161.
Ungoliante 180.

V

Valandil 386.
Valanya adj.: 427.
Valar 'Powers, Authorities, gods, Rulers':
146, 149, 193, 198, 235.

Valimar 186.
Valinor 148, 150, 151.
vanimálion 'of beautiful children':
(308)/448.
vanimar 'beautiful ones': (308)/448.
Varda 'Lofty': 206, 282.
Vilya 186.

Y

Yavanna 285, 335.

Sindarin

A

a 'and': (308)/448.
a 'O': (308)/448.
Adan, (pl.) **Edain** 'fathers of men':
282.
aglar'ni 'glory to the': (308)/448.
Aglarond 282.
alfirin 'immortal': 248, 402.
Amon Uilos 278.
anann 'long': (308)/448.
-and, **(an)** 'land': 383.
Anduin 157.
Angerthas 222.
annûn 'west': (308)/448.
Aragorn 104, 426.
aran 'king': 426.
ardor Theoretical real Sindarin name
of Arnor: 428.
argonath 'the group of (two) noble
stones': 427.
arn(a) 'noble': 427.
Arnor 'royal land', due to a blending
of Quenya *arnanórë* with
Sindarin *arn(a)dor > ardor*: 157,
428.
Arthedain 426.
Arvedui 199.
Arwen 160.
-ath a collective or group suffix: 427.

B

Balrog 180.

*Belain a theoretical form of Quenya
Valar, "but no such form existed":
427.
Beleriand 334.
Beren 130, 149.
Berhael 'Samwise': (308)/448.
Berúthiel 217.
born 'hot, red': 426–7.
borñgil 'Borgil': 427.
Boromir 79.

D

Daur 'Frodo': (308)/448.
Denethor 197.
Dior 193.
Dol Guldur 290.
Dor 'Land': 417.
Dorthonion 334.
-dur see Quenya *-(n)dur*.

E

eglerio 'glorify (them)': (308)/448.
êl, (pl.) **elin** 'star': 281.
el, **ell-** 'star or elf': 281.
elanor 106, 248.
Elbereth 'Star-lady': 206, 282.
eledh, (pl.) **elidh** 'elf', passed out of use
among the Sindar: 281.
Eledhwen 'Elven-fair': 281.
Elladan 'elf-Numenorean': 193, 282.
Elrohir 'elf-knight': 193, 282.
Elrond 'the vault of stars': 104, 122,
149, 152, 282, 423.
Elros 'star spray': 154, 282.
Elwing 'Elf-foam': 150, 282.
en '(of) the': (308)/448.
en, **ened** 'middle, centre': 224.
-end, **(en)** ending for lands: 383.
enedwaith 'middle people or region':
224.
Ennor 'Middle-earth': 384.
ennorath 'Middle-earth, collective
plural of Ennor': 224, 384.
ennyn Durin 426.
ered (pl. of *orod*): 263.

Eregion 152.
Eryn Lasgalen 382.

F

fan 'white, the whiteness of clouds (in the sun): 278.
Fangorn (Forest) 216.
Fanuilos 278.
Faramir 79, 80, 104.
Fëanor 148, 150.
Forochel 'Northern Ice': 199.
Forodwaith 'north-region': 224.

G

galad 425.
galadh 'tree': 426.
Galadriel 'Glittering garland, Maiden crowned with gleaming hair': 104, 423, 428.
Gebir 76.
Gilgalad 'star-light, Star (of) brilliance': Also *Gil-galad*: 152, 279, 426.
Glorfindel 'golden-hair': 423.
golas, -olas 'collection of leaves, foliage'. Also *go-lass*: 282, 382.
Gondolin 21, 130, 150.
Gondor "'Stone-land' sc. 'Stone (-using people's) land'": 79, 104, 157, 409.
govannen 'met': 308.
Gyrth 'Dead': 417.

H

Haradrim 'the Southrons': 178, 241.
hir, hîr 'master, lord': 282, 382.
Húrin 130, 150.

CH

chuinar 'live', in *i chuinar* 'that live': 417.

I

i 'the': (308)/448.
i 'that': 417.
iâ 'void, abyss': 383.
Idril 193.

Imladris 'Rivendell': 152.
Ithilien 76, 79, 97.
Ithryn Luin 'the Blue Wizards': 448.

C/K

calen 'green': 282.
Calenarðon 'the (great) green region': 383.
celeb 'silver': 426.
Celebdil 'Silvertine': 392.
Celeborn 425.
Celebrían 'silver-queen': 193, 423.
Celebrimbor 77, 110.
Cirith 247.
Kirith Ungol 76, 79, 82, 92, 104, 106.
Conin 'princes': (308)/448.
cuio 'live long!': (308)/448.

L

laeg 'green', seldom used, usually replaced by *calen*. "'viridis' fresh and green': 282, 382.
laegolas 'green-leaves', proper Sindarin form of the name *Legolas* (*q.v.*): 282, 382.
las(s) 'leaf': 282, 382.
Lothlórien 216.
Luin 'Blue': 263, 448.
Lúthien 130, 149, 150.

M

mae 'well': 308.
mallorn 248.
mallos 248.
mellon 'friend': 424.
Minas Ithil 76.
Minas Morghul 76, 79, 80.
Minas Tirith 'Tower of Vigilance': 104, 158.
Mindolluin 206.
môr 'dark(ness)': 308, 382.
Morannon 'Black Gate': 97, 178.
Mordor 106.
Morghul 76, 79, 80.
Morgoth 78, 85.

Telerin

Woodland (Silvan) Dialect

Common (Primitive) Elvish

*AYAR 'Sea'. "Primarily applied to the Great Sea of the West, lying between Middle-earth, and *Aman* the Blessed Realm of the Valar." Q. *eär*, S. *aear*. Called a C.E. stem: 386.

*Balaniā adj. 'Valanya'. Older form of Q. *Valanya* (*q.v.*): 427.

eledā/elenā 'an Elf'. "The Elves were called *eledā/elenā* because they were found by the Vala *Oromë* in a valley under the star-light; and they remained always lovers of the stars. But this name became specially attached to those that eventually marched West guided by Oromë (and mostly passed Oversea)." Q. *Elda*, S. *eledh*, pl. *elidh*: 281.

*ĕlĕn, pl. **elenī** 'star'. S. *êl, elin* "in primitive Elvish": 281.

*galadā 'tree' [< √GAL] [> Q. *alda*, S. *galadh*] One of "2 ancient words in Elvish for tree": 426.

*gond(o), ***gon(o)** 'stone'. Q. *ondo*: 410.

*gwa-lassa/*gwa-lassiē 'collection of leaves, foliage'. Q. *olassiē*, S. *golas, -olas*: 282.

khēr, kherū 'master'. Said to be "Prim. Elvish". Q. *hēr, hĕru*; S. *hir*: 282.

*kyelepē 'silver'. "The words for silver point to an orig.: **kyelepē*". Q.*tyelpe*, S. *celeb*, T. *telepi*: 426.

*laikā 'green' [< LAY]. Q. *laica*, S. *laeg*, W. *leg*: 282.

*lassē 'leaf'. Q. *lasse*, S. *las(s)*: 282.

*mori 'dark(ness)'. Q. *more*, S. *môr*: 382.

*mornā adj. 'dark'. Q. *morna*, S. *morn*: 382.

oio 'ever'. Marked "Primitive Elvish": 278.

*orne 'tree' [< √OR/RO] [> Q. *orne*, S. *orn*] One of two ancient words in Elvish for 'tree': 426.

*rokkō 'swift horse for riding'. Q. *rokko*, S. *roch*: 382.

*rondō 'cavern'. *Cf. Nargothrond, Aglarond, Elrond*. A "prim[itive] Elvish word": 282.

*rossē 'dew, spray (of fall or fountain)'. *Cf. Elros*: 282.

*θaurā adj. 'detestable' [< √THAW]: 380.

*θaurond- 'detestable' [< **θaurā*]. Q. *Sauron*: 380.

*yagā 'void, abyss' [< √YAG] [> S. *iâ*]: 383.

Elvish Roots

ata 'two'. A numerative dual, said to be for Quenya: 427.

EL 'star'. "As a first element in a compound *el-* may mean, (or at least symbolize) 'star' and 'elf'.": 281.

ER 'one, single, alone'. An important element in Elvish: 384.

fan- 'white, the whiteness of clouds (in the sun)': 278.

gal A stem more or less synonymous with *kal*, corresponding with *gil*: 278.

√GAL intransitive 'grow': 426.

gil A stem only applied to 'white or silver light': 278.

kal Usual stem for words referring to light: 278.

kher- 'possess': 178.

LAY Basis of **laikā, lairë* 'summer': 282.

los(s) 'white, as snow': 278.

√MOR 'dark, black': 382.

√NAR 'fire'. *Cf. Narsil*: 425.

(N)DIL 'to love, be devoted to'. *Cf. Mardil*: 386.

ndor, nor, (n)dor 'land, country': 308, 383.

-(n)dur 'to serve'. *Cf. Arandur* 'king's servant, minister': 386.

√**ndū, nu,** √**NDU** 'going down; below, down, descend': 303, 361.

√**OR/RO** 'rise up, go high'. A very frequently used stem. *Cf. ortani* 'raised': 426.

√**SIL** as in *Silmarilli*, not *Isil*: 425.

√**talat** 'slipping, sliding, falling down'. *Cf. Atalantië*. Stated to be a Quenya stem: 347.

√**THAW** 'detest'. > *θaurā*: 380.

√**THIL** 'white light'. As in *Ithil, Isil*: 425.

TIR 'watch, gaze at, etc.': 427.

ū Indicates a pair. *Cf. Aldūya*. Preferred after *d/t* in a stem: 427.

√**YAG** 'void, abyss': 383.

Notes on Grammar

101. The difference between Quenya *Isil* and Sindarin *Ithil* is due to a change of þ (*th*) > *s* in the Quenya of the Exiles: 425.

102. Quenya had a regular syncope of the vowel in a sequence of two short vowels of the same quality (as *e* in *tyelpe* < **kyelepē*): 426.

103. In Telerin the syncope of a second vowel in a sequence of two short vowels of the same quality was not regular, but occurred in words of length such as *Telperion*: 426.

104. The variation *g/k* in *gal/kal* is not to be confused with the grammatical change of *k, c* > *g* in Grey-elven, seen in the initials of words in composition or after closely connected particles (like the article). So *Gil-galad* 'starlight'. *Cf. palan-díriel* compared with *a tiro nin*: 278–9.

105. Quenya makes a distinction in its dual inflection, which turns on the number of persons involved; failure to understand this was "a mistake generally made by mortals": 447 n. 205.

106. Originally the Quenya duals were (a) purely numerative (element *ata*) and (b) pairs (element *ū* as seen in *Aldúya*); but they are normally in later Quenya only usual with reference to natural pairs, and the choice of *t* or *ū* was decided by euphony (*e.g. ū* was preferred after *d/t* in a stem): 427.

107. In Sindarin duals of nouns or pronouns early became obsolete, except in written works. A case occurs in ***Orgalaðad*** 'Day of the Two Trees', but since these Sindarin nouns were all derived from Quenya names of the six-day week, brought from Valinor, it may be due to an attempt to imitate Quenya duals such as *ciriat* 'two ships'. In any case *-d* was later lost, and so we have *argonath* 'the group of (two) noble stones' instead of **argonad*: 427.

108. ***ath***. Though it could be a Sindarin form of Quenya *atta* '2', it is in fact not related, nor a sign of a dual. It was a collective or group suffix, and the nouns so formed were originally singulars. But they were later treated as plurals, especially when applied to people(s). For example, *Periannath*, the Hobbit-folk, as distinguished from *periain* hobbits, an indefinite number of 'halflings': 427.

— *continued on page 13.*

Essitalmar

The Roots of Middle-earth Names and Places

A column by Tom Loback

This is a forum for the readers of VT *to submit their ideas and thoughts about names, both of people and places; their meanings and the story that they tell. All are encouraged to submit inquiries, short interpretations and discussions thereof, particularly those names still undefined. Send all correspondence for this column to the editor at 152 West 26th St., #36, N.Y. City, NY 10001, USA.*

This column is dedicated to the memory of Taum Santoski, the great fan. It is to be hoped that he dwells now in that place of imagination he so loved.

Dor Gyrth i Chuinar
'Land of the Dead that Live' — JRRT 1972

i-cuilwarthon	[LT2:368]	
(i-)guilwarthon	[LT2:368]	
cuilwarthien	[SM:133]	(name used by Men)
Gwerth-i-Cuina	[SM:179]	(name used by Elves)
Land of the *Cuilwarthin*	[SM:224]	
Gwerth(< *Gwaith*)*-i-Cuina*	[SM:230, 233]	
Gwerth-i-Cuina	[LR:305]	(name used by Gnomes)
Gwerth-i-Guinar	[LR:313]	(name used by Gnomes)
Gyrth-i-Guinar	[LR:305]	(name used by the Noldor)
Dor Firn i Guinar	[Et:381–2]	
Dor Firn-i-Guinar	[S:188]	
Dor Gyrth i chuinar	[L:417]	

This phrase could serve as a road marker for the long trail of the Grey-elven languages. Its permutations raise many interesting points about the Sindarin group, but only one will be dealt with here. The final *-r* in *cuinar*, when it appears, is maintained thereafter. To hazard a guess, based on the rather vague evidence of *gar* on Thror's Map and *hinar* in the *Nebrachar* poem (MC:217), and even less certainly on *pennar*[1] in some versions of *A Elbereth* (*e.g.* RS:394), this final *-r* might be a plural marker on the 3rd person verb. What reasoning there is goes like this: in Ilkorin in *Etymologies* the 3rd person ends in *-a*, and the 'dead' referred to in the place-names above are plural (Beren and Lúthien). Noldorin, too, shows an example of 3rd person impersonal that ends in *-a*: *thia* 'it appears' (Et:392).

Hanging this thought in midair, examine two known verb tenses from *lin-* 'sing' in the 1st person:

---

[1] Negative evidence, in that the published final version has 3rd singular, *penna* (I:394).

linnon	*'I sing'	[LB:354]	(present)
linnathon	'I will sing'	[I:250, R:72–3]	(future)

From these it can be inferred that *-on* marks the 1st person and that *-ath-* indicates the future tense. It might be that *-ath-* is a lenition of *-as-*. Consider the stubbornly untranslatable:

> *diragas•venwed*
> *diragath•telwen*   [RS:451]

Excerpting this section of the phrase emphasizes the similarity of the two groups. Once again a guess is ventured that *diragas* and *diragath* are the same word and are verbs. Supporting the notion that they might be the same word is the dot that separates each from the following word. This dot, when used elsewhere, is an indication of lenition or mutation; *e.g. i•dal* (LR:298) (perhaps the - seen in places is a variation of this). If so, these four words are most interesting in that, for some reason, in the first pair *-s* does not change, but *v-* must be from original *m-*, *i.e.* *menwed*; whereas in the second pair *-s > -th* while the original *t-* of *telwen* remains unchanged. If this guess is correct, then *diragas*/*diragath* could be the bare future tense:

Annon	**porennin**	**diragas•**	**venwed**
Gate	?	?-will	?
diragath•	*telwen*	*porannin*[2]	*nithrad*[3]
?-will	?	?	?

More simply put, this could be the form of the future tense used when the subject precedes, as in:

Maglor linnas 'Maglor will sing'
Maglor linnath i laer Cu Beleg 'Maglor will sing the song of the Strong Bow'.

When the subject does not precede, the future is marked by the pronominal suffix, 1st person singular *-on*, 3rd person singular *-a*. Further, if *-r* marks the plural the results are:

linnathon	'I will sing'
linnatha	'he will sing'
linnathar	'they will sing'

---

[2] In the Sindarin spoken by Sam in the Third Age, *tiro nin* = 'watch over me'. So *poran-nin* may be related to *an + men = ammen* 'for us' (RS:463, note 14) and *an + im = anim* 'for myself' (III:342).

[3] Again in Sam's invocation, in *sí di-nguruthos*, *di-* is translated as 'beneath' (R:72). If *di-* and *ni-* are cognates, then given *athrad* 'crossing, ford' and *ostrad* 'a street' (Et:383 *s.v.* **RAT-** 'walk'), *nithrad* may indicate an underground passage or tunnel.

Given all this, perhaps the delivery of a long-awaited letter can be anticipated with some highly speculative construction:

Q. ***esta-*** 'to name' (Et:356 *s.v.* **ES-**), N **est*[4] >
*esta 'he names'
*estatha 'he will name'
*estar 'they name'
*estathar 'they will name'

It is not possible at this time to integrate this into the idea of previous columns where the theory of two main branches of Sindarin were examined, except to point out the difference between 3rd person in Ilkorin and Noldorin.

It is notable that when **-r** is added to ***cuina*** its next appearance also ascribes it to Noldorin and drops the term "Gnome", thereby marking another point on the Great Divide where the Ship of Middle-earth casts off yet another of the direct lines mooring it to this world. And that ship sets out on the sea of imagination to seek its own destiny separate from this world. But, still visible with long sight down the straight road that world hovers beyond our reach and on its own. For as Tolkien says, in deep sorrow, near the end:

> "there is no *Dor Gyrth i chuinar*, the Land of the Dead that Live, in this Fallen Kingdom of Arda…"

---

[4]   *Cf.* Q ***ista-*** 'to know', N *ist* 'knowledge' (Et:361 *s.v.* **IS-**)

Elvish Source List from Letters   *— continued from page 10.*

109.   The lenitions or 'mutations' of Sindarin were deliberately devised to resemble those of Welsh in phonetic origin and grammatical use; but are not the *same* in either phonetic origin or grammatical use. Thus ***ost-giliath*** 'fortress of the stars' in which the second noun functions as an uninflected genitive shows no mutation, *Cf.* **ennyn Durin**. In Sindarin this absence of mutation is maintained (a) in compounds and (b) when a noun is actually virtually an adjective, as in ***Gil-galad*** 'Star (of) brilliance': 426.

110.   In Sindarin initial **g** was retained in composition where a contact **n + g** occurred. So ***born*** 'hot, red' *+ gil* to ***borñgil***; ***morn*** 'black' *+ dor* to ***morñdor***; the triconsonantal group then being reduced to **rg**, **rd**: 426–7.

111.   In Sindarin **t > þ** (**th**) is the nasal mutation, and so appears after the plural article in: ***thîw***, ***i Pheriannath***. ***palan-ñriel*** should phonetically > **-thíriel**, past participle 'having gazed afar'; but grammatically before actual forms of verbs, the soft mutation only was normally used in later Sindarin, to avoid confusion with other verb stems, and the soft mutation of $m > \tilde{v} > v$ was also often used for the same reason: 427.

Words and Devices
A column by Carl F. Hostetter and Patrick Wynne

"It is said also that these Men had long ago had dealings with the Dark Elves east of the mountains, and from them had learned much of their speech; and since all the languages of the Quendi were of one origin, the language of Bëor and his folk resembled the Elven-tongue in many words and devices." (S:141)

The purpose of this column is to examine words and other linguistic features in Tolkien's Secondary-World languages that have Primary-World cognates and analogues. Comments and contributions are encouraged: send them to Carl F. Hostetter, 2509 Ambling Circle, Crofton, MD 21114, USA.

The Quick and the Dead

As detailed in this issue's *Essitalmar*, the name **Dor Firn i Guinar** 'Land of the Dead that Live' in its various incarnations has an appropriately long-lived history in Tolkien's writings, from the *Book of Lost Tales* to the *Silmarillion* and perhaps beyond, being variously ascribed to the Gnomes or Noldor[1], to Men, or to the Eldar[2] as the narratives evolved. If it is a "road marker for the long trail of the Grey-elven languages", so too does it mark an important juncture on the oft-intersecting paths of the Eldarin and Indo-European languages. In particular, the words *i Guinar* 'that Live' and **Firn** 'the Dead' demonstrate a genetic relationship between these languages.

The first element in the phrase *i Guinar* 'that Live' is probably the Noldorin cognate of the Quenya relative particle *i* 'who, that', as in *i Eru i* 'the One who' (UT:305) and *nai* (< *nā-i*) 'be it that' (R:60). The second element is apparently the present-tense 3rd-person plural of the Noldorin verb **cuino** 'to be alive', with **cuinar* '[they] live, are alive' becoming **guinar** due to the 'Initial Variation of Consonants' that occurred in Exilic Noldorin. In *The Lost Road* Christopher Tolkien describes this phenomenon, "whereby a consonant at the beginning of the second element of a compounded word (or of the second word in two words standing in a very close syntactic relation, as noun and article) underwent the same change as it would when standing in ordinary medial position." (LR:298) Apparently the relative particle followed by a verb was considered a "close syntactic relation", and since *k > g* in medial position was usual in Noldorin (*e.g.* **akrā* > N *agor* 'narrow', LR:348), *i Cuinar* became *i Guinar*.

The verb **cuino** 'to be alive' is listed together with **Dor Firn i Guinar** in the *Etymologies s.v.* **KUY-** 'come to life, awake', which is the source of such familiar words in the late corpus as Q **Kuiviénen** 'Water of Awakening' (S:48) and the Sindarin imperative **cuio** 'live [long]!' (as in French *vive!*) (III:231). Tolkien

---

[1] Even though we dispatched it last issue, the mistaken belief that the word **Noldor** 'the Wise' is unrelated to the Indo-European languages has been resurrected. **Noldor** comes from the base **ÑGOL-** 'wise, wisdom, be wise', and we hope that by noting once again the IE root **gnō-** 'to know', whence *gnome* and both *knowledge* and *ignorance*, this notion may be sent to its final rest.

[2] "The Eldar afterwards called that country Dor Firn-i-Guinar..." (S:188)

probably intended **KUY-** as the original source of the Indo-European root **g^wei-** 'to live', whence Latin *vīvere* 'to live' (> French *vivre*) as well as Old English *cwic* and Modern English *quick* 'living, alive'. **KUY-** and its derivatives (with their connection to Indo-European) occur throughout the history of the corpus. The *Qenya Lexicon* (*c.* 1917) lists a root **KOYO** 'have life' (LT1:257) with derivatives including *koiva* 'awake' (*cf.* Lat. *vīva* 'living, alive'), and the Gnomish Lexicon has among its derivatives *cwiv-* 'be awake' and *cuith* 'life, living body' (*cf.* Lat. *vīta* 'life'). In a letter dated 24 January 1972 (L:417), among Tolkien's last writings, **cuinar* occurs in yet another variant of 'Land of the Dead that Live', **Dor Gyrth i chuinar.** Here **cuinar > chuinar* is probably an example of the nasal mutation. This occurred in Sindarin following the plural article, *e.g.* **Ernil i Pheriannath** 'Prince of the Halflings' (III:41) < **Ernil in Periannath* (*cf.* LR:361: "N *i-* 'the', plural *in* or *i-*."). Thus *i chuinar* probably resulted from **in cuinar*, with **in* the plural form of the relative particle or definite article *i* (*cf.* Old English, in which the definite article can also function as a relative pronoun).

Firn 'the Dead' is the plural of N *fern* 'dead (of mortals)', from the base **PHIR-.** Other derivatives of this base include Q *fire* 'mortal man' (pl. *firi*) and *firya* 'human', as well as N *feir*, pl. *fîr* 'mortals' and *firen* 'human'. The *Etymologies* does not provide a translation for **PHIR-**, but it must mean the same as the verb stem *fir-* 'die, fade' cited in Tolkien's notes to *Oilima Markirya 3* (MC:224) and also seen in S *firith* 'fading' (III:386), the Elves viewing natural death among Men as the result of a gradual fading of vitality. Tolkien seems to have deliberately designed **PHIR-** and its derivatives to be cognate with Old English *firas* 'men, human beings' (Hall 119). That Tolkien intended this is evident from his use of *firas* in Ælfwine's OE translation of the *Quenta Noldorinwa* (SM:206; the translation is our own):

> Elfe and Fíras (þæt sindon men) onwócon ǽrest on worolde æfter þára Valena cyme. Ealfæder ána geworhte Elfe and Fíras ond ǽgþerum gedǽlde hira ágene gifa; þý hátað hí woroldbearn oþþe Ealfæderes bearn.

> 'Elves and Humans (that are Men) first awoke into the world after the coming of the Valar. The Allfather alone created Elves and Humans and on both bestowed their own gifts; thus they are called the children of the world or the Allfather's children.'

OE *firas* is thought to be derived from *feorh* 'life, soul, spirit'[3], but the etymology of *feorh* and its Common Germanic root **ferhwa* is, as de Vries generously describes it, "unclear".[4] It is tempting to relate *firas* and *feorh* to Irish *fear* 'man', pl. *fir*, but this is phonologically implausible. Ir. *fear* derives from IE **wī-ro-** 'man', which in turn is thought to be a derivative of IE **weiə-** 'vital force', whence Lat. *vīs* 'force'. Thus *fear* is cognate with Latin *vir* 'man'; and the equivalent OE form derived from **wī-ro-** is in fact *wer* 'man', not *feorh*. The resemblance between N *feir*, pl. *fîr* 'mortals' and Ir. *fear*, pl. *fir* 'men' is even more striking, but the two cannot be cognates since they derive from distinct roots, N *feir* < **PHIR-** 'die, fade' and Ir. *fear* ultimately < **weiə-** 'vital force'.

---

[3] Hall 115; see Campell 59 n. 3 for an explanation of the phonological relationship.

[4] 125 *s.v.* **fjǫr.**

Indeed, with **PHIR-** Tolkien once again seems to be providing a "missing link" in the etymology of OE *firas, feorh* < **ferhwa* — a recurrent refrain in our cross-etymological studies. According to de Vries, one theory suggests that **ferhwa* is related to Latin *quercus* 'oak', "since [in Norse mythology] mankind was supposed to have originated from trees", a reference to the first humans *Askr* 'Ash' and *Embla* 'Elm' animated from these two trees.[5] This is especially intriguing because *quercus* comes from the IE root **perk^wu-** 'oak', from which our own tree-name *fir* derives (such variation of *genera* is not uncommon among etymologies of tree-names), and **perk^wu-** bears a strong resemblance to the Eldarin base **PHER-, PHÉREN-** 'beech', which in turn could be an ablaut variant of **PHIR-** 'fade'. The sense-connection between 'fade' and 'beech' may be that the beech is a common deciduous tree whose leaves fade and fall every autumn (S *firith* 'fading' was the name of the fourth season in the Eldarin solar year, coming between *iavas* 'autumn' and *rhîw* 'winter' and also known as *lasse-lanta* 'leaf-fall' in Quenya).

Another proposed source for **ferhwa* noted by de Vries is a postulated IE root **perk-** 'surround, enclose', whence Old Irish *párśu* 'rib', with evidence of an extension to 'soul' as a hidden animating force. The derivation of *firas* 'men, human beings' from *feorh* 'life, soul, spirit' implies that *firas* is literally "those who possess souls". There is some evidence that this was Tolkien's interpretation from a note (SM:211) that *Fíras* "includes both Men and Elves", in apparent disagreement with its more restrictive use in Ælfwine's translation, where it is distinct from *Elfe* 'Elves'. Following this note is a list in Old English titled **Fíra bearn**, which begins with a list of the Three Kindreds of the Elves. It seems that Tolkien was here using *firas* to denote all sentient beings, *i.e.* "those who possess souls", rather than simply mortal Men.[6] The word *bearn* 'children, offspring' reinforces this notion, for Elves and Men together are *Ealfæderes bearn*, the Children of Ilúvatar.

With *i Guinar* and *Firn*, the Quick and the Dead, Tolkien fastened two more direct lines to the Ship of Middle-earth, mooring it and binding its destiny securely to our own world, which it thus imbues with the wonder of his imagination; and keeping it within our ready reach, plainly visible to those who will only look with unobscured gaze. For this "Fallen Kingdom of Arda", this Middle-earth, "is not…a never-never land without relation to the world we live in", but rather it is our own.

Bibliography

Campbell, A. *Old English Grammar*. Oxford: Oxford University Press, 1962.

de Vries, Jan. *Altnordisches etymologisches Wörterbuch*. Second corrected ed. Leiden: E.J. Brill, 1977.

Hall, J.R. Clark. *A Concise Anglo-Saxon Dictionary*. Fourth ed. Toronto: University of Toronto Press, 1984.

Watkins, Calvert, ed. *The American Heritage Dictionary of Indo-European Roots*. Boston: Houghton Mifflin, 1985.

---

[5] *Æsc*, the Old English form of *Askr*, is written above *Ermon*, one of the two Men awakened by Nuin 'Father of Speech', on the manuscript of *The Book of Lost Tales* (LT1:245); the other is *Elmir* (*ibid.* 237), which is transparently equivalent to *Embla*.

[6] In this moral connection, it is also interesting to note the similarity of N *firen* 'human' to OE *firen* 'sin' (Hall 119), also of uncertain etymology (de Vries 121 *s.v.* **firn**). After all, *errāre hūmānum est*.

Transitions in Translations

A column by Arden R. Smith

The purpose of this column is to examine peculiarities in translations of Tolkien's works: mistranslations, unusual translations, interesting solutions to the problems of translation, and other curiosities in foreign editions. Ideas and contributions are encouraged: send them to "Transitions," c/o Arden R. Smith, P.O. Box 4395, Berkeley, CA 94704-0395, USA.

How Many *Meilen* are in a *Lár*?

In these days when the metric system is used in pretty much all of the world, we may tend to forget that there was once a time when units of measurement differed from country to country, even from city to city. When these units, originally based on such imprecise measures as the length of barleycorns or body parts, became standardized, different regions had different values for cognate words. A single word in a single language could even have different values in different political regions, *e.g.* the gallon: 3.78533 liters in the United States, but 4.54596 liters in the British Empire.

Such differences in value may lead to problems in translation. Vague measures like "many leagues" can be translated in terms of rough equivalence without any resulting inaccuracy, but the more precise the measurement, the more precise the translation has to be. Perhaps the greatest precision of all is required when translating a text discussing values of units of measurement. Such a text is found in "Númenórean Linear Measures", the appendix to "The Disaster of the Gladden Fields" (UT:285–7).

Let's examine a key section of this appendix:

> "Measures of distance are converted as nearly as possible into modern terms. 'League' is used because it was the longest measurement of distance: in Númenórean reckoning (which was decimal) five thousand *rangar* (full paces) made a *lár*, which was very nearly three of our miles…. The Númenórean *ranga* was slightly longer than our yard, approximately thirty-eight inches, owing to their greater stature. Therefore five thousand *rangar* would be almost exactly the equivalent of 5280 yards, our 'league': 5277 yards, two feet and four inches, supposing the equivalence to be exact." (UT:285)

In the German version by Hans J. Schütz (*Nachrichten aus Mittelerde*. Stuttgart: Klett-Cotta, 1983, p. 377), this becomes:

> "… >Meile< wird benutzt, weil es das längste Maß für Entfernungen war: in númenórischer Rechnung (die auf dem Dezimalsystem beruhte) ergaben 5000 *rangar* (volle Schritte) ein *lár*, was fast genau drei heutigen Meilen entspricht…. Die númenórische *ranga* war ein wenig länger als

unsere Elle, annähernd 38 Zoll, infolge ihres größeren Körperbaus. Folglich entsprächen 5000 *rangar* beinahe genau 5280 Ellen, unserer >Meile<: 5277 Ellen, zwei Fuß und vier Zoll, angenommen die Entsprechung wäre exakt."

First of all, it should be noted that none of the numbers have been changed. This implies that the English units have the same values (or at least the same ratios to one another) as the German units used to translate them. But are they really equivalent? *Zoll* is used to translate *inch*. This is fitting, with the *inch* having a value of 2.54 cm and the *Zoll* ranging from 2.3541667 cm in Leipzig to 2.6341858 in Austria.[1]

The *Fuß*/*foot* correspondence is also appropriate, with this unit equivalent to twelve *Zoll*/*inches* (though the *Fuß* was equal to ten *Zoll* in some parts of Germany).

The translation of *yard* as *Elle* is a little more problematic. The value of the *yard* (36 inches) is 91.44 cm, whereas the *Elle* ranged from 54.728 cm in Frankfurt-am-Main to 120 cm in the Rhenish Palatinate. The English cognate of *Elle*, namely *ell*, also falls within this range, but with a different value from that of the *yard*: 45 inches in England, *i.e.* 114.3 cm. So would a German reader interpret *Elle* as an English *ell*, an English *yard*, or something else?

Even if the German reader equates the *Elle* with the *yard* (Muret-Sanders does in fact equate *yard* with *englische Elle*), that still leaves us with the problem of the *Meile*. And in this translation it *is* a problem. Note that the German text states that 5000 *rangar* (one *lár*) was nearly three *Meilen*, but a few sentences later states that 5000 *rangar* was almost exactly 5280 *Ellen* (*i.e.* yards), "our *Meile*". *Meile* is thus used to translate both *mile* and *league*! It should be pointed out that the German *Meile* was neither one mile nor three, but *over four and a half miles* (7.4204296 km; a mile is 1.609 km, a league 4.827 km). So how many *Meilen* are in a *lár*? Three? One? Or is the correct answer 0.6502276?

Review: The Russian *Lord of the Rings*
by David Doughan

VLASTELIN KOLETS: *The Lord of the Rings*, translated by Natalya Grigoryeva and Vladimir Grushetskiy, published in Leningrad (= St. Petersburg) by Severo-Zapad, 1991. 1005 p + 1008–1105 p.

Here it is at last, in one volume (with selected Appendices in a separate pamphlet), while Volume 3 of the Muravyov version has yet to appear. So what's it like?

---

[1] Values of British measurements are in accordance with the 1963 Weights and Measures Act; see R. D. Connor's *The Weights and Measures of England* (London: Her Majesty's Stationery Office, 1987). The ranges of German values are taken from the 19th Century values in various German-speaking areas given in Hubert Jansen's "German, Austrian, and Swiss Measures, Weights, Coins" in *Muret-Sanders Encyclopædic English-German and German-English Dictionary* (Berlin-Schöneberg: Langenscheidt, [1906]).

First, the bad news. The translator's preface includes some odd statements, the oddest being that Tolkien was known as "J.R.R." to his friends. More seriously, there is a distinct tendency to leave bits out, or to paraphrase slightly. Though there is some improvement over the nomenclature used by Muravyov (*e.g.* instead of "Hobbitania" for the Shire, they use "Shir", which has the advantage of sounding very Russian — though with implications of wide open spaces), many undesirable features are retained — like Thingol's daughter "Lúchien".

However, with the above reservations, this is a translation which can definitely be recommended. Certainly, it is far more faithful to Tolkien than Muravyov and Kistyakovskiy, and not just in word-for-word literalness. There is more variation of tone, and the style is "plainer" (in the best Tolkienian sense) yet more varied than the somewhat racy one of the earlier publication. In short, it reads more like Tolkien himself than an imaginative Russianising adaptation of his work. Also, the book itself is extremely well produced (apart from slight variations in paper weight and colour). It is attractively and legibly typeset, and lavishly illustrated in black and white throughout by Aleksandr Nikolayev, whose worst drawings are tolerable, and whose best are excellent. Furthermore, the very handsome dust-jacket has two beautiful colour pictures by Denis Gordeyev (of Kheled-zaram and Galadriel in a swan boat) which should increase its deserved popularity.

Except, of course, that its popularity needs no increase. I gather that this edition has already sold out, in a couple of months, and a new edition in three volumes, illustrated throughout by Denis Gordeyev, is in preparation. I look forward very much to seeing it; for although the translators generously state that there is a need of several translations to reflect the different aspects, for me, despite its (relatively minor) imperfections, this is definitely the best Russian translation so far.

More Russian Translation Notes
by David Doughan

I have received a copy of a new(ish) translation of *The Hobbit*, by "V.A.M." [Valeriya Aleksandrovna Matorina, very well known in Russian fan circles], published in Khabarovsk last year by "Amur" Publishing House. This differs considerably in detail from the 1976 Rakhmanova/Komarova translation. I have not had the time to make exhaustive comparisons, but it seems to be about as accurate and (in its own way) as well-written as the previous version — with the exception of the verses — alas, here I find Komarova far superior to V.A.M. And it isn't illustrated. By the way, I gather that V.A.M.'s translation of *Lord of the Rings* is due to be published in the course of the next couple of years… that makes FOUR!

Regular readers of this column may remember my account of an awful translation of *Leaf by Niggle*. I have now belatedly seen issue #6/1990 of a serious fantasy/literary paper from Khabarovsk (only slightly west of Vladivostok) called *Publikator*, which contains a translation of *Leaf by Niggle* which is really excellent. However, the translator is completely unacknowledged! I've written to the magazine in the hope that we can be put in touch with someone whose feeling for Tolkien is so profound, and whose knowledge of English is so good.

Again belatedly, I have a booklet of *Songs from the Red Book* (Песни Алой Книги), published for the 1990 Krasnoyarsk Hobbit Games by "Jabberwockey [*sic*] SF", which contains translations of poems from *The Lord of the Rings* (generally much better than those in the Muravyov/Kistyakovskiy translation), as well as original poetry on Tolkienian themes.

I've recently been sent a brand new, *good* translation of *Farmer Giles* (by G. Abramyan), published by a "little" Leningrad publisher unimaginatively called "*Peterburg*". It has copious notes (by M. Kapustina) for Russian readers on such background matters as Geoffrey of Monmouth, Saints Hilarius and Felix, *etc.*, which are (with a very few minor exceptions) not only learned but accurate. The wildly inappropriate (albeit decent) cover illustration is by Aubrey Beardsley!

Even more interestingly, the above firm's 1991 list includes a translation of Tolkien's "*Silmarion*" [*sic*]! If I discover more, I'll let you know.

The trouble about good translations is that I can't find much more to say about them than that they are good. Not so a new 500 page "re-telling" of the *Lord of the Rings* which has recently been published in Russia. Natalya Prohorova tells me that we can learn many hitherto unsuspected facts about Middle-earth from it. For instance, did you know that the Winged Crown of the Kings of Gondor had long been in Mordor, in the hands of Sauron? He, it seems, feared to put it on because it possessed the property of incinerating any wearer without royal blood. One wonders how Tolkien was so unobservant as to miss that important detail.

Finally, back to them thar Grand Dukes of Gondor and Arnor. My reference to them was obviously expressed badly, and Nathalie was right to pick it up. In fact, I was not thinking of 19th Century buffalo-hunters, or indeed of Parisian taxi-drivers of the 1930s, but precisely of the mediaeval rulers of Kiev Rus' and Muscovy, and especially Vladimir (Volodimir), who is the Charlemagne/Arthur figure of many былины (folk epics). The title Великий Князь is without doubt steeped in the authentic traditions of ancient Rus — and there's the rub, because *The Lord of the Rings* is steeped in a very different set of traditions. The point I was attempting to make, in an excessively elliptical sort of way, is that this sort of "Russification" is a perilous path for a translator to tread. It is a bit like calling the leading characters in *War and Peace* Lord Andrew Stockley, Lord Nicholas and the Hon. Nancy Grew, and Peter Earless....

Trivia Question

Q: What is the term used to translate 'goblin' in the Dutch *Hobbit*?

A: *Aardman*, meaning 'earth-man' (*De Hobbit*. Translated by Max Schuchart. Utrecht: Het Spectrum, 1976).

Next Issue

Special for the Centenary — Tolkien on Tolkien Translation

Publications of Interest

Due to space limitations, the editor cannot thoroughly review all publications received; the following reviews emphasize those publications and items which the editor feels would be of special interest to members of the Elvish Linguistic Fellowship. BIA = Back Issues Available.

Cirth de Gandalf: Cercle d'etudes de Tolkien en Belgique. Published bimonthly.
    Editor: Nathalie Kotowski. *Subscriptions to*: the editor at 25, rue Victor Gambier,
    1180 Bruxelles, Belgium. *Annual subscription*: Belgium 400 FB, 450 FB
    elsewhere.
    No. 16, September 1991: Continues the presentation of *Le Quenya: une grammaire*,
    Nathalie's French translation of Nancy Martsch's "Quenya Language Lessons"
    from *Beyond Bree*. *Leçon 16: Le Passé*. "Combat entre Thingol et Boldog" by
    Tom Loback, with *cirth*. Obituary for Taum Santoski.

The Father Christmas Letters

ed. by Baillie Tolkien

reviewed by Carl F. Hostetter

Boston: Houghton Mifflin Company, 1991. $10.95. ISBN 0-395-59698-X.

    The reissue in softcover of *The Father Christmas Letters*, which has long been out of print in the United States, is appropriate to both the Tolkien Centenary and to the season. The contents of the book are unchanged from the previous edition, which unfortunately means that the pages are still unnumbered.... However, the cover of the reissue features the watercolor of Polar Bear's Fall from the letter of 1928, instead of the Northern Lights from that of 1926.

    Of course, this reissue has a special significance for linguists, since *The Father Christmas Letters* contains the only known example of the Quenya-like language Arctic: **"*Mára mesta an ni véla tye ento, ya rato nea*"**, 'Goodbye till I see you next, and I hope it will be soon', which is given in the Appendix along with the odd, anthropomorphic alphabet created by Karhu from Goblin markings he found on cave walls.

    These delightfully drawn and wittily written missives from Santa should certainly give pause to those of us who barely manage even to *address* our Christmas cards before Dec. 24th!

Vinyar Tengwar

The bimonthly 'news-letters' of the Elvish Linguistic Fellowship,
a Special Interest Group of the Mythopoeic Society.

Editor: Carl F. Hostetter, 2509 Ambling Circle, Crofton, MD 21114, USA.

Proofreaders: Arden R. Smith and Patrick Wynne.

Masthead: by Tom Loback.

Tengwar numerals: from Lawrence M. Schoen's *Moroma* PostScript *Tengwar* font for the Mac, available on disk for $6.00 from PsychoGlyph, P.O. Box 74, Lake Bluff, IL 60044.

Subscriptions: Subscriptions are for 1 year (6 issues) and must be paid in US dollars.

$12.00   USA
$15.00   Canada (sent airmail) and Overseas surface mail
$18.00   Overseas airmail

Back issues available: Individual copies of back issues are available at the current per-issue subscription price: $2.00 USA, $2.50 Canada and Overseas surface mail, $3.00 Overseas airmail. Deduct 25% if ordering a complete set of back issues. *All costs are postpaid.*

Payments: All payments must be in US dollars. It is recommended that overseas members make payments via international postal money order.

Make all checks payable to Carl F. Hostetter.

Submissions: Written material should in some manner deal with Tolkien's invented languages. All submissions must be typed, or must be exquisitely legible: the editor will not decipher lower-glyphics. The editor reserves the right to edit any material (except artwork) for purposes of brevity and relevance. Ilúvatar smiles upon submissions on 400K or 800K (3.5") Macintosh or 720K (3.5") MS-DOS formatted disks in PageMaker, Microsoft Word, Microsoft Works, WordPerfect, MacWrite, DCA, or RTF formats, or as unformatted ASCII text files. Artwork should be Tolkienian in nature.

The deadline for VT #21 is January 1, 1992.

Bibliographical Abbreviations

H	*The Hobbit*	LT2	*The Book of Lost Tales, Part Two*
I	*The Fellowship of the Ring*	LB	*The Lays of Beleriand*
II	*The Two Towers*	SM	*The Shaping of Middle-earth*
III	*The Return of the King*	LR	*The Lost Road*
R	*The Road Goes Ever On*	RS	*The Return of the Shadow*
S	*The Silmarillion*	TI	*The Treason of Isengard*
UT	*Unfinished Tales*	WR	*The War of the Ring*
L	*The Letters of J.R.R. Tolkien*	QL	*The Qenya Lexicon, App.* LT1 & 2
MC	*The Monsters and the Critics*	GL	*The Gnomish Lexicon, App.* LT1 & 2
LT1	*The Book of Lost Tales, Part One*	Et	*The Etymologies, in* LR

Vinyar Tengwar is produced by the editor on an Apple Macintosh II personal computer, using a LaCie Silverscan scanner, Microsoft Word 4.0 and Aldus PageMaker 4.0. VT is printed on an NEC Silentwriter2 Model 90 laser printer.

Printed in Poland
by Amazon Fulfillment
Poland Sp. z o.o., Wrocław